HT

D1121183

2001

Reforming Chile

PATRICK BARR-MELEJ

Reforming
Chile

Cultural

Politics,

Nationalism,

and the

Rise of the

Middle

Class

THE UNIVERSITY OF NORTH CAROLINA PRESS

Chapel Hill and London

Designed by Heidi Perov
Set in Legacy Serif and The Serif
by Keystone Typesetting, Inc.

Manufactured in the United States of America

The paper in this book meets the guidelines for permanence and
durability of the Committee on Production Guidelines for Book
Longevity of the Council on Library Resources.

P. iii: Ahumada Street, Santiago, 1930. (Courtesy Consorcio
Periodístico, S.A. [Copesa], and *La Tercera,* Santiago)

Portions of Chapters 3 and 4 appeared in slightly different form in
"Cowboys and Constructions: Nationalist Representations of Pastoral
Life in Post-Portalian Chile," *Journal of Latin American Studies* 30
(February 1998): 35–61. Used by permission of Cambridge University Press.

LIBRARY OF CONGRESS CATALOGING-IN-PUBLICATION DATA
Barr-Melej, Patrick.
Reforming Chile: cultural politics, nationalism, and the rise of the middle class /
Patrick Barr-Melej.
p. cm.
Includes bibliographical references and index.
ISBN 0-8078-2604-9 (cloth: alk. paper)—ISBN 0-8078-4919-7 (pbk.: alk. paper)
1. Middle class—Chile—History—20th century. 2. Chile—Politics and government—
20th century. 3. Education—Chile—History—20th century. I. Title.
HT690.C5 B37   2001
305.5′5′0983—dc21   00-051218

05 04 03 02 01   5 4 3 2 1

for Abraham Melej Nazar and

Violeta González Ossandón,

abuelos queridos/beloved grandparents

Contents

Illustrations

Acknowledgments

The principal questions in this book germinated from seeds of curiosity that Arnold J. Bauer and I scattered to the wind as we walked to a café on a mild springtime day in Davis, California—a day quite similar to those in Santiago around October, minus the smog. Over the years, a great many people in the United States and Chile stimulated, conditioned, and facilitated this study's evolution. I take great pleasure in expressing my gratitude to them here with the practical realization that I cannot possibly thank all my teachers, colleagues, and students who have enriched my academic life.

First and foremost, this book could not have been completed, and my life would not be complete, without my wife, Melissa Barr. With love, patience, and kindness, she has always supported and encouraged my desire to study history in a world that seems to value more "practical" professions. While I toiled with this manuscript, she graciously took upon her shoulders a disproportional amount of child rearing, though the author's increasing dexterity allowed for typing with one hand and keeping our rather spirited toddler, Eva, out of trouble with the other. I wish to express loving appreciation to my father, Roger Barr, an avid reader whose passion for history and taste for books surely had something to do with my career choice. I profoundly thank my mother, Cinthia Melej de Barr, for giving me the *rincones chilenos* that I will forever hold dear. Over the course of three decades, my parents have improved the lives of many thousands of Mexican farmworkers in California, and I am inspired by their collective sense of purpose and dedication.

I warmly thank my mentor at the University of California at Berkeley, Tulio Halperín-Donghi, for his thoughtful help. As thematic and methodological "flavors of the month" come and go, his immense knowledge and wide-ranging interests are examples for us all. Arnold Bauer at UC Davis, my friend and teacher, assisted me during the entire course of this project, always making time to review chapter drafts meticulously and, perhaps best of all, to exchange thoughts over some glasses of the latest vintage of Dos Patos. I am also grateful to Julio Ramos for sharing his insight into Latin America's literature and intellectual milieu, and Charles Walker for teaching me a great deal about the academic scene and for hearing me out when I was flustered. Margaret Chowning, a keen reader and critic, always offered sage advice and kind words of support. My gratitude goes to James Cane, who can put complex things in the clearest of terms. Jim's friendship and tremendous intellect enriched my doctoral study at Berkeley and contributed in no small way to the making of this book. Claudio Robles Ortiz shared with me his knowledge of Chile's academy and historiography and graciously read the manuscript while busily working on his dissertation. He always makes that thin land on the edge of the earth seem much closer. I also thank William Skuban, Andrew Wood, Paula De Vos, Vera Candiani, and Jaime Aguila for their comradeship. Moreover, I cannot go without relaying my deep appreciation to Lee Terkelsen, who taught me how to ask important questions, and to F. Roy Willis, whose poetic and illuminating lectures on modern European history helped bring motivation and resolve to a once indifferent undergraduate.

While researching in Santiago, I spent many hours engaged in absorbing discussions with Professors Bernardo Subercaseaux, Alfredo Jocelyn-Holt, Luis Ortega, Eduardo Devés, and Florencia Mallon, to whom I express appreciation. In addition, Luis Durand Jr. and the distinguished author Luis Merino Reyes—still without a much deserved National Literature Award— kindly accepted interviews that enriched my understanding of Chilean culture and its crafters. My thanks go to the staff of the Archivo Nacional de Chile, including María del Carmen Montaner; the personnel of the Archivo del Siglo XX, especially Sandra Godoy; Carlos Oyarzún and Carmen Morandé at the Biblioteca del Congreso Nacional; and the staff of the Biblioteca Nacional, especially Juan Camilo, director of the library's Sección de Referencias Críticas. More than a dozen people at these sites patiently accepted countless photocopy requests and carted around hundreds of dusty volumes. Many months of research would have been fatiguing without the camaraderie of Claudio Barrientos, whose intellect and sense of humor made for memorable (and pleasantly long) lunches on smoggy afternoons, as well as the love and hospitality of my family in and around Santiago. Carlos Zenteno of the University of Chile also became a supportive friend. I also am indebted to María Soledad de la Cerda at the Consorcio Periodístico de Chile, the functionaries at the Archivo Fotográfico of the Museo Histórico Nacional, and Fernando Purcell.

Financial support from Berkeley in the form of a Graduate Opportunity Fellowship funded much of the research for this study. I am also grateful to the Mellon Foundation, which generously supported the earliest incarnations of this project with a dissertation prospectus fellowship and dissertation write-up fellowship. In addition, Berkeley's Center for Latin American Studies funded exploratory and preliminary research, as did a Humanities Research Grant from the Graduate Division of the university.

Many of the people mentioned above kindly read and commented on chapter drafts. Those who initially read the manuscript for the University of North Carolina Press offered valuable comments and suggestions that most certainly improved it. Press editors Elaine Maisner and Pamela Upton, who make difficult jobs appear easy, patiently helped me through the publication process. This book also benefited greatly from the skillful and thoughtful review of UNC Press copyeditor Grace Buonocore. Of course, any lingering errors are mine.

Abbreviations

AEN	National Education Association (Asociación de Educación Nacional)
AGP	General Association of Teachers (Asociación General de Profesores)
AL	Liberal Alliance (Alianza Liberal)
APL	People's Liberation Alliance (Alianza Popular Libertadora)
CORFO	Production Development Corporation (Corporación de Fomento de la Producción)
FECh	Chilean Federation of Students (Federación de Estudiantes de Chile)
FOCh	Chilean Workers Federation (Federación de Obreros de Chile)
FP	Popular Front (Frente Popular)
FRAP	Popular Action Front (Frente de Acción Popular)
IWW	Industrial Workers of the World
MNS	National Socialist Movement, or Nazi Party (Movimiento Nacional Socialista)
PC	Conservative Party (Partido Conservador)
PCCh	Chilean Communist Party (Partido Comunista de Chile)
PD	Democratic Party (Partido Democrático)
PL	Liberal Party (Partido Liberal)
PLD	Liberal-Democratic Party, or Balmacedists (Partido Liberal Democrático)
PN	Nationalist Party (Partido Nacionalista)
POS	Socialist Workers Party (Partido Obrero Socialista)
PR	Radical Party (Partido Radical)
PS	Socialist Party (Partido Socialista)
SNA	National Agricultural Society (Sociedad Nacional de Agricultura)
SNP	National Society of Teachers (Sociedad Nacional de Profesores)
SOFOFA	Manufacturing Promotion Society (Sociedad de Fomento Fabril)

UN	National Union (Unión Nacional)
UNA	Nationalist Union (Unión Nacionalista)
UNA/PN	Nationalist Union/Nationalist Party (Unión Nacionalista/ Partido Nacionalista)
UP	Popular Unity (Unidad Popular)

Reforming Chile

Las ideas adquieren alas potentes y veloces, no
en el helado seno de la abstracción, sino en el
luminoso y cálido ambiente de la forma.

JOSÉ ENRIQUE RODÓ, *Ariel*, 1900

Introduction

Strolling down a sidewalk along Santiago's lively Alameda de las Delicias
(now the Avenida del Libertador General Bernardo O'Higgins) during the
latter years of the so-called Parliamentary Republic (1891–1925), the casual
observer witnessed numerous indications of a modern nation in the making.
The crisp ring of a trolley's bell sounded the call of progress. A dozen different newspapers of various political persuasions dangled from clothespins
at a corner kiosk, and passersby glanced at the latest headlines. A bookstore's
window near the University of Chile seemed more crowded with new titles.
The observer could hear the giggles and chatter of children as they made
their daily pilgrimage from a working-class neighborhood to a recently established primary school. Near busy Ahumada Street, yet another fashionable department store serving an affluent, exclusive clientele drew the spec-
tator's attention, if only for a brief moment. A foundry's plume of smoke
that billowed in the distance, or perhaps the increasingly long lines of people
waiting outside the doors of a law office, a notary public, an accounting firm,
and a medical practice, also beckoned glances. These and other obvious
reflections of modernization's impelling force—aspects of a once traditional
society becoming something else—touched the lives of many thousands of
urban Chileans during the early decades of the twentieth century.

Amid the low rumble and rhythmic bustle of this urban environment,
there emerged from within Chile's burgeoning middle class a nationalist
reform movement with far-reaching political and cultural implications.

During the first half of the century, as oligarchs anxiously sought to prevent the corrosion of their power and working-class groups armed themselves with revolutionary concepts and combative rhetoric in a highly conflictive ideological arena, influential people of the middle class negotiated an intermediate position between the sociopolitical forces of Right and Left. They endeavored to sculpt a nation distanced from the predominance and pretentiousness of aristocrats, safeguarded from proletarian insurrection, and a Chile in which their ideas and values formed the collective *mentalité*. At the heart of this movement were intellectuals, educators, bureaucrats, and politicians who articulated an agenda of cultural politics and elaborated a nationalist imagination that altered Chile's cultural landscape, infused politics with a new constellation of images, symbols, and meanings, and influenced how many Chileans thought about themselves and their nation.

This book examines the rise of the middle class and the confluence of culture, politics, and nationalism in a rapidly changing Latin American society. It focuses on the perceptions, voices, and actions of liberal reformers who contributed in significant ways to the shaping of modern Chile during the five decades spanning the founding of the Parliamentary Republic through the Popular Front (Frente Popular, or FP) presidency of Radical Party leader Pedro Aguirre Cerda (1938–41). Its principal purpose is to illustrate and interpret the intricacies of a political-cultural project as it was being manufactured by elements of a class intimately tied to the varied consequences of capitalist modernization. Doing so necessarily entails positing important questions that have not been addressed, much less formulated, about twentieth-century Chile and, arguably, its least studied social constituency: the urban middle class, or "mesocracy" (*mesocracia*, a term used in Chile for much of the century, underscores the middle stratum's social importance by suggesting authority, legitimacy, and posture). What political concerns and aims motivated middle-class reformers, and why were those concerns and aims unique to their social layer? Why and how were such ideological underpinnings manifested culturally? What role did nationalism play in early-twentieth-century Chile's public sphere in general, and the middle-class milieu in particular? What impact did reform-minded nationalists have on politics, culture, and identity? Were Chilean "mesocrats" simply consorts of the traditional elite, as some would have us believe? Were they, instead, genuinely antioligarchic and committed to far-reaching reform? The chapters hereinafter approach the cultural and political ideas and practices of middle-class reformers by way of literary culture and public education. Both cultural environments—one artistic and aesthetic, the other official and programmatic—are equally important in this story and together impart a multidimensional view of a movement contrived by Chileans who saw themselves as centurions of culture and "authentic interpreters of nationality [and] the national spirit."[1]

Through political will and efficient organization, middle-class reformers with either direct or informal ties to the Radical Party (Partido Radical, or PR), a political body founded by "radical" liberals in the mid-nineteenth century, became the dominant interest group in national affairs by the end of the 1930s. Their ascendance, however, did not come quickly or easily. For much of the nineteenth and early twentieth centuries, an upper class composed largely of wealthy landowning and mine-owning families maintained control over the political system. But while the mesocracy expanded and the PR increased its representation in the Senate and Chamber of Deputies after the War of the Pacific (1879–84), reformers came to wield a considerable amount of power in the area of cultural production and reproduction, as aristocrats demonstrated only moderate interest in matters of domestic culture. Members of the middle class soon commanded the literary marketplace as the culture industry matured, and public education at the bureaucratic and classroom levels became their nearly exclusive domain by the second decade of the twentieth century. These cultural environments also constituted political environments in which middle-class reformers expressed the fears, hopes, and ideas they shared about such things as class conflict, social solidarity, liberal democracy and democratization, and the "Chilean race."

Such culturally active reformers expressed deep-seated concern about what they deemed obvious symptoms of national decline. Fueling such worry was the "social question," or the problem of worsening living and working conditions in the country's mining centers and major cities, especially Santiago and the port city of Valparaíso, and the associated proliferation of working-class radicalism. Chile's anarchist and communist movements were in nascent states during the earliest years of the twentieth century, but reformers nonetheless were keenly aware of the possibility of social revolution and viewed the social question as a powder keg for just such an explosion. To make troublesome matters worse, reformers surmised, the upper class remained unresponsive to the social question despite harboring anxieties about insurrection, propagated a certain institutional inertia that stifled broad-based government-sponsored reform, and was simply aloof from the nation's autochthonous culture and cultural needs. Thus, through narration, debates, and policies, mesocrats with cultural capital in literature and pedagogy addressed aspects of the social question, strove for the ultimate decomposition of the elite's power, and propelled their own national project based on reformist cultural and political ideas that were enveloped in a nationalist discourse with strongly liberal democratic overtones. These nationalist reformers, in short, exploited culture's dualistic essence as a mechanism of liberation and authority in the name of inclusive democracy and the *patria* (fatherland or homeland). While doing so they broke new cultural and political ground upon which subsequent movements, including Salvador Allende's Popular Unity (Unidad Popular, or UP) of the 1960s and early 1970s, erected their national projects.

This study does not purport to be a definitive examination of the middle class, nor does it discuss in detail all the social actors who contributed to the country's cultural and political life during and immediately following the Parliamentary Republic. Rather, it seeks to discern how certain Chileans understood the world around them, why and how they charted and navigated courses in response to it, and how those responses shaped the history of twentieth-century Chile. Accordingly, attention is focused on those Chileans of "middle" standing with greatest cultural and political power between the 1890s and early 1940s: reformers who stood firmly between revolution and reaction. It must be noted here that as Chile's sociopolitical landscape continued to diversify in the 1930s, the loyalty of many middle-class people (including Allende's) came to rest in the organized Left, and the budding Socialist Party in particular. But recognizably "middle-class" Marxists remained in lesser positions in the culture industry, the political system, and in the broader national context during the period under consideration. That is not to say that historians should only study people with the greatest power, leaving the rest behind as inconsequential or, at least, less interesting. On the contrary, we should be sensitive to the undertakings of the powerful to understand better the opportunities, challenges, and dilemmas faced by the less powerful and powerless.

Class, Culture, and Hegemony

In my effort to establish an analytical and interpretive framework that may help us understand the rise of the mesocracy and the cultural politics and nationalism that permeated it, I have found great utility in thinking about "class" and "hegemony" as historical processes. It is more than reasonable to assert that in the twentieth century no other identity marker proved more compelling among Chileans and more pervasive in their political culture than the idea of class. On the surface of things, the relationship between class divisions and political ideologies broke down, in general terms, as one might imagine in a "textbook" sort of way during the first half of the century. That is to say, the upper class remained traditionalist despite its party variation (namely, its division into Liberal and Conservative camps), though some deserters joined the reformist cause; the bulk of the middle class was reformist, cautious, and concerned with furthering its own social and political power; and members of the increasingly radicalized popular classes found leadership in men with middle-class pedigrees who had chosen the path of social revolution (Luis Emilio Recabarren and Allende, for instance). This relationship between social circumstance and ideology lends a degree of insight into the importance of class in the present examination.

The historian E. P. Thompson offered a most succinct, insightful, and adequately malleable definition of "class" in his 1963 trailblazing study on the making of the English working class. He explained that "class happens when some men, as a result of common experiences (inherited or shared), feel and articulate the identity of their interests as between themselves, and as against other men whose interests are different from (and usually opposed to) theirs. . . . Class consciousness is the way in which the experiences are handled in cultural terms: embodied in traditions, value-systems, ideas, and institutional forms."[2] Class, then, is not a static "thing" but rather an unfolding drama of consciousness, organization, and activity that is expressed and reproduced culturally. Thompson eloquently conveyed the significance of culture in the construction of class by noting, "I am convinced that we cannot understand class unless we see it as a social and cultural formation, arising from processes which can only be studied as they work themselves out over a considerable historical period."[3] In the context of twentieth-century Chile, I am, accordingly, convinced that we cannot begin to comprehend social and cultural formations without addressing class and, specifically, the middle class's station between the elite on the one hand and the working class on the other. As literary critic and educator Angel Rama reminds us, classes with distinct "cultural ways" have found themselves in "a struggle won or lost on the chessboard of history."[4]

Latin America's middle classes coalesced in the nineteenth and early twentieth centuries—some later than others depending on national contexts—as sectors indelibly linked to capitalist modernization and "classical liberal" projects that fostered international trade, domestic commerce, and internal migration. These factors created the necessary conditions for the proliferation of middle-class professions in such areas as governmental bureaucracy, accounting, small business, teaching, journalism, and so forth. Yet, when considering the Chilean case, defining who composed the middle class is a complicated endeavor because "class," as Thompson and Rama indicate, is not merely a socioeconomic category but a cultural one as well. In early-twentieth-century Santiago, for example, it was not entirely uncommon to see the progeny of the upper class take jobs as journalists, teachers, or bureaucrats, join the PR, and, in general, immerse themselves in, and contribute to, a characteristically mesocratic cultural milieu. In this changeful urban setting, genealogy did not necessarily correlate with a distinct lifestyle, ideology, or identity; many mesocrats-by-choice shared with mesocrats-by-station certain cultural tastes and ideological sympathies that, in many ways, differed significantly from those of aristocrats. A mesocrat's being in the world, then, was not solely the function of economic activity and a comparable social standing; it also was tied to cultural norms and a cultural outlook. That is not to say that middle-class Chileans, especially notable professionals, never circulated in high society's cultural medium (a good number of social climbers could not have wished for anything better). In short, it may be argued that locating and identifying a mesocracy during this period by, say, examining employment data or breakdowns of occupations in census reports would not take into full account the pliability of "class" and, for that matter, the significance of culture and cultural practices in the elaboration of classes and identity.

Long before the appearance of Thompson's widely praised work, Antonio Gramsci noted in 1920 that a class, "just as it has thought to organize itself politically and economically[,] . . . must also think about organizing itself culturally."[5] Gramsci's argument for culture's pertinence in the organization of classes was a departure from prevailing Marxist thought. As Raymond Williams explains, in pre-Gramsci Marxist ideology "no cultural activity is allowed to be real and significant in itself, but is always reduced to a direct or indirect expression of some proceeding and controlling economic content, or of political content determined by an economic position or situation."[6] Marx stipulated that social being (or class) above all shaped consciousness—whether political or cultural. Gramsci, however, essentially argued that culture is an integral component (and not merely a shallow reflection) of social being. He took this very convincing analysis a step further by underscoring the importance of culture in the building of hegemony. Originally formulated by Lenin and Russian Marxists before the Bolshevik Revolution of 1917 and furthered by an incarcerated Gramsci in the 1920s and 1930s, the concept of hegemony has exerted a great deal of historiographical influence in recent years as the conventions of orthodox Marxist historiography have faded.[7] Gramsci exploded Marxism's "base/superstructure" correlation, which subordinated culture to social being, by arguing that culture, like politics and economy, is a critical component not only of class but of hegemony, or the direction of a social group realized through coercion and consent at all levels of interpersonal organization.[8] Williams added to Gramsci's formulation of hegemony by arguing that "a lived hegemony is always a process. It is not, except analytically, a system or structure."[9] Thus, "we have then to add to the concept of hegemony the concepts of counter-hegemony and alternative hegemony, which are real and persistent elements of practice."[10] It was, moreover, Gramsci's contention that a "war of position"—that is, the aggregation of battles between class-based interests seeking to preserve, topple, or realize hegemony—would largely be waged on the field of culture.[11] On a more general level, it is significant for the Chilean case that Gramsci attempted to explain why and how a bourgeois hegemonic project had successfully mitigated class struggle in early-twentieth-century Italy, thus derailing what once was a promising proletarian movement. As we shall see, culturally and politically active elements of Chile's middle class pursued an alternative hegemony that, aside from undermining the preeminence of the oligarchic establishment, sought to suppress working-class radicalism. Collectively, the above formulations of class and hegemony, originally conceived by Marxist thinkers who had working classes and proletarian struggles in mind, resonate in this study of Chilean society's middle sector and its complicated relationship with competing class interests.

The Politics of Prose

Writing in 1915, one Chilean reformer described art as a "social reality" that "can be the source of the elevation of character and harmony in the collective organism." He went on to explain that "the formation of a national art, or at least the stimulation and cultivation of the artistic faculties of the race, is a labor that is eminently nationalist."[12] As this statement indicates, at the center of every modern culture are artistic creations—paintings, sculptures, novels, short stories, poems, and the like—that carry with them meaning and intent. It therefore stands to reason that such cultural products may reflect ideological currents and interpretations of prevailing conditions in a society at a moment in time. In literary culture, art takes form as words, which, far from being definite and unchanging, convey opinions and perspectives conditioned by, and indicative of, social, cultural, political, and economic circumstances. Of most interest to us here is the relationship between art and ideas and, specifically, that of literary culture and political ideology.

As the nineteenth century drew to a close, Chilean literature underwent significant shifts in style, content, and function, as new market and cultural conditions gradually created an expanded readership. This era saw the specialization of the intellectual enterprise throughout Latin America, as fiction writers, poets, or literary critics came to earn professional livelihoods. As Argentine literary scholars Beatriz Sarlo and Carlos Altamirano explain, there appeared an "interaction between the writers and the market starting with the moment in which the production and distribution of the book was converted into a branch of the general production of goods."[13] Rama, moreover, notes that this "period of modernization brought a stronger emphasis on specialization, a more rigid division of intellectual labor . . . appropriate for societies that now confronted demands for various kinds of complex knowledge."[14] The prevalence of relatively affordable paper-bound books, higher literacy rates, and greater demand spurred by a literature-hungry urban population signified that literary culture was moving further away from its earlier, exclusive purpose as a diversion of and for the elite. Novels, poetry, short stories, and newspaper serials were increasingly being written and read by intellectuals, civil servants, accountants, journalists, teachers, politicians, and businesspeople of a middle class eager to define and fortify its own cultural presence in society. The most widely read and praised fiction trend of early-twentieth-century Chile was *criollismo* ("creolism"), a predominantly middle-class genre that combined stylistic and thematic sensibilities inspired by European naturalist writers allied to the liberal cause, especially the celebrated Frenchman Émile Zola, with native—or criollo—settings.

Criollismo emerged at the turn of the century as a cultural creation with ideological overtones. Contributors to the genre, including members and fellow travelers of the PR, revealed a nationalist, reformist, and populistic disposition in works that placed lower-class Chileans in the cultural and national limelight and pushed the aristocracy out of it. In a manner similar to that of important English, Irish, and Argentine intellectuals of the 1920s and 1930s, Guillermo Labarca Hubertson, Mariano Latorre, Luis Durand, and other *criollistas* saw nationness in the countryside, among campesinos (country folk) whom the urban elite essentially thought of as bumpkins.[15] The genre's contributors believed that *chilenidad* ("Chileanness" or "Chileanity") was not an inherent quality of the cosmopolitan elite; rather, it was ingrained in such figures as the *huasos*, or horsemen service tenants, of the Central Valley's sprawling haciendas, who shared a more wholesome and genuine existence, or so the *criollistas* sustained. By divulging the (supposed) characteristics and day-to-day experiences of society's underbelly, and by negating high society's cultural and national distinction, the *criollistas* contributed to a middle-class reform movement that included the popular sector in a national and nationalist project. But any change was to occur on terms set by reformers, and there were limits to the lower class's political options in this newly reimagined community.[16]

The process of discerning a discourse of cultural and sociopolitical consequence in a literary medium does not come without some methodological and theoretical pitfalls. What, for example, may a collection of fictional short stories and novels filled with hundreds of plots and protagonists tell us about the contours of a reformist ideology rooted in the middle class? Leo Lowenthal, a sociologist of literature, observed that "literature is a particularly suitable bearer of fundamental symbols and values which give cohesion to social groups, ranging from nations and epochs to special social subgroups and points in time. . . . Literature tells us not only what a society was like in a past age, but also what the individual felt about it." Analyses of literature may therefore reveal "those central problems with which man has been concerned at various times, permitting us to develop an image of a given society in terms of the individuals that composed it."[17] For our purposes here, should we then perceive literature as an artsy expression of ideology? If so, would art then cease to be art and simply become aestheticized politics?

In his theory of the "transindividual subject," Lucien Goldmann drew a direct correlation between an author's position in society and the type of literature that he or she yields.[18] Although it is tempting simply to interpret an author's literary production as an expression of his or her subject position, we must be wary of such a static and undynamic relational certainty. Pierre Bourdieu tells us that investigators often sloppily choose samples of a literary movement that express class-based interests and ideas, putting aside more marginal authors whose works may cast doubt on a direct author-class nexus. Bourdieu also states that strategies and trajectories of authors tend to be independent and differentiated among those of similar social origin.[19] However, Bourdieu may be overly swift in his rejection of the author-class nexus. Certain tendencies are, in fact, discernible within a given genre that may link, on a "macro" rather than "micro" level, more than one author to a class and class interests. Such links may not be overt and thus beckon excavation. In their works, the *criollistas* demonstrate commonalities that not only are stylistic and structural but also political and functional. In essence, this book's treatment of *criollismo* assumes the middle ground between Goldmann and Bourdieu, where art can be for art's sake and art can be for politics' sake. As Gramsci observed when writing on culture and ideology, "given the principle that one should look only to the artistic character of the work of art, this does not in the least prevent one from investigating the mass of feelings and the attitude towards life present in the work itself."[20]

Although scholars have produced many important contributions to our understanding of modern Chilean literature, *criollismo*'s ideological morphology remains unexplored. The few existing references to *criollismo*, which demonstrate the genre's aesthetic commitment to themes and settings associated with the lower classes, emphasize that its proliferation signaled the emergence of a new urban type—the professional writer—who was a product of economic modernization and social change. Indeed, this is an important aspect of late-nineteenth- and early-twentieth-century literary culture, but sidestepped in such studies is *criollismo*'s place in a middle-class reform movement with hegemonic intent and a new vision of the nation and its culture. This book, therefore, treats *criollismo* not only as a literary form with a peculiar style but also as a collection of historical texts that disclose an agenda of cultural politics anchored by an emerging nationalist imagination.

Ideology and Cultural Politics: Lessons from the Classroom

The elaboration of the culture industry and the diversification of cultural production paralleled significant developments in pedagogy, which, like literary culture, was a medium for the cultural politics and nationalist principles of middle-class reformers. As Chile's bureaucratic state expanded to meet the demands of a modernizing society during the late nineteenth and early twentieth centuries, public education became an important part of governance, as was the case in other Latin American nations, North America, Britain, and continental Europe. The mesocracy's leverage in Chilean public instruction dates from the final years of what is often called the Portalian Republic (1831–91), named after its principal architect, the trader Diego Portales. A sharp increase in education spending during the presidency of José Manuel Balmaceda (1886–91) produced a need for more teachers and ministerial bureaucrats. Middle-class personnel, many of them Radicals, filled such posts in large numbers, thus establishing a reformist presence that guided public instruction for many decades. For the historian, early-twentieth-century Chilean pedagogy is a rich depository of ideas and practices that were strongly "mesocratic" and reformist in character and was a cultural space in which leading reformers, including Aguirre Cerda and a young Arturo Alessandri Palma, implemented a cultural political agenda and espoused nationalist principles.

The rise of an increasingly politicized Chilean working class and the persistence of oligarchic power convinced reformers of the Parliamentary Republic that cultural democratization in the form of compulsory primary instruction and the spread of an inclusive nationalism among students were pedagogical imperatives. In public debate over the amplification of public education, reformers gave shape to a strongly nationalist discourse when criticizing traditionalists allied to the Catholic Church, who objected to the secularization of pedagogy through the expansion of state-executed schooling, and others outside religious conservatism (especially Liberals of the Parliamentary Republic establishment) who were critical of Radical reformism. Meanwhile, the diffusion of nationalism in the classroom, reformers thought, would inculcate workers, their families, and other Chileans with cultural and political demeanors that would contribute to the mesocracy's hegemonic project and the perpetuation of liberal democracy. Indeed, Basil Bernstein notes that in any society "the structuring of knowledge and symbol in . . . educational institutions is intimately related to the principles of social control."[21] Among the concepts and constructs propagated in decrees and protocols issued by Chile's education bureaucracy was a mestizo (mixed-blooded) racial identity, which reformers employed to champion unity during this period of heated social conflict.

In general, historians of Chilean education have not examined pedagogical manifestations of nationalism, though the middle class's important place in the evolution of public education has been documented. Discussions of Parliamentary-era debates over a proposed law of obligatory primary instruction, for example, do not locate and explore a nationalism that informed that dimension of reformist cultural politics. No study, moreover, traces the evolution of policies and protocols governing nationalist teachings in Chile that were formulated and implemented, in large part, by middle-class reformers between the turn of the century and the 1940s. Such guidelines demonstrate that reformers actively and imaginatively employed public schooling as a conduit for a nationalist sensibility that permeated the middle class's milieu; they wielded the cultural capital associated with an elevated status in the pedagogical bureaucracy to manipulate the construction of a collective identity. E. J. Hobsbawm, in his widely read book on nationalism, calls such manipulation "ideological engineering." Its success, he explains, is directly related to the capability of the state's bureaucracy to touch the lives of all or most citizens in a uniform manner.[22]

A Historiographical Path Less Traveled

How middle-class reformers interlaced cultural politics and nationalism for hegemonic ends is a complex issue that has gone without investigation. More broadly speaking, scholarship on Chile's mesocracy, its cultural history, and nationalist impulse is scant. Notable non-Chilean historians have, in general, devoted their intellectual energies to subjects other than the middle class since Chile's history began drawing considerable academic interest in the 1950s and 1960s, and Chilean scholars also have applied their intellectual energies elsewhere owing, in large part, to changing sociopolitical circumstances during the course of the twentieth century. All the while, the study of Chilean nationalism has taken a course that, it may be argued, diminishes the utility of "nationalism" as an analytical category.

John Johnson's 1958 study *Political Change in Latin America* identified, for what may be the first time in "foreign" scholarship on the region, the presence of powerful middle sectors whose constituents expressed and executed far-reaching progressive agendas based on principles of democratization and inclusion. Johnson credits middle-class movements for promoting domestic economic development, fostering literacy by expanding public education systems, and pursuing the construction of modern welfare states. His positive assessment of twentieth-century Latin America's middle layers did not go unchallenged. Frederick Pike, in his article on class relations in Chile published in 1963, essentially argues that the middle class was but an appendage of the elite, was bereft of its own cultural attributes, and shared high society's opprobrious view of the lower classes.[23] Pike reached this conclusion by identifying members of a nineteenth-century "middle class" who, after striking it rich as mining entrepreneurs, merged socially, politically, and culturally with Liberal and Conservative aristocrats. These nouveaux riches, he further explains, were the same "middle class" people who, in the early twentieth century, demonstrated the "tendency to shun the lower mass and embrace the aristocracy" while developing "very little consciousness of themselves as members of a distinct class." In fact, Pike found it "extremely difficult to detect opinions, customs, and value judgments in Chile that are demonstrably middle class."[24] It will become clear that Pike's "middle class," quite simply, is not necessarily the same middle class explored in the following chapters, though some offspring of the nineteenth century's social climbers, including notable educators and a prominent *criollista*, contributed to the mesocracy's hegemonic project. The present study seeks to demonstrate that middle-class reformers were fundamentally antioligarchic without breaching the parameters of democratic demeanor; they successfully expanded a recognizably mesocratic cultural domain, forged a nationalist discourse that celebrated the lower class, and, at least symbolically, included Chileans of lesser status in an imagined community.

Pike's skepticism of middle-class dynamism was soon shared by a generation of Marxist historians of Latin America influenced by the emergent *dependentista* paradigm who believed that fundamental change could only be realized through social revolution, and certainly not by way of middle-class liberalism. As David Parker explains, moreover, very different portraits of Latin America's middle layers were painted by the 1970s. Aside from those like Pike, who viewed mesocrats as consorts of the elite, some argued that middle sectors demonstrated both progressive and traditionalist tendencies over extended periods—progressivism in their struggles against oligarchies (good) and traditionalism when they sought to consolidate their hard-won sociopolitical gains (bad).[25] Yet another group of scholars more convincingly explained such an apparent duality by arguing that older, established middle sectors gravitated toward authoritarian principles, while emergent middle layers maintained a decidedly progressive mentality.[26] One gathers from such investigations that, despite their progressivism and discourses of democratization, Latin America's middle classes were either incapable or unwilling to enact wide-ranging and long-lasting change in their respective societies; democracy faltered, and poverty and injustice persisted either by defeat, design, or default.

Aside from Pike's article, historians interested in Chile have not explored these and other important issues related to the mesocracy. When appraising the body of literature published by non-Chilean scholars, we find important studies on the political and intellectual foundations of the nation-state; works related to economic issues, especially themes associated with development; valuable contributions to our understanding of rural society; significant studies on the working class; and other examinations that do not directly address the middle class's pivotal role in modern Chilean history. It may very well be the case that an overriding sense of Chile's historical

exceptionalism—probably shared by more non-Chilean than Chilean scholars—accounts for this historiographical lapse. The country's unusually stable political system in the nineteenth century, the prevalence of a thor-
oughly integrated landed aristocracy, its world-renowned nitrate boom, and
the dramatic (and ultimately tragic) course of its particularly successful
working-class movement are lightning rods for academic interest, over-
shadowing the urban mesocracy and its significant place in Chilean society
and history. Another factor, however, may be more consequential when assessing why the Chilean middle class (and other Latin American middle
classes) continues to receive little attention: a latent contempt for liberalism.
To Pike and other historians, middle-class liberals, by virtue of ties to the
liberal elite, simply buttressed an ideology that, when practiced in Latin
America, was a pillar of aristocratic power and a sham. In sum, it remains
clear that the middle class—a decisive social, political, economic, and cultural presence in national affairs since the Parliamentary Republic—has not
received the historiographical attention it warrants among historians outside Chile.

A similar problem characterizes the scholarship of important Chilean
historians of the mid- and late twentieth century, whose works have largely
steered clear of society's middle stratum. During the nineteenth and early
twentieth centuries, historical investigation was in the hands of upper-class
Chileans who wove grand narratives about colonial society, the struggle for
independence, and the country's unique experience with "constitutional
authoritarianism" during the Portalian Republic.[27] Great men, politics, and
international and civil wars dominated the thematic stage. The revered historian Diego Barros Arana, for example, expressed little interest in matters
outside of elite politics.[28] This is completely understandable given that politics was almost exclusively in the elite's hands until the late nineteenth
century. By midcentury, however, important sociopolitical and cultural developments, including the democratization of public education, had transformed the composition of the country's academy and, in turn, Chilean
historiography. "History" changed from being an elite's avocation to a pro-
fession of trained scholars, many of them from the middle class.

There emerged from outside the elite such scholars as Jorge Barría Serón,
Julio César Jobet, and Hernán Ramírez Necochea, three of Chile's leading
Marxist historians, who burst onto the academic scene in the 1950s and
1960s as university professors with interests related to the evolution of the
working class and its sociopolitical institutions. Their influential books on
the radicalized labor movement shifted, to a certain degree, the locus of

Chilean historiography from the elite to workers, thereby leapfrogging the middle class as an object of historical study.[29] It must be stated here that these and other leftist historians also harbored suspicions of liberal democracy, the political expression of capitalism. This translated into their less-than-positive opinions of a notably liberal democratic middle class, though some Marxists scholars—especially those with ties to UP—held more favorable, or at least tolerant, views of political liberalism. In the years leading up to the election of UP candidate Salvador Allende in 1970, then, Chilean historiography took on a somewhat Marxist hue.[30] After the 1973 military coup that toppled Allende and the *"vía chilena al socialismo,"* an influential cadre of younger Chilean historians on the left found little purpose in continuing to write blow-by-blow narratives of a defeated working-class political project. Scholars such as Gabriel Salazar judged the works of Barría, Jobet, and Ramírez as reductionist and unable to relay the compound experiences of *"el bajo pueblo."* They sought to escape the constraints of a "top-down" analysis by focusing on the day-to-day lives—the social history—of the popular sectors.[31] They, too, sidestepped the mesocracy. In short, when assessing the long-term trajectory of Chilean historiography, we see that while thematic and methodological perspectives shifted within the academy, the middle class largely remained in the dusty corners of historical inquiry.

Studies of Chilean nationalism, like those on the middle class, are few. Ernst Halperin and Carl Solberg offered two of the earliest assessments of it in the mid-1960s and early 1970s. Halperin approached the topic in his *Nationalism and Communism in Chile* (1965) by looking at economic policy and issues related to development. Chilean nationalism, Halperin explained, was developmentalist and anti-imperialist; it could be detected in the public policy of the Popular Front (a Radical-led coalition of the Center and Left) in the late 1930s and early 1940s, the Christian Democrat administration of Eduardo Frei Montalva (1964–70), and the program of the Left's Popular Action Front (Frente de Acción Popular, or FRAP). Halperin, therefore, essentially confined his investigation of Chilean nationalism to the economic realm.[32] The analysis offered by Solberg examines the relationships between immigration and nationalism in both Chile and Argentina between 1890 and 1914. His 1970 study, though certainly more elaborate than Halperin's, nevertheless echoes *Nationalism and Communism in Chile* by asserting that Chilean nationalism "concentrated primarily on economic problems."[33] Although Solberg focused on reactions to immigration that emerged from society's middle strata, his study's temporal span ends exactly when middle-class Chileans asserted themselves in national affairs to a greater degree. Solberg, therefore, missed the era in which nationalist ideas rapidly matured. Moreover, Solberg did not consider the existence of competing nationalisms within each country and chose instead to formulate a comparative exercise involving two seemingly uniform nationalisms, one "Chilean" and the other "Argentine." Nationalism's rich complexity is, therefore, largely left untapped, though his study certainly provides a more robust analysis than Halperin's.

In more recent years, Chile's experience with military dictatorship has led historians in and of that country strictly to equate nationalism with authoritarianism, thereby denying the existence of alternative nationalisms.[34] I am suggesting here that recent scholarship on Chile recognizes nationalism as a singularly elitist and fundamentally antidemocratic sensibility, which justifies chauvinism, belligerence, and intolerance on the grounds of national salvation and renovation. One gathers, furthermore, that Chilean nationalism's historical trajectory may be traced from Jorge González von Marées's National Socialist Movement (Movimiento Nacional Socialista, or Nazi Party) of the 1930s to the horrific Directorate of National Intelligence (Dirección de Inteligencia Nacional, or DINA) of the 1970s and is best symbolized by the stern look on General Augusto Pinochet's face.[35] To be sure, this describes *a* nationalism that was especially real to the many thousands who faced the atrocities of dictatorship in the 1970s and 1980s. It does not, however, describe all species of Chilean nationalism. Historians have not ventured to ask if a criollo variant of what Hobsbawm has called "democratic-revolutionary nationalism" developed in Chile's crowded ideological arena.[36] Was Chilean nationalism naturally bereft of the Enlightenment's liberal commandments? Is it possible to identify an early-century "progressive" nationalism—an alternative nationalism that challenged the oligarchy's power, offered a democratized vision of the imagined community, and defended the precepts of liberal democracy?

This book is organized as follows. Chapter 1 examines urban social transformations brought on by the export economy and the early phases of industrialization, the amplification of electoral politics and sociopolitical contestation, the rise of middle-class reformism, and the cultural practices of the elite during the Parliamentary Republic. It seeks to orient the reader within the changing environment of Chile's troubled belle epoque. Chapter 2 presents a schematic history of Chilean patriotism and nationalism and then embarks on an interpretation of early-twentieth-century nationalism(s) in that country. Keeping in mind class interests and the malleability of nationalist discourse, it explores the articulation of two strains of nationalism and, in general, seeks to orient the reader within the densely wooded and somewhat foggy forest of Chilean nationalism.

Chapter 3 opens this book's discussion of middle-class literary culture, nationalism, and cultural politics by focusing on the first generation of *criollistas* (ca. 1900–1920), its rewriting of what may be called the "national narrative," and the accompanying phenomenon of rural aestheticism in Chile's urban space. Chapter 4 examines the historical trajectory of *criollismo* and the steady diffusion of *criollista* ideas in the public sphere from about 1920 to the Aguirre Cerda presidency. It argues that nativist imagery had become an important component of opposing political discourses by the 1930s and that the Radical-directed Popular Front was particularly attracted to the national narrative introduced by literary *criollismo*'s progenitors.

The subsequent three chapters look at middle-class cultural politics and nationalism from a different angle: public education. Chapter 5 explores the motives and aims of Parliamentary Republic reformers who endeavored to democratize culture by way of obligatory primary education, and Chapter 6 examines the development of nationalist teachings in Chile's newly amplified pedagogical complex. The latter chapter emphasizes the central role played by reformers in the promulgation of decrees and protocols that were designed to foster nationalism in public schools and by extension realize middle-class hegemony. Chapter 7 demonstrates how reformers, seeking to build consensus among fellow Chileans regarding concepts such as *patria*, *raza*, and citizenship, relayed their ideas by way of ministry-approved textbooks that were assembled for all levels of state-directed schooling. Concluding this study is an epilogue in which the ramifications of middle-class reformism, its cultural politics, and its nationalism are assessed.

Un viento de revolución soplaba en el país.

ALBERTO EDWARDS, *La fronda aristocrática*, 1928

A Troubled Belle Epoque 1

The Parliamentary Republic, like the deity Janus, bared more than one face. It was an era of long-term economic growth based on incipient industrialization and the geologic exploitation of northern Chile's arid expanses. Party politics operated relatively unfettered when compared with other Latin American nations, and aristocrats sipped imported tea in salons while conversing about issues of the day and the latest Parisian publications. The wealthy enjoyed trips to the Old World, department stores showcased the latest European fashions for men and women, and, by the 1920s, the growing middle class began expanding its barrios in Santiago and other cities. It was not uncommon for the elite to boast about their fine country. One conservative newspaper, for example, claimed in 1908 that Chileans—especially affluent and demure women—were recognized throughout the world for their "morality" and elegant wardrobe.[1] But all was not well in the republic. The century's early years saw bloody confrontations between workers and the state, abject squalor in working-class neighborhoods and mining communities, one of the world's highest infant mortality rates, a ravaging plague of tuberculosis, short-term economic crises, and legislative, ministerial, and administrative inaction that hampered the development of initiatives to deal with profound socioeconomic and demographic transformations. A critic in the reformist newspaper *La Lei* captured the darker side of the Parliamentary Republic on Independence Day in 1903: "The decline of the nation is clear in politics, in administration, in wealth, and morality in general."[2] Contrasting accounts of the period are littered throughout the press and other chronicles of public life. While the oligarchy praised itself for having created a criollo belle epoque, reformers of the mesocracy pointed to the upper class's ineptitude and a pressing social question that, if left unaddressed, eventually would lead to revolution.

This chapter examines sociopolitical tensions associated with economic modernization as well as the Chilean elite's cultural practices between the 1890s and the 1920s to establish a context for subsequent discussions of the reformist movement's mission to displace oligarchic power and mitigate the social question through the democratization of culture and the propagation of an alternative nationalism. It does so in a general, schematic way by discussing the republic's political environment; the rise of the Radical Party (PR) as a potent political player; the social question's emergence in urban society; and the elite's cultural tastes and habits. Throughout this chapter, a narrative fabric is woven that connects many lines of analysis, varying issues, and a diverse assortment of actors to offer a tapestry of political, social, and cultural patterns.

The Portalian Project, José Manuel Balmaceda, and Civil War

After achieving independence in 1818, Chileans experienced more than a decade of the intraelite political turmoil common to nearly every nascent Latin American republic. General Bernardo O'Higgins, the illegitimate son of an Irish-born bureaucrat who governed colonial Chile in the late eighteenth century, assumed the reigns of the new government after the cessation of hostilities. At first, the bulk of the elite accepted O'Higgins's mix of liberal notions and authoritarian practices, but his ouster came in 1823 when supporters grew weary of his quasi-dictatorial demeanor. The presidencies of O'Higgins (1817–23), the genuinely liberal Ramón Freire (1823–27), and Francisco Antonio Pinto (1827–29)—a span during which the country had four constitutions—caused a great deal of frustration among conservatives. The early republic lacked the confidence of many members of the new republican political aristocracy and informed citizens who considered the infant state dysfunctional. News of civil war in Argentina, moreover, fed fears of chaos and anarchy in Chile. Using a dispute over the vice presidential elections of 1829 to their advantage, conservative interests (known collectively as the *pelucones*, or "big wigs") headed by Valparaíso businessman Diego Portales launched a revolt that ended the liberal regime in April 1830, terminating the project initiated by O'Higgins. Portales's hand-picked nominee for president, Joaquín Prieto, took power in 1831, thus beginning the so-called Portalian Republic. The constitution of 1833, which swept away the liberal constitution of 1828, was then promulgated.

Centralized executive authority formed the basis of the new constitution. Political might flowed from Santiago, and the executive possessed emergency powers to govern the nation whenever he deemed it necessary. However, it should not be inferred that executives of the Portalian period matched the brutality of Argentine caudillo Juan Manuel de Rosas or other similar characters. Simon Collier explains that "Chile managed to put a stop to disorder without accepting a personal tyranny. By creating a strong but impersonal authority, the Chileans were able to pave the way for later constitutional government and the establishment of a genuinely democratic tradition."[3] While the power brokers of the Portalian system recurrently disregarded the political principles of liberalism (jailing opponents was not extraordinary), they oversaw a steady growth in foreign trade—an ingredient of economic liberalism—from the 1820s to the 1870s. The value of external trade in 1825, for example, stood at $7.5 million. The figure increased to $74 million by 1875. Led by the bustling and economically critical port of Valparaíso, Chile's prolonged economic expansion would not have occurred without advances in infrastructure. The government and private Chilean investors, for instance, together financed the important Santiago–Valparaíso railroad line built by North American Henry Meiggs. Foreign investment, however, remained meager before the nitrate era.

Sturdy but adaptive, Portales's constitutional system weathered the assassination of its master builder (Portales was shot in 1837), a protracted international conflict in the 1830s, and two civil wars in the 1850s but eventually succumbed to intraelite discord over the distribution of political power. By the late 1880s, as the spoils of victory in the War of the Pacific began paying their financial dividends to the treasury, conflict mounted between the Portalian system's defenders and a section of the political hierarchy that wanted to limit presidential authority and expand legislative influence. After the hard-fought election of Chile's first Liberal president in 1861, Liberal and Conservative notables maintained an arrangement regarding presidential succession that propelled members of each party to the presidential palace. This Liberal-Conservative amalgam contributed to political stability for much of the second half of the nineteenth century, though presidential elections did not go without heated political firefights. Tensions were especially acute during the presidency of José Manuel Balmaceda (1886–91), a Liberal and defender of the constitution's stress on executive prerogative.

Nitrate production in the once Peruvian and Bolivian arid north spurred economic growth and government spending during the 1880s. Export taxes on the fertilizer yielded just over half of all government revenue in 1890, as nitrate mining enterprises, like those owned by the Englishman John Thomas North, earned huge profits. Between 1886 and 1890 alone, twenty-one British-owned operations were started in the nitrate zone.[4] Accordingly, populations swelled in northern mining hubs such as Antofagasta, which saw its population climb from 5,384 in 1875 to 21,213 in 1885.[5] The growth of urban centers in the north and the conglomeration of thousands of workers and their families in poor living conditions led to the proliferation of political movements and ideologies that, by the first decade of the twentieth century, prompted violent crackdowns that left hundreds dead and thousands more deeply resentful of the oligarchic establishment's heavy-handed approach to the social question.

As Chilean demographic and economic patterns changed in the 1880s, the need for investment in vital public works and other infrastructure became apparent to many. Fifteen new railroads spanning more than 1,150 kilometers were constructed in the Norte Chico, the Central Valley, and southern provinces during the Balmaceda administration. Fifty-six new primary schools were constructed between 1886 and 1888, partially helping expand the total student population nationwide from 79,000 to 140,000. In addition, a new medical school, a hospital, and an art school were among the many major public projects in the capital that were sponsored by the Balmaceda administration.[6] Although Balmaceda's accomplishments looked good on paper, the manner in which he exercised power progressively crippled his ability to keep his political friends, including interests (such as the PR) that had supported his candidacy in 1886.

By the second year of the Balmaceda administration, deep resentment was evident among *parlamentarios* who complained of the executive branch's meddling in elections, the president's taste for decrees rather than legislative policy making, and his rhetoric regarding the possible expansion of the state's role in nitrate production. On the first two counts, Alberto Edwards commented that the nineteenth century had seen a gradual democratization of the political system; Balmaceda, however, swam against this tide—a "law of history"—and, ultimately, was defeated in his attempt to continue the "monarchical tradition" of Spanish colonialism and Portales.[7] There is much to Edwards's observation. In the wake of Chile's midcentury civil strife, an agreement was established in 1861 that loosened the executive branch's grip on political power without eschewing its central role in government decision making. Electoral reforms, which included the expansion of suffrage to all males over twenty-five years of age, followed during the administrations of the 1870s and early 1880s. But Edwards, anti-Balmacedist to the last, displayed a flair for exaggeration when he fastened the badge of Hispanic monarchism on Balmaceda's presidential sash.

The issue of nitrates, a major point of contention between Balmacedists and their enemies in the Congress, became paramount by 1887. When Balmaceda opened the new legislative session on June 1 of that year, he suggested that his government would adopt a new way of dealing with foreign interests involved in nitrate production: "Ideas are being entertained [within the administration] regarding means that would permit the nationalization [not state ownership but ownership by Chilean nationals], to the extent it would be practical, of Chilean industries that today bear fruit principally in the hands of foreigners."[8] Balmaceda's detractors in the Congress harshly criticized the president's inflammatory rhetoric in such newspapers as the conservative *El Independiente* and *El Estandarte Católico*, both of Santiago. Fearing the possible loss of their investment capital and their high earnings, British entrepreneurs (such as North) rallied support among parliamentarians in defense of laissez-faire. The growing rift within Chile's political elite over nitrate capital and revenue capped a process that saw the Liberal-Conservative amalgam dissipate, for the time being.

The political and constitutional situation worsened in 1890, when the president looked to pick a successor to win the upcoming election of 1891—a Portalian custom. Liberal and affluent landowner Enrique Salvador Sanfuentes was Balmaceda's man. In light of the fact that Sanfuentes had enemies within his own party, not to mention among conservatives, an open struggle ensued within the political hierarchy over presidential succession and the nature of supreme authority in general. Tired of the president's tactics, a congressional majority agreed that Balmaceda was no longer fit to serve. Balmaceda's reference to the legislative body as a "bastard parliamentary system" only inflamed the situation.[9] To make matters worse for Balmaceda, heightened political tensions in Santiago were matched by growing unrest in the nitrate centers in 1890 when a cyclical downturn in the mining economy prompted large demonstrations in the northern region. When tensions within the political leadership reached an apex in late 1890 and early 1891, a civil war erupted.[10] It lasted nine months, costing the lives of some ten thousand Chileans and marking the end of the Portalian system. The heyday of Chilean nitrates, in short, saw the most violent outbreak of civil hostilities since the 1850s.

As the guns fell silent and Balmaceda lay dead from a self-inflicted gunshot wound, such notable parliamentarians as Joaquín Walker Martínez, Isidoro Errázuriz Errázuriz, and Manuel José Yrarrázaval (also spelled Irarrázaval) began formulating a new parliament-centered system of governance under the authority of a provisional junta. Months later, naval captain Jorge Montt became the first post-Portalian president and later tabbed PR figure Enrique Mac-Iver, a Balmaceda supporter-turned-enemy, to head the Ministry of the Treasury (the highest appointment for a Radical to that date). In December 1891, the president openly discussed amnesty for all civil war combatants. After two amnesty laws were issued in 1893, the toned-down Balmacedists were soon involved in the workings of government once more via the Liberal-Democratic Party (Partido Liberal Democrático, or PLD), which became a significant player in parliamentary politics. Stability, it seems, had returned. Yet, as the new parliamentary order matured, other social and political actors, including the PR, rose to challenge it.

The New Republic

The period known as the Parliamentary Republic (the name derives from the legislative branch's primacy in governmental affairs) began with the ouster of Balmaceda—the last "Portalian" executive—and ended with the promulgation of the constitution of 1925 and political intervention by the Chilean military. The executive, who enjoyed wide powers under the Portalian system, was stripped of supreme authority by the victors in the 1891 conflict, and most of the decision-making powers of the government shifted to the Chamber of Deputies and the Senate. But without clearly defined leadership emanating from the executive branch or a cloture rule in either legislative body, parliamentary debates seemed endless and useless.[11] Political parties (none with an outright majority in the Chamber or Senate) were, according to critics, often consumed by self-interest and scheming for the next election.[12] In mid-1893, only two years after the civil war, Radical deputy Francisco Puelma Tupper, appearing at a party assembly in Santiago, expressed growing rancor within the PR toward parliamentary politics by stating that he dreaded more the "dictatorship of the families Yrarrázaval or Walker Martínez" than the "dictatorship" of Balmaceda.[13]

Parliamentary stalemates caused by ratification procedures for ministerial appointments and repeated standoffs over the national budget translated into continual chaos within the executive branch. Some eighty-nine different cabinets were formed and dissolved over the course of seven presidential administrations between 1891 and 1925, and, without a powerful executive to serve as a political rudder, some sixty different ministries were formed between 1891 and 1915, each with an average life of only four months. Blakemore notes that "Chile experienced in these years neither dictatorial government nor military intervention, and these were part of a valuable historical tradition which the parliamentary period underlined. But the price was stultification of ministerial initiative [and the] lack of long-term planning. . . . It's not surprising that the strains on the social fabric of Chile were acute by the end of the period."[14]

The legislative branch's centrality in the Parliamentary Republic established a medium for the proliferation of party politics. The electoral old guard of the Portalian years (the Conservative, Liberal, National, and Radical parties) was now accompanied by the Balmacedist Liberal-Democrats and, perhaps more important, two political parties that changed the tone of Chile's political conversation. As the newest players in the political game, the Democratic Party (Partido Democrático, or PD), led by the lawyer Malaquías Concha, and the Socialist Workers Party (Partido Obrero Socialista, or POS) of former Democrat Luis Emilio Recabarren brought greater attention to the ongoing social question. Radicals, meanwhile, slowly increased their representation in the Chamber of Deputies and Senate. The Democrats, an ensemble of artisans, workers, and former Radicals who had grown tired of the PR's centrism but remained committed to reform, established their party in 1887 in the name of the "political, economic, and social liberation of the people."[15] The PD largely remained on the margins of liberal coalitions until the 1920s, and aspects of its platform (which included planks regarding obligatory education and economic protectionism) were championed by more significant parties, including the PR. Recabarren's POS, a predecessor of the Chilean Communist Party (Partido Comunista de Chile, or PCCh), also failed to rally much electoral support during the Parliamentary years, though its activities among labor unions made it an influential minor party. Founded in 1912, the POS sought radical social change through proletarian activism and, after its first congress in 1915, actively engaged in the organization and radicalization of trade unions. Recabarren, who some believe met Lenin during a European trip, became a symbolic leader for the mid- and late-twentieth-century Chilean Left after his death in 1924.

Statistics show a steady increase in the electoral pull of the Democrats after the turn of the century, while the POS lagged behind. PD candidates for the Chamber of Deputies garnered 4.2 percent of the vote in 1912 (suffrage was limited to males over the age of twenty-five), 7.9 percent in 1915, 6.5 percent in 1918, and 12.4 percent in 1921. During the same period, the PR maintained electoral supremacy over the Democrats, boasting 16.6 percent of the vote in the Chamber elections of 1912. That figure doubled in 1921, eclipsing the showing of the giant Conservative Party (Partido Conservador, or PC) by some 10 percent.[16] While both the Conservative and Liberal parties showed a long-term decline in their electoral support within the Chamber during the Parliamentary Republic, the Radicals and Democrats enjoyed opposing trends. The leaps shown by Radicalism during the Parliamentary years were clearly the result of some important factors: the creation of a political machinery based on local assemblies, youth groups, social clubs, and clientelism, as well as the expansion of the Chilean bureaucracy. As the government grew and the liberal professions boomed in civil society, an ever increasing number of mesocrats turned to a well-organized PR for solutions to the myriad of political, socioeconomic, and cultural problems of the day.

Birth and Growth of Chilean Radicalism, 1850s–1890s

By the second decade of the twentieth century, the PR stood firmly in the center of the political spectrum, sandwiched between anarchist, communist, and socialist groups on one side and the traditional parties of the elite on the other (the Conservative, Liberal, and Liberal-Democratic parties). It formed alliances, negotiated some legislative compromises, and added a measure of stability to a parliamentary system that often stood on the verge of collapse owing to congressional stalemates and ministerial turnover. The party's moderate or centrist posture during the Parliamentary Republic was relatively new, in a manner of speaking. For much of its history, the PR constituted what could be considered the Left and operated on the margin of the political arena until the latter third of the nineteenth century. Inspired by European republicanism and the Revolutions of 1848, Radicals erected an edifice of ideas and programs on a foundation established by the philippics of Francisco Bilbao, one of the most notable figures—along with José Victorino Lastarria and Venezuelan-born Andrés Bello—of nineteenth-century Chile's political and intellectual circles. Bilbao lashed out against the legacies of Hispanic colonialism in the newspaper *El Crepúsculo* in the mid-1840s, criticizing the Catholic Church and much of the governmental

superstructure for their conservatism. Moreover, Bilbao, along with Santiago Arcos and the Matta brothers, established the Society of Equality, an
important organizational precursor to the PR, in 1850. The society, drawn to
the liberal principles of the French abbot Lamennais, openly and vociferously criticized the existing Portalian order and the administration of President Manuel Bulnes (1841–51) at public gatherings and demonstrations. In
response, Bulnes's intendant of Santiago outlawed the group, and the regime cracked down on the opposition press, ending the Society of Equality
but not the movement it spawned. The administration's quick reaction to
the organization attests to the concern generated among conservatives by
the liberal firebrands.

A rebellious fragment of the Liberal Party (Partido Liberal, or PL), the PR
coalesced during the 1860s in the wake of two civil wars that shook the
republic's foundations, and it came to be a more powerful political force
than its organizational predecessor, the Society of Equality. Established in
1861 and led by such figures as Guillermo Matta and Pedro León Gallo, the
PR experienced a steady rise from relative obscurity. In 1863, the first Radical
Assembly was held in the city of Copiapó, an important mining hub in the
desert north. Assemblies then followed in La Serena in the Norte Chico and
later in the southern city of Concepción in 1865. Radicals, after becoming
important players in coalition politics by the early 1880s, threw their support
behind Balmaceda's candidacy in 1886 but later withdrew their allegiance
because of the president's defense of executive privilege. Enrique Mac-Iver
and another Matta brother, Manuel, were among the more notable Radicals
who fought on the side of parliamentarism during the civil war of 1891.

Early Radicalism's base of support largely came from members of the
urban elite discouraged by the PL's traditionalism, southern landowners
who had grown tired of the Central Valley landowning oligarchy's strangle-
hold on Chilean politics, and mining entrepreneurs. Only decades later did
the party adopt a firmly urban, middle-class base and identity. As modernization accelerated after the War of the Pacific, urban professionals (teachers,
lawyers, accountants, journalists, bureaucrats, and so forth) increasingly
turned to the PR as the most appropriate representative of their interests. By
the end of the nineteenth century, as Alberto Edwards eloquently explains,
Radicalism's rank and file consisted of "men of recent origin—without he-
reditary ties that bound them to the soul of the old culture—educated in the
ideas of liberty."[17]

In 1888, the party held its first national convention, which was attended by
such standouts as Mac-Iver, Manuel Matta, Eduardo de la Barra, Valentín

Letelier, and Pedro Bannen. The meeting, held in Santiago, touched on a variety of social issues. On the topic of public education (one that was certainly on the back burner of the oligarchy's legislative agenda), the Radicals called for a law mandating free, obligatory, and secular primary instruction. The party also aimed for the "improvement of the legal condition of women" and "the improvement of conditions for the proletarians and laborers."[18] The need for reform measures from above to stall more radical ideas for social change that were beginning to surge from below was the underlying theme of convention discussion. While espousing a rhetoric of reform, the party lacked a clearly articulated program. Although it adopted a platform that briefly mentioned workers and alluded to their poor living conditions, the convention remained relatively silent regarding the working class and the social question—a fact that may have contributed to the steady growth of Malaquías Concha's PD.

Apparent during and after the 1888 convention was Radicalism's attention to "order" and "progress." Drawing on notions of social evolution and the sociological positivism of Comte and Littré, the Radicals explicitly rejected violence as a means of social change but, unlike more orthodox positivists in Latin America, did not find abstract, metaphysical, and universal concepts, such as liberty, equality, fraternity, or the republican spirit, anachronistic. In the first issue of the Radical newspaper *La Lei* in 1894, the party pledged to follow a course of social reform without breaching the political norms of republican constitutionalism, calling the preservation of "legal and social order" a "great cause."[19] The key to maintaining social peace was fundamental reform through the evolution of political institutions. Without rejecting their positivist dedication to order and progress, many Radicals endorsed a "socialist" disposition during the first decade of the century. At the PR's third national convention held in Santiago in 1906, a tendency in favor of a so-called *socialismo de Estado*, or "state socialism," emerged; it prompted the most heated debates over the party's ideological foundation to that date. Spearheaded by the former rector of the Pedagogical Institute, Valentín Letelier, a Radical bloc touting "socialism" proposed increased government intervention in social and economic affairs and, in general, espoused a nebulous but powerful notion of a criollo gemeinschaft, of sorts. Chile's long-standing tradition of upholding free trade as an economic pillar was among the primary targets of the party's Letelierian branch. Letelier, an admirer of Otto von Bismarck's Germany (a system he witnessed firsthand in the late 1880s), argued on the convention floor: "All of the cultured peoples of the world have at this moment something of socialism, in the sense that they look out for the interests of society. . . . There is no reason to be puzzled when the Radical Party is called socialist; when it was born in political life it was also branded, ironically, as socialist and also communist and *sansimoniano* [followers of the intellectual Saint-Simon]; aren't we accustomed to epithets being put on us?"[20]

Led by Mac-Iver, Radicalism's conservative wing ardently opposed the "state socialist" tendency mounting within the party. The Mac-Iverist faction maintained that Radicals should preserve their "individualist" posture when addressing vital national issues. Mac-Iver also argued in favor of keeping the state away from economic affairs and, as a more moderate Radical on the issue of clerical power, feared that Letelier was showing his "Jacobin" stripes when he virulently criticized church-state ties.[21] At one point, Mac-Iver and his followers at the convention threatened to break with the PR if the "socialist" plank passed. The party, however, managed to weather the storm intact. When the rain clouds cleared from the convention floor and the air calmed, Letelier's position emerged victorious. The PR's 1906 declaration of principles emphasized the state's responsibility in improving conditions in such areas as health and education, calling such involvement a "moral duty." In addition, it called upon the state to "dictate laws and create institutions that would be necessary to better the conditions" of the working classes, which could raise the laboring poor to a more equitable social level.[22] All told, the essence of the 1906 platform remained a central component of Radical discourse and public policy in later decades.

Radicals who championed the Letelierian line were careful to distinguish between their form of socialism and revolutionary ideologies, specifically communism and anarchism. Armando Quezada Acharán, a Letelier supporter at the 1906 convention, explained that Radical reform efforts, especially those directed at easing the plight of the working classes, should not be confused with "systematic socialism that, among other things, aspires to collectivize property."[23] Years after the convention, the Radicals remained on the defensive regarding their adoption of "state socialism." A 1909 newspaper editorial, worth citing at length, defined Radicalism's "socialist" sensibility in the following terms: "Socialism contributes to the union of everyone for the general good; it is equal justice, it is defense of the weak against the strong, it is protection of the workers against the abuses of capital. . . . It is not, then, a threat to the State or the Government, whatever it may be; it does not aim to get rid of property nor be involved in anyone's life. It only aspires to produce the greatest wellness and the greatest accumulation of benefits, dividing them among the greatest possible number."[24]

Outnumbered in the Congress for most of the Parliamentary Republic, Radicals could only hope to realize such goals by building alliances with other parties. The organization agreed to enter the first Liberal Alliance (Alianza Liberal) during the presidency of Federico Errázuriz Zañartu (1871–75), joining the National Party (secular conservatives) and Liberals. During the administration of Federico Errázuriz Echaurren (the son of the afore-mentioned president) at the end of the nineteenth century, Radicals were members of an opposition alliance along with a number of liberal factions, including the Balmacedist PLD and Concha's PD. The ruling "Coalition" bloc during the Errázuriz Echaurren years included the Conservatives and traditionalist Liberals. By the end of the twentieth century's first decade, Radicals and Balmacedists were at the head of a newly refurbished Liberal Alliance (or AL), which also counted the National Party and yet another liberal splinter group as partners. Although Radicals were leaders in the civil war that toppled Balmaceda, they soon harbored no animosity toward the Balmacedists and considered them valuable allies. A 1908 *La Lei* editorial, in the wake of the PLD's national convention, explained that "an inspired and patriotic impulse swept though the whole assembly. The last thought of Balmaceda seemed to have arrived like a breath of fire in the hearts of his political heirs."[25] Never mind that one of Balmaceda's last thoughts proba-bly was an unkind epithet directed to Radicals who took up arms against him in 1891.

After throwing their support behind Liberal candidate Germán Riesco Errázuriz, who emerged victorious in the presidential election of 1901, Radi-cal leaders enjoyed ministerial offices, such as Justice and Public Instruction, Treasury, and War and Navy, in six of the administration's seventeen cabi-nets. Radicals occupied ministerial posts from time to time after the Riesco administration as well, but in proportionally fewer numbers. Between 1906 and 1915 (during the presidencies of Pedro Montt and Ramón Barros Luco, both Liberals), only nine Radicals—six as ministers of industry, public works, and railroads, one as minister of war and the navy, and one as minister of the treasury—served in twenty-six cabinets. It was not until the presidential administration of Juan Luis Sanfuentes (1915–20) did Radicalism emerge as the nation's outright leader in coalition politics.

A veteran of the parliamentary machinery, Sanfuentes defeated Javier An-gel Figueroa Larraín, who had garnered the support of Radicals and dissi-dent Liberals (more progressive members of the PL), in 1915. To Radicals the victory of Sanfuentes may have, at first, signified the continuation of the oligarchic establishment, but the government later demonstrated nuances that enthused many Radical *correligionarios* (party members often called one another "coreligionists"). After Sanfuentes's first cabinet—composed almost entirely of Liberals and Conservatives—collapsed shortly after his inauguration, Radicals became important players in ministerial administration. Radicalism was represented by Armando Quezada Acharán (Treasury and Interior), Eduardo Suárez (Foreign Relations), Pedro Aguirre Cerda (Justice and Public Instruction), Daniel Feliú (Foreign Relations), Ramón Briones (Industry, Public Works, and Railroads), Ruperto Bahamonde (Foreign Relations), Víctor Robles (War and Navy), Luis Aníbal Barrios (Treasury), the author Luis Orrego Luco (Justice and Public Instruction), Luis Serrano (Interior and Industry, Public Works, and Railroads), Anselmo Hevia (Interior), Pablo Ramírez (Justice and Public Instruction), Enrique Oyarzún (Treasury), and Javier Gandarillas (Justice and Public Instruction).[26] More Radicals served under Sanfuentes than in any other five-year administration. Furthermore, significant electoral gains registered by the PR in the parliamentary elections of 1918 strengthened the opinion within the oligarchy that Radicalism was a movement to be taken with absolute seriousness. In sum, the shifting of some degree of political influence from the oligarchy to reformist mesocrats is evident during the Sanfuentes administration, although much of the existing historiography suggests that 1920 was the pivotal year of transition. (The president went so far as to tab PD leader Malaquías Concha to serve as minister of industry, public works, and railroads in October 1918 and again in March 1920.)

A deep split was apparent among Chilean liberals and the parliamentary leadership at large as the presidential election of 1920 neared. Within the Liberal Party, dividing lines were drawn over the issue of state intervention in social and economic matters, with dissident Liberals on one side and traditionalist Liberals on the other. Radicals joined dissident Liberals, Concha's Democrats, and Recabarren's POS in a new incarnation of the AL and backed the candidacy of a politically experienced and populistic grandson of an Italian immigrant, Arturo Alessandri Palma. A senator, lawyer, and former congressional deputy, Alessandri (along with such personalities as Eliodoro Yañez, the founder of the dissident Liberal newspaper *La Nación*) broke from traditionalist Liberals during the second decade of the century because of the PL leadership's aloofness regarding the country's socioeconomic problems. It was Alessandri's self-appointed goal to save liberalism from itself. In a March 1920 letter to Radical leaders, including his friend Aguirre Cerda, Alessandri wrote: "I have initiated a campaign before the country to defend what I believe are the genuine interests of democracy and liberal-

Arturo Alessandri Palma upon his victory in the presidential election of 1920. (Courtesy of Eduardo Devés)

ism."[27] Although Radical support of Alessandri did not come without grumbles from some party members, his campaign echoed the basic tenets of PR doctrine: order, progress, social evolution, reform, justice, and democracy. A Radical, Héctor Arancibia Laso, ran Alessandri's campaign, while another PR *correligionario*, the poet Víctor Domingo Silva, wrote propaganda for the AL in the daily *El Mercurio*.

By a narrow margin, Alessandri emerged victorious over the *parlamentarista* candidate, Luis Barros Borgoño, and immediately set out to further the democratization of politics, formulate reform proposals, and fight conservative senators (who remained in control of the body) over legislation. We shall return to the elections of 1920 and the social milieu of the late Parliamentary years in subsequent chapters, but it is important to state here that the Alessandri years represented a fundamental departure from *parlamentarismo*, though the system remained structurally intact until after Alessandri was pushed out of power by the military in 1924. The opening to reformism that appeared during the Sanfuentes years widened during the early 1920s, and the lower classes quickly took advantage of their newly gained political influence. Never again would the aristocracy and its political oligarchs possess exclusive control of the political arena.

As Radicals became dynamic and influential actors among the Parliamentary Republic's movers and shakers, they continued to complain loudly that oligarchs were slow to respond to the mounting social problems that arose from modernization. Whether revolutionary, reformist, or conservative, all the major political parties of the era addressed, in one way or another, the myriad of problems that stemmed from socioeconomic and demographic shifts that changed the face of Chilean society, though Radicals would have their compatriots believe they were the sole voices of sympathy and sources of action. The most pressing matters of national concern were issues related to the working class, which had grown from 75,000 people in 1879 to some 350,000 by 1920.[28]

The Social Question: Workers, Reformers, and Oligarchs

During the latter decades of the nineteenth century, significant structural changes in the economy had profound repercussions on social relations. The mining economy's rapid growth in the north and incipient industrialization in northern and central regions established a new pattern of conditions that incited working-class activism as well as fear of social revolution within more affluent strata. The social question—an umbrella term first employed in the mid-nineteenth century to denote the varying points of discord between workers and *patrones* (bosses or employers)—became the paramount concern in fin de siècle Chilean politics. Given both the existing historiography's detailed documentation of Chile's social question and this study's scope, we need only discuss the social question in broad terms to establish the circumstances that contributed to worker unrest and, in turn, the varying interpretations of, and responses to, the phenomenon during early decades of the twentieth century.

The Parliamentary Republic saw socioeconomic change not unlike that of nineteenth-century Europe, the United States, and neighboring Argentina, as well as an urbanization boom that permanently altered the country's human geography. Tens of thousands migrated from rural areas to northern mining camps to feed the nitrate industry's ever increasing hunger for labor, while thousands more campesinos moved to Santiago, Valparaíso, and other industrializing cities in search of higher wages. According to census data, the population of Antofagasta (the main port of the nitrate-rich province sharing its name) swelled from 13,500 in 1895 to 33,000 in 1907. In 1920, the port counted more than 51,000 residents. Santiago's population nearly doubled between 1885 and 1920, growing from 256,403 to 507,796. The magnitude of urbanization is best weighed when one considers rural population figures for the same period. The city of Talca (in the center-south's province of

Maule) registered 33,323 inhabitants in 1895 and only 36,079 in 1920. Chillán, the capital of the province of Ñuble, saw its population decline from 33,386 in 1895 to 30,881 in 1920.[29]

Laborers arriving in mining districts and cities faced harsh working and living conditions—the underpinnings of the social question. Housing for the working class, for example, varied from unhealthy to truly squalid. Workers crowded into one- and two-story *conventillos* (tenements) in the capital and Valparaíso. Some *conventillos* housed dozens of families at one time. It is estimated that the adobe or brick walls of some 2,000 *conventillos* in 1911 were home to 130,000 *santiaguinos*, a figure that translates to 40 percent of the city's total population. The average single-family room measured 19.64 square meters and averaged four residents in 1910.[30] It was not uncommon for *conventillo* beds to be used around the clock, as families split their labor between night and day shifts. In Antofagasta, moreover, the housing situation was called "the most painful insult to human sentiment" and "inadequate for human beings" by one working-class organization.[31] Cramped living conditions facilitated the rapid spread of disease, leading to infant mortality rates that ranked among the world's highest during the first decades of the twentieth century.

Official figures of fatal disease are staggering. Chile's infant mortality rate in 1909—31.5 percent dead before reaching one year of age—equaled that of Russia, eclipsed Italy's, Argentina's, or France's by 50 percent, doubled the rates of Uruguay and Great Britain, and was 200 percent higher than the mortality rate in New Zealand. Infant mortality rates in the small provincial cities of Curicó and San Felipe were higher than that of Bombay, while rates in Valparaíso, Talcahuano, and La Serena surpassed Calcutta's. Of the 626,623 deaths nationwide between 1905 and 1910, 303,417 were children who failed to reach the age of five.[32] Health officials were especially concerned with a tuberculosis epidemic that gripped the country's major urban centers. Spread through the air mostly indoors, the respiratory ailment claimed the lives of thousands of children and adults. Between 1915 and 1920 alone, respiratory diseases caused an average of 33,000 deaths per year. In 1921, a study of 1,064 children found that 296 suffered from tuberculosis or other respiratory diseases. Only 52 were considered "healthy." A smallpox epidemic in Santiago, moreover, killed 1,000 residents per month in 1921.[33] Of course, upper-class Chileans were susceptible to disease, but working-class neighborhoods, many of which had sewer water draining down their streets, were zones of extreme risk. Compounding the situation were preventable maladies, such as alcoholism and venereal diseases, that swiftly made their way through the urban working class.

If health and housing situations were poor for laborers during the Parliamentary Republic, working environments fared no better, especially in nitrate zones. The labor intensity of nitrate mining and refining as well as the isolated nature of the northern *oficinas* (nitrate production centers) presented laborers with formidable challenges. *Oficina* bosses, for example, often issued their own form of currency (*fichas*, or tokens) to their workers, forcing them to purchase only goods offered in the company-owned store. It was also not uncommon to see many thousands of children under sixteen years of age engaged in dangerous mining operations under the watchful eyes of *oficina* administrators who, in the words of one foreign visitor, wielded immense power over their respective "small kingdoms."[34] Moreover, the value of the money earned from working under the Atacama Desert's sun evaporated like sweat. As wages remained stagnant between 1890 and 1910, the peso's long-term devaluation eroded the purchasing power of workers seeking to buy basic foodstuffs, including sugar, bread, milk, meat, and potatoes, that tripled in price during the same twenty-year period. Workers, moreover, complained of poor or nonexistent medical care and the lack of cemeteries.

A working-class family's situation obviously took a turn for the worse when unemployment struck. Oscillations in the international nitrate trade often entailed massive layoffs in the *oficinas*. The first major downturn in nitrate production came between 1896 and 1898 and led to the reduction of the nitrate workforce from 22,485 to 15,955.[35] One *santiaguino*, writing in the Radical newspaper *La Lei*, reflected on such problems in the following terms: "There isn't mail from the provinces of the north that does not bring us documented complaints stated with fiery and sincere language about the very sad situation, in terms of economy, in which the workers have been placed." He went on to call the *oficinas* outposts of "feudal servitude" and placed blame squarely on the shoulders of nitrate magnates and complicit oligarchs of the Parliamentary Republic's leadership who together believed that "force is the adequate method" for handling issues pertaining to the working class and the social question.[36]

As laborers massed in cities and mining communities, found common ground with others, discussed the problems they shared, and looked to better their situations, organized elements of the working class became competitors in politics for the first time. Once dispersed on the rural landscape or sprinkled about the cities, thousands of workers found themselves in close quarters—spaces in which ideas moved with fluidlike properties from worker to worker, *oficina* to *oficina*, dock to dock, and factory to factory. From within this new environment there emerged a "new democratic conscience," as historian Julio Heise González puts it. The ideological confluence of "democracy" and "liberty" that prevailed among the republic's founders during the early nineteenth century gave way to that of "democracy" and "equality," especially among emerging middle- and working-class groups.[37] Equality was what union leaders like Valentín Arce of the Society of Shoemakers desired: "The working class is waking up everywhere. . . . The workers look as though they are finally dusting off the apathy that kept them submerged in indifference. . . . The time of vindication is nearing."[38]

Three types of working-class organizations emerged during the late nineteenth century: trade unions; *mancomunales* (or fellowships that functioned much like mutual aid societies); and anarchist-led "resistance societies" (largely composed of artisans, shop workers, and dockworkers in Santiago, Valparaíso, and Antofagasta). Along with the Democrats and Recabarren's POS (which became the PCCh in 1922), these groups permanently changed the nature of Chilean politics. Trade unions before 1900 did not champion Marxist ideology and generally responded to local grievances rather than national ones. This would change during the first decade of the twentieth century, when the trade union movement meshed with the *mancomunales* and members of the POS to form the first major umbrella union in the country's history, the Chilean Workers Federation (Federación Obrera de Chile, or FOCh) in 1909. The FOCh quickly gained a large following—one hundred thousand members by 1920—and adhered to communist principles. In fact, members of the FOCh stopped carrying the Chilean flag in its rallies in 1919, opting instead for a red banner.[39]

Reformist mesocrats harbored a much deeper fear of anarchists, who burst onto the turn-of-the-century political scene and persisted until the late 1920s, than of communist trade unions. Chilean anarchists allied themselves with the Industrial Workers of the World (IWW) after that organization was founded in London in 1919, and they established such unions as the Regional Workers Federation of Chile (Federación Obrera Regional de Chile) and the Chilean Federal Union (Unión Federal Chilena). Radicals talked about Chilean anarcho-syndicalism in an almost desperate tone: "The thrones and societies of Europe find themselves threatened by anarchism. . . . When the atmosphere is impregnated by invisible atoms that create vice and corrupt, there is a germination and propagation of calamity," a concerned Radical explained. Anarchists, he resolved, use the social question to spread "nihilism," which is a "monster that sinisterly frightens" law and order.[40] Another Radical *correligionario* troubled by both anarchism and the diffusion of Marxist ideas explained, "There is no other solution to the frightful problem that exists in the nitrate region but justice. We need to resolve it promptly, adopting just resolutions that the injured cry of the enslaved worker demands, and only then we will see the red and black phantasm [the colors of communism and anarchism, respectively] disappear, emblems of blood and death that roam throughout the nitrate lands and are formed from the cries of the worker who agonizes while trapped in the burning chains of a servitude that does not release him until when he is returned inanimate to the bosom of the Earth."[41] To Radicals, the ideas of law, order, progress, and democracy left no room to stomach worker-sponsored violence (among other things), but the PR tolerated strikes resulting from specific points of discord between patrons and employees. "Justice," though presented as an amorphous, vague notion by the columnist quoted above, nonetheless translated into specific reforms (such as education reform) down the line, which, it was hoped, would stem a tide of anger among Chilean workers. Such Radicals believed that reform, rather than state-sponsored violence, was the key to ensuring social peace and curbing further working-class radicalization.

In March 1921, interior minister Aguirre Cerda was informed that "Bolshevism" was spreading among workers of the Nitrate and Railway Company of Agua Santa in the northern desert. A company administrator in the port of Caleta Buena reported that workers gathered in the plaza to hear a student named Triguiño and a worker not of the company (both apparently from Iquique) espouse "ideas completely Bolshevist, very hostile toward the government and capital, that reached the point of recommending contempt toward the *patria*. They have left seeds of discontent among our workers who have become very impressed by such speakers."[42] The next month, Aguirre Cerda received a letter from the Radical Assembly of Curanilahue (near Concepción) with news that three Radicals were killed during various days of conflict between PR members and radicalized workers. The report, moreover, stated that party members were the targets of threats, a conspiracy, and a boycott at the hands of the local branch of the FOCh. Local PR chiefs complained that the union was persecuting Radicals "for no other reason than for not accepting its [the union's] violent or revolutionary methods" for ameliorating the social question. Examples of alleged union aggression included a boycott of businesses owned by the González brothers, Marcial

Martínez, Luis Arriagada, Manuel Contreras, and Carlos Roberto Saavedra, as well as plans to burn down or blow up houses owned by the aforementioned Radicals.[43] Such cases of confrontation between reformers and
working-class organizations with more revolutionary agendas were not
uncommon during the Parliamentary Republic. Frustrated with the reformers' ties to a state that openly attacked workers with brutal force on
numerous occasions, working-class interests remained hostile toward Radical intentions.

The most notable instances of labor unrest occurred during the first decade of the century, when workers in mining districts, Valparaíso, and Santiago organized strikes and demanded better working and living environments, payments in national currency, expanded health services, and other
reforms. After the nation's first general strike in 1890, a slew of worker-
patron confrontations provoked concern among reformers and *parlamentarista* traditionalists. Most labor conflicts were confined to the northern
nitrate zone, where workers often took to the streets. When violence spread
to other regions, political leaders in Santiago placed the social question at
the center of national debate. In May 1903, soldiers and gunfire met striking
port workers in Valparaíso who demanded a wage increase and fewer hours.
Nearly three dozen strikers were killed and more than eighty wounded. As
one Valparaíso native later recalled, "The city was an encampment the following day. Amid the ruins and clouds of smoke one could see the tents and
armaments of the soldiers who had arrived from Santiago and Limache."[44]
Four years later, an immense strike in the nitrate port of Iquique ended with
hundreds of dead workers after a military assault on a school, the Escuela
Santa María, where strikers had gathered.

Though they agreed that organized activism was the mother of political
change, the issue of strikes and other forms of pubic manifestations complicated matters for Radical reformers. Radicals, in general, supported what
they viewed as "just" or "orderly" strikes and social protests and assigned
such activism sociopolitical significance, while oligarchs overwhelmingly believed that strikes were but "rebellions of rabble."[45] Despite the fact that
Radicals supported strikes in principle, they disapproved of strikes that
spread to workers without direct ties to the foundry, factory, *oficina*, or port
where a given instance of patron-client disagreement originated. General
strikes were, therefore, simply considered by most Radicals as dangers to
social order. According to reformers, instances such as those in Valparaíso
and Iquique exemplified *parlamentarismo*'s failures: "We believe the moment
has arrived in which the men of state begin to concern themselves with the

questions posed by the current social and political situation. . . . We should take advantage of the lesson . . . and we should not remain blinded by egoism and ineptitude."[46]

The Radical press constantly defended the idea of social evolution by way of measured reform as a potion to treat the social question, and overt and subtle critiques of the oligarchy were almost always included in Radical diatribes about the ongoing problem. Radicals seemed cognizant that social change was proceeding at a faster pace than legislative solutions and that liberal democracy risked being swept away unless lawmakers could somehow keep up with the revolutionary momentum gaining within the urban lower class. As *La Lei* solemnly stated in the spring of 1907: "Whether you like it or not, with our wishes or against our wishes, the force of things has made it be that a new form of relation between laborer [*operador*] and boss [*patrono*], between employee and employer, has imperceptibly been elaborating."[47]

The social question dominated discussion at a special Radical congress in 1912, which gathered many of the party's top young (and some not so young) thinkers to discuss policy options. Among delegates at the First Congress of the Radical Youth of Chile were Aguirre Cerda, the authors Orrego Luco and Guillermo Labarca Hubertson, Armando Quezada Acharán, and educator Darío Salas. The president of the organizing committee, Armando Labra Carvajal, opened the convention by noting, "It is not possible to forget that the latent question in the entire world is that of the worker, who provokes so many doctrines and engenders in his spirit the concepts of solidarity to raise the great problem that is called the social question." Radical concern over the social question had come a long way since the 1888 convention, when the party glossed over the issue with general statements regarding the "improvement of conditions." This time, Radical delegates explicitly pinpointed an enemy to shoulder the blame for the social question's persistence: "Whereas the oligarchy is one of the insuperable obstacles to the free development of the principles of equality and democracy, Radicalism should accentuate its antioligarchic tendency as a means to realize its political aspirations."[48]

While reformers complained of the oligarchy's blindness toward serious political and socioeconomic problems, the republic's defenders offered their own interpretation of the social question and promoted elixirs to ameliorate it. Through its press apparatus, the oligarchic establishment demonstrated that it was not an undynamic bloc but rather one capable of molding its language to suit the political moment. Conservatives, for example, talked about economic problems, social despair, disease, housing problems, and working conditions and, at times, supported strikers against bosses. Their stance on the social question, which clearly differed from those of reformers and revolutionaries in matters of policy, was captured by Alejandro Huneeus, a congressional deputy in 1903, and is worth quoting at length:

> I am ... profoundly convinced of the great importance of that social question that has attracted universal attention to it; that question that exists not only in Europe but also in our own Chile, and that is intimately linked not only to the moral and religious order, but also the political and economic one. Just as I consider the worker and social question of primordial importance, I also consider that it is an imperative necessity, an inescapable duty that weighs on all the men of government to worry about it in a preferential manner. Hopefully what is happening in Europe does not happen in Chile, that which was allowed to happen by a liberal optimism and by the ideas of extreme individualism, and that maintained an indifference toward the labor movement only to wake up when the existing institutions were threatened by death and when the frightful problem of social salvation presented itself in all its magnitude.[49]

Huneeus called for laws to protect workers from overly demanding and unfair employers and foreshadowed some of the themes championed by the *falangistas* of the 1930s, who emerged from conservative circles and later formed the core of the Christian Democrat Party. It would, then, be incorrect to assume that conservatives turned a blind eye to the crisis confronting the lower reaches of society. With an expanding electorate, a more complex arena of party politics, a growing middle class, and a rising number of voting-age workers, conservative Chileans had little choice but to ease their obstinate language, especially during the latter years of the Parliamentary Republic.

Catholicism was a guiding sensibility among conservatives who could no longer ignore deepening social tensions. Pope Leo XIII's 1891 encyclical *Rerum Novarum*, which assigned to the Catholic Church a crusade against lower-class despair, proved highly influential in Chile and informed many of the Conservative Party's social, political, and economic ideas. The notion persisted among Conservatives that the biblical principle of humanism and religious brotherhood were key factors in easing social divisions and working-class plight. It is important to note here that the issue of church-state linkage was a central point of contention between Conservatives and Liberals of the elite during much of the nineteenth and early twentieth centuries, and certainly until the constitution of 1925 officially divided religion from affairs of state. It is not surprising, then, that despite sharing with

Conservatives the goal of maintaining the sociopolitical status quo, Liberals remained quite skeptical of Conservative calls for a more religious or Christian way of confronting the social question.

The leading conservative intellectual of the era who addressed the social question was Juan Enrique Concha, who meshed Catholic social philosophy and papal dictum with personal observations of the Chilean condition in his published materials and public statements. Concha and like-minded conservatives did not understand the social question as a purely economic concern but rather as a "psychological, moral, and religious question to which a solution will be found, the world willing, only in the teaching of Christ, practiced by the individual and respected and supported by the State and by laws."[50] In essence, the social question could be mitigated in the cultural realm; it was as much (or more) a question of ethos, he argued, than a question of socioeconomics. Monseñor Rafael Edwards also addressed the economic problems facing the working class (specifically inflation), but like Concha he also stressed the primacy of spiritual and moral concerns, among them the idea of family values: "The question of the price of goods constitutes, without a doubt, one of the factors [contributing to the social question], and is not one of the least considerable, of the discontent of our working classes; but, if one looks closely, this discontent also stems from more profound causes, more serious ones that have their roots in the peoples' own habits. In this way my personal conviction is that this crisis, as much a moral one as a material one, which is borne by the working class, comes from the bad state that dominates the constitution of the family." The family (and thus the working class), the cleric explains, is damaged not by macroeconomic structures but by the "father [who] does not perform his duty to allot the product of his labor to the maintenance of his home." The remedy from above, he goes on to state, is simple: "a continuous and patient labor of education, of charity, of Christian social action without self-interest."[51] The conservative elite essentially viewed Catholicism as the prime sociocultural instrument to soothe the apparent moral and religious crises that gripped the nation; they cast the social question as an important cultural concern rather than a purely socioeconomic one.

Amid the diatribes of reformers and working-class groups, conservatives believed that people who spent their time complaining about socioeconomic problems were not doing a service to society. Thus, beneficence was seen as a positive labor—a moral mission upon which many aristocrats embarked. Upper-class women, in particular, formed beneficence societies to improve the material conditions faced by workers and their families. One such group was the National Children's Foundation (Patronato Nacional de la Infancia), which conservatives believed was an exemplary organization that worked to relieve social strife, thus qualifying it as the antithesis of unions with pernicious revolutionary programs. The conservative press observed that "the foundation gathers the donations of the kind poor person and the generous rich, of the employee and the financier, for the children and mothers who they do not know but who they know suffer from poverty and pain. The parents and husbands of those children and women speak up in their lairs against the society that helps them in these ways, against those who have and give, against those who work and produce . . . but many workers with healthy souls, when they give their modest offerings, have understood the falsehood of the black picture of the society that is exhibited in the assemblies and meetings in which the red evangelism is preached."[52] The antirevolutionary and, indeed, antiliberal message of this crusade is clear: those who did not address the spiritual problems of the downtrodden masses were merely involved in pestilential, anti-Christian political rabble-rousing.

Radicals, who maintained an ardent secular plank and complained loudly of the church's power in Chilean society, naturally rejected the Catholic option outright. Traditionalist Liberals, too, were uneasy about the congregationalist road to social peace, though, at least during the Parliamentary Republic, this difference of opinion did not necessarily negate other common interests. Quite simply, Radicals believed that Catholic *parlamentaristas* were ignoring society's basic problems by shrouding them in clerical robes. This is not to say, however, that Radicals eschewed the importance of culture in society. On the contrary, they also saw the social question as a cultural one but certainly not a religious one. Indeed, middle-class reformers denounced conceptions of culture shared by the elite and pursued their own cultural remedies to the social question. More generally speaking, they believed Chile was in need of recasting, of democratization, of secularization, of "Chileanization" in response to the prevailing conditions of their day.

Aristocratic Culture in the Time of Nitrate

While economic modernization in late-nineteenth- and early-twentieth-century Latin America entailed the diversification of production, markets, and labor and political development meant competition between more parties, there existed a semblance of transnational uniformity in terms of the elite's cultural conventions, consumption patterns, and sociability. The

Chilean elite basically shared the same cultural goods and practices as the Carioca aristocracy in Brazil, wealthy landowners and merchants in Buenos Aires, the *comerciantes* of Lima, or the Porfirian elite in Mexico. Western Europe served as their cultural model, and France, in particular, was highly regarded by aristocrats for its refined cultural ways and commodities. Quite simply, members of Latin America's upper classes understood cultural cosmopolitanism as a means of civilizing their respective countries and what they considered a barbarous continent.

Outside the commotion of party politics and inside the tranquil sitting rooms, department stores, and theaters of the Parliamentary Republic, Chilean aristocrats—whether Conservatives or Liberals, clericalists or secularists, Balmacedists or *parlamentaristas*—together apportioned cultural capital among themselves and established modes of sociability that perpetuated a privileged cultural space. While many thousands of Chileans lived in squalor and thousands died in infancy, an obsessive attention to consumption and style (*la moda*) permeated the aristocracy as it replicated in the cultural realm the hierarchy of politics and economy. The elite dismissed the cultural practices of Chile's lower classes as pedantic, choosing instead to adopt, emulate, and cherish the cultural artifacts and rituals of the Old World (and the United States to some extent). They believed that valuable cultural practices could not come from sectors of society that did not stand as the "best examples" to "inspire proper ideas about Chile."[53] Manuel Vicuña observes that "the elite, in general, attributes to itself a set of virtues or values. . . . In contrast to the popular classes [*el pueblo*], which represent the chaos and the dark call of passions, the ruling group is order or, perhaps more exact, the conscience of the nation."[54] A controversy over Chile's planned pavilion for the Exposition of 1900 in Paris clearly exposed the aristocracy's opinions regarding what should be considered Chilean culture. As the Santiago newspaper *El Porvenir* explained, "Certain entrepreneurs of spectacles are preparing to take a group of Araucanians [Indians from the country's south] to the Grand Exposition in Paris. This deed awakens the tenacious opposition of one newspaper in the capital. It alleges that it . . . discredits the country: 'What national interest does it serve to cart around, in order to exhibit in Paris as a sample of Chile, a handful of Indians who are almost savage, brutalized, degraded, and repugnant in appearance?'"[55] True culture, aristocrats believed, existed within their own purview. In essence, the upper reaches of society looked down on lower-class cultural practices—and, indeed, members of the lower classes—with a notable degree of haughtiness.

The Parliamentary Republic's aura of cultural cosmopolitanism emanated from affluent *santiaguinos* whose cultural telos was "ostentation and pleasure."[56] Historian Fernando Silva explains that "by the end of the nineteenth century and likely since the end of the war [the War of the Pacific] there were symptoms of an inflexibility of the sectors of Santiago's high society expressed by a distant valorization of things not belonging to them. The trips, the long-term stays of Chilean families in foreign countries, especially in Paris, and . . . a spirit of imitation contributed to this phenomenon."[57] Aristocrats, then, defined their favored place in Chilean society not only by pedigree or genealogy but also by their cultural tastes and through public displays of culture, or what they considered proper cultural practice. It was important to possess certain cultural markers of socioeconomic status—ones that could not be obtained by those of more modest means. Differences in class were characterized by the presence of discernible cultural cleavages. This certainly holds true when considering variations in cultural practices between the upper and working classes, but it should not be overstated given that people of the highest reaches of the middle class could mingle in the elite's social circles, purchase fine imported goods, perhaps carry on conversations in French, and matriculate their children at leading private schools.

The public display of culture through conspicuous consumption was a hallmark of the aristocratic lifestyle during the Parliamentary Republic, especially after the turn of the century. Aristocrats, for example, flocked to the opulent clothing store Gath y Chaves, established in downtown Santiago in 1910, to see and be seen. The grand opening of Gath y Chaves was a memorable cultural event for well-to-do *santiaguinos*; it was a thrilling public spectacle for affluent Chileans starved for high-quality foreign brands and another location for socializing. The department store essentially represented a new Chile, the Chile of modernity, of consumption, of beauty—a nation amid its belle epoque. One contemporary recalled, "The opening of Gath y Chaves has remained in memory as one of the explosions of curiosity and enthusiasm that have swept us. We all felt that something better was coming. A herald of progress. The era was good."[58] In 1921, Gath y Chaves inaugurated a daily "five o'clock tea" for its patrons, hoping that such sociocultural gatherings would make the department store appear even more "worldly" and of "high quality."[59] Another of the fashionable, first-class department stores and shops that served the elite's tastes was Casa Pra, owned by the Pra brothers of France. A Pra sibling apparently owned a "magnificent residence" in Paris and "upon his death on 1938, the sale of his works of art, more than awaken the interest of the great collectors of Europe,

yielded many millions of francs."[60] Other businesses that catered to aristocrats and the upper middle class were Umlauff jewelers, the clothier Las
Novedades Parisienses, the hat merchant Dumas, the tailors Pinaud and
Bouzigue, and the Bazar Alemán de Krauss, a favorite of children. The acquisition of imported goods, such as French perfume or English textiles,
could only be eclipsed, in terms of cultural significance, by purchasing such
items while traveling in Europe. Those who ventured abroad, as Silva comments, often "returned with the latest clothing fashions, furniture, car-
riages, new servants, and books."[61]

These same aristocrats viewed the construction of ornate European-style
homes and the mastery of Paris's Eiffel and Company's workmanship on the
Estación Central, or Central Station (a principal railway station in downtown Santiago), to be vital ingredients in the creation of a more cosmopolitan capital. One Chilean diplomat, so impressed during his residence in
France, went so far as to design his new Santiago home after a Parisian
hotel.[62] In short, Chilean aristocrats understood they were not, and could
never truly be, Europeans; they therefore opted for the next best thing. They
consumed like Europeans: dressed how the English dressed; read what the
French read; and discussed what Old World aristocrats discussed.

Beyond material matters, the elite's cultural practices also included exclusive spectacles of entertainment. In Santiago, the lavish Municipal Theater
was a prized stage of aristocratic sociability before, during, and after the
Parliamentary Republic. Opera was the venue's specialty, and the Chilean
elite filled the theater to witness French companies starring Lucien Guitry,
André Brulé, and Vera Sergine. Not going to the opera, according to one
contemporary, was just as bad as missing mass.[63] It was simply a sin to fail to
witness productions that had appeared at the Metropolitan Opera House in
New York City or Milan's historic Scala. In addition to the opera, the advent
of motion pictures after the turn of the century brought images of foreign
cultures, peoples, technology, and cities to Santiago movie houses. Chileans
flocked to see the latest Yankee film releases advertised daily in *El Mercurio*,
the country's largest daily newspaper, and many other publications. Affluent
Chileans also assembled to enjoy some jazz or a polka, perhaps while sipping
a cocktail or two.[64] At this time, the sensual tango was making its way back
to the Southern Cone from France and was highly regarded in Chile. Foreign
music, often enjoyed by way of imported phonographs and radios, brought
with it the proper accompanying dances. Parliamentary-era dance halls, for
example, commonly played host to "flappers," who demonstrated a most
alluring form of foreign popular culture: the "Charleston."[65] Eduardo Bal-

maceda Valdés recalls one *"gran baile"* at a Santiago mansion in 1912: "In those days, a dance corresponded to its name; people danced through the night, mainly the one-step; later came the fox-trot and the tango."[66] While the public, conspicuous consumption and reproduction of culture were important endeavors within aristocratic circles, there also existed a private sphere of cultural practice—yet another mode of aristocratic sociability— that flourished during the era. Private cultural venues included the *salones*, living rooms, and dining tables of the *tertulianos* (participants in *tertulias*, or discussion groups), as well as social clubs, such as the capital's famed Club de la Unión, or Union Club.

Inspired by eighteenth- and nineteenth-century French café and salon culture, the *tertulias*, as sociologist José Joaquín Brunner describes, were "spaces of private conservation with public influence."[67] Each evening for much of a century (roughly 1850 to 1950), affluent Chileans, including the aristocracy's leading intellectuals and, by the early twentieth century, highly regarded mesocrats, assembled after dinner to discuss books, politics, economic matters, or perhaps the geographic origin of the coffee or tea they calmly sipped. The *tertulia* La Picantería in the 1860s, for example, drew a collection of notables that included Miguel and Gregorio Amunátegui, José Miguel Balmaceda (the future president's brother), the author Alberto Blest Gana, Radical leader Pedro León Gallo, Eusebio Lillo, and Eduardo and Augusto Matte. Other nineteenth-century *tertulias* were sponsored by the historian Diego Barros Arana, Benjamín Vicuña Mackenna, Domingo Santa María, Federico Errázuriz Echaurren, Ramón Barros Luco, and Pedro Balmaceda, who held *tertulias* in the presidential palace during his father's (José Manuel's) administration.[68]

Women were important contributors to the *tertulias*. At the turn of the century, this arena of interaction became one in which women voiced their opinions in an otherwise male-dominated setting. In fact, women-led *tertulias* were some of the most widely attended and admired discussion groups. Lucía Bulnes de Vergara (daughter of the mid-nineteenth-century president) founded her mixed-sex *tertulia* circa 1880 in her Monjitas Street home in downtown Santiago. Luis Orrego Luco, a writer of aristocratic origin but of mesocratic demeanor, praised Bulnes's *tertulia* as "one of the most interesting that has ever existed in Chile, one of those centers of superior culture, of ingenuity, and of good taste that contributed in the formation of the spirit of our old society."[69] Marina Barros de Luco (daughter of the historian Barros Arana and spouse of Liberal leader Augusto Orrego Luco) also hosted *tertulias* attended by the poet Diego Dublé Urrutia, Luis Orrego Luco, Adeodato García (future leader of the Masons), and the young lawyer Alessandri, who discussed the works of Balzac, Hugo, Daudet, and others.[70]

The *tertulia* was but one private space in which Chile's affluent sector interacted on the cultural level. Clubs, such as the prestigious and exclusive Union Club, were places where both political and business deals meshed with cultural practices. In a stately home on the corner of Huérfanos and Bandera Streets in downtown Santiago, Union Club members consumed fine foods and alcoholic beverages, lounged on lavish furnishings, browsed in the club's library, and, in general, pursued the sensation of being associates of a Parisian jockey club or an English rowing club.[71] The families of the male-only membership regularly attended the club's events, which included banquets and balls where Chilean aristocrats mingled with ambassadors and other foreign dignitaries.[72]

Such cultural practices complemented the elite's social, political, and economic power during the Parliamentary Republic. Distinguished politicians, prominent landowners, and wealthy entrepreneurs (one person could be all three) maintained access to a privileged cultural space and perpetuated the marginalization of lower-class cultural practices, while defining "Chilean culture" as their own constellation of cultural tastes, habits, and rituals. When certain mesocrats began to question the cultural preferences of the elite, they did so in conjunction with blistering attacks on the structural joists of *parlamentarismo* and, accordingly, the oligarchic establishment. Radicals took the lead in criticizing the status quo.

Questioning the Republic

The Parliamentary Republic was an oligopoly, not a dictatorship. Its leadership did not openly repress prominent opposition parties or "disappear" their organizers. Criticism, whether on the floor of the Chamber of Deputies, in *tertulias*, in speeches, or out on the street, was an accepted by-product of emancipation from Portalian authoritarianism as long as such talk did not, of course, escalate into a general strike or armed revolutionary struggle. The reader need only recall the formation of Recabarren's POS and the FOCh to appreciate the political pluralism of the era. Such movements were generally given wide berth, but events on the order of the Iquique massacre of 1907 unfolded if they breached the elite's threshold for social criticism.

The Radicals were particularly quick to criticize the very system they fought to establish in 1891. "Could there be any more anarchy?" A Radical *santiaguino* journalist posed this question in 1906 when commenting on the political landscape of the Parliamentary Republic.[73] The anarchy that piqued the writer's query was not the organized anarchist movement orchestrated by working-class groups that aimed to topple the Chilean oligarchy from political power but rather the systemic "anarchism" of party politics. As a reformer frustrated with the legislative and bureaucratic inertia of aristocratic interests, he believed that "anarchism from above"—a pathological trait of *parlamentarismo*—was just as dangerous as the anarchism surging from below.

During the Parliamentary Republic, Radical *correligionarios* generally maintained the same dualistic posture toward oligarchic political groups that they had during the formative years of their party in the mid-nineteenth century. While they accepted and promoted political alliances with more traditionalist parties (notably the PL), Radicals maintained a critical posture toward politics as usual. This was evident during the Parliamentary Republic, a period of constant debate over the constitutional order, economic policy, and other elements vital to the nation's future. Although it had pledged its support for a more parliament-oriented order at its national convention in 1888 (during the crisis of the Balmaceda years), the PR did not hesitate to criticize the new system and its decidedly oligarchic ambience.[74] During the presidential election of 1896, for instance, Radicals slammed *parlamentarismo* for its obvious inadequacies: "In the political order [the oligarchy] kills the doctrine of progress, which is the liberal [doctrine], and produces stagnation, the basis of conservatism. Founded on the memory of a fratricidal war, sad for all good Chileans, that [parliamentary] system looks for its nourishment and its life in social division and the perpetuation of hatreds."[75] It was suspected that parliamentarism's systemic inertia played into the hands of conservatives and other oligarchs who wished to stultify what the Radicals envisioned as "progress": social evolution guided by a paternalistic state. The PR and its liberal-minded allies were, on the other hand, on a "patriotic" mission to transform Chilean society. In short, suspicions existed within reformist circles that oligarchs were actively sabotaging the spirit and political workings of a new republic bought with the blood of thousands of their compatriots.

Ideas of moral crisis and social decay were also quite apparent in turn-of-the-century Radical discourse, and again oligarchs were to blame. Mac-Iver, of Radicalism's old guard, spoke to a gathering of friends and foes in 1900 about what may be called Chile's dilemma of ethos. When reflecting on the spirit of his day, Mac-Iver regretted, "It seems to me that we are not happy;

one takes notice that discontent does not come from a certain class nor from certain regions of the country, but from all of the country and from the bulk of the people who live in it." In a somewhat vague manner, Mac-Iver described what he inferred as a pessimistic sensibility that gripped the nation, one that not only damaged Radical optimism in "order" and "progress" but also contributed to the intensification of the social question. It was Mac-Iver's (and the Radical) view that there was a dire need for identifying "the vices and the social and institutional defects to put yourself in the position to correct and mend them."[76] A nationwide sense of insecurity, in short, bothered Mac-Iver and his *correligionarios*.

During the Riesco presidency, which Radicals initially supported, the pro-Radical *La Lei* questioned the motives of flamboyant oligarchs in the government, noting in 1903 that personal grandstanding and egoism were demoralizing Chilean politics: "The man of true merit is humble, is estranged from honors and only through the force of instances in which he cannot negate patriotism, he moves to break with his life and his modest customs."[77] In 1905, the newspaper commented that parliamentary *politiquería* ("politicking") was the principal disorder behind the republic's symptoms of systemic "anarchy" and instability. It argued that "personal ambitions" and "political intrigue" were working against the "noble and patriotic" politics of those seeking fundamental social reform.[78] It should be mentioned here that turn-of-the-century Radicals respected the term *"política"* when used as a noun (as in *"la política chilena"*) but scorned it when employed as an adjective (*"una propuesta muy política"*); *"política"* the noun was patriotic, whereas the adjective suggested that personal or interest-group gains were prevailing motives. This overtone persists today.

The PR found itself in a peculiar position during much of the Parliamentary Republic. As the Radicals' participation in the executive branch expanded (especially during the Sanfuentes years) and their representation in Congress increased markedly, they became critics of the system they helped establish and under which they flourished like never before. They complained, among other things, of party politics' debilitating effects on the legislative process and the ministerial musical chairs being played in La Moneda, the presidential palace. Radicals believed that parliamentary party politics and a politically sluggish and backward oligarchy were blocking "progress." Thus, the party launched harsh attacks on the republic it once pledged to uphold. In addition, parliamentarism, though scored by the Radicals, entailed a noticeable degree of political tolerance among the time-tested and foremost parties (this group, of course, did not include the anarchists or early communists). Radicalism's ability to compete with the parties of oligarchs without fear of repression fed a certain confidence and forcefulness among PR leaders who addressed the parliamentary system's political impasse, oligarchic power, and what were perceived to be the important social and cultural illnesses of the period. They came to call oligarchic *parlamentaristas* "traditional adversaries."[79]

Radical politicians were members of a larger and sociopolitically diverse assembly of Chileans from which condemnations of *parlamentarismo* emanated. Nicolás Palacios, Francisco A. Encina, Tancredo Pinochet Le-Brun, and Alejandro Venegas (also known as Dr. Julio Valdés Cange), among others, formed a chorus—with varying political voices—that questioned the foundations of Chile as they understood them. Palacios, Encina, Pinochet, and Venegas expressed their views of national reality, examined the evidence before them, assessed where responsibility for society's ills was to be placed, and offered alternatives to the status quo. Although they approached the myriad of problems facing the nation from different perspectives, one fundamental element linked them: they made appeals in nationalist terms. Our discussion must now turn to the issue of nationalism and its important place during the Parliamentary Republic. It will become apparent in the chapters to come that the ideas and language of nationalism crossed the boundaries of class and party with remarkable fluidity and versatility.

Defendamos al pueblo de Chile; son nuestros
hermanos; ellos son el fundamento de nuestro
organismo social i político.

DR. NICOLÁS PALACIOS, *Raza chilena*, 1904

Nationalists

2

Entrenched but under bombardment atop the socioeconomic and political hierarchy of the Parliamentary Republic, the oligarchic establishment found itself in crossfire. Not only did Radicals, dissident Liberals, and revolutionary interests voice their objections regarding the status quo, but some Chileans with more conservative dispositions also questioned the policies of parliamentary leaders, especially their guiding economic principles. During Chile's troubled belle epoque, many critics with diverse socioeconomic pedigrees and political allegiances expressed nationalist principles in their appeals for varying degrees of change. Indeed, intertwined branches of nationalism surfaced in response to the economic, political, social, and cultural conditions of the era, and nationalist discourses became conspicuous and respected components of day-to-day debate. A burgeoning intellectual milieu largely sustained by the urban middle class incited and conditioned nationalism's rapid diffusion. An explosion of new periodicals, a sharp increase in book and pamphlet publication, and an improving literacy rate amplified this space of interaction—part of a maturing public sphere.[1]

From the turn of the century to the outbreak of World War I in Europe, there existed in Chile a circle of nationalists whose ideas mingled and crossfertilized. Leading nationalist thinkers, including Nicolás Palacios, Tancredo Pinochet Le-Brun, Alejandro Venegas, and Francisco A. Encina, each located areas of policy in which *parlamentarismo* had failed their nation, and they became widely known for propagating what may be called a "culture of criticism" that survived into the early 1970s. But by the final decade of the Parliamentary Republic, when middle-class reformers stood on the brink of claiming supreme political power, Chilean nationalism had branched into two dominant species: a reformist strain or "progressive nationalism" harshly critical of the oligarchy, and a "conservative nationalism" that betrayed a more traditionalist hue. The principal roots of progressive nationalism were in the middle-class reform movement associated with the Radical Party (PR); this variant of nationalism drew on the rhetoric of Bilbao and other nineteenth-century "radical" liberals, and reformist mesocrats espoused it as they negotiated a path between revolution and reaction. Nationalism's conservative variety emerged as a critical discourse elaborated by intellectuals and politicians such as those associated with the Nationalist Union (Unión Nacionalista, or UNA), a small yet consequential party that supported the candidate of the oligarchy's National Union (Unión Nacional, or UN) in the 1920 presidential election. As it matured during the 1920s and 1930s, conservative nationalism found a significant place in public debate as a discursive tool of the oligarchic establishment. All the while, progressive nationalism and the reformist mesocrats who promoted it came to exert great influence in society, especially in the cultural sphere. The published works of interest here underscore the complexity, maturity, and discursive flair of early-twentieth-century Chilean nationalism. It was as pliant as it was powerful.[2]

Origins of Nationality

If the nations of Latin America are, indeed, imagined communities, then these communities began to be imagined during the colonial period, well before the geographic limits of countries were set and nation-states formed. David Brading shows that regional identities were present in the intellectual circles of the New World as early as the sixteenth century, and the earliest expressions of "Creole patriotism" came from colonists frustrated with the Spanish Crown's policies to curb their capacity to consolidate personal power.[3] Thus began an intellectual tradition based on regionalist and localist tendencies that developed alongside colonial institutions and administration for three centuries. Brading notes that "no matter how much Spanish America depended on Europe for its art forms, literature and general culture, its chroniclers and patriots succeeded in creating an intellectual tradition that, by reason of its engagement with the historical experience and contemporary reality of America, was original, idiosyncratic, complex, and quite distinct from any European model."[4] Creole patriotism took firm root in Chile, a land with small populations of colonists and Indians on the very edge of Spain's vast empire.

The Spanish noble Alonso de Ercilla's epic *La Araucana*, a sixteenth-century poem written with classical flare, may be considered one of the first examples of "Chilean" nativism, which developed into Creole patriotism. Unlike other narratives of the early colonial era, Ercilla's writings focused on the native element of the great encounter and, specifically, the Araucanian Indians of the southern region who heroically defended their land and life-ways against the Spaniards. The poem, a result of Ercilla's personal recollections of events he witnessed in the 1540s, describes the Araucanians as freedom fighters who thrived on the valiant struggle against the Iberian invaders (led by Diego Hurtado de Mendoza). It also touches on Governor Pedro de Valdivia's inability to curb Spanish oppression of the indigenous population. The execution of Caupolicán, a leading Araucanian war chief, is among many examples of Spanish excess decried in the poem. Although it would be foolish to label Ercilla a Creole patriot (he was certainly Spanish of peninsular origin and not "Chilean" or Creole), it is certain that sentiments related to the singularity of the "Chilean" experience expressed in *La Araucana* shaped much of what became Creole patriotism. As the independence revolution approached, Creoles in Santiago and elsewhere were keenly aware of their status as Americans with an American heritage and, specifically, as Chileans with a Chilean heritage.

Creole patriotism in Chile evolved during much of the colonial period. Distanced from the centers of colonial power in the New World, conquerors and settlers were surrounded by the world's most arid desert to the north, a towering mountain range to the east, and Araucanian resistance to the south. What resulted was a tightly knit colonial society that developed in the Central Valley region, where Creoles intermarried and a "Chilean" aristocracy coalesced.[5] In the mid-seventeenth century, Father Alonso de Ovalle nostalgically reflected on this new, Chilean colonial society in his *Histórica relación del Reyno de Chile* (1646), which, as Simon Collier explains, is a seminal work of a "local and distinctly Chilean patriotism."[6] By the latter half of the eighteenth century, Chilean colonists had amassed a substantial collection of patriotic writings, including those of Juan Ignacio Molina and Felipe Gómez de Vidaurre, who drew on the spirit of Ercilla's *La Araucana* when they presented Chile's indigenous population in a positive light. By doing so, these intellectuals demonstrated the sharp distinction between what was

European and what was American. Chile, they believed, was not truly Spanish and never was; this "garden of South America" was something exotic and unique, partially owing to its resourceful indigenous inhabitants.[7] Juan Egaña, for example, wrote in 1804 that "the fame of the riches and fertility of Chile, and of the genius of its inhabitants, was resounding throughout Europe when the gross and uncivilized Russians were unknown even to their neighbors."[8]

Chilean revolutionaries later touted the image of the heroic Araucanian after Napoleon's invasion of Spain in 1808 threw colonial administration into crisis, setting the stage for Latin American independence. Creole patriotism was strong during the turbulent years of the independence campaigns and the so-called Old Fatherland, or Patria Vieja (1810–14), as revolutionaries rushed to legitimize their authority on the grounds of identity and nationhood (casting royalists and the Spanish Crown as foreign). General Bernardo O'Higgins challenged Creoles to support the noble cause of independence by asking: "How could you forget that you are Chileans, our brethren, from the same homeland and with the same religion, and that you must be free despite the tyrants who are deceiving you?"[9] Creole patriots joined O'Higgins's effort in large numbers, but the lowest sectors of colonial society provided the royalist cause with many foot soldiers. Thus, one infers that patriotism or a national identity did not permeate Chilean colonial or early national society but rather was confined to the Creole aristocracy, from which revolutionary leaders emerged.[10]

The Portalian Project and State-Based Patriotism

The Portalian system, as described in the previous chapter, was a significant anomaly in nineteenth-century Latin America. While Argentines, Mexicans, Peruvians, and other Latin Americans experienced *caudillismo*'s disruptive effects on economy and politics, the Portalian Republic's elite oversaw steady economic growth and political continuity, though not without civil unrest and violence. Affluent Chileans traveled throughout Latin America and witnessed ongoing tumult, then returned home to compare their country's stability with chaotic happenings elsewhere when conversing with friends and political leaders. Notions of singularity and Chile's privileged position as the "model republic" of Latin America (as the elite reminded others) reinforced what Eric Hobsbawm calls in the European context a "state-based patriotism." As Hobsbawm explains, state-based patriotism is a force that is not "necessarily ineffective, since the very existence and functions of the modern territorial citizen-state constantly involve its inhabitants [the elite, in this case] in its affairs, and, inevitably, provide an institutional or procedural 'landscape' which is unlike any other such landscapes and is the setting for their lives, which it largely determines."[11] Of course, not all were enthused by Portalianism's "procedural landscape," but, in general, liberals of the elite found the republic to be a relatively amiable place for the development of an intellectual tradition, especially after the 1850s. They certainly were involved in the functions of the "citizen-state" as state-based patriotism made significant inroads in Chile's political culture. Outstanding intellectuals of the mid-nineteenth century, some of whom were embroiled in bitter debates, did not examine *lo chileno*, or what is Chilean, as some would later do, but nonetheless touched on notions of identity and patriotism.[12] Figures such as José Victorino Lastarria (a liberal romanticist) and Andrés Bello (a historical traditionalist along the lines of Van Ranke in Germany) were among the most respected intellectuals of the era.

Bello's adherence to the scientific study of history through archive-based sources and thick description tended toward the marginalization of national identity. History, to Bello, was to be kept separate from contemporary matters—whether political, social, or otherwise. Lastarria, on the other hand, championed the centrality of history and historical study in the creation of a collective sense of community. Although historians, such as Allen Woll and Gertrude M. Yeager, have asserted that Bello's view eventually prevailed in Chilean scholarship, Lastarria's influence should not be understated. Lastarria and his liberal successors, including the influential historian Diego Barros Arana (author of the landmark *Historia jeneral de Chile*, published between 1884 and 1902), contended that national identity should be based on the perpetuation of a pantheon of national heroes—mainly Creole Chileans—and that such an identity should underscore Chile's liberal tradition. When discussing Barros Arana, Yeager aptly states that "a major purpose of the *Historia jeneral* was to instill a sense of nationalism, of national collective consciousness, and to identify liberals as the proper custodians of common national interests [though Barros Arana also drew much from the more conservative Bello]. The book is introduced as an effort to define the *patria*; in a sense to define the Chilean national character and to trace its geographical and historical origins."[13] Barros Arana, Lastarria, and their liberal cohorts essentially envisioned the heart of the *patria* as the enlightened liberal elite—the liberal intelligentsia who founded the nation and those who had championed liberalism since independence. (Barros

Arana broke from his liberal colleagues by arguing that roots of Chilean liberalism could be found during the Bourbon reforms in the mid- to late eighteenth century, a period he described in rather positive terms). Thus, Lastarria and Barros Arana were inclined to consider national identity as something intrinsically bound to liberal politics and republicanism rather than culture, ethnicity, or other traits that establish and buttress profound national bonds. Lastarria and Barros Arana were, in essence, concerned with the origin and nature of their citizen-state, which many celebrated with pomp and circumstance.

A vital component of state-based patriotism was pageantry. Vibrant and colorful commemorations of Independence Day (September 18) drew large crowds, including members of both the urban and rural lower classes, whose *patrones* gave permission for their attendance. In 1834, the country's coat of arms ("By Reason or By Force") was coined, as the Latin Americanism of such independence leaders as Bolívar waned across the continent. A victorious war against the Peru-Bolivia Confederation (1836–39), which included the long-remembered Battle of Yungay (January 20, 1839), only fanned the flames of Chilean state-based patriotism. Yet it would not constitute a conceptual leap to assert that the concept of nationality largely remained confined to the upper reaches of Chile's social layers throughout the nineteenth century despite lower-class participation in the war against the Confederation and subsequent celebrations of it. Some historians speculate that a distinct sense of *chilenidad* did not spread from aristocratic circles to the lower classes before the War of the Pacific.[14] But when considering the nature of state-based patriotism and the intellectual production of the period, one arrives at the conclusion that developed concepts of *chilenidad* were also absent from the aristocracy. Indeed, *chilenidad* became a national and nationalist concern during the Parliamentary Republic, when notable mesocrats were at the forefront of defining and disseminating conceptions of "nation" and national culture.

State-based patriotism, a sociopolitical mortar of sorts during the Portalian Republic, could not rescue the constitutional authoritarian system from impending structural collapse. The civil war that toppled Balmaceda and damaged the country's legacy as a "model republic" profoundly affected ideas about the state and nation. Soon, many Chileans grew concerned about the relative absence of nationalist sentiment within the Parliamentary Republic's oligarchic establishment. Periodic economic crises contributed to their uneasiness. They began looking to factors of their reality (or perceptions of it) as they confronted the needs of a rapidly changing country, and they couched their criticisms and proposals in nationalist language.

Certain intellectuals complained of a weakened national *geist* and bemoaned the fact that their compatriots were ignorant of the interests of the *patria*. As a maturing culture industry facilitated the spread of ideas, numerous publications expressing nationalist principles appeared. The Parliamentary Republic, an era of economic and cultural cosmopolitanism, saw the elaboration of nationalist discourses that differed substantially in scope and essence from the state-based patriotism of the Portalian Republic. Some nationalist intellectuals criticized the economic principles guiding decision making at the highest levels of government, while others questioned the political system and rigid social divisions. Still others addressed cultural conditions. Within this dynamic environment, different species of nationalism emerged as ideological alternatives. A seminal work of early-twentieth-century Chilean nationalism was Nicolás Palacios's *Raza chilena* (1904), which informed the discourses of many nationalists—both progressive and conservative—for many years.

Politics, Nation, and Race

As classical liberalism and positivism swept through Latin America during the latter decades of the nineteenth century, national elites adopted strategies of open immigration to transform societies weighed down by the legacy of Spanish colonialism. Their collective goal was to create modern, cosmopolitan nation-states. Governments of the Parliamentary Republic actively encouraged European immigration to the cities and countryside and went so far as to establish recruitment centers in major capitals of the Old World. Some critics were convinced that the oligarchy's immigration policy and the aristocracy's preference for all things foreign (culture, genes, markets, and so on) perpetuated a certain anti-Chileanism that served to undermine national identity and cohesion. One of the most outspoken intellectuals who challenged the elite's conceptions of "nation" was Palacios, a widely respected turn-of-the-century intellectual whose radical notions related to *mestizaje* (racial mixing between Iberians and Native Americans) predated those of a more widely recognized Latin American thinker, the Mexican José Vasconcelos.

Palacios (1854–1911), a physician who practiced in the northern nitrate zone during the late nineteenth century, published his book "in the precise instance in which the great moral and material crisis reached its apogee," as one admirer recalled.[15] *Raza chilena*, a history and sociology of the Chilean "race," became an instant best-seller that influenced Chilean politics and culture for many decades. Drawn to Darwinist concepts of species differentiation, the racial ideas circulating in Europe, and, it seems, the heroic image of the Araucanian perpetuated by Ercilla's sixteenth-century epic *La Araucana*, Palacios meticulously traces the origin and evolution of Chile's mestizo population. The native of Colchagua was a critic of both revolutionary ideas and the privileges of aristocrats and elaborated a political ideology based on the notion that Chileans had a peculiar genetic heritage. Class conflict and oligarchs, Palacios claimed, endangered the "race."

Angered by the Riesco administration's preference of Europeans to settle Chile's southern frontier (below the Bío-Bío River) rather than middle- or lower-class Chileans hoping to become small landowners, Palacios constructed a complicated polemic of xenophobia, nativism, racial theory, and biological determinism. Chileans, as natives and mestizos (people produced by *mestizaje*), were the rightful heirs to the southern frontier, not the foreign-born settlers of European blood.[16] In the preface of his lengthy book, Palacios condemns Chilean officials for "handing the nation's land to families of a race foreign to our own."[17] He defines the "Chilean race"—one superior to European and other Latin American races alike—as the birth child of Visigothic conquistadores (the father) and noble Araucanian Indians (the mother). Chileans are, in fact, not descendants of pure Spaniards but rather the offspring of a peculiar group of Spaniards whose roots extended to north-central Europe before the Moorish conquest of Iberia in the eighth century, he sustains. Thus, Chileans are more German than Latin—a difference that put Chileans one step higher on the racial ladder than other Latin Americans. In fact, Palacios calculates that only 10 percent (at most) of the conquerors and earliest settlers were of Latin origin. He arrives at this conclusion only after spending a great deal of time reviewing portraits and surviving descriptions of these Europeans. In the mid-eighteenth century, Palacios goes on to explain, an influx of Latin blood (including that of Basques) made little or no impact on a heavily Germanic mestizo population numbering approximately five hundred thousand.[18] Although he offers a racial theory that identifies Germanic chromosomes as half of Chile's genetic makeup, the doctor also asserts that European blood is inferior to that of the *raza chilena*; the noble and heroic blood of the Indians gave the Chilean race its singularity and eminence.

Nicolás Palacios, physician and author of *Raza chilena* (1904). (Courtesy of Eduardo Devés)

To prove his case of the Chilean race's superiority, Palacios compares criminality rates of native-born Chileans with those of foreign nationals residing in the country. According to 1896 figures cited by Palacios, fewer than 1 percent of "nationals" (all defined as mestizos) were guilty of deeds identified by law as criminal behavior, whereas three times as many foreign-born residents were apprehended for such illegal activities.[19] The folly in the doctor's logic is clear: the data do not stipulate the exact racial compositions of those considered native-born; Palacios assumed that all "nationals" in the data were mestizos. Furthermore, Palacios's formulation conjures up the image of foreigners flooding into Chile from every possible direction. Yet census figures show that although the number of *extranjeros* (foreigners) increased in the late nineteenth and early twentieth centuries, outsiders constituted only a relatively small percentage of the total population. In 1895, there were 79,056 *extranjeros* in Chile, or about 3 percent of the total population. The census of 1907 showed 134,524 *extranjeros*, or roughly 4 percent of the 3,249,279 people counted.[20] Of course, not all the foreigners listed in the census were of European or North American origin. Census figures included visitors from neighboring Latin American countries, including Mexicans, Argentines, and Peruvians, who, in Palacios's mind, most likely did not threaten the purity and success of the *raza chilena*.

Radicals, who later incorporated much of Palacios's language of race into their political and cultural discourses, were quick to criticize discrimination against native-born, would-be Chilean settlers of the southern frontier. A year after Palacios's book appeared, *La Lei* argued that the oligarchy's preference of immigrant settlers was simply "shameful" and that Chileans facing discrimination in their own country were settling in Argentine Patagonia instead. Moreover, the newspaper complained that state-owned southern lands were illegally being dealt to foreigners who were "useless elements—when they aren't damaging—for our population."[21] Given Radicalism's liberal pedigree and the fact that Latin American liberals enthusiastically backed the arrival of newcomers as an impetus for modernization, such a negative reaction toward immigration is an interesting twist and demonstrates the nationalist element in the PR's liberal ideology. One may comprehend this apparent contradiction in light of the fact that many European immigrants in Chile were, as Carl Solberg has shown, of middle-class stock and therefore competed against middle-class Chileans for both southern lands and urban jobs. Sensing the shifting tide of public opinion, the government changed its tune on the issue by 1910 and gradually began to encourage native ownership of southern lands. A committee assigned to study the issue in 1913 quickly concluded, as Solberg explains, that "national interest required the government to favor the native born."[22] Even the traditionalist Liberal *El Mercurio*, a longtime supporter of open immigration, admitted, "Instead of immigration we ought to prefer the protection and betterment of our own people."[23] The government almost immediately granted land titles to more than a thousand native-born squatters while curtailing grants to foreigners (only twelve were issued during the years 1912–13).[24]

Aside from responding to issues related to immigration, Palacios also took it upon himself to revise Chile's national identity. Since independence, intellectuals had tended toward the marginalization of the popular masses in matters of national identity and, in some cases, expressed contempt for *mestizaje* and the nation's indigenous legacy despite the resurgence of Ercilla's *La Araucana* during the independence campaigns. Barros Arana, for example, exhibited his distaste for Chile's mestizo heritage in the multivolume *Historia jeneral de Chile*. In the words of one historian, "though [Barros Arana] had found the *mestizo* a natural transition from barbarism to civilization in the sixteenth century, he concluded that by 1810 the *mestizo* had inherited the deficit qualities of both races. . . . For Barros Arana, the Creole elite were emphatically the conservators of Chilean virtues and the defenders of natural liberties."[25] Such a sentiment, as the reader will recall from the previous chapter, prompted certain members of high society to question the proposal to include indigenous people in the country's pavilion at the Universal Exposition of 1900. Thus, Palacios's ideas were revisionist in that they clearly identified "Chilean" as something other than what contemptuous Europhiles thought it was or should be.

Soon after the appearance of *Raza chilena*, Palacios was enthused about the spirit of change surrounding Liberal leader Pedro Montt's presidential campaign. Reformers, led by the PR, found Montt's agenda quite appealing, though they later criticized the president for falling short in areas of public policy and for buttressing the oligarchic system. Montt's campaign of "regeneration" in 1906 sought to shake up *parlamentarismo* by proposing remedies to economic problems, including measures to curb inflation, as well as political reforms and a "restoration of morals." But Palacios, like many others, became profoundly disappointed with the shortcomings of *monttismo*. In the end, the Montt episode only strengthened the belief among reformers that oligarchs were involved in a carefully executed plan to stonewall reform within the government and in civil society.[26] Palacios made this frustration clear in a conference he presented at the University of Chile in 1908, which soon after circulated in printed form as the essay "Decadencia del espíritu de nacionalidad" (Decline of the spirit of nationality). The speech did not rehash the racial thesis of *Raza chilena* but rather focused on economic issues in the background of his monumental book, specifically those associated with "the scarce development of the instinct of national preservation."[27] Foreigners, especially those involved in commerce, were the principal topic of Palacios's talk. He argued that "utilitarian" immigrants were replacing native Chileans in urban professions and threatened to extinguish all sentiments related to *lo nacional*, or what is national. Palacios explained that "the antisocial utilitarian doctrines have opened up an ample breach in the sentiment of *patria* among the Chilean people." That sentiment of *patria*, he suggested, was central in the maintenance of social peace across class lines: "The tie that unites the thousand private reasons for discontent is, then, the sentiment of nationality, the magnificent developed instinct of *patria*."[28]

Palacios's death in 1911 ended his short but highly influential presence on Chile's intellectual stage. One writer assessed the doctor's effect on national identity and morale by asking, "Who could deny an honored place . . . to the illustrious author of *Raza chilena*, tireless worker, example of those who fight without other weapons but intelligence and faith, wise eminence, example to the studious youth and teachers, fervent apostle of the very noble cause of defending the people from the hateful accusations and the Chilean citizen who pronounced the nobility of his race with words that have been heard by the entire world?" He also noted that "the work of Dr. Palacios, in whatever areas of human and national activity, is so broad and beautiful that analysis becomes difficult when attempting to make an orderly explanation of it."[29] Palacios's racial ideology was exactly what many Chileans tired of the oligarchic establishment and fearful of revolutionary politics wanted to hear. It indicated that the race, if united, could overcome the problems vexing it, including class conflict. Indeed, by questioning the assumption that immigration was a valuable chisel in the sculpting of society, he pointed out that racial (and thus national) improvement needed to come from within rather than from without. He also suggested that the elite did not hold a monopoly on who constituted the nation; aristocrats and oligarchs were simply members of a larger community—defined by genotype—which should be proud to be mestizo and criollo. As we shall see, the idea of *"raza chilena"* became a mainstream locution interchangeable with "nation" during the Parliamentary Republic, and reformist intellectuals, educators, bureaucrats, and politicians of the mesocracy regularly expressed a racial identity in their political and cultural discourses.[30]

Parameters of "Progressive Nationalism"

Palacios's considerable influence in Chile's intellectual milieu became especially visible as the centennial of the country's independence drew nearer. The 1910 celebration, organized with precision by the oligarchy, was a gala of remarkable opulence and affectation. Aristocrats put on an ornate show for both themselves and foreign dignitaries who wished to bask in the glory of the belle epoque. In essence, the fanfare marked the one hundredth anniversary of the Chilean elite and the nation they created. But all did not share in the euphoria. In fact, the years around 1910 witnessed a flurry of criticism by intellectuals opposed to the Parliamentary Republic's leadership and the elite's power. Two intellectuals of this movement were Tancredo Pinochet Le-Brun (1879–1957) and Alejandro Venegas (1871–1922), both public schoolteachers. Articulating a nationalist discourse with progressive overtones and demonstrating the lasting influence of Palacios, they touched on issues such as parliamentary politics, the oligarchy's attitude toward national development, and the elite's frail sense of nationality.

In 1909, Pinochet published *La conquista de Chile en el siglo XX*, which produced shock waves within intellectual and political circles. In it, the author questioned *parlamentarismo*'s economic and social pillars, while blaming oligarchs for a weak state of nationalism that had turned Chile into a nation dominated by *extranjeros*. The *patria*, he strongly suggests, had been led astray by Europhiles looking to hide their Chilean origin. These aristocrats sought to consume their way to modernity, Pinochet contends, and desired to make Chile less Chilean, to move it away from its natural pathology as a community with singularities worthy of preservation and perpetuation. "Our government, our educational institutions and almost all our upper class in general seem to manifest a deep obligation to the downfall and ruin of national interests and of all the national ideals in order to be replaced by foreign interests and ideals," he wrote. "It is not only a question of lacking the nationalist egoism inherent to all of the well-established nations; it is a question of our contempt for our race and that we Chileans find ourselves outside of our *patria*."[31] Demonstrating the influence of Palacios on his ideological formation, Pinochet later states, "There is already in the soul of our race a contempt for what is our nation [*lo nacional*]. One hears all the time that we're off to Europe to look for a *patria* deserving of our spirit and many Chilean students become dual citizens in Paris for that reason. . . . [In France] they do not feel a nostalgia for their distant *patria* that has entrusted to them the mission to contribute and make us better and more dignified."[32] The elite, he explains, were guilty of perpetuating a national amnesia toward things Chilean: "Every day we go on losing more respect and love for what is national, whether they are men, customs, traditions, our language, the land or flag."[33] Pinochet, in short, argues that Chilean aristocrats had knowingly facilitated another European "conquest" of Chile—an economic and cultural one—during the Parliamentary Republic.

Pinochet also expressed a strong economic nationalism by calling for protectionism and the "Chileanization" of foreign-controlled industries. In a language that would later be identified with the sociopolitical conflicts of the 1960s and early 1970s, Pinochet argues in *La conquista de Chile en el siglo XX*, "It is necessary that we soon adopt a politics of Chileanization of our riches because we do not want to convert the Chilean race into an inferior one, into a slave race, in the service of other races that have in their possession our ground and our riches."[34] He goes on to blame the elite's consumption patterns for underdevelopment. It is here that Pinochet overtly expresses a rather poor opinion of the aristocracy. To those of high society, Pinochet states, all material goods must come from foreign lands from birth to death, from the "bronze cradle [that] is sold by Buquets, Seckel, Lumsden" to the tombstones fabricated by Ceppi or Botinelli "with the Latin inscription

Requestad in pace." He explains, "All that they spend, from the cradle to the grave, goes to the foreigner; all what they earn comes from the Chilean who, tied to the land, has his bronzed arms drenched by the blazing sun."[35] The Chilean lower class, in essence, pays the price for aristocratic indulgence.

When assessing *La conquista de Chile en el siglo XX*, it would be unfair to characterize Pinochet as a rampant nativist bent on the extirpation of all foreign elements in Chilean society. Rather, he proposed a scheme of selective acculturation. Pinochet thought that Chile was being made stronger by a foreign "civilizing" presence but that an unchecked proliferation of *lo europeo*, or what is European, endangered the nation's unique hybrid character. In a revealing statement, Pinochet states, "We, then, need to civilize ourselves, that is to say we need to Europeanize; we need to assimilate all the knowledge of European civilization, all of its virtues, all of its aptitudes that are not strange and are necessary to live. . . . We should not end up being a colony for Europe, we should not bring European bosses who would command us for the good of their civilization. . . . We should continue being Chileans, respecting all of the Chilean virtues and assimilating European virtues, [while] resisting its [Europe's] vices."[36] In essence, Pinochet was not anti-European. He surely savored French wine, wore fine English textiles, and enjoyed other imports of his day. What Pinochet envisioned was a nation in which inherent qualities and sovereignty were not eclipsed by cosmopolitanism and foreigners.

In the spirit of Pinochet's *La conquista de Chile en el siglo XX*, Alejandro Venegas (also known as Dr. Julio Valdés Cange), one of the most recognized and outspoken intellectuals of the period, also expressed disgust with the oligarchy's regime. If one publication best relates the frustration that beset many intellectuals of the Parliamentary Republic, it is Venegas's *Sinceridad: Chile íntimo en 1910*. The book is a compilation of letters Venegas wrote to President Ramón Barros Luco, a traditionalist Liberal, in response to the euphoria felt by oligarchs as the centennial anniversary of independence neared. Each piece is a bitter indictment of *parlamentarismo* and expresses the need for a nationalism that is more substantive and democratic than the superficial patriotism demonstrated by aristocrats. Such a shallow patriotism was visible during the centennial celebrations, which, in Venegas's eyes, were absurd and ironic: Chilean independence—in the twentieth century—was the furthest thing from the minds of the republic's leaders. Sincerity about Chile's problems, the longtime educator believed, was a true sign of nationalism and a sparse commodity in the parliamentary system. The anthology opens with a preface that boldly states his intentions: "I want to take a sincere offering to the altars of the *patria*, which perhaps will be the only one seen."[37] Liberal historian Domingo Amunátegui Solar noted that candor was absent in Chile "since the time of Francisco Bilbao and Santiago Arcos [both founders of Chilean Radicalism]" and that "no one preached with the same frankness" as did Venegas.[38]

Venegas directs one of his first salvos at members of the oligarchic establishment who "do not view us down below and believe that they are not seen by us, but fortunate for the *patria*, there is no reciprocity in this; the people see with admirable clarity the greed, the degenerate ambitions, all of the crimes and all of the vices of those up above."[39] High society, Venegas later states, is primarily driven in all aspects of life by the private acquisition of wealth, not by the creation of a prosperous nation. It is for this reason, he contends, that Chile has only two classes: the exploiters and the exploited. Venegas, in an interesting twist, states that no discernible "middle class" exists in Chile—the center portion of society is composed of people "in transit" from the exploited class to the exploiting one. Society, then, is simply based on the shallow need of aristocrats and social climbers to accumulate wealth, and this mentality is anathema to national unity: "The Chilean aristocracy is based almost exclusively on wealth; money is nobility, and from this major drawbacks are born. All of the means of gaining wealth are held in esteem, almost without any limitation; and society looks with disdain at one of its members that has gone to jail for a swindle or a dishonest act; it's not the fault of his morality but his clumsiness. They respect and consider talent, scientific and literary knowledge, university degrees, only if it is to pave the way to acquiring a fortune. But pure science, the love of art for art's sake, are currency that are not tender in this blessed land of Chile."[40] The purveyors of "degenerate ambition" are the same oligarchs who, when peering out over their nation, only recognize a selected few as their compatriots, as fellow Chileans, and forget the majority.[41] What is lacking is a democratized national consciousness, he suggests. It is not surprising, then, that Venegas, who like Palacios supported the *monttista* option in 1906 but soon was angered by the regime's inertia,[42] joined the author of *Raza chilena* and Pinochet by promoting a positive vision of the "race" that undermined the aristocracy's hegemony and expressed a certain hope and confidence intrinsic to progressive nationalism. "I have faith in the lively forces of our young race, I have faith in that there are many damaged elements that can be regenerated," Venegas writes.[43]

Venegas's sense of frustration is quite reasonable. Chile's centennial independence in Santiago, an occasion for the celebration of all things Chilean, was, in fact, rather cosmopolitan in nature. The elite gave foreign guests, such as the Uruguayan intellectual José Rodó, a proponent of Latin Americanism, a great deal of attention, while the state dinner at La Moneda featured the finest in French cuisine.[44] Although an array of patriotic festivities were organized (including homage to Bernardo O'Higgins, military parades, and inaugurations of monuments), there was something oddly foreign about the very Chilean holiday. Reflecting on the observances, Venegas lamented, "We finished celebrating our centennial and we are left satisfied, very complacent with ourselves. We have not expected for our visitors to return to their own countries and give their opinions."[45] He hints that such opinions would not be overwhelmingly positive.

The nationalist criticisms articulated by Palacios, Pinochet, and Venegas—intellectuals who preferred to refrain from joining political parties—reflected an antioligarchic conviction that was prevalent within the mesocracy during the Parliamentary Republic, especially among Radicals and dissident Liberals. Encina (1874–1965), who borrowed much from Pinochet, also became a leading voice of Chilean nationalism during the same period. As we shall see, however, Encina's nationalism and politics took an unambiguously conservative turn as the presidential election of 1920 drew closer and Chilean intellectuals and voters chose sides in a bifurcated political environment. Tried-and-true traditionalists may have found some of Encina's ideas unappetizing, but the species of nationalism he professed—one born amid the political struggles of the 1910s—developed into a rhetorical and ideological pillar of the oligarchic establishment during the eventful 1920s and 1930s. As this transpired, the progressive nature of Pinochet's, Venegas's, and middle-class reformism's nationalist discourse became unmistakable.

The Roots of "Conservative Nationalism"

The economic structure of the Parliamentary Republic, like the elite's cultural sensibility, was cosmopolitan, that is to say, open to relatively free contact with the modern world and its increasingly global marketplace. The nitrate-driven export economy propelled Chile's first phase of modernization, as foreign capital, in the form of investment in the northern *oficinas*, railroads, and communication technology, increased during the latter years of the nineteenth century and under *parlamentarismo*. Important intellectuals grew concerned with such factors as the backwardness of domestic industry and the country's reliance on overseas capital. Encina, a conservative landowner who later became a prominent historian, was a leading critic of the oligarchy's acceptance of classical liberalism's "invisible hand."

Perhaps the Parliamentary Republic's most recognized critic of national life, Encina published *Nuestra inferioridad económica* in 1911, a book that paints a pessimistic portrait of a Chilean economy and society dominated by "superior" foreign civilizations that retarded the development of domestic industries and nationalism. In this foundational work of economic nationalism, the native of Talca (a provincial capital of the Central Valley) asserts that "our economic development has manifested in recent years symptoms that show a real pathological state" and that "foreign penetration, realized by way of books and, to a lesser extent, travelers" had negatively impacted "the spirit of nationhood."[46] Encina, who owned a *fundo* (a hacienda or sizable plot) near the town of Buin and was a member of the protectionist National Agricultural Society (Sociedad Nacional de Agricultura, or SNA), goes on to state that "among the determined causes [for a debilitated nationalism during the Parliamentary Republic] should be included the intense penetration of stronger civilizations into our national spirit" and that "the will of the inferior weakens and becomes subordinate to the superior. Not only does admiration for the science, arts, institutions and the civilization in general develop [among the inferiors], but he [the inferior] also shares the same vital interests that pertain to the superior."[47] Recognizing the government's failure to create the proper environment for domestic economic development, Encina essentially called for economic nationalism to end Chile's subordination to the "superior." Yet "superior" peoples were not the sole cause of the nation's inferiority.

A native, psychological component to Chile's underdevelopment is clearly identified in *Nuestra inferioridad económica*. Encina, especially in his later writings (such as the multivolume *Historia de Chile*), tended to demonstrate a certain low opinion of lower-class Chileans and suggested that the elite, a predominantly Basque aristocracy, was the standard-bearer of civilization and the civilizing project. *Nuestra inferioridad económica* calls attention to the rural and urban worker whose psychological traits supposedly include the incapacity for methodical labor, a weak spirit of cooperation and association (an ironic observation when one considers the rise of unionization during this era), and a talent for wasting time. Encina concludes that such traits, coupled with an ineffective education system and a government that gazes toward foreign lands for inspiration in matters of economy, society, and culture, have led to the "loss of the position we held in South America."[48] He therefore paradoxically suggests that Chileans should become more "European" (i.e., industrialized, civilized, modern, motivated) by being less economically cosmopolitan.[49]

Compounding Chile's problems were "sociological and socialist doctrines" that directly endangered the "spirit of nationality," Encina contends.[50] In an uncompromising tone, he dismisses ideas of international solidarity proposed by such nineteenth-century thinkers as the Frenchman G. L. Duprat, who came to view "society" as a transnational entity. While doing so, Encina links the Chilean aristocracy's cosmopolitanism to European notions of a global community, which, he insists, produce damaging results. Moreover, he indicates that socialism lacks tremendous support in Chile but remains lurking in the shadows, ready to pounce at a moment's notice. According to Encina, the labor unrest of the Parliamentary Republic is a manifestation of working-class anger, which is a direct consequence of underdevelopment. He was not exaggerating the relative absence of organized socialism at the end of the century's first decade, though his negation of ideology as a guiding element of the working-class movement is unfounded. Thus, while the Radicals were embracing Valentín Letelier's notion of socialism—their *socialismo de Estado*—during the first decade of the century, Encina remained a fervent opponent of collectivist notions that, in his words, were detrimental to the "sentiment of nationality."[51] Letelier, as we shall see in a subsequent chapter, believed that a *socialismo de Estado* would, in fact, reinforce national bonds.

In 1913, Encina moved to apply his ideas in electoral politics by forming the UNA, which eventually changed its name to the Nationalist Party (Partido Nacionalista). Along with such allies as diplomat Alberto Edwards, Germán Riesco, and educator Luis Galdames, Encina and Guillermo Subercaseaux, a conservative congressional deputy and professor of economics at the University of Chile, chartered the organization devoted to "nationalizing" the industrializing economy and implementing reforms to spur domestic economic development. Economic nationalism, above all else, stood at the center of the party's conservative nationalist agenda (well before protectionism became widely popular during and after the Great Depression of the 1930s). Yet Encina, like Balmaceda, did not envision the state as the owner of industry but instead believed that "Chilean" industries should be owned by Chilean entrepreneurs.

In a 1916 manifesto, the UNA, a body that attempted to incorporate aspects of traditionalist liberalism and conservatism under the banner of nationalism, displayed nostalgia for the Portalian years, blaming the parliamentary system for, among other things, "ministerial crisis" and "the impotence of the state to carry forward reforms for national progress." Such mismanagement, the UNA claimed, allowed for the power of foreign capitalists to expand with remarkable speed on Chilean soil at the expense of national producers. Thus, the UNA called for the "broadening of executive power [and] the restoration of the principle of authority without throwing out individual liberties and the political rights that we have managed to conquer with the blood of our fathers and brothers." Overall, the UNA platform consisted of twelve major planks: the separation of religion and politics; the protection of domestic industry; the nationalization of industry; state action to improve the condition of the working class; the development and expansion of domestic commerce; the strengthening of commercial ties with Chile's neighbors; monetary reform (an obsession of Subercaseaux); tax reform; the establishment of obligatory primary education; the expansion of vocational or "technical" education; a commitment by the University of Chile to investigate objectively and report the nation's problems; and, last, the amplification of executive authority within the government.[52]

The language used by UNA members often took on an antiliberal inflection, though the party's program was quite liberal in some ways. Subercaseaux, for example, stated in 1913 that liberalism and individualism fostered by the Parliamentary regime were good and necessary for progress but had gone too far: "the absolutism of liberalism's individualist principle has produced . . . an alarming weakening of the nationalist spirit."[53] Liberals were uncomfortable with such rhetoric and dismissed the suggestion that liberalism was antinationalist. One Liberal Party (PL) organization argued in *El Mercurio* that "nationalist ideas figure in the programs of today's parties."[54] In the same edition, another Liberal argued that the UNA did not demonstrate convincingly a commitment to secularism and that no good-hearted liberal would join it. The UNA responded to such attacks by declaring, "The country . . . looks with terror at the abyss to which it is being taken by our politics, which is corrupted by everything; and the birth of the Nationalist Union is nothing but a waking up of a healthy and patriotic opinion."[55] In 1916, after the UNA published its first substantive platform, traditionalist Liberals struck a more conciliatory tone regarding the new party, to which some in their cohort, including former president Riesco, gravitated. *El Mercurio* observed that the UNA "will be heard and will find strong sympathies in the country."[56]

The conservative *El Diario Ilustrado* expressed strong support for the UNA. One contributor found the group's nationalism refreshing. In the short series "Rumbos Nacionalistas," Eliodoro Astorquiza wrote in June 1913 that nationalism "tells us now to set aside the books and press of Europe, to observe the Chilean reality and fix our laws and institutions to conform to it." The nationalism conveyed by the UNA, which Astorquiza praised for its "conservative tendency," was unlike that of France, where it was reduced to the hatred of Germans or scorn toward Jews, or that of England, where it was manifested as imperialism, he argued. Encina and other like-minded nationalists, Astorquiza explained, scientifically identified the Chilean mentality and the country's ills, whereas others never adopted "a Chilean point of view to judge national problems."[57] Praise for the organization continued in the columns of *El Diario Ilustrado* in 1915, when the newspaper explained that UNA members were "patriotically inspired" and that "we already have many parties and now another one is born. Yet, even though the multiplication of parties is a bad thing, we will celebrate if this new party becomes organized and grows.... It talks to us about many problems closely tied to the nation's progress."[58] Much was changing in Chile and in the warring world in 1915, and the conservative newspaper's warm reception of Encina's and the UNA's criticism reveals that the oligarchic establishment was undergoing somewhat of a discursive overhaul. Nationalism was in style.

The UNA became a consequential, if minor, player in the political fray largely owing to the personal success of Guillermo Subercaseaux, the maternal grandson of nineteenth-century president José Joaquín Pérez. After serving as a finance minister in 1908 during the Montt administration, he once again assumed that post during the Sanfuentes government (the highest government position given to a member of the UNA, which never gained representation in the Congress). In 1920, the trained engineer served on the so-called Tribunal of Honor, a council convened to decide the final outcome of that year's presidential election in light of the very slim electoral margin between the candidates. Although the UNA (which by now called itself the Nationalist Party, or PN) emerged as an organization critical of the Parliamentary elite, it ultimately demonstrated its support for the ancien régime by allying with Luis Barros Borgoño and the UN in the election.[59] Yet, in a surprising turn of events, Subercaseaux gave his support to Alessandri—the eventual president—in the Tribunal of Honor. In response, the UNA/PN summarily canceled Subercaseaux's membership. In 1923, a grateful Alessandri handed a cabinet post (finance minister) to Subercaseaux, who also became a member of the PL (and presumably an ally of its dissident, *alessandrista* sect). Subercaseaux, it seems, sensed the political limitations of the conservative-oriented UNA/PN, recognized the growing power of *alessan-*

drismo, and saw that nationalism was a welcomed sensibility among Chilean liberals.

While the UNA/PN, which disappeared from the political scene in the early 1920s, moved toward the oligarchic establishment during the Sanfuentes administration, progressive nationalists continued their attacks on the Parliamentary Republic's traditionalists. In 1917, Pinochet, who respected Encina and drew much from the landowner's ideas, contributed to this ongoing chorus of discontent by publishing a sequel to his renown *La conquista de Chile en el siglo XX*. Pinochet's antioligarchism, though easily inferred from *La conquista de Chile en el siglo XX*, is substantially amplified in his *Oligarquía y democracia*. The book, which opens with a prologue by Dr. Carlos Fernández Peña, president of the National Education Association (Asociación de Educación Nacional, or AEN), expresses progressive nationalist sentiments that later pervaded Arturo Alessandri Palma's 1920 presidential campaign.

In a stinging indictment of aristocratic rule, rigid social divisions, and socioeconomic injustice in Chilean society, Pinochet asserts, "The separation of castes in Chile is well defined, and the government strives to maintain and develop it. We are accustomed to not think of the poorer classes as Chileans."[60] Members of the working class, he argues, are not lackadaisical and uncooperative, as Encina portrayed them in *Nuestra inferioridad económica*. Without naming specific culprits, Pinochet explains that high society believes "the factory worker is lazy. The *inquilino* of the hacienda is lazy. Any foreign worker produces more. The Chilean laborer hates work." Refuting the idea that working-class Chileans are predisposed to such unproductive tendencies, he contends that "the exploited Chilean worker, with a salary that is not sufficient to live, the farm hand paid around sixty cents per day, gives only the minimum of his effort for the minimum salary he is paid. . . . He loves work when he obtains value from it. . . . The Chilean race is not one of loafers, it is not one of lazy people."[61] Given that Pinochet was a teacher and a member of the AEN, it is not surprising that he promoted education as means through which disadvantaged Chileans could better their socioeconomic and cultural standings.

Pinochet found oligarchic power, with its social, economic, and political pillars, simply abhorrent. As the title of his book demonstrates, the educator was convinced that a struggle between the forces of oligarchism and democracy was at hand, but it was not necessarily a fight to the death. In a manner that reflected ideas of evolution and peaceful progress espoused by many reformist mesocrats of that era, Pinochet went about his indictment without calling for the elite's destruction. He was not a revolutionary by any means. The book, of course, is not titled "Oligarquía o democracia." To Pinochet, building a democratic Chile entailed the decomposition of aristocratic power, rather than the destruction of a social sector from which the founders and consolidators of the republic emerged. The transition from oligarchism to democracy, Pinochet suggests, is merely a matter of political and social will on the part of reformers: "At the beginning of the nineteenth century, our country felt it necessary to break the chains of slavery and wished to become a republic, and it became a republic. At the beginning of the twentieth century, our country now feels the necessity to become a democracy, and it will become a democracy."[62]

Pinochet and other progressive nationalists—and, to some extent, conservative nationalists—expressed concerns similar to those that circulated among the embryonic Left's intellectual leaders during the Parliamentary Republic. They, too, were troubled by the oligarchic establishment's intransigence and were concerned about their country's productive future. But whereas progressive and conservative nationalists called for a more prevalent sense of *nacionalidad*, the intellectual leader of the early-twentieth-century Chilean Left, Luis Emilio Recabarren, critically assessed what both Palacios and Encina called the "sentiment of nationality." This is not to say that Recabarren did not envision a "national" project but rather that he was aware that nationalism was a cornerstone of antirevolutionary discourses.

The Proletariat and the *Patria*

Nationalism, as we have seen, was ingrained in the political dialogue of the Parliamentary Republic. Palacios, Pinochet, Venegas, and Encina expressed nationalist principles and appealed to sentiments of nationality to rally support for their agendas, and all firmly believed their criticisms and ideas were in country's best interest. Luis Emilio Recabarren, however, thought otherwise. Although his Socialist Workers Party (POS) called for some of the same policies proposed by leading nationalists, including obligatory primary education, Recabarren recognized that a major pillar of Chilean nationalist thought was an antirevolutionary conviction. In contrast to the internationalist ideas of Marxists, nationalists profess that the nation, rather than a class, is the principal unit of analysis, identity, and historical development. Thus, Recabarren understood nationalism as a bourgeois ideology that perpetuated an oppressive capitalist system. But Recabarren was a complex man and found some redeeming value in what he considered truly "patriotic" service on behalf of the working class.

Consumed with the social question, intellectuals of the revolutionary Left were active writers and publishers during the era of *parlamentarismo*. Born in 1876, Recabarren, whose publications far outnumber those of any other Chilean Marxist of his time, began publishing columns in working-class newspapers in Santiago—*La Tarde* and *La Democracia*—during the last decade of the nineteenth century. In 1901, his opinions appeared in *El Trabajo* of Iquique and by 1905 dotted newspapers in the cities and towns of Antofagasta, Casablanca, Chañaral, Concepción, Coquimbo, La Unión, Lebu, Nueva Imperial, Taltal, and Tocopilla. In 1906, Recabarren was elected to the Chamber of Deputies but almost immediately was dismissed from his seat. He went on to found the POS in 1912, which became the Chilean Communist Party (PCCh) in 1922, and ardently fought for working-class interests until his surprising suicide in the capital in 1924.

Given Radicalism's commitment to gradual social evolution rather than revolutionary change, as well as the oligarchy's failure to confront the social question by way of direct state action, Recabarren and others on the left assumed a cynical posture toward the nationalist rhetoric that emanated from the middle and upper reaches of society. It is apparent from Recabarren's published works that while significant intellectuals embraced nationalism after the turn of the century, the ideological artifice did not enthuse Chile's Marxist leadership in any profound way, at least during the first two decades of the century. By the 1930s and the Popular Front era, however, nationalist rhetoric and principles flowed from the Left as part of *frentismo*'s antioligarchic and anti-imperialist discourse in what was a very different national context.

In 1910, amid the celebratory atmosphere of the centennial, Recabarren indicated that he not only was without nationalism but was without a nation as well. In the *folleto*, or pamphlet, "Ricos y pobres" (The rich and poor), he explains, "I look at the past through my thirty-four years and I cannot find in all of my life one circumstance that convinces me that I have had a *patria* or that I have had liberty."[63] As a defender of the lower classes, Recabarren believed—and rightly so—that he and his movement were outside the *patria*'s conceptual borders, as they were envisioned and established by the elite. Pinochet argued a similar point about the marginalization of the lower classes in *Oligarquía y democracia*, as did Venegas in *Sinceridad*. Yet it would not be inconsistent to conclude that Recabarren was also frustrated by progressive nationalists such as Pinochet and Venegas, who easily could have been construed as promoters of bourgeois hegemony. This point is buttressed by the fact that Recabarren, tired of middle-of-the-road politics, had split from the more moderate Democratic Party, which, under Concha, had formed from a rib of the PR.

In the leftist press, Recabarren published very few articles that address the concept of nation or *patria*.[64] One piece, published in a 1909 edition of the newspaper *El Trasandino* of the town of Los Andes, contends that elite- and bourgeoisie-sponsored celebrations of independence were simply charades. The other, a poetic commentary titled "A mi patria" (To my fatherland), expresses bitter resentment toward what the *patria* has and has not done for the popular classes. Both deserve some attention here. The *El Trasandino* article appeared during the *dieciocho* (Independence Day, September 18) festivities in 1909 and resonates with estrangement from *lo nacional*. Here, Recabarren castigates members of the working class who joined in the celebration of "bourgeois" rule. On the issue of class-based oppression, Recabarren states that nothing changed with independence: "The working class lived through centuries of Spanish slavery and tyranny, and when Chile sounded what was called the hour of liberty . . . it was only for the bourgeois and moneyed class, but in no case was it for the people who continued being a slave of the new class that set itself up as the government of Chile."[65] Moreover, when discussing working-class festivity, Recabarren flatly remarks that revolutionary intellectuals feel a "profound weight when we see the working class participate in a celebration that is not its own and feel merriment for a so-called national independence that has brought no real liberty for the producing people." In short, "the people, in reality, have nothing to celebrate."[66] The misery of working-class living and labor conditions, according to Recabarren, conferred a certain absurdity to any celebration of "independence."

Recabarren's "A mi patria" is a much more complex and acrid assessment. Adopting the voice of a worker and with a flair for verse and a sardonic tone, he offers a long list of questions, each beginning with the phrase "How can't I love you, my *patria*." What follow are dark reflections on working-class life: "How can't I love you, my *patria*, if now at my mature age, I carry with love the chains of capitalist exploitation, putting up with salaries that are not enough for food, nor to dress, and putting up with being treated like a beast, all to resign myself like my holy Catholic religion commands. . . . How can't I love you, my *patria*, if you teach me to be generous, when you make me give my labor to the *patrón* [landowner], to the businessman, to the authorities, immortal glories of the *patria*."[67] The *patria*, constituted and perpetuated by the exploiting classes, is the antithesis to justice, Recabarren contends. Furthermore, his prose suggests an awareness of nationalism's growing popularity in the public sphere, and he challenges blind love for the *patria* by referring to specific aspects of the social question. Regardless of his disposition in "A mi patria," Recabarren did endorse a precise utilization of patriotism.

Though Recabarren affirmed in "Ricos y pobres" that he was a man without a *patria*—as were all proletarians—he nevertheless made reference to a particular form of patriotic service in the *folleto* "Patria y patriotismo." In this widely cited essay, he implies that Marxists alone were engaged in a patriotic endeavor to right social wrongs and improve the lives of workers: "That is the labor we call patriotic, and working for the disappearance of vices is how we give utmost proof of our real patriotic love, perhaps quietly, but more real and effective than those who shout a lot about patriotism."[68] Recabarren, in essence, equates patriotism with a will to alleviate the predicaments of the working class. Indeed, he suggests that workers are the real *patria*, and, accordingly, correcting their circumstance is the hallmark of genuine patriotism. For most, the distinction between patriotism and nationalism is admittedly difficult to discern, and much of it boils down to a semantic factor; what some Chileans dubbed "patriotism" before World War I was called "nationalism" during and after the conflict. That aside, Recabarren reasoned that two basic patriotic or nationalist currents prevailed in his day: one that served the interests of the aristocracy and bourgeoisie, and another that evoked unambiguous obligation to the "producing people." The coming decades, however, saw divergent conceptions and applications of nationalism among middle-class reformers and defenders of the oligarchic establishment, and Recabarren's understanding of the ideological landscape certainly bears interpretive weight when one considers the antirevolutionary convictions of both groups.

What once was a somewhat undifferentiated nationalist impulse had, by the presidential election of 1920, branched into "progressive" and "conservative" variants that were espoused by social interests locked in direct competition over power. Both forms of nationalists agreed that Chile's industrializing economy should more or less be protected from foreign interests, but the Alessandri–Barros Borgoño clash demonstrated that progressive and conservative nationalists agreed on little else. In essence, the most rancorous election of the Parliamentary Republic exposed nationalism's pliancy. This book revisits the 1920 presidential race—a pivotal juncture in modern Chilean history—at a later time. Middle-class reformers who were purveyors of progressive nationalism believed that actualizing their "national" vision involved shaping the cultural sphere in accordance with their cultural and political values. It is to the manifestations of their ideology in literary culture and public education that we may now turn in the remaining chapters. By way of short stories, novels, essays, public debate, ministerial directives, and textbooks, reformers introduced their compatriots to a fundamentally different way of thinking about the Chilean nation and its cultural core and did so in pursuit of hegemony.

Describer un paisaje o interpretar un estado

de alma es, en el fondo, lo mismo si el escritor

lo ha visto con sensibilidad artística.

MARIANO LATORRE, *Autobiografía de una vocación*, 1954

Rewriting Chile

3

Criollismo and the Generation of 1900

Celebrated Chilean novelist José Donoso once said that a writer does more than answer questions. He or she asks them.[1] Authors are not merely witnesses to society who wisely expose what others may not see but actors in society whose inquiries spark personal or collective inquest and introspection. In the literary environment of early-twentieth-century Chile, the architects of the genre known as *criollismo* both asked and answered two interrelated questions associated with the nation and culture: What is Chile? Who are Chileans? *Criollismo* created a fundamental break in Chilean cultural development when it questioned the value of narratives that rarely ventured from the pursuits of the privileged few. As conveyors of a reformist sensibility and progressive nationalism, the *criollistas* called the elite's legitimacy into question by weaving a populistic and more "national" narrative that focused on lower-class people who exemplified *chilenidad* and were worthy of a country's admiration. One *criollista*, when reflecting on his artistic motivation to uncover the authentic Chile, observed, "A profound love for the disinherited made me write with sincere emotion, and if something I have done is worthwhile, I owe it to those with uncompensated heroism."[2] As a rising middle class staked claims in society, culture, and politics, *criollismo* pronounced that the aristocrat no longer would be the locus of the nation, as a juridically and culturally constituted entity; high society was simply not worthy of dominion and prestige. In other words, by undermining the positions of the elite's literature and the elite in literature, *criollismo* offered a new portrayal of national life—a democratized one that challenged the legitimacy of the Parliamentary Republic's aristocracy and oligarchic establishment by devaluating their cultural precepts.[3]

Meanwhile, the *criollistas*, many of them with familial ties to a sector of small landowners in the center-south, did not affirm inspirations of proletarian revolution by undermining liberal ideals of order, progress, and democracy. The genre's short stories (*cuentos*) and novels delicately impart a code of conduct for the lower class as the social question intensified and unionization touched the countryside during the Parliamentary Republic; the truly Chilean laborer is respectable and assiduous and remains unmoved by the ideas and catechists of revolution. Most urban and rural workers may not have been reading *criollismo*, but middle-class reformers as well as more affluent and conservative readers certainly were, and the genre reinforced both sectors' views of worker radicalization. In essence, *criollismo* may be considered both antioligarchic for its delegitimization of high society's preeminence and antirevolutionary for its representations of labor—a dualism congruent to the sociopolitical position of reformist mesocrats and one that sheds light on the important link between culture and class. Broadly speaking, then, the genre's founding cohort of intellectuals, members of the so-called literary Generation of 1900, demonstrated inclinations and imparted convictions in line with those expressed by reformers of and outside the Radical Party who sought to remake Chile.[4]

The *criollistas* exhibited the penetrating influence of European "naturalist" writers and the rigor of Comtean positivism by approaching literature with a scientific disposition. Theirs was a project of documenting what they discerned as day-to-day aspects of life—qualities, attitudes, passions, concerns, hatreds, loves, problems—present within Chile's social underbelly between the late nineteenth and mid-twentieth centuries. Some *criollistas*, such as Baldomero Lillo, wrote widely popular stories about miners and urban workers, but most of the genre's contributors concentrated on rural themes and campesinos, to whom the authors ascribed cultural worth and national significance. One of *criollismo*'s main personalities is a campesino horseman, or *huaso*. This *criollo* cowboy emerged in Chilean culture as a complicated representation of a service tenant (the *inquilino de a caballo*) common to the Central Valley's archipelago of haciendas. Small property owners and any rural person with a horse were sometimes called *huasos* during our period of interest, though such usage was less prevalent. Regarded as a bumpkin by urban Chileans of the nineteenth century, the *huaso típico* (or stylized *huaso*) became a prominent example of *chilenidad*, a cultural symbol, and a national character by the Popular Front (FP) era in large part owing to the literary exploits of the *criollistas*.[5]

In light of *criollismo*'s ideological weight, not only should we understand the genre's content and style, but we should also examine the personal histories of its crafters, their basic cultural and political principles, and what proved to be a receptive audience. This analysis must begin with a discussion of the nineteenth century's intellectual atmosphere—an exclusive space of and for the wealthy and educated few—that flourished during the Portalian Republic. The foundations of Chile's national literary culture lay in the coalescence of what has been called the "movement of 1842" and the subsequent "realist" movement (1860s to 1890s). It will become apparent that although *criollismo* offered new aesthetic, thematic, and ideological perspectives to the reading public, it nonetheless upheld a cardinal rule of most postcolonial Chilean literature: stylistic inspiration could come from abroad, but subject matter was to be Chilean. "Chilean," of course, meant different things to different people in the nineteenth and twentieth centuries, and this discrepancy informs our story.

Literature and Nation-State Formation

Chile's independence from Spain in 1818 brought with it the prodigious task of creating a country from a colonial region. After more than a decade of intraelite political conflict, the conservative Portalians emerged victorious in 1829. Four years later, a new constitution established the structural foundations of a relatively stable political system. In cultural circles, intellectuals recognized the importance of domestic literary production in the ongoing process of building a nation-state and initiated the composition of a "national" literature and a Chilean intellectual tradition. In the words of José Victorino Lastarria, one of the leading intellectuals of the mid-nineteenth century, "no nations in the entire world have the imperious need that Americans have of being original in their literature."[6] For this reason, many young intellectuals from affluent families became enthused during the late 1830s and early 1840s with the "romantic" literary trend in Europe, which, by that time, was in its twilight. The late-eighteenth- and early-nineteenth-century romantics, especially those in France, were theorists of nationalism who held that literature was "defined by its national affiliation and should embody the unique characteristics of the nation. The underlying premise of the literary nationalists was that humanity is naturally divided into homogeneous, but distinctive groups marked by a unique set of values and concerns and by a distinctive 'national character.' "[7] Chile's movement of 1842—a diverse grouping of intellectuals and statesmen that included Lastarria, the widely celebrated Andrés Bello, José Joaquín Vallejo (known as "Jotabeche"), Francisco Bilbao, Eusebio Lillo, and Guillermo Matta—accepted romanticism's functional definition of literature (though Bello preferred the neoclassical style) and sought to describe the "realities of the country."[8] Although many of its members were not Portalian conservatives, the movement of 1842 reinforced the state-based patriotism of the Portalian Republic.

The first years of the Manuel Bulnes presidency (1841–51) were "favorable for the letters," Lastarria observed. "Those years saw a certain intellectual movement come to pass in an unimpeded and comforting way."[9] Lastarria (1817–88), a liberal, accomplished lawyer, historian, leader of the country's positivist school, and fiction writer, took advantage of this creative aperture. In the tradition of leading nineteenth-century intellectuals, the Rancagua native entered public life at a young age, joining the Interior Ministry at twenty-six. Later, at age thirty-two, he was elected to the Congress. Lastarria, as Allen Woll notes, was the first intellectual to discuss the country's need for a "national" literature based on Chile's historical experience. Lastarria's often-cited friendship with exiled Argentine Domingo Faustino Sarmiento in the 1840s and polemical conflicts with the more conservative Bello at midcentury served to strengthen his vision of a modern nation.[10]

One of the nation's first *cuentistas* (storytellers), Lastarria possessed an "ardent desire, very common in new nations, to earn a place alongside other civilizations and hold their head up proudly before European philosophers" and for Chilean literature to be, above all else, "useful and progressive."[11] Though committed more to historical, political, and philosophical endeavors, Lastarria published examples of fiction and historical fiction that garnered critical acclaim, such as his first short story, "El Mendigo" (1843), and later "Rosa" (1848). Both *cuentos* have independence battles as settings and concentrate on the heroic Creoles' struggle against royalists. "El Mendigo," first published in the progressive newspaper *El Crepúsculo*, is a love story that unfolds in the capital. Its protagonist is a Creole veteran of the Battle of Rancagua, which was fought in April 1814 between Chilean troops under O'Higgins and General José Miguel Carrera and forces loyal to King Ferdinand VII. Lastarria tells the story of what amounts to Creole valor and nostalgia, but he also includes passing references to the emerging country's beauty. His descriptions, for example, of the Mapocho River and shepherds leading their flocks on the sides of San Cristóbal Hill anticipate *criollismo*'s penchant for depicting the landscape. The *cuento* "Rosa" first appeared in the newspaper *El Aguinaldo* and likewise relates to the process of nation founding and nation building by tying sentimental characters to the Battle of Chacabuco and the declaration of independence from Spain. Given that the independence campaigns were led by enlightened Creoles, Lastarria's stories tend to display an elite-centered interpretation of national struggles and national life. (Politics on the national level, moreover, also emerged as an important theme of Chilean romanticism, which only fortified the movement's tendency to cast "elite" themes as "national" ones.)

The Lastarrian and movement of 1842's perception of literary production as a central tenet of nationality established the intellectual foundations for *criollismo*'s later emergence, but the *criollistas* offered a different interpretation of *lo nacional* in their "national" literature. As romanticism waned at midcentury, Chilean practitioners of another European cultural innovation produced works that also influenced the *criollistas*. Writers found inspiration in the penetrating realism of the Frenchman Honoré de Balzac's social novel and emulated his style with aptitude and precision between the 1860s and the turn of the century. Alberto Blest Gana (1830–1920), the greatest novelist of nineteenth-century Chile, is generally credited with bringing Balzacian style to Santiago in the form of his 1862 novel *Martín Rivas*. Although it did not revolutionize *criollo* literary culture, the realist movement certainly molded it, opening the way for the "naturalism" of the *criollistas*, who drew much from French writer Émile Zola, among others. In other words, Chilean realism, aside from its inherent merit, was as a stylistic bridge between the movement of 1842 and *criollismo*'s Generation of 1900.

Literary "Realism": Alberto Blest Gana and *Martín Rivas*

Domingo Amunátegui Solar, aristocrat, Liberal, and intellectual of the early twentieth century, called Chilean realism "a faithful portrait of society."[12] It certainly is not surprising that a man like Amunátegui, a member of an affluent family of Basque immigrants, would make such an assertion. The novels of Blest Gana and other realists rarely ventured from urban settings and the experiences of relatively affluent protagonists—Amunátegui's "society." Like the generation of writers that preceded it, the realist movement was committed to the exploration of Chile's early national experience and perpetuation of a national intellectual tradition but did not necessarily include the lower classes in its vision. However, what set realism apart from the movement of 1842 was its commitment to observing and analyzing what were, at that time, everyday aspects of contemporary life in a relatively stable, modernizing country, rather than the writing of stories related to nation founding and nation building. In this way, realism set the literary stage for naturalism and the *criollistas*, who maintained realism's affinity for "the real" but turned their attention to the social underbelly.

Blest Gana served as ambassador to the United States in the 1860s and won a congressional seat in Colchagua, while publishing books and composing articles for newspapers in the capital and Valparaíso. Two attributes distinguish Blest Gana's realism from the movement of 1842: the narrative attention he gives to Chile's nouveaux riches and his predilection for social criticism. Both qualities are prevalent in the novel *Martín Rivas* and reflect Chile's new social, political, and economic realities after the civil wars of the 1850s. In *Martín Rivas* we catch a glimpse of a product of modernization—the nouveaux riches, or an urban pseudobourgeoisie—who, like the country's aristocracy, do not hold the lower classes in high regard. It is a novel that criticizes snobbery, materialism, and wasteful elegance in Santiago, where money was the "idol of the day."[13] In this way, Blest Gana anticipates *Casa Grande*, the 1908 novelistic bombshell by Radical Party member Luis Orrego Luco, which expressed a similar opinion.

Blest Gana's Martín Rivas is a common man from the provinces whose shortcomings are brought to his attention by the capital's elite (the Encina family) and "gente de medio pelo," or members of what can be called Chile's new "shabby" middle class. They look upon the lower classes with scorn but often are too poor to achieve incorporation into the "buenas familias," or good families.[14] This sector, as Blest Gana observes in *Martín Rivas*, is "situated between a democratic disposition that despises [the *buenas familias*] and those *buenas familias* who fill them with jealousy and who they ordinarily want to copy."[15] One character *de medio pelo*, the young man Amador, enthusiastically remarks to his mother that marriage would usher them into the Encina family, and thus into aristocratic social circles, within a year.[16] For this reason, Best Gana sees the culture of the nouveaux riches as hybrid—an amalgam of "popular customs" and sociocultural traits of the "top of the social hierarchy."[17]

The stark division between Chile's provincial and urban spheres is an underlying theme of the novel, but a message stressing the potential for national unity is woven into the text.[18] Martín Rivas is not a social derelict but a provincial figure of modest means who seeks education and self-improvement in the capital. Martín falls in love with an aristocratic girl, Leonor, the daughter of landowner Dámaso Encina, who gives Rivas a job. It soon becomes evident to Rivas that his love for Leonor may be impossible. The divisions between classes, and provincial and urban life, seem like impenetrable barriers, but Martín's wholesome ways gradually claim Leonor's attention and, in the end, her affection.[19] The city, hints Blest Gana, is less "real," less dignified than the provinces, where good people like Rivas are the rule rather than the exception. In addition, Blest Gana offers a criticism of the city's cosmopolitanism and the Frenchification of Chilean culture, which was already under way before the Parliamentary Republic. For example, Leonor's brother, the dandy Agustín, enjoys adding French phrases to conversations to demonstrate his cultural status.[20]

Bumpkins and Backwardness

Despite Blest Gana's subtle doubts about the validity of urban life, his literature never truly ventures beyond the city's edge in search of attributes worthy of admiration. The *criollista* Mariano Latorre accounted for Blest Gana's hesitance by noting that the urban sphere was the only environment Blest Gana truly understood, and this kept the realist from painting a more substantive portrait of Chile's postcolonial experience.[21] But one does find campesinos and *huaso*-like figures with traits somewhat like Rivas's in almost all of Blest Gana's novels and short stories. Yet, as Latorre explained, for Blest Gana "the *huaso* was nothing but a personality who had not evolved, very interesting due to his customs, clothes, and ways of expressing himself. That was the understanding of the upper class, Frenchified and Anglo-Saxonized, of the *huaso*."[22] Such less-than-favorable opinions of the rural lower class may be discerned from a wide selection of nonfiction and non-*criollismo* fiction of the nineteenth and early twentieth centuries. Literary critic Ricardo Latcham notes that a "majority of nineteenth-century writers viewed rural life with disdain and preferred the city in their novelistic descriptions and plots. In the best of cases, *lo rural* [or 'what is rural'] constituted a decorative frame or a place of rest for a romantic figure who would flee to a sedate atmosphere to forget about problems of the heart or to admire nature."[23]

In an interesting manner, the 1905 memoirs of Liberal aristocrat Benjamín Vicuña Subercaseaux exemplify how many *santiaguinos*—of high society or the middle class—viewed rural life. Vicuña briefly discusses the presence of

Chileans in Paris who were there to see and be seen during the 1850s. Among them were questionable characters (most likely *hacendados*, or owners of haciendas) whom he identifies as *"huasos* in Paris." The connotation here is of backwardness and a certain degree of confusion experienced by such *"huasos"* amid the grandeur of Parisian life. In short, Vicuña calls some of his upper-class brethren *"huasos"* to expose their lack of truly cosmopolitan tastes. But when discussing the first decade of the twentieth century, Vicuña is quick to state, "No longer is there anything in Paris that could startle a *santiaguino*. That is why there no longer exists a savory type like the *huaso* in Paris, whose mishaps have been . . . the topics of great horselaughs."[24] Many urban Chileans, however, believed that such laughable traits remained very alive within the rural lower class, and a fictional story about a *huaso* named Lucas Gómez certainly reinforced that sentiment.

Accompanying *Martín Rivas* and other examples of nineteenth-century fiction on the market were *folletines*, inexpensive publications of lesser print quality reproduced for widespread consumption among an increasingly literate public. A favored *folletín* was Mateo Martínez Quevedo's *Don Lucas Gómez, o sea un huaso en Santiago*, which appeared in the 1880s (two decades before *criollismo*'s inception).[25] As the title suggests, the story follows a *huaso*'s journey from the small rural settlement of Curepto (in the province of Maule) to Santiago, where he is faced with a troubling situation. Lucas Gómez's *santiaguino* brother, Genaro, attempts to hide the true, rural origin of his horseman sibling. The *huaso* Gómez, according to Genaro and his urban relatives, is a comical, backward representative of an underdeveloped countryside. Genaro, who most likely had emigrated to the capital from the *campo*, had become civilized by urban society. In short, the *huaso* embarrasses Genaro for being too *huaso*. After achieving some notoriety, the story became a theatrical production in the 1890s and was performed from time to time in Santiago and other major cities well into the twentieth century. *Don Lucas Gómez*, in essence, demonstrates in a fairly accurate manner the prevailing "urban" attitude toward "the rural" in the late nineteenth century, regardless of how many *hacendados* resided in Santiago. The story suggests that people like the *huaso* Lucas weigh down a modernizing nation but remain interesting "others" with rustic cultural ways that are worth chuckling about (the second and final act of the stage production ends with a traditional *zamacueca* folk dance).

The *criollista* Mariano Latorre recognized the laughable backwardness of Lucas Gómez as a grave flaw in Chilean national identity. Writing in his memoirs, Latorre laments that Chileans in the nineteenth century developed no heroic rural type, as did the Argentines. Absent was a figure similar to José Hernández's gaucho Martín Fierro, the protagonist in the author's 1872 lengthy poem by the same title. Gómez, Latorre explained, was "a farce of a personality who doesn't know what electric light is and doesn't want to take his spurs off to enter a home."[26] Like the character Gómez, Latorre went to Santiago from the countryside and most likely was personally insulted by Martínez Quevedo's story (though Latorre certainly was not a *huaso*). Joaquín Edwards Bello, a member of *criollismo*'s second generation, added that the story of Lucas Gómez fits the "place it has in time," suggesting subsequent changes in national identity and urban perceptions of rural existence.[27]

Often situated behind modern typewriters and aided by the radiance of Edison light bulbs in their comfortable Santiago homes, *criollismo*'s contributors interpreted and portrayed a rural landscape that seemed distant—conceptually more than geographically—to many urban Chileans. As artists seeking subjects, the *criollistas* turned to campesinos, and especially "*huasos*," for characteristics that supposedly revealed *chilenidad*. Before delving into *criollismo*'s stylistic, thematic, and cultural/political dimensions, we must pause to examine the history of Chilean rural society and accounts of life on Central Valley haciendas in the nineteenth and twentieth centuries. In particular, the development and circumstances of rural labor lend some insight into the *criollistas'* subject matter and their understanding of "nation" and culture. As Angel Rama explained when describing intellectual production and cultural nationalism in early-twentieth-century Latin America, "myths start from something real, but they constitute more wishful thinking than accurate depictions of the way things really function."[28]

The Campo and Campesinos

When Pedro de Valdivia and his followers reached and settled what is now central Chile in the 1540s, two factors aided in the rapid formation of a powerful landowning elite. First, central Chile's considerable distance from Lima—the Spanish Crown's bureaucratic and administrative center for the entire western coast of the Americas at that time—allowed settlers the opportunity to intimidate or simply ignore royal representatives, since the powers of enforcement were many thousands of miles away. Second, as gold mining in Mesoamerica and the Andes drew the attention of the Spanish Crown, only small gold deposits were found in Chile. The region simply did not pique the monarchy's monetary interests, relatively speaking. Without a strong royal presence, *encomenderos* (Spaniards who were granted *encomiendas*, the widely applied system of allocating indigenous labor characteristic of all major Spanish inroads in the New World) wielded great power in matters of conquest and settlement.

Grants of *encomienda* did not satisfy colonists who ambitiously sought a more feudal station atop Chile's nascent rural society.[29] Indeed, *encomiendas* dealt only with half of the seigniorial recipe. In the seventeenth century, the acquisition of fertile land in the Central Valley region became a prime interest of Spanish colonials. As Spaniards added American Indian lands to their holdings, the native population's subsistence disintegrated, and landless Indians settled on estates for survival.[30] The uprooting and transplantation of the indigenous population from villages to haciendas produced precisely what the Spanish Crown had sought to avoid in the New World—the mixing of Iberian and American Indian blood. Increased day-to-day interaction and close living quarters contributed to *mestizaje*, or the creation of the mestizo race in Chile. In the Andes and Mesoamerica, unlike Chile, the autonomy of Indian villages remained relatively intact until after independence. This division of races is reflected in contemporary Mexico and the Andean zone, where a large number of campesinos are predominantly, and many times exclusively, of pure American Indian descent (this is much more the case in Peru, Bolivia, and Ecuador).

The evolution of Chile's landowning aristocracy, whose members enjoyed spending time in their Santiago homes when not overseeing estate activities, was concurrent with the development of a diverse labor pool. Transient laborers (*afuerinos*) accompanied stable wage laborers (*peones*) and service tenants (*inquilinos*) on Central Valley haciendas. In the early nineteenth century, Frenchman Claudio Gay observed the poor conditions that all rural laborers experienced. Many *inquilinos*, for example, could not afford the necessary tools to farm plots granted to them by their *hacendados*.[31] In addition, since the campesinos constructed their own small shacks, the abodes were "very sincere, quite dirty, without a single commodity though they would be easy to procure."[32]

Horsemen *inquilinos* were indispensable on Central Valley haciendas during the Portalian Republic. In a manual about proper hacienda management published in 1875, Manuel José Balmaceda (father of the president) favors horsemen over "*inquilinos* on foot," or second-class service tenants. Not only did the landowner recognize the practical importance of service tenants with horses, but he also valued these *huasos* as "more decent, more honorable" campesinos.[33] The horsemen *inquilinos* joined vaqueros, another type of cattlemen, in traversing "the hills from day to day, looking for the sick and maimed as far as possible, protecting very young calves from attacks of condors, and driving stragglers within the boundaries of the hacienda again."[34] During the fall, duties in the rodeo primarily consisted of herding livestock from an estate's vast expanses to corrals for counting. The rodeo also was a time of festivity. Campesino families gathered at the corrals to enjoy watching cowboys display their horsemanship and roping skills. Landowners often joined these "dark and swarthy" *huasos* "with beards and heads uncombed" to celebrate the rodeo.[35]

At the core of *inquilino*-landowner relations was an informal system of deference and paternalism that tied *inquilinos* to estates and made landowners responsible for their workers' well-being. For example, one mid-nineteenth-century traveler notes that if a *patrón* (landowner) was notified that a worker took ill, the landowner "strives to get him to the nearest town; but, as with workers everywhere, they have a dread of hospitals, and so great is their repugnance that few can be induced to go from the country."[36] Gay suggests that Indian blood pulsing through *inquilinos* produced such a "repugnance" toward "social life" away from their respective haciendas.[37] Whatever the source for this sentiment—biological or psychological—it reflects the common *inquilino*'s strong ties to the hacienda. As another observer noted, "The *huaso* does not know his roots or from which nation he originated. He does not know if he descends from the Spanish or English, from the Russians or Chinese. . . . The *huaso* thinks of himself as indigenous to his hacienda, and that is enough for him."[38] In short, the *huaso* or *inquilino* entertained no conception of the Chilean *patria* during the early national period. The hacienda, a microsociety with a social life of its own, was his *patria*, and its borders were his borders.[39]

The close association between *inquilino* and *patrón* was necessary in order for the landowner to preserve an adequate supply of reliable and skilled labor. In the 1870s, for example, commercial expansion threatened to sap the Central Valley of its labor force and cripple production on the great haciendas. On the issue of rural labor needs, a British visitor commented in 1876, "In addition to emigration abroad, agriculturists in this country have lately had to contend with an increasing tendency on the part of laborers to migrate from their native fields in the central provinces to the mining districts of the north, or the coal fields of the south, or to hire themselves out as navvies on the railway, and other public works in progress in various parts of the Republic."[40] The collapse of world wheat prices in the late 1870s only aggravated the situation in the countryside. Booming wheat production in Russia, Australia, North America, and other regions of Latin America increased the grain supply and drove prices lower. Chilean wheat remained land- and labor-intensive and soon lost its export market.[41] The migration of labor from the Central Valley to growing commercial centers, especially those in the northern nitrate zone, increased after Chile's victory in the War of the Pacific. The country's demographic center of gravity, then, shifted to an increasingly dynamic urban society, which stood in contrast to "rural stagnation, so far as the lives of its peasantry were concerned."[42]

After the turn of the century, urban reformers and Marxists addressed the circumstances of rural labor and landowner power. As Thomas Wright explains, they viewed the countryside as a "feudal society . . . inadmissible in a democracy and inconsistent with their respective visions of the ideal society."[43] Radicals joined the chorus. As early as 1912, the Radical Party (PR) had a plank concerning the plight of the rural working class and the need to correct it. The year before, the National Agricultural Society, which became a voice of more "progressive" landowners as the century went on, described the condition of rural labor as "simply monstrous" and "unworthy of a civilized country and an affront to the Chilean landowner."[44] In 1916, Tancredo Pinochet Le-Brun offered a more harsh assessment of rural life in his *Inquilinos en la hacienda de Su Excelencia*, which describes working conditions on the *fundo* of President Sanfuentes.[45] Moreover, urban political groups encouraged by the election of Arturo Alessandri Palma in 1920 identified Central Valley *hacendados* as "villains" and members of the "squandering class" in the press and elsewhere.[46]

In the 1930s, as Brian Loveman notes, "the hacienda-resident labor system still dominated the Chilean countryside, though increasing numbers of temporary and seasonal wage hands presaged some alteration in the basic arrangement."[47] While this may be the case, new and significant laws regarding rural labor were in place, including a 1924 measure that regulated landowner-worker relations. In addition, the Labor Code of 1931, issued during the dictatorship of Carlos Ibáñez del Campo (1927–31), was the most notable government action related to *inquilinos* and other campesinos during the early decades of the century. Article 76, for example, stipulated that landowners were to provide "adequate" and "clean" housing on their haciendas. In addition, the code "exposed landowners to legal labor petitions,

Huasos go about their work in the countryside of the southern Central Valley, ca. 1920. (Courtesy of Eduardo Devés)

strikes, and unionization by rural labor and obligated them to deal with these situations, at least formally, as stipulated in the Labor Code."[48] Yet, landowners commonly evaded compliance by capitalizing on the Labor Department's failure to enforce the code fully.

Though politicians in Santiago began to deal with agrarian issues during the first decades of the century, *inquilinos* and other rural workers did not see consequential improvements in terms of living conditions and workloads. Most *criollistas* understood the difficult reality of campesino life. Mariano Latorre, for example, was born and raised in Maule, a poor province of the center-south, where modern commodities were scant and most livelihoods depended on good harvests (Latorre's father went bankrupt after a poor lentil crop). The *criollistas*, like the European naturalists, were not hesitant to describe the challenges faced daily by those of society's underbelly, but they also identified traits worthy of national celebration when they thought about Chile's rural space. A curious mix of naturalism, nationalism, and what is a "rural aestheticism" binds *criollismo*; the genre's architects saw the countryside as a place where hardship and fatalism were not uncommon, but a domain in which *chilenidad* maintained cohesion.

The Generation of 1900: Founders and Formula

As one sociologist of literature has observed, "national literatures, like nations, are created by the cultural work of specific people engaged in an
identifiable set of activities."[49] The *criollistas* were among such engineers of
national culture, and together participated in the most important and popular literary enterprise of early-twentieth-century Chile. Nearly all were
members of an expanding middle class, and many were either directly or
loosely affiliated with the leading reformist political association of the era,
the PR. While Lastarria wrote about heroic protagonists of the independence campaigns and Blest Gana entered the homes of the urban elite and
nouveaux riches in the nineteenth century, the *criollistas* proposed that the
real Chile and *chilenidad*—including authentic cultural practices—were to be
found among the lower classes, especially in the countryside. They found
chilenidad in the experiences and lifeways of forgotten "others," rather than
at five o'clock tea at the posh department store Gath y Chaves or at social
events at the Union Club.

The journalist and literary critic Ernesto Montenegro, an acquaintance of
Guillermo Labarca and other *criollistas*, eloquently described the genre in the
following terms: "*Criollismo* is an historical concept, a social phenomenon,
and a literary mode. At first, the *criollista* sensibility germinated as a repudia-
tion of foreign influences that threatened to choke traditional traits and
customs of a people. . . . The *criollismo* that concerns us here is the deliberate
tendency to preferentially valorize in our literature stories pertaining to
campesinos and popular sectors, regional traditions and legends, and the
customs of the land. This literary *criollismo* supposes that in our way of being
and in our beliefs inherited from our elders are found inherent and exclusive
virtues that possess superior merit, beauty, and singular enchantment."[50]
Cosmopolitanism, Montenegro explains, was seen by the *criollistas* as an aristocratic cultural practice with debilitating effects on *chilenidad*. Indeed, the
criollistas often questioned high society's cosmopolitanism through subtle
inference rather than overt attack, choosing instead to focus their narrative
energies on lower-class individuals and their national significance. Their
position as intellectuals seeking to widen the mesocracy's political and cultural spaces and promote a new national and nationalist agenda shaped
their critique of aristocratic cosmopolitanism. The *criollistas* thus demonstrated a "nationalist sensibility . . . inspired by positivist humanitarian-
ism"[51]—an ideological orientation shared by Pinochet, Venegas, and other
progressive nationalists.

Blest Gana's *Martín Rivas*, which forged a new current in Chilean literature, anticipated some central characteristics of *criollismo*, save *criollismo*'s dedication to exploring lower-class lifeways in rural society. Realism, unlike romanticism, dealt exclusively with interpersonal interaction in the context of everyday life. Moreover, it infused literary culture with a critical spirit that mirrored the rising tide of sociopolitical criticism within Chilean society in the 1850s and 1860s. By the first decade of the twentieth century, when the Parliamentary Republic's social, economic, and political problems were manifest, the first *criollistas* shaped a genre that combined Blest Gana's Balzacian eye for the "real" and the stylistic and thematic modes of such European naturalists as Zola, Guy de Maupassant, and Alphonse Daudet. In an all-too-common twist in Latin American intellectual and cultural history, foreign innovations inspired authors of a "national" literature.

Although *criollismo* is generally considered a genre devoted to the investigation of rural life, one of the movement's founders, Baldomero Lillo (1867–1923), exposed readers to the working and living conditions of the mining poor. The *"cuentos mineros"* of his book *Sub-Terra* (1904) drew the acclaim of social reformers and literary critics and inaugurated a relatively short but successful literary career. A native of Lota, a small coal-mining community near the city of Concepción, the sickly Lillo began holding miners in high esteem at a young age and was always a "penetrating observer of life," as his brother, the author Samuel Lillo, recalled.[52] After graduating from the secondary school in nearby Lebu, the young Baldomero briefly held a white-collar job at a local mine before leaving for Santiago in 1900 after a disagreement with a "gringo" administrator.[53] He found employment, as did his brother, as an insurance agent before becoming interested in the prospect of writing. *Sub-Terra*, a collection of stories about coal miners, was Lillo's first major publication, and it was soon followed by the sequel *Sub-Sole* (1907). When reflecting on *Sub-Terra*, literary critic Raúl Silva Castro wrote that in Lillo's literature "there is more than a love for the worker, for the abandoned, and for those offended by all the injustices; there is a mingling of spirits, and this is the way in which Lillo becomes a spokesman by way of his art."[54] *Sub-Terra* caused a commotion in Chilean literary circles. A collection with such acrimony had never before been read. He wrote about hard lives in a tough place far from the Santiago sitting rooms so visible in Blest Gana's realism. On the heels of the very popular *Sub-Terra*, other authors with similar motives and stylistic interests turned to rural themes, including Lillo's good friend Guillermo Labarca.[55]

Guillermo Labarca Hubertson (1878–1954), who sometimes wrote under the pseudonyms Valdvino, Atalaya, and Huelén, produced some of the earliest examples of rural-oriented Chilean *criollismo*. Born in Santiago in 1878, he was captivated by literature and politics while completing his education at the Pedagogical Institute at the University of Chile. The first decade of the new century brought with it many new opportunities for this young member of the PR, who seemed to take advantage of all of them. In 1903, he met his future wife, Amanda Pinto Sepúlveda, who later became the renowned educator Amanda Labarca Hubertson (she adopted both of his last names). Two years later, he joined the staff of the new magazine *Zig-Zag* and, in 1906, became secretary of the incipient Chilean Federation of Students (Federación de Estudiantes de Chile, or FECh) at the university. Guillermo Labarca was then appointed to teach history to girls at a Santiago secondary school in 1906, where he served for four years.[56]

While wearing many different hats, he found time to write short stories about a place so unlike the bustling city that was his home. Imagining the countryside may have helped Guillermo Labarca escape from an urban environment consumed by "doubt, indecision, and pessimism." He explained in a 1907 speech that urban society was a place where the social question was unmistakable and oligarchs turned their back to the lives and concerns of workers: "We realize that a social problem is upon us. New demands, new ideas have made it necessary to reform the current condition of the masses. Let us go to the *pueblo*, let us look for it, and if we know that we march in unity, we will be able to raise the level of our culture, quickly learn what its necessities are, [and] learn about how to exalt work and not money. . . . Such conduct would create sympathies between workers and ourselves and mutual respect."[57] The *criollista*'s journey "to the *pueblo*" is symbolically expressed in and through his literature, which was heavily influenced by Zola.[58] Along the way, he sought to understand the common Chilean—the authentic Chilean *outside* the plagued city. Literary critic Raúl Silva Castro later observed that the cofounder of *criollismo* "fell in love with the countryside. . . . He dedicated attentive observation to the landscape to the extent that his tales do not lack details about colors."[59] Through understanding the lower classes, as Guillermo Labarca suggests in his speech, comes social enlightenment and change. Here, again, the sway of Zola is strong. Like Zola, who achieved fame as a naturalist author and outspoken critic of the French government during the Dreyfus Affair, Guillermo Labarca came to see art as a means of exploring society, especially its underbelly.

The Radical's first short stories appeared in the magazine *Luz y Sombra* in 1900 and later in *Zig-Zag*, an urban favorite.[60] But it was not until the publication of *Al amor de la tierra*, an anthology of short stories published in 1905, that Guillermo Labarca gained recognition as a serious author.[61] *Al amor de la tierra*, which stands as his only published collection of *cuentos*, blends portraits of campesino lifeways with the aesthetic marvel of a bountiful countryside. As examples of early *criollismo*, his stories do not rely on substantive dialogue; they mostly relay information about settings, emotions, and predicaments through third-person description. One of the anthology's most telling *cuentos* is "Después del Trabajo" (After work), which describes a day in the life of Olegario, an *inquilino* (or *huaso*) on a Central Valley hacienda, and his family (wife Mercedes and sons Eugenio and Ignacio). When the day is over and the burning sun sets, Olegario goes home to his *ranchito* (a small house or hut), where his wife and children await him. The *inquilino* is content with his honest labor and relaxes with his wife while peeking at the infant Ignacio. Guillermo Labarca writes: "And there they stayed for a long time, both of them enjoying the placid and enviable happiness of a day now done, which seemed to float over the tranquil shack. The sanctity of a rest well earned filled their souls with an ineffable joy."[62] Like Olegario and his wife, another campesino couple—recently married—also take great enjoyment from time alone after their daily labor on the *patrón*'s land in the *cuento* "La siembra" (The sowing of seeds, a title with hints of a double meaning). As the narrator states, "and what happiness is felt by one who is next to his beloved wife after work!"[63]

In the *cuento* "Vida de campo" (Rural life), Guillermo Labarca tells of Pedro Juan, quite possibly a horseman *inquilino*, who fell in love with Filomena, a resident of a neighboring town. While visiting Pedro Juan's *ranchito*, the story's narrator learns from the campesino that a city man courted Filomena and eventually took her to the capital: "[Pedro Juan] was the same as always ... very tranquil from the look of it, just a little older, that's all. ... I asked him about Filomena, believing that she would be his woman by now. His face turned pale, his chest swelled and I'm not sure if he breathed. 'She left, *patrón*. ... They say she's been seen looking elegant in Santiago.' There he remained staring at the still poplars and the hills of Chanqueahue, which were beginning to become covered by the shadows."[64] The campesino, though saddened by Filomena's flight to *santiaguino* society, continues his noble work and seems to find solace in gazing over a rural landscape that will never leave him.

Al amor de la tierra convinced many readers that Guillermo Labarca had a promising future as a fiction writer. Many intellectuals, such as Silva Castro and Ernesto Montenegro, praised the author's flare for description, but not all readers were impressed with the Radical's work. Fernando Santiván, a self-proclaimed Tolstoyan who also dabbled in *criollismo*, found *Al amor de la tierra* "pedantic." Writing in the Radical newspaper *La Lei* only weeks after the book's publication, Santiván called one *cuento* a "literary abomination" and added that the *criollista* wrote nothing but "simple scenes." He found the anthology's final *cuento*, which includes the verses of a *zamacueca* folksong, especially repulsive.[65] Indeed, Guillermo Labarca wrote *cuentos* with little, if any, explicit social commentary and compelling drama, but he nevertheless was a principal figure in the elaboration of a new national narrative with profound cultural implications. Santiván's bitter assessment aside, Guillermo Labarca earned recognition as a *criollista* with "penetrating intelligence."[66]

After publishing his only novel, *Mirando al océano*, in 1911, Guillermo Labarca gravitated toward a career in politics. In 1915, he took a position at *La Opinión*, a Santiago newspaper founded by Tancredo Pinochet Le-Brun, and never again returned to *criollista* fiction as a vocation or an avocation. He joined the reformist National Education Association (AEN) and, along with close friend Pedro Aguirre Cerda, became a member of the National Society of Teachers (Sociedad Nacional de Profesores), one of the nation's largest teachers unions, in the early 1920s. All the while, the *criollista* rose in the ranks of the PR and assumed important governmental posts. In 1924, he became Alessandri's minister of justice and public instruction and later served as Santiago's mayor in the mid-1930s. After the FP's victory in 1938, he accepted Aguirre Cerda's invitations to head the ministries of War and the Interior and then became president of the PR in 1941. Moreover, the *criollista* wrote columns in the capital's *El Mercurio* and the Radical-oriented *La Hora* before his death in 1954.[67]

Joining Guillermo Labarca as a founding father of *criollismo* was his nephew, Rafael Maluenda Labarca (1885–1963). Maluenda, who also published short stories in the press under the pseudonym "Pedro Franco," is best known for his *Escenas de la vida campesina* (1909), an anthology dedicated to the campesinos who embody, according to the book's preface, the "strength and consolation" of the nation.[68] He began his writing career as a contributor to the PR's *La Lei* at the turn of the century and then moved for a brief time to the conservative *El Diario Ilustrado* circa 1910. Maluenda published *cuentos* from time to time in the magazine *Zig-Zag* and, in 1920, went to work for *El Mercurio*, which he later directed during the 1950s and 1960s. His movement from one newspaper to the next reflected a political disposition in flux. Maluenda, like his uncle, began his political life as a Radical and became a strong supporter of Alessandri's brand of antioligarchic liberalism in the 1920s.[69] But while writing for *El Mercurio* in the 1930s, Maluenda demonstrated that his Radical days were clearly over. He adopted a more conservative posture (as did Alessandri) as socialism and communism made inroads in the Chilean body politic. In 1938, Maluenda offered a warm endorsement of the Liberal-Conservative candidate, Gustavo Ross Santa María, who was engaged in a tight electoral battle with Radical and FP leader Aguirre Cerda.[70] Maluenda's support of Ross undoubtedly made for entertaining debates around the Labarca clan's dinner table (his uncle was a high-ranking PR official at that time) and may have strained a family as it did a nation. Although Maluenda drifted into more conservative circles as the century progressed, he was firmly in the reformist, Radical corner when he began his literary career.

Demonstrating an aesthetic sensibility similar to his uncle's, Maluenda's *cuentos* in *Escenas de la vida campesina* seek to portray the day-to-day activities of campesinos, including *huasos*, who are hardworking, honorable, and, at times, mysterious.[71] One cuento, "Ño Pancho" (a derivation of "Don Pancho"), tells of an old *huaso*-like campesino who becomes upset at the now dead *patrón*'s son, a landowner of modest means who is selling tracts of hacienda land in order to purchase equipment to modernize production. The old man, in Maluenda's words, "detested these new acquisitions for changing the stretch of land that he considered his."[72] Modern machines and production techniques, the protagonist believes, are disrupting the normal rhythms of rural life; elements of the "outside" are encroaching upon authenticity and tradition. The old campesino does not necessarily express an antimodern political ideology, nor does he engage in metaphysical reflections on modernity. Rather, the campesino simply sees that the young heir is undoing all that the deceased *patrón* and his workers accomplished and is forgetting about the blood, sweat, and tears it took to run a *fundo*. In addition, the old man may also be lamenting that machines, rather than campesinos, will now be the locus of rural life. Something original, something *criollo* is being lost. In all, the story is about the feelings of a campesino who, it seems, is being cast aside by a young landowner seeking to maximize his wealth (and possibly enter the ranks of Santiago's nouveaux riches?).

Although Maluenda went on to publish twelve novels and anthologies during his long and celebrated literary career, *Escenas de la vida campesina* stands as his most memorable work. *El Mercurio* literary critic Emilio Vaisse (who wrote under the name Omer Emeth) described the collection of *cuentos*, which touches on topics ranging from banditry to love, as "an expression of the Chilean countryside." He observed that "all of that book is distinctly

Chilean; valiant boys and frolicking girls, the intrepid bandits and their tenacious pursuers who are evaded. . . . Loves and hates, fatalistic patience and indomitable value, everything there grows from Chilean land and takes with it the indelible mark of its origin."[73] Vaisse and others praised Maluenda (along with his fellow *criollistas*) for promoting a compelling vision of campesino life—an authentically Chilean existence. Campesinos are not portrayed as rustic simpletons but as humans with emotions, desires, and opinions. Maluenda's and Guillermo Labarca's literary explorations of rural life gave shape to the embryonic genre during the first decade of the century. However, no figure of the *criollista* Generation of 1900 proved more influential than Mariano Latorre Court (1886–1955), whom intellectuals recognized as "the most outstanding interpreter of the Chilean countryside" and "the most Chilean of our national authors."[74]

Latorre's first book, *Cuentos del Maule* (1912), is a quintessential example of early *criollismo* that inaugurated a four-decade-long literary career marked by more than a dozen novels and anthologies and a seemingly endless string of short stories published in leading periodicals. Latorre, who deemed authors "objective interpreters or sociologists of Chilean life in the countryside and the city,"[75] was born in the town of Cobquecura in the province of Maule, a riverine region some 250 miles south of the capital. His father, a Balmacedist and member of the Civil Guard of the Revolution during the civil war of 1891, went bankrupt after a crop failure in 1895. The family soon moved to Parral (also in Maule Province between the cities of Chillán and Linares), where his father worked for the municipality before the family relocated to the port city of Valparaíso. The elder Latorre enrolled his son at Santiago's prestigious National Institute (Instituto Nacional) in 1897, where Mariano received his secondary education. After graduation, the younger Latorre entered the Pedagogical Institute at the University of Chile, where he earned his education certificate. While publishing his examples of *criollismo*, Latorre taught Hispanic literature, served as rector of the Pedagogical Institute in the 1920s, was appointed ambassador to Colombia by Aguirre Cerda in 1939, and won the first National Literature Award in 1942. He also was a member and general secretary of the National Association of Free Thinkers (Asociación Nacional de Libre Pensadores).[76] While juggling many responsibilities, the *criollista* was a strong proponent of reformism and was counted among the fellow travelers of the PR, though he was known to be wary of engaging in political activism outside the literary medium. One Latorre friend explained in the late 1930s that the *criollista* is a "socialist without a party [and] could have been a member of all or neither of them."[77] (The reader will recall that Radicals often identified themselves as "socialists," though they were not referring to any sort of Marxist socialism.)

The Maule native started writing at an early age and began publishing short stories in *Zig-Zag* after the turn of the century. He later recalled that his motivation for writing stemmed from a spiritual (and physical) proximity to campesinos and a desire to expose their human faces and cultural/national worth, which persisted despite the tyranny of some landowners.[78] As a boy in Parral, Latorre said in a 1943 interview in the newspaper *Las Últimas Noticias*, he grew close to the countryside and its *huasos*. Latorre remembered, "We stayed in Parral for many years, and there I came to know the countryside of my *patria* in all its moving and dramatic expression. It was the Chile of *huasos*! . . . So Chilean like an old *poncho* . . . the Chilean countryside and its people entered me through my eyes, my ears and mouth, and renovated my blood. . . . Without being a *campesino*, I made a *campesino* of myself."[79] Elsewhere Latorre recalled, "[I wrote] . . . for the people who love those of our race who are so rich in vitality and in unbreakable perseverance."[80] Latorre essentially found *chilenidad* among the rural poor, not "the parties of the aristocrats and the *nouveaux riches*, their social scandals, their shady deals, and their crimes," as he explained.[81] Moreover, Latorre's friend Domingo Melfi wrote that the *criollista* "incited love for the country" that "snobs despised" and "is a believer of Chilean life and each one of his books is a support of *criollo* values."[82]

Like others in the *criollista* cohort, Latorre drew stylistic inspiration from the European naturalists, especially Zola. "We knew Zola's definition of a work of art by memory," Latorre explained. "*Novel, poem, portrait or sculpture are but a refuge of nature, seen through a temperament.* One had to observe nature to become acquainted with it or look for it within the pool of our sensations, and finally live it. . . . We borrowed from [Zola] more than anyone."[83] Moreover, Latorre was a great admirer of Bret Harte, who crafted tales about the North American frontier, as well as Mark Twain.[84] In short, the *criollista* fused foreign literary style with Chilean substance, and, in the words of one literary critic of the era, convincingly conveyed "the traditions, legends, and customs of the land."[85]

Cuentos del Maule, a collection of seven short stories that relate the rural experience in his native province, is one of his many books that introduced his Chilean compatriots immersed in the bustle of city life to campesinos and the panorama of the center-south. Known to sport *huaso* attire when writing, Latorre saw Maule as a bastion of Chilean authenticity and values, where the complexities of urban life are distant and workers confront the

The most widely recognized writer of the *criollista* movement, Mariano Latorre drew on his childhood and adolescent memories of Maule Province while crafting stories about the Chilean countryside. Latorre, a teacher by training, became a diplomat after the election of Pedro Aguirre Cerda in 1938. (Courtesy of the Archivo Fotográfico, Museo Histórico Nacional, Santiago)

forces of nature and *patrón* power.[86] As an admirer of the naturalists, Latorre sought to portray the pain and anguish sometimes suffered by the campesinos of his native province. The *cuento* "Sandías ribereñas" (Riverine watermelons) describes the experience of *inquilinos* during a drought when "that sad landscape has a primitive desolation: the poverty of the land puts in the eyes of men that same tranquil resignation shown by the old horses and oxen."[87] The *campesinos* weather such changes of fortune and remain on the *fundos*. They suffer, but Latorre suggests that suffering is a component of a real Chile beyond the understanding of affluent city dwellers; the anguish of campesinos is authentic.

"Un hijo del Maule" (A son of the Maule River) ventures beyond description of campesino life to include the demeanor of visitors to Maule. Here Latorre addresses rampant *snobismo* and elitism by way of a first-person narrative strategy. In the summertime, the narrator Latorre explains, vacationers from the city travel by railroad to Maule's beaches and rivers, where they exercise "a pernicious influence over the customs of my land."[88] The narrator then bemoans a consequence of such infiltration. He notes that some *maulinos* "had assumed that aristocratic sense of superiority and it was great comedy to see them strut about the streets of the town, at the beach, on the pier: anxious to be mistaken . . . [for] those who fill the hotels and the bed-and-breakfasts in the summertime."[89] One infers that those *maulinos* anxious to become cultured along urban lines were akin to the nouveaux riches or the *gente de medio pelo* criticized by Blest Gana in *Martín Rivas*—not the *inquilinos* or other campesinos of the region.

Many found this message and Latorre's literary style immensely attractive. Luis Durand, a second-generation *criollista* and disciple of Latorre, called the *maulino* a "novelist and storyteller of authentic Chilean stock, due to the love he shows for things that he embosses in his vigorous tales—men, landscapes, and animals—and for an exact understanding of the psychology of his characters and the milieu he describes."[90] Literary critic Silva Castro stated that "the literature of Mariano Latorre, which has sought the face of Chile and its Chileans in the mountains and on the sea, has gained importance as a testament about the race. There does not exist another author with a deeper nationalist sentiment."[91] But Silva Castro did express some reservations, noting that many of Latorre's characters are "beings without spiritual, emotional or sentimental attractions."[92] Hernán Díaz Arrieta, who wrote under the pseudonym "Alone," was more direct; he found the *criollista*'s work "boring and uninteresting."[93] Even so, Latorre's mark on Chilean literary culture was a prominent one, and it remained well into the second half of the twentieth century.

While Latorre mingled with intellectuals in Santiago circa 1912, he came across a self-proclaimed bohemian from a landowning family, Federico Gana (1867–1926), whom the *maulino* had first met as a boy. Gana had also been writing *criollismo* but was yet to publish a book. He was an interesting and generous character, as Fernando Santiván recalled, who often went to his retreat in the countryside of the center-south to work on stories destined for Santiago periodicals.[94] Politically speaking, Gana was a Balmacedist. His father, Federico Gana Munizaga, owner of the *fundo* El Rosario and cousin of Alberto Blest Gana, was imprisoned by anti-Balmaceda forces during the civil war of 1891—an act that spawned the younger Gana's disgust for the Parliamentary Republic. In addition, the younger Federico's mother, who was his father's cousin, was the daughter of a government minister under Balmaceda.

Born in Santiago, Gana remained in the capital to enroll at the National Institute and pursue a legal education; he then served as secretary of Chile's legation in London during the Balmaceda administration. After traveling in Europe in the wake of the civil war, Gana resettled in Santiago to practice law, and literature soon became his avocation. Gana published *Días de campo* in 1916, an anthology of short stories that first appeared in turn-of-the-century periodicals, which examines the customs he deemed native to rural life. Though it stands as Gana's only book, its *cuentos* were described by contemporaries as the best written to that date, and they earned him notoriety more than a decade before they were assembled as a book (and before the first books by Lillo, Guillermo Labarca, Maluenda, and Latorre).[95] In the words of the critic Alone, Gana "discovered the Chilean countryside."[96] After the *criollista*'s death in 1926, moreover, the newspaper *La Nación* observed that "Federico Gana was the first to cultivate [a ruralesque literature] with love and the true style of an artist."[97]

Gana's anthology includes the *cuento* "Confidencias," which opens with a description of a rural worker who had just completed his day's duty: "There, he heard the soft rustling of the stream's waters slithering smoothly, kissing the damp roots of the large weeping willows. All was tranquil, sweetness, preludes to the deep silence of the night."[98] Many similar depictions of tranquility and simplicity are found in *Días de campo* and the entire *criollista* genre for that matter. But clearly lacking here is something on par with Latorre's thinly veiled contempt for *snobismo*'s purveyors—the unwelcome visitors and their local mimickers who bring an air of haughtiness to an otherwise down-to-earth countryside. That is not to say that Gana's *cuentos* are devoid of ideological depth. One may easily infer from Gana the notion that urban society's worst qualities, including the political forces responsible for his father's jailing, are far away from the peace of the campo.[99] Indeed, the countryside's physical and conceptual distance from urban life is one of *criollismo*'s underlying themes, which says much about the turbulent politics and social problems in Santiago and elsewhere in Chile during the Parliamentary Republic.

The cohort of writers discussed in the preceding pages not only brought a new dimension to Chilean culture but also proposed a different way of imagining their national community. The *criollistas* of the Generation of 1900 collectively secured a place in the Parliamentary Republic's cultural and political dialogue when they conveyed sentiments and images that repudiated aristocratic values and assigned significance to lower-class lifeways. Thus, the early *criollistas* extended to readers an inclusive and critical discourse three decades before the Left (and such authors as Pablo Neruda and Vicente Huidobro) established a firm voice in literary culture.[100] A second generation of *criollistas*, including Luis Durand, Marta Brunet, and Joaquín Edwards Bello, added to the genre's substance in the 1920s and 1930s by shaping stories with more complex dialogue and sharper descriptions of their protagonists' singularities. During the rise of the Popular Front in the mid-1930s, and especially after Aguirre Cerda's presidential victory in late 1938, *criollista* ideas about "nation" and culture were privileged elements of antioligarchic discourses. But conservative landowners, their traditionalist Liberal allies, and other detractors of *frentismo* ("Popular Frontism") did not allow middle-class reformers and their allies to monopolize ruralesque, nationalist expression.

El amor a la patria es un rasgo vigoroso

y acentuado de nuestro carácter nacional.

ALBERTO CABERO, *Chile y los chilenos*, 1926

Prose, Politics, and *Patria* from Alessandri to the Popular Front

4

Carlos Valdés Vásques, a young Chilean musician with artistic tastes rooted in rural folk culture, appeared in urban theaters during a nationwide tour in 1930 and proved to be a sensation in a metropolitan environment that had become estranged from campesino lifeways since the mid-nineteenth century. Dressed as a *huaso*, with his characteristic poncholike *chamanto*, black riding boots, silver spurs, and flat-brimmed hat, Valdés strummed his guitar and sang *zamacuecas*, folk songs of the Central Valley countryside. In attendance at one Santiago performance was a critic for the conservative and pro-oligarchy daily newspaper *El Diario Ilustrado*, who apparently found more than technical merit in Valdés's spectacle. The artist, he wrote, "[made] us remember that we are Chileans" and that "if there were many people in Chile like Carlos Valdés Vásques that were concerned with what is ours, we could aspire to create a solid race, rooted in tradition, truly Chilean, truly *criollo*." The reviewer went on to state, "Now is the time to begin a difficult task: to dignify this music, make everyone understand it, realize its miracles that make us proud, and for the country to adopt it and reject the intrusive *tango* and the petulant fox-trot."[1] Valdés's representation of "*huaso* culture" was, in the observer's mind, indelibly linked to a peculiar existence that resonated with *chilenidad*. The urban elite of the 1930s, it would seem, were beginning to look fondly upon popular traditions that would have made turn-of-the-century patrons of Gath y Chaves or members of the Union Club grimace with embarrassment, though wealthy landowners certainly appreciated and valued their rural socioeconomic base. *Criollismo's* imagery had gradually become ingrained in the public sphere over the course of three decades. Aside from the reformist application of the genre's aestheticism, there emerged an equally ruralesque response from the traditional elite, who, like other political interests of the 1930s, desired to be seen as legitimately *chileno* in light of changing sociopolitical and electoral conditions.

On a warm evening in January 1939, associates and friends of the ruling Popular Front (FP)—the political alliance of the Radical, Socialist, and Communist parties that rose to power in 1938—gathered at Santiago's Caupolicán Theater for a special gala sponsored by the Alliance of Intellectuals, an organization that included Pablo Neruda, Vicente Huidobro, and Pablo de Rokha. In an article announcing the event, the newspaper *Frente Popular* noted, "The program has been studied and prepared in order to give the presentation as much popular significance as possible. Thus, all of the artists who will participate in this true celebration of *criollo* grace are only the most representative and distinctive of our environment." What and who were deemed most representative of *lo criollo*? "The Four Huasas and their guitars," the newspaper explains, and "the *huasos* of Chincolco competing in an elegant rodeo arena."[2] For its organizers and those in attendance, what *Frente Popular* called a "great folkloric act" served to construct and strengthen a symbolic link between the governing coalition and the lower classes it claimed to valorize and represent. It also underscored *frentismo's* nationalism and anti-imperialism during an era in which Latin American governments were rethinking their nations' place in the world. The presence of the *"huasas,"* furthermore, suggests that lower-class women (certainly not women aristocrats!) exhibited elements of the national soul, and one *criollista* active in the 1920s and 1930s had much to say in this respect.

The two spectacles described above, as well as others explored in this chapter, suggest that by the 1930s literary *criollismo* had influenced—at some consequential level—the ways an array of Chileans imagined their nation and viewed its cultural idiosyncrasies. Owing to the interpretative dimension inherent in fiction literature, competing social sectors came to understand *criollismo* in different manners and expressed those understandings in their corresponding nationalist political discourses. More than one social constituency looking to legitimize its sociopolitical agenda did so by incorporating interrelated notions of *lo rural* and *lo chileno*. Political leaders and intellectuals from left to right reasoned that the more *criollo* they sounded or seemed, the more respectability and power their respective movements would garner. What could be more *criollo* than exhibiting close ties to the campo and campesinos? Despite the fact that different groups employed rural-oriented nationalist imagery to varying degrees, the production of *criollismo* largely remained within the intellectual purview of middle-class *santiaguinos* after the election of President Arturo Alessandri Palma in 1920. The rapid expansion of the sociopolitical power of middle-class groups after Alessandri's victory accompanied an explosion in the number and variety of *criollista* works circulating in the cultural marketplace, as *criollismo* solidified its place as the country's leading fiction genre.

A second generation of *criollista* intellectuals, including Luis Durand, Marta Brunet, and Joaquín Edwards Bello, merged in their works the aesthetic sensibilities of Guillermo Labarca, Maluenda, Latorre, and other members of the Generation of 1900 with more active characters and dialogue with greater substance. Their narratives, which are diverse and wide ranging, place *huasos* ahead of most other pastoral figures as protagonists that embody *chilenidad*; these *huasos* are poised and pragmatic. As we shall see, the *huaso*'s popularity as a national and cultural character expanded rapidly in the 1930s. Indeed, during the presidency of Radical Party (PR) leader Pedro Aguirre Cerda (1938–41) *criollismo*'s rural imagery and the cowboy construct were heralded within an "official" nationalist discourse, one that essentially codified progressive nationalism as the guiding nationalist sensibility of the opening years of the FP government.[3]

Criollista literary production and the widespread use of nationalistic representations of rural society in the 1920s and 1930s did not come to pass in a vacuum but instead were concurrent processes of broader sociopolitical, economic, and demographic transformations that continued to alter life's rhythms for the vast majority of Chileans. Such developments constitute integral parts of this unfolding story about the country's (symbolic and linguistic) *"vuelta a la tierra,"* or "return to the land," as one periodical called it.[4] Thus, as we examine *criollismo* from Alessandri's first presidency through Aguirre Cerda's FP administration, we must remain conscious of the important changes in society that exerted some influence on the genre in terms of thematic emphasis and cultural-political intent, as well as how *criollismo* was perceived and applied in Chile's public sphere.

The Turbulent 1920s

Alessandri's victory in the presidential election of 1920 gave new vigor to a reform movement that had grown tired of the Parliamentary Republic's legislative inertia and structural chaos. Aguirre Cerda ascribed historical meaning to the shifting tide in Chilean society, noting that the "old regime" was "abandoned once and for all."[5] Radicals were vital members of the Liberal Alliance (AL), the political coalition that brought the relatively young Alessandri, a dissident Liberal, to power by defeating the Conservatives and traditionalist Liberals of the National Union (UN). Hopes among reformers for a more effective government and the amplification of Chilean democracy, however, were dashed before Alessandri was able to complete a full five-year term in office. The intensification of class conflict, the ouster of Alessandri in 1924, the president's resignation in 1925, the resignation of an ineffective successor in 1927, the four-year dictatorship of Carlos Ibáñez del Campo, and the proclamation of a short-lived but inspiring "Socialist Republic" in 1932 made the "long" decade of 1920–32 the most turbulent in Chilean history between the civil war of 1891 and the 1960s. All the while, most *criollista* intellectuals expanded the scope of their *cuentos* and remained committed to expressing their politics and nationalism through the subtleties of narration.

Alessandri, who was elected senator from Tarapacá in 1915 after serving in the Chamber of Deputies, was a gifted public speaker and political organizer. With his party split, Alessandri's bulk of support came from the Radicals, but only after Radicalism's old guard, led by Enrique Mac-Iver, became convinced that the Liberal's rhetoric was in line with Radical principles.[6] When he entered office, Alessandri immediately went about rewarding Radicals for their warm support during the 1920 campaign. He offered Armando Quezada Acharán, president of the PR and friend of Alessandri since both were in law school, the office of interior minister (the top cabinet position). Quezada, however, declined the appointment. His decision opened the way for an up-and-coming Radical, Aguirre Cerda, who soon assumed the post. By 1922, however, Radicals and other members of the AL, including the Democrats, had chosen to pursue their own agendas. The alliance slowly crumbled, as did Alessandri's presidency.

The political environment of 1920–24 in many ways mirrored that of 1886–91, when the Balmacedists faced strong opposition from oligarchs in the government's legislative branch. Alessandri's win in 1920 over UN candidate Luis Barros Borgoño exemplified both the possibilities and limitations of the parliamentary order. The Parliamentary Republic witnessed the most rapid diversification and amplification of the political arena in Chilean history to that time, while it also perpetuated an oligarchic power base that Alessandri's dissident Liberals and the Radicals found hard to crack. In large part, Alessandri and his AL supporters encountered stiff opposition in the Senate, where the UN used its majority to put up legislative roadblocks. The administration's most notable legislative failure was its proposed labor code and social security provision (Código del Trabajo y Previsión Social). The joint measure was introduced in the Congress on June 1, 1921. Led by Ladislao Errázuriz Lazcano and Rafael Luis Gamucio, the UN tenaciously battled the measure in the Senate, and Alessandri responded with complaints about his opponents' obstruction of "justice and social redemption."[7] The AL's efforts and Alessandri's vocal support could not overcome the reality of party politics; the labor code and social security measure faltered.

Growing rifts among members of the AL further complicated policy making. After the AL won majorities in both houses of the legislative branch in early 1924, Radicals gradually withdrew their support for Alessandri. A fracture occurred during the 1924 nationwide congressional contest, when Alessandri broke a long-standing presidential tradition by engaging in campaign activities on behalf of the AL. Alessandri, like Balmaceda, was accused of abusing executive power. Criticism came not only from UNistas but also from many Radicals who found Alessandri's electoral antics unattractive. Radicals, as previously noted, enjoyed control of the Chamber of Deputies and certainly did not want to see meddling by the executive branch despite Alessandri's intentions. By mid-1924, Radicals were openly criticizing the administration. Thus, UNista obstructionism was, in retrospect, only one part of Alessandri's political problems. The eventual loss of Radical support doomed the so-called Lion of Tarapacá.

A sharp economic downturn after World War I certainly did not help matters for Alessandri's administration. As Harold Blakemore explains, the accumulation of large nitrate stocks in consuming countries and Germany's development of a synthetic alternative exacerbated Chile's postwar depression.[8] Public demonstrations increased in mining centers, Santiago, Valparaíso, and other urban areas as economic hardship worsened. The government's office of labor reported a total of 66 strikes involving 23,529 workers in 1919. In 1920, the number of strikes swelled to 105 and strikers to 50,439.[9] By comparison, there were only 17 strikes involving 10,490 workers in 1913. Although the populistic Alessandri called for the amelioration of the social question, there was a limit to how much labor unrest his government would

tolerate. In 1921, less than six months after Alessandri took office, government troops killed more than forty unemployed workers at the nitrate
oficina San Gregorio, southeast of Antofagasta in the province of Tarapacá,
after being fired upon by a union leader.[10] The military's bloody response
only strengthened Recabarren's and the Chilean Left's opposition to *alessandrismo*, which they believed was an oligarchic wolf in a reformist sheep's
clothing. Radicals, however, remained relatively quiet about the massacre in
light of the fact that Aguirre Cerda was interior minister at the time. In
addition, when Héctor Arancibia Laso (the Radical who headed Alessandri's
campaign in 1920) ran for the senate seat in Tarapacá the same year of the
San Gregorio incident, he simply—and rather diplomatically—stated that
both workers and the state were to blame for such "painful deeds."[11] If
Arancibia had taken Alessandri's side, the move would have been perceived
as an endorsement of state-directed violence, while throwing support behind Recabarren's position would not have squared with the PR's antirevolutionary rhetoric. The Radicals, quite simply, desired to maintain their
position on middle ground.

On September 5, 1924, military leaders responding to the "serious political,
social, and economic conditions of the post World War I decade, and the failure of the government to ameliorate them," toppled the Alessandri government.[12] Alessandri sought refuge in the U.S. embassy in downtown Santiago
and soon fled the country. "My pain is that of all Chileans," he solemnly
stated after resigning under pressure.[13] The resourceful Lion of Tarapacá
managed a brief comeback in March 1925, during which he chose a young
colonel, Carlos Ibáñez del Campo, to serve as minister of war. Alessandri
opted to appoint a special commission to write a new constitution instead of
reconvening the Congress, which was closed during the coup of 1924. The
document was finished by the spring of 1925, was promptly approved in a
national plebiscite, and remained intact until the military coup of September 1973. The 1925 constitution greatly expanded the power of the executive
branch at the expense of the Congress, though the legislative branch was not
left crippled. The new constitution did not represent a return to the Portalian system but certainly altered the state's institutional foundations.

Alessandri's return to power also entailed a violent crackdown on workers
in the northern nitrate zone. In June 1925, soldiers opened fire on more than
twelve hundred demonstrators at La Coruña, killing and injuring scores.
Artillery barrages destroyed working-class dwellings. Memories of San Gregorio flashed through the minds of many. It has been suggested that Ibáñez
was the mastermind of the massacre at La Coruña and that Alessandri tried

to prevent the incident. Alessandri did, in fact, ask Ibáñez to resign over the massacre, but the minister of war refused. In the face of Ibáñez's steadfastness, Alessandri promptly resigned for the second time in less than two years. His government was succeeded by the brief civilian administration of Emiliano Figueroa Larraín before Ibáñez seized power in 1927, inaugurating Chile's first military dictatorship since independence. Alessandri, of course, developed a deep hatred of Ibáñez: "The country ended up in the hands of an irresponsible dictatorship of a man who was replacing the constitution and laws with his sovereign will, like all dictators."[14] Although some reformers were pleased to see Ibáñez implement sweeping changes in public education and the expansion of public works, his heavy-handed dealings with unions and the opposition movement in general drew the ire of many Radicals. Some, such as Aguirre Cerda, were briefly exiled, but others managed to remain politically active.[15] Moreover, the *criollista* Guillermo Labarca, who served as minister of justice and public instruction under Alessandri, loudly and clearly stated his opinion of *ibañismo*. The Radical called the Ibáñez administration a "tyrannical regime" and said the dictator's supporters derogatorily referred to Radicals as "socialists" (he took this as an insult even though Radicals often lauded their "state socialism").[16]

The Great Depression's devastating effects on Chile's economy and violent street demonstrations doomed Ibáñez's regime, which ended in the leader's exile in 1931.[17] A flurry of short-lived governments followed, including the so-called Socialist Republic of 1932 led by Air Commodore Marmaduke Grove. After decades of political marginality, leftists, including notable military officers of middle-class stock, took advantage of an unstable situation after Ibáñez's departure, but their success was ephemeral. The Socialist Republic survived for little more than three months, during which no lasting revolutionary policies were implemented. Yet the Socialist Republic had consequential effects on the body politic. The Liberal Party (PL), for example, made a sharp turn toward the right in light of both the Socialist Republic and the subsequent founding of the Socialist Party of Chile (Partido Socialista de Chile, or PS) in April 1933.

Stability Returns?: Politics and Society in the 1930s

After more than a year of political tumult after Ibáñez's ouster, Alessandri returned to Chile from exile and announced his candidacy for the presidential election of late 1932. The Radicals, who increasingly became concerned about the threat of social revolution during and after the Socialist Republic, were quick to hail Chile's return to "democracy" and immediately declared their support for Alessandri, who also gained the backing of his PL and the Conservative Party (PC). This unexpected but understandable political triumvirate coalesced to combat the candidacies of PS candidate Grove and Chilean Communist Party (PCCh) leader Elías Lafertte. Alessandri received more than 54 percent of the nearly 340,000 votes cast, while Grove and Lafertte shared roughly 20 percent. Alessandri, though armed with the populistic and reformist rhetoric of his first administration, soon demonstrated that his second government would be more conservative and would, in fact, *be* the oligarchic establishment. His swing mirrored that of his party and did not come as a surprise to the Left, which remembered Alessandri's ties to the massacres at San Gregorio in 1921 and La Coruña in 1925. The most important political consequence of Alessandri's ideological shift was his loss of Radical support (again) at midterm.

The Chile Alessandri governed in the 1930s was, of course, not the Chile of his first term. The Left, divided into mutual aid societies and relatively small parties during the final years of the Parliamentary Republic, had matured into well-organized Socialist and Communist parties. The non-Socialist Left immediately felt Alessandri's heavy hand. When he assumed the presidency, Alessandri set out to extinguish the possibility of another coup. Tired of ousters and short-lived governments, Alessandri's allies in the Congress passed a measure granting the president "extraordinary powers" to deal with his enemies on the left. He used presidential authority from April to October 1933 and December 1933 to June 1934 to close newspapers and jail leaders of the PCCh and the Chilean Workers Federation (FOCh).[18] In response, the Radicals, led by party president Aguirre Cerda, approved a resolution at their 1933 convention calling for the repeal of the executive's extraordinary powers. Although Alessandri did not appreciate the gesture, he nonetheless maintained relatively cordial relations with the PR until 1934.

Amid demonstrations and violent clashes in Santiago, Valparaíso, and Concepción that involved both leftists and members of the newly established National Socialist Movement (Movimiento National Socialista, or MNS), Radicals called on Alessandri to implement an economic reform program stipulated in their party's platform. The Great Depression was at hand, and the social question deepened. Sensing the PR's lack of support, Alessandri immediately ordered the resignation of all Radicals in his cabinet.[19] The subsequent cabinet was Alessandri's first without PR representatives. Furthermore, Radicals increasingly had become uneasy with participating in a government that included Conservative luminary Gustavo Ross Santa María, who, as Alessandri's finance minister, implemented austerity measures to combat high unemployment and a robust budget deficit. By the late 1930s, Chile's macroeconomic situation was much improved, but the Alessandri administration seriously compromised living standards among the working poor when, as part of Ross's program, it devalued the national currency in order to bolster agricultural and industrial export production. This, of course, made food, clothes, and other common products more expensive for Chileans of meager means and was construed by the administration's detractors as a get-rich-quick plan hatched by and for the elite. Meanwhile, the reformist and leftist press called Alessandri and Ross "oligarchs," "reactionaries," and "antidemocratic," and they bestowed upon Ross the honorary title of "minister of hunger."

The growing split between Radicals and Alessandri opened the way for the PR's eventual entrance into the FP. Conceived in 1934 by the Third International in Moscow in response to European fascism, the Popular Front strategy was played out in a unique way in Chile. Founded by Communists in early 1936, *frentismo* took on a Socialist hue after the larger PS joined soon after. The Left sought to include reformist elements in order to build an electoral majority and immediately looked to the PR for support. In March 1936, the Radical Assembly of Santiago, estranged from *alessandrismo* and influenced by the entrance of Spanish and French reformist parties into similar coalitions, decided to run party members on the FP's slate in the upcoming congressional election (Alessandri's Liberals and Conservatives won control of both houses). The final breach between the PR and the *alessandristas* occurred on May 23, 1937, when, after a brief return to the government, Radicals pulled out of the president's cabinet, never to return. That same day, PR boss (and future president) Gabriel González Videla called the FP a national movement in "defense of democracy."[20] The PR, the most experienced and powerful party within the FP, immediately claimed leadership of the coalition. Héctor Arancibia Laso, the Radical who spearheaded Alessandri's 1920 campaign, was elected to head the FP in early 1936. With Radicals in top positions, the coalition's candidate for the presidential election of 1938 naturally came from within the PR camp. In April 1938, Aguirre Cerda, a lawyer and teacher who had served in both Alessandri governments in varying capacities, was named the FP's presidential candidate.[21] He immediately took to the campaign trail against the *alessandrista* candidate, Ross.

Aside from the PR-*alessandrismo* divorce, one of the more interesting political novelties of the 1930s was the founding of the MNS, or Chile's Nazi Party, in 1932. Led by the charismatic, volatile, and belligerent führer criollo, Jorge González von Marées, the National Socialists never became a formidable electoral force but further stirred the turbulent waters of Chilean politics over the course of a decade. They were anti-Masonic, anticommunist, foes of "international Judaism," critics of capitalist magnates, and they expressed a certain contempt for party politics. Yet the Chilean Nazis, seeking to woo middle-class supporters, characterized themselves as democrats and anti-imperialists, while distancing their movement from European fascism.[22] The MNS's ideological and discursive diversity, which made for unpredictable twists and turns, appealed to many nonleftist, urban Chileans disillusioned with *alessandrismo* and the country's return to traditional party politics. In addition, the MNS's ability to adapt to changing political circumstances gave it a certain knack for survival.

Without any hope of winning the presidency on their own, the National Socialists threw their support behind none other than Carlos Ibáñez del Campo, who had returned from exile and had become the candidate of the newly formed People's Liberation Alliance (Alianza Popular Libertadora, or APL) during the early stages of the 1938 race. In September 1938, a month before the election, some thirty thousand supporters of Ibáñez, National Socialists among them, demonstrated in the streets of the capital in protest of the Alessandri administration. The *nacistas*, who proved more bellicose than Ibáñez's followers, mounted a putsch on September 5 to overthrow the government, seizing the University of Chile and the Social Security (Caja de Seguro Obligatorio) building near La Moneda. Inside the Social Security building, National Socialists killed a carabinero (state policeman) and occupied the seventh floor before being captured by carabineros who stormed the locale. Meanwhile, six *nacistas* who had taken control of the university were killed, and more than two dozen survivors were taken the Social Security building, where a total of sixty-one National Socialists were summarily executed. The downtown massacre, however, did not mean the end for González von Marées's MNS. In an amazing turn of events, the MNS and the APL pledged to vote for the antifascist (but anti-Alessandri) FP less than a week before the 1938 election. After experiencing the government's repressive capacity, the Nazis quickly realized their short-term fortune was very much tied to that of the opposing coalition.

The National Socialists are significant players in this story not only for their political ties to the FP but for their nationalist sensibility as well. The MNS brandished a particular variant of nationalism that may be called "authoritarian nationalism," which differed from the "conservative" and "progressive" varieties in one important way: the *nacistas* condemned the precepts and rhetoric of liberal democracy and the constitutional/political system to which conservative and progressive nationalists adhered (whether they complained about it or not). The National Socialist press, for example, pointed to the "misery" of the Chilean masses and blamed an impotent political system led by "autocrats" who incessantly extolled "democracy" and "liberty" to maintain "order." The newspaper *Trabajo* explained, "The people cannot take it any more. We have a glorious tradition, we have a history that is the most virile and beautiful in the universe, and Chile should wake up. 'Democracy' is exploiting the people. 'Order' is killing the people."[23]

On the economic front, the MNS complained—as had Francisco A. Encina, Tancredo Pinochet Le-Brun, the Radicals, and others—of foreign control of Chilean export production and the frail state of domestically owned industry. Encina, as the reader will recall, pushed for the development of domestic industry in the name of nationalism in his *Nuestra inferioridad económica*. The Nationalist Union (also known as the Nationalist Party) and such influential members as Guillermo Subercaseaux soon echoed Encina's sentiments during the final decade of the Parliamentary Republic. At the same time, Pinochet and other progressive nationalists expressed similar concerns and laid the early groundwork for measures championed by the Radical-led FP in the late 1930s and early 1940s that bolstered national industrial development after the economic ruin of the Great Depression. In short, Chileans with otherwise divergent ideologies converged on economic nationalism as a policy initiative during the first half of the twentieth century.

Authoritarian nationalism and National Socialist discourse in the 1930s also reflected the diffusion of Palacios's racial formulations in the public sphere. Largely brought to the fore by progressive nationalists and sometimes expressed by more conservative thinkers like Encina, the notion of "*raza chilena*" and a distinct racial identity were applied in the Nazi press. Like Palacios and others, the *nacistas* used "*raza chilena*" to describe the *pueblo* as a whole. They argued that the race suffered from "hunger" and "misery" and faced "destruction" at the hands of Alessandri.[24] González von Marées referred to the "soul" of the Chilean race when criticizing "materialism" and "libertarianism": "It is the soul of the race that returns . . . shielded by the gray legions of Nazism."[25] Moreover, in an interesting turn, the Chilean Nazis broke ranks with Hitler's Germany by openly proclaiming that they were not anti-Semitic and that the *raza chilena* contained the blood of Jews together with the Araucanians, Spaniards, Anglo-Saxons, and Germans.[26] It

becomes clear that nationalism—and economic nationalism in particular—
was a fundamental ideological and discursive component of contrasting and
competing political constituencies in a relatively crowded electoral arena. In
1938, that arena played host to the most heated and contested presidential
race since the Alessandri-Barros Borgoño clash of 1920.

Despite the threat of government repression, the *frentista* press pulled no
punches when discussing the Alessandri government and Ross's presidential
bid. In mid-1938, the newspaper *Frente Popular*, which tended toward a more
communist posture than other procoalition publications, called Ross "public enemy number one" and flatly stated that "those who are not with
Aguirre Cerda are committing treason against the people."[27] Aguirre Cerda
told his supporters that Chile's governmental apparatus was a tool of "arro-
gant oligarchs" and that the people were "waking up."[28] The pro-Alessandri
El Diario Ilustrado responded to such sentiments by characterizing all *frentistas* as "materialists" who harbor contempt for "religious ideals." The newspaper, moreover, derogatorily referred to Radicals as "communists."[29]

Aguirre Cerda defeated Ross in the October election by a small margin
(220,892 ballots cast for Aguirre Cerda versus 213,521 for Ross).[30] The rural
vote predominantly went to Ross, while urban voters (including National
Socialists and supporters of the APL) secured Aguirre Cerda's and the FP's
victory. But *governing* as a coalition proved quite different than *campaigning*
as coalition. As the Radical, Socialist, and Communist parties began to pursue their own agendas as early as 1939, the FP lost cohesion and, ultimately,
collapsed for all intents and purposes. That is not to say the FP was impotent. Interparty cooperation and the coalition's control of both congressional houses led to measures that strengthened the state's presence in the
economy and society during Aguirre Cerda's presidency. In 1939, for example, the government founded a state development agency (the Corporación
de Fomento de la Producción, or CORFO) to oversee and spur domestic
economic growth. Moreover, the *frentistas* made significant headway in areas
of public education and health.[31] Addressing urban and rural labor concerns
also was a high priority, though, as we shall later see, the matter of labor
unrest in the countryside exposed tensions within the FP.

Criollismo: The Next Generation

The rapidly changing social, political, and economic circumstances of the
late 1920s and 1930s were topics of debate in the daily press, nonfiction

books, local coffee bars, and elsewhere. In other words, many Chileans were aware that their country was experiencing accelerated transformations that affected their lives. In the realm of fiction literature, *criollismo* did not undergo any profound shifts in terms of basic subject matter—the campo persisted as its narrative keystone. What changed, however, were the genre's structural and stylistic components. By the end of the Parliamentary Republic, the *criollistas* were combining tried-and-true naturalism with a central element of the bourgeois novel, substantive dialogue, thus, in a sense, adhering to a literary precept of Blest Gana's Balzacian realism. Campesinos no longer were the objects of depiction and description but rather subjects involved in verbal action and interaction. Quite simply, the once quiet campesinos now had voices of their own and important things to say. The second generation of *criollistas*, moreover, were witnessing the rapid upsurge of working-class radicalism and the organization of leftist parties, which, as middle-class reformers temporarily forged an alliance with oligarchs, apparently exerted degrees of influence on some of the genre's contributors.

Any discussion of *criollismo* in the 1920s and 1930s must necessarily return to one of its founders, Mariano Latorre, who was among a handful of writers who propelled the genre's narrative evolution. The genre's second full decade was inaugurated by Latorre's first lengthy novel, *Zurzulita* (1920), which enters rural life by way of a love story. *Huasos*, in general, are in the background of the novel, but Latorre includes narrative gems that underscore *criollismo*'s major tenets. Latorre, furthermore, demonstrates in *Zurzulita* that the predilection for *cuentos* that inspired *Cuentos del Maule* no longer constituted the driving force behind his ever popular *criollismo*. As a committed naturalist, however, he again crafted a story in which the narrator remains a detached observer—the "objective" conduit of facts and occurrences linking characters and context to the reader. Over the course of more than three hundred pages, Latorre tells of Mateo Elorduy, a twenty-year-old from the town of Loncomilla in the center-south, who travels to the countryside of Maule Province after his father's death. During the liquidation of his father's estate, Mateo ends up in possession of the hacienda Millavoro and has no idea what to do on it and with it.

Mateo, the author suggests, is out of place on the rural landscape but soon is convinced that the countryside offers an opportunity to put city life behind him; it is a place to start anew. "His eyes," Latorre writes, "were filled with new sensations, they boldly took account of all things. The campo awoke the man in him, and a simple thing such as living made him feel happy."[32] His insertion into rural life does not come easily. "I don't understand a thing about the campo," Mateo explains upon his arrival.[33] But after meeting Milla, a local campesina and young schoolgirl, Mateo is motivated to stay and learn about rural ways because of the "primitive passion" that she engenders (a positive thing).[34] All the while, he faces campesinos who view him as an unwelcome outsider, including Millavoro's longtime administrator, Carmen Lobos, who competes against Mateo for Milla's heart. As Milla falls in love with Mateo, the new *hacendado* manages to push Lobos out of his job and off the property. Lobos is enraged and, in the end, contracts a local bandit, Juan Rulo, to kill Mateo. Milla finds Mateo's corpse—disfigured by hungry animals—three days later.

Latorre, I believe, does not want to suggest that rural society simply is the hearth of pestilent ruffians that tend to murder outsiders, though one may easily arrive at that interpretation. Instead, it becomes apparent from descriptions and dialogue that Mateo, the urban man, lacks a fundamental understanding of the campo, and this ignorance prevents him from dealing with Lobos and his love for Milla with greater skill and caution. From the beginning, Mateo sees himself, and is seen, as a being out of place in the countryside. A conceptual and cultural gulf between urban and rural life lies at the center of the novel, and Latorre aims to educate his urban compatriots about the latter environment in order to bring them closer to *chilenidad*. Authentic passions and, at times, tragedy are components of this typically Chilean existence, Latorre suggests. Equally evident in *Zurzulita* is the theme of masculinity, which permeates this and other examples of the genre. Mateo's catharsis—the countryside awaking the "man in him"—underscores the maleness of the campo, a sometimes rough-and-tumble place where Mateo, perhaps, is not enough of a real man to survive.

In what is certainly a character-driven book, Latorre also adds descriptions that most certainly qualify as social criticism. As the narrator notes on numerous occasions, Mateo becomes aware of the material reality of rural life: "The poverty of the countryside made him feel down."[35] Latorre, moreover, makes a passing reference to the country's demographic change (and the socioeconomic conditions causing it) during the late nineteenth and early twentieth centuries—a fundamental transformation with effects that were most apparent in the 1920s and 1930s. The narrator suggests that the ongoing shift away from rural labor is damaging to the nation but that campesinos are not to blame. Mateo, when he confronts a campesino youth, takes notice that "he was one of the few young men in the countryside. The rest migrated to more fertile pastures or to the El Teniente [copper] mine, which pays fabulous wages."[36] The implication here is that rural wages are far below pay levels at the mines (and they were) and that landowners are responsible for rural poverty and the waves of campesinos entering the cities and mining zones.

After the appearance of *Zurzulita*, Latorre encountered many of the same criticisms that circulated after the appearance of *Cuentos del Maule* nearly a decade earlier. When recalling some negative comments leveled against Latorre's style, Joaquín Edwards Bello observed that "they [some literary commentators] had unjust criticisms about Latorre's *Zurzulita*. They said it was excessive, its descriptions were overwhelming. . . . Mariano said 'the public's stomach is weak. It can't digest such a large stew as *Zurzulita*. Give them small plates so they aren't frightened. Give them light foods.'"[37] Indeed, *Zurzulita* stands among the most appetizing and satisfying examples of *criollismo*.[38] The book's success and wide distribution demonstrates the *criollistas'* ability either to alter or to keep up with literary tastes in the cultural marketplace by adjusting the genre's form without changing its basic aesthetic appeal. *Zurzulita* and its predecessor, *Cuentos del Maule*, together exerted significant influence among members of the genre's second generation, including Luis Durand (1895–1954), a friend and disciple of Latorre who helped expand *criollismo's* appeal.

The journal *Atenea* explained in 1954 that Durand "didn't need to go to the countryside to make literature. He carried the countryside in his heart."[39] Indeed, literary critic Raúl Silva Castro recalled overhearing the *criollista* talk about that place in his heart: "One day I heard him say: 'I really like *huasos*, the humble people of the countryside without any of the pretense of city life. . . . All of my *cuentos* are dedicated to them, in payment of a debt: what I know of life I have heard from them, or I have captured from seeing them live, because sometimes they are quiet and don't say anything.'"[40] Durand, however, found much to say about the countryside in dozens of books and short stories published in Santiago periodicals between the 1920s and 1940s. His works, in short, added a fresh voice to the widely popular genre.

Born in Traiguén, a small town on the Traiguén River between the cities of Los Angeles and Temuco, Durand concentrated most of his artistic attention on the countryside of the southern Central Valley, like numerous other *criollistas*. After attending primary school in Traiguén, he moved to Santiago and enrolled at the National Institute. But Durand soon returned to Traiguén, where he entered an agricultural school with the hope of finding work as a *fundo* administrator, which he later did in nearby Quechereguas—a less-than-ideal experience that influenced a change of careers. Durand moved back to Santiago, where he began to write short stories at age thirty while working as a postal administrator. He also joined the Masons, becoming acquainted with Lodge notable Aguirre Cerda, but did not formally register as a member of a political party until after Aguirre Cerda's abbreviated presidency. Like others of the middle class, Durand's political sympathies rested with *alessandrismo* in the 1920s and early 1930s and Radicalism in the late 1930s and early 1940s, before he gravitated further to the left.[41]

A portly man who wore round, thick glasses, Durand first published some short works in such magazines as *Zig-Zag* during the mid-1920s. His 1927 *cuento* "Humitas"—named after a corn dish cooked inside dried husks—tells the story of the upstanding *huaso* Miguel Rodríguez, who travels in order to court a *"chiquilla,"* or young girl, named María Pochard. She is the rather attractive daughter of French immigrants, who as *colonos* (or settlers) acquired a small *fundo* near a town called Reihue (presumably in the southern Central Valley because of accompanying descriptions of the landscape, Durand's constant attention to his native region in his literature, and the considerable presence of foreign-born *colonos* in that area during the early decades of the century). Rodríguez, Durand writes, "is a young man with masculine and amiable aspects, dressed in the countryside manner. . . . He gazes out on the peacefulness of the afternoon that falls sweetly over the countryside."[42] The *huaso* Rodríguez feels both a love for rural life and a growing attraction toward María. One obstacle, however, stands between María and the *huaso*: Señora Pochard, the mother. Some dialogue between the mother and Rodríguez centers on *humitas* (the following excerpt begins with Rodríguez, then alternates with statements by María's mother):

> "You, too, like *humitas*?"
> "Of course, who doesn't like good things! María makes good ones because she was taught by Rosalía, the cook we once had."
> "I suppose you will invite me to sample them some day."
> "I would be delighted, but who knows if you would like *humitas* made by gringos."[43]

María's mother, with a hint of animosity, suggests that Rodríguez could identify *humitas* that are not authentically Chilean. *Humitas* (or material culture in general) produced by foreign hands have different, even alien, characteristics that are noticeable to an authentic *chileno*, a *huaso*. Durand's nationalism is clearly evident: Rodríguez represents Chile's cultural singularity among those unacquainted with *chilenidad*.[44] In the end, Rodríguez finds the family's *humitas* appealing, but only because María sits across from the *huaso* at the dinner table—their eyes meeting with fixed gazes.

To Durand, *huasos* like Rodríguez embodied a uniquely Chilean experience. The *criollista* presented similar opinions in two anthologies of essays published late in his life. Durand reflects on the "real" *huaso* in *Alma y cuerpo de Chile* (1947), noting that the cowboy's life was not without rest and pleasure. In this way, Durand echoed the *criollismo* of Guillermo Labarca, who underscored the relaxing side of an otherwise stressful and challenging environment. "Below the protective shade of a tree with his horse nearby," Durand states, "the *huaso*, in this land of sunshine, sleeps, after having drank some cups of *chicha* [an alcoholic drink made from grapes in Chile or corn in the Andean zone] or wine together with his plate of meatballs . . . or some very spicy beans."[45] Moreover, in his *Paisajes y gentes de Chile* (1953) Durand observes that "the *huaso* of Chile's Central Valley has the rejoicing happiness of an orchestra of rural birds in complete liberty. . . . The *huaso*, until now, aside for all egoism, maintains his air of confidence, of tranquil moderation, in the way he speaks and the way he steps."[46] Durand also praises the cowboy's cultural traits, especially his music: "The guitars are strummed and the light air of the springtime becomes dense with the buzzing of large flies [*moscardones* and *coliguachos*] and bees."[47] The *huaso*'s music, it seems, is part of a larger rural symphony of sight and sound that pleases Durand's senses.

Similar flavors and sentiments permeate "Humitas," making the *cuento* an important example of the genre. But there is a peculiar element to the story of the *huaso* Rodríguez: this cowboy freely consorts with the daughter of French immigrants and routinely visits the Pochard *fundo*. A horseman *inquilino* interacting with such a fine young woman? In her parents' home, no less? At work here is an interesting narrative element indicative of some second-generation *criollismo*—an infrequent juxtaposition of *huaso* characteristics and characters more akin to (moral and uncorrupted) small landowners and cultivators than *inquilinos*. The reader will recall that Durand, like Latorre, was born and raised in the southern stretches of the Central Valley. There, in that region rich in grain and livestock, families of small landholders (many of them with immigrant roots, such as the Durand's and Latorre's) were common and, generally speaking, gave long-term electoral support to the reformist agenda during the late nineteenth and early twentieth centuries. Indeed, southern small landowners, together with urban professionals, formed the backbone of the PR. In the case of "Humitas," then, one detects Durand's high regard for typically *huaso* traits and his ties to a landscape occupied by small landowners—longtime sociopolitical rivals, if not enemies, of the more conservative landowning aristocracy to their north. By understanding Durand's personal background, his reformist sympathies, and the prevailing political environment, we may arrive at some understanding of Rodríguez, a complex literary amalgam. (Small-scale landowners of today's Central Valley continue to be called *huasos.*)

Aside from his commitment to *criollista* literature, Durand also contributed editorial pieces to the Santiago press during the 1940s and published *Don Arturo* (1952), which contains reflections on political developments and his tenure from 1932 to 1936 as a private secretary for Alessandri during the president's second term. Like many members of the urban mesocracy, Durand was mesmerized by Alessandri's candidacy in 1920 and believed the Liberal possessed a political will and "messianic" personality that could fundamentally change Chilean society by sweeping away the oligarchy's power. As Durand recalls, "It was in 1920 when there suddenly appeared a man who picked up the faded flag of confused aspirations of the working masses and the middle class that languishes. . . . Alessandri embodied, at that time, all of the longing that the immense majority of the Chilean public does not know how to put into words with clarity and certainty."[48] Durand also favorably assesses Alessandri's second administration, which was, at first, warmly supported by the reformers of the PR. Yet, like the PR, Durand fell away from *alessandrismo* during the second half of the 1930s. Though he does not discuss this estrangement in *Don Arturo*, Durand is known to have supported the FP and the candidacy of Aguirre Cerda in 1938 rather than his former employer's handpicked candidate, Ross.[49] Durand was not the only *criollista* to participate actively in the Alessandri administration while engaged in the literary sphere.

Marta Brunet (1897–1967), a fellow traveler of the PR and the most notable woman author of *criollismo*, worked for a time in the Alessandri administration's Cultural Extension Department of the Ministry of Labor.[50] A native of Chillán, an important agricultural hub of the center-south, Brunet dedicated much of her literary energy to portraying the area's environment and lifeways of its people. Her first book, the short novel *Montaña adentro* (1923), appeared on the heels of her arrival in Santiago at age twenty-six after witnessing the loss of her family's fortune. *Montaña adentro*, a widely praised example of *criollismo*'s second generation, inaugurated a long and successful literary career that culminated with the National Literature Award in 1961. She died in Montevideo, Uruguay, doing what she most surely enjoyed, lecturing on the history of Chilean literature. Brunet was distinguished not only for her gender in an overwhelmingly male culture industry but also for adding depth to a genre that, during the Generation of 1900's heyday, put pastures before persons and descriptions before dialogue.

For its short length, *Montaña adentro* demonstrates narrative complexity and depth. Its characters—mostly *peones* and *afuerinos* (migrant laborers)—face the difficult conditions of rural life and the abusive demeanor of their *fundo*'s administrator. In general, then, *Montaña adentro*'s plot is not terribly different from those of its *criollista* cousins. What truly sets the book apart is that women are particularly visible in the book. If there were a gender-oriented message, it would be that working *campesinas* face the same material and emotional challenges as *campesinos* but brave life's difficulties with more grace than do men.[51] Leading critics (all men) believed Brunet's placement of women at the center of *Montaña adentro* and subsequent books, such as the anthology *Reloj del sol* (1930), was a refreshing departure from the genre's accepted narrative boundaries (one need only recall the masculine overtones of earlier *criollismo*, including Latorre's *Zurzulita*, to appreciate Brunet's innovation). But critics praised Brunet for being a woman who did not impart a feminist political disposition in her literature. In fact, one reviewer enthused by *Montaña adentro* considered her an honorary male: "It looks like the work of a man, but of a man with great talent who knows the Spanish language with depth and also Chile's popular language. . . . This is a male writer [*escritor*]; this is not a female writer [*escritora*], even though the writer is a young lady. . . . We have not read something so genuinely Chilean in a long time."[52] Another critic noted that Brunet was "very male when she writes and a lovable and spoiled little girl the rest of the time."[53] Apparently, her *criollismo* was of a quality befitting a male! Such fine work was not expected of women. Feminist or not, Brunet wrote women into the national and nationalist narrative of *criollismo* and thus acknowledged their meaning in the imagined community. Critics undoubtedly recognized this but instead chose to question publicly her maturity and undermine her cultural authority as a woman author.

Though committed to relaying the experiences of rural women, Brunet's literature also includes male protagonists with emotional substance. A very short story published in 1925 tells of a sickly old *huaso*, who confides to his dog that his granddaughters will not let him leave the confines of their *rancho* (small house or hut) to mount his horse. He complains of aches and pains, but his deeper wounds correspond to his separation from nature—the open *campo*. A *huaso* without a horse, it seems, is a *huaso* without a soul: "It was a sense of humiliation which made him look with sad eyes at the horse, the dog, at the entire *campo*. . . . The dog looked at him from a distance, and slowly approached to sniff him. When the dog neared his face, he began to lick the silent tears that ran down the old man's cheeks."[54] The *huaso*, with

Marta Brunet became a significant member of the *criollista* cohort upon the appearance of her first work, *Montaña adentro*, in 1923. The native of Chilláan was best known for her narrative emphasis on women in her *cuentos* and novels. (Courtesy of the Archivo Fotográfico, Museo Histórico Nacional, Santiago)

anger building inside, unties and kicks the horse, which gallops away. Brunet's prose reinforces *criollismo*'s message that campesinos, though poor, are nonetheless physically and metaphysically linked to the rural landscape—a space that is authentically Chilean.

Brunet contributed in no small way to *criollismo*'s popularity among urban readers in the 1920s and 1930s. Yet some Chileans lamented the lack of a single, great work of fiction on par with Argentine *criollista* Ricardo Güiraldes's *Don Segundo Sombra* (1925) that could capture the authentic Chile in a definitive way. *El Diario Ilustrado*, which published numerous *criollista* short stories and serials in the 1930s, praised *Don Segundo Sombra* as the "magnificent novel of the [Argentine] pampas, which has made us think, almost with melancholy, of that great Chilean novel, a synthesis of the spirit of our race, which is so late in arriving."[55] In 1934, the *criollista* Joaquín Edwards Bello made reference to José Hernández's classic nineteenth-century Argentine poem *Martín Fierro* when he complained: "What do we have to compare to it? No, *Don Lucas Gómez* doesn't work."[56] Despite the lack of Chilean heroes like the gauchos Segundo Sombra or Martín Fierro, the *criollistas* already had begun to reshape Chile's national identity.

A 1929 article in the *Revista de Educación* by one PR *correligionario* recognizes the importance of *lo rural* in Chilean national identity. Citing Latorre, Gana, and other authors, the reformer explains, "Now that Chileans begin to look with loving eyes upon the landscape our countryside offers, the beauties of our ocean and all the magnificence of our native mountains, the writers that have put forward this admiration feel the jubilation in what is in them a flame of enthusiasm and love of this rugged land." He goes on to state, "[These] writers have drawn close to their heart the native landscape, with its trees, characteristic types, and customs that form the racial idiosyncrasy in which an able pupil can find all of the avenues on which the highest of emotions travel."[57] In an article concerning "*la chilenidad literaria*," one critic in *El Diario Ilustrado* stated in 1931 that "it seems as though the place where *chilenidad* is most notably manifested is among the lower class, especially in the countryside" and that *criollismo*'s goal was to produce "books that are specifically national."[58] Some forty years earlier, the semibarbaric, embarrassing, and ridiculed campesino Lucas Gómez (the character in Martínez Quevedo's *Don Lucas Gómez, o sea, un huaso en Santiago*) was a widely popular representation of the rural underclass's characteristics. *Criollismo* did much to change perceptions of the campo and campesinos in urban society.

The *criollista* literature of Joaquín Edwards Bello bolstered the genre's place in Chile's cultural life during the 1920s and 1930s. The great-grandson of Andrés Bello, Edwards Bello (1887–1968) was a member of the affluent Edwards clan that owned, and owns, the newspaper *El Mercurio*. He was raised in Valparaíso before moving to Santiago, where he began a long career as a journalist and writer of fiction and nonfiction. Coming from the country's major port, he arrived in the capital already aware of the social question and its many implications. Outside *criollismo*, Edwards Bello expressed his views while working as a columnist for *La Nación* (his weekly columns were quite popular). A member of the PR since 1912, he regularly echoed the ideas of his party on issues such as education, national characteristics, and patriotism, though he, like Latorre, claimed to be "apolitical."[59] Edwards Bello became a widely recognized author upon the publication in 1920 of his first major book, *El roto*, a short *criollista* novel set in urban society that exhibits naturalism's considerable penetration into Chilean literary culture.[60]

El roto's appearance coincided with the fervor of a presidential election in which the AL and Alessandri ran a populistic campaign, and the novel certainly has something to say about socioeconomic and political problems addressed by the reformist *alessandristas*. Filled with descriptions of characters and objects, the novel focuses on "humble" Chileans, the author explains. These are the "*rotos*"—urban and rural mestizos, including *huasos*, miners, and even ruffians—who are subject to the imperious power of the elite.[61] Indeed, *roto* means "broken" or "damaged." They are the broken peo-

A reformer of aristocratic stock, a young Joaquín Edwards Bello published his first major work, *El roto*, in 1920 and became one of the foremost Chilean intellectuals of the 1930s and 1940s as a newspaper columnist, essayist, and novelist. (Courtesy of the Consocio Periodístico, S.A. [Copesa], and *La Tercera*, Santiago)

ple. They are men like Esmeraldo and Fernando. Esmeraldo's mother raises him in a brothel, while Fernando is a hard worker with hope for a better life but learns that upward mobility is illusory in the rigid hierarchy of a traditional society. The elite, meanwhile, is frivolous and corrupt, as demonstrated by the character Pantaleón Madroño, a senator, whose morality (public and private) is quite clearly "broken."[62] As one literary critic noted, such aspects of society (especially those associated with its underbelly) were unknown to, or ignored by, the residents of Santiago's finest neighborhoods and most opulent homes.[63] The *criollista* thus expanded the narrative parameters of Chile's social experience and, in the form of the *roto*, offered readers a complex look at *chilenidad*. One also understands from Edwards Bello that many of the *rotos'* negative traits, such a propensity toward violence, gambling, and sexual hedonism, can be attributed to the prevailing socioeconomic, political, and cultural circumstances of the Parliamentary Republic. Conditions associated with the social question, for example, loom over the underclass in *El roto*. Edwards Bello, who is known to have anonymously wandered through poor neighborhoods to witness living and working conditions for himself, continued to write about this subject in later years.

In 1933, Edwards Bello blamed the ongoing social question on a central flaw of the Chilean character. While acknowledging the material differences among social groups, he explains that "it is easy to live one's life protesting" and that in Chile "everyone wants what they do not have." He essentially states that a solution to the social question lay not only in material matters but also in attitude.[64] A 1932 column explains that a principal national characteristic is envy, which only leads, "bit by bit, to ruin." Another trait is a proclivity for disorder, which fertilizes revolutionary thought among workers. Edwards Bello suggests, however, that Chilean workers are not to blame: "At heart, our *pueblo*, our popular masses have great worth, more than what people think. But yes, it is a pueblo poisoned by the evil prophets [perhaps communists?]. . . . In general, our *pueblo*, that is so say, the worker, is basically bourgeois, in the deepest sense."[65] The notion that Chilean workers are good but easily misled commonly circulated among reformers during this era. As we shall see in subsequent chapters, reformers considered public education a sphere in which Chileans could be led down a more correct path through the dissemination of culture and the spread of a nationalist sensibility.[66]

The aristocracy was not immune to character flaws either, Edwards Bello argued. In a 1937 column, the *criollista* criticized the elite who found no redeeming values in Chilean civilization—those who ventured abroad and criticized their homeland. "The Chilean only rarely knows how to give himself importance," he explained. It was common, moreover, for those of the elite to value Paris or London more than Santiago, and Edwards Bello makes an example of a "young girl [who] pretends to be *chic*, elegant, and modern. Please don't think she is a stupid *huasa*!"[67] With wit and a sharp tongue, Edwards Bello suggests that the young girl does not want to be identified with a typical Chilean, a *huasa*, but rather with a culture foreign to her. Like Latorre, who in *Cuentos del Maule* described Chileans who want to act European, Edwards Bello demonstrates a nationalism that values, in a roundabout way, Chile's authentic traditions and heritage; the *huasa* is *lo chileno* and should not be the subject of ridicule.

The notion of authenticity lies at the heart of *La chica del Crillón*, which, in large part, won Edwards Bello the 1943 National Literature Award. The novel helped lift *lo rural* (or urban perceptions of it) and the *huaso* mystique to national attention and acclaim in the 1930s. *La chica del Crillón* (the Crillón was a French-style luxurious hotel in downtown Santiago) is the story of an upper-class urban girl, Teresa Iturrigorriaga (not her real name, she admits to the reader), who attempts and fails to maintain the flamboyant and expensive lifestyle typical of the capital's elite after her father's financial ruin and her mother's death. Near the end of the novel, Iturrigorriaga, on her journey near the coastal city of Viña del Mar, confronts Ramón Ortega Urrutia and is swept off her feet by this man of the countryside with an inner strength characteristic of *criollismo* protagonists. He wears *huaso* attire and, as the author describes, is a species far "healthier and stronger . . . than the weak and sickly men of the city."[68] One of Edwards Bello's contemporaries, Raúl Silva Castro, commented that Ortega appears in the story as a supernatural apparition, helping the young woman to fend off the cruelties of life.[69]

Ortega's kind demeanor toward the helpless—or hapless—Iturrigorriaga represents a provincial morality that stands in sharp contrast to the decadence of Santiago.[70] Iturrigorriaga warmly describes Ortega in this way: "His words were so filled with nobility and security, that I threw caution to the wind and, sitting on the haunch of his horse, I grabbed the reins and began to gallop."[71] From the back of a horse, Ortega introduces Iturrigorriaga to a wondrous environment she had never explored. As the urban girl states when Ortega makes his way off into the countryside at dusk, "An immense, unknown tenderness made my heart swell. I lay down on the ground without a word; I saw nothing but his shadow slowly getting further away; the stars were near, near, more near than ever before. A great smell of the countryside, of grass, of nature, induced sleepiness; far-away frogs sang at the stream and, at the same time, other sounds of waterfalls, of broken branches, of nocturnal rodents, of the horses who stomped around searching for grass, formed a concert infinitely more dignified than a *jazz* band."[72] To Iturrigorriaga, the harmonies of pastoral life are decidedly more Chilean than those of the saxophone or trumpet. Like the music of the *zamacueca* (or *cueca*, for short), the symphony of nature is authentic and comforting. Thus, Ortega, to whom the author ascribes *"huaso"* traits, and his environment exemplify what Edwards Bello and others hailed as features of *chilenidad*.

The Ortega character devised by Edwards Bello is certainly not a "common" *huaso*. This horseman is not a poor campesino but rather a more affluent *huaso* (similar to Durand's Miguel Rodríguez in "Humitas") and even bears the maternal last name Urrutia, an uncommon name among the lower classes. Ortega is, in fact, not only the "bourgeois" campesino Edwards Bello imagined in his 1932 column in *La Nación* but also a landowner with workers under him. How can we explain Edwards Bello's literary construction of a well-to-do *huaso*? We see in Ortega the fusion of lower-class, *"huaso"* characteristics that *criollistas* cast as typically *chileno* (including the horseman's clothes that make Teresa swoon) with a more affluent representative of the rural populace—the blending of a populistic and mesocratic construction with a more prosperous persona. It is clear from his many writings that Edwards Bello held a high opinion of Chile's popular classes but also respected the participation of landowners and other elements of the elite in a democratic society. Reformers generally shared this view but certainly envisioned themselves in charge. Of most interest here, however, is the fact that when Edwards Bello was writing *La chica del Crillón*, reformers were coalition partners of Alessandri and had joined Liberals and Conservatives against the rising Socialists and Communists in the election of 1932. Indeed, the negative vibes of worker unrest in the countryside form a component of Edwards Bello's novel, which says much about the reformers' and traditionalists' meeting of the minds on the issue during the 1930s.

Much to the chagrin of Iturrigorriaga, the campesinos of the region between Santiago and Viña del Mar are in rebellion, and to make things worse, there is a railroad strike brewing, making it difficult for people to flee the instability. In fact, Iturrigorriaga finds herself stranded on a train with danger all around (campesinos armed with rudimentary weapons!) until she is rescued from the predicament by Ortega, who comes into sight on horseback and takes the naive *santiaguina* to safety. These campesino rebels stand in sharp contrast to Ortega, who, Edwards Bello suggests, is more "Chilean"—more *huaso*—than those incited to insurrection (perhaps by communist agitators or leftist politicians such as Grove or Lafertte?). Thus, this literary complexity rather effectively reflects the broader political situation at the time, which saw increased labor unrest in the countryside and a short-lived Radical-Liberal-Conservative antirevolutionary alliance immediately after the failed Socialist Republic.

A columnist who reviewed *La chica del Crillón* for *El Diario Ilustrado*, a journalistic voice of the Right, wrote: "Teresa Iturrigorriaga . . . ends up as a good young lady in a home without fantasy and with a man in whom she sees certain moral traits. . . . Does all of this represent a return to the countryside?"[73] It did, symbolically speaking. *El Diario Ilustrado*'s praise of *La chica del Crillón* and the newspaper's periodic printing of *criollista* short stories in the 1930s points to a significant development in the history of genre: the diffusion of its images and sentiments throughout the public sphere. A nation's symbolic "return to the countryside" was at hand, and *criollismo*-inspired rural aestheticism was to play different roles for competing political interests.[74]

Interpreting *Criollismo*: Urban Politics and Visions of the Countryside

During most of the Parliamentary Republic, three major parties formed the core of Chile's political arena: the PL, the PC, and the PR. By the 1930s,

Socialists and their largely middle-class leadership had joined the ongoing contest, as had the PCCh and the small but boisterous MNS. Thus, politics became a much more crowded place after the Parliamentary Republic, and competitors were anxious to build or augment solid electoral constituencies. Images and sentiments like those captured in print by the *criollistas* became components of an array of political discourses as interest groups sought to legitimize further their agendas and ideologies by demonstrating their approximation to *chilenidad*. During the 1930s both Right and Left constructed derivatives of an aestheticism that had originally emerged as a narrative projection of middle-class reformism. This diffusion demonstrated the genre's far-reaching influence in Chilean society, as democratized concepts of who and what constituted Chile proliferated across class and party lines, at least discursively. Groups staked claims to the *huaso* construct (as well as the generic *"roto"* to some degree) and asserted that they understood the rural existence more than their competitors. No longer were inferences to authentic *huasos* and campesino lifeways merely facets of a subtle narrative strategy infused with a unique cultural and political sensibility. They became overt components of political discourses and the symbolic universe of popular culture, and the once ridiculed campesino and his cultural heritage came to represent *lo chileno*.

In newspapers, magazines, speeches, school textbooks, and other media, urban Chileans of many political persuasions established discursive and symbolic ties to a rural existence that many had never directly experienced. In some cases, a rural identity was manifested in indirect and humorous ways. Political cartoons in the satirical magazine *Topaze*, for example, used *huaso* figures to represent political groups and often dressed caricatures of well-known Chilean politicians in *huaso* clothes. One 1936 cartoon shows *huasos* representing both the PC and the FP engaged in a *zamacueca* folk dance with a young lady, the PR. Radicals, *Topaze* suggests, have no problem socializing with more than one political group, and both Conservatives and *frentistas* gaze upon the PR as a possible consort.[75] Moreover, Alessandri and Aguirre Cerda appeared often in *Topaze* cartoons. A cartoon published in 1938 depicts Aguirre Cerda—with spurs, a *chamanto*, and the typical *huaso* hat—on horseback attempting to rope a steer labeled "Ibañismo" during a rodeo. The cartoon pokes fun at Aguirre Cerda's move to gain the support of Ibáñez and the APL in the 1938 presidential election and presents the nation's political sphere as a rodeo arena—a rough place with untamed animals.[76] Nearly all prominent political leaders are depicted in *huaso* attire at one time or another in *Topaze*, which demonstrates quite effectively two developments: the infusion of a rural identity into the overwhelmingly urban political conversation of the early twentieth century, and signs that "*huaso*" was becoming a term that also suggested legitimacy. *Topaze*, it should be added, poked fun at all political persuasions and was probably the most humorous political publication of the era.

Of central importance here is how and why political interests constructed rural identities for themselves and on their own terms. The ensuing tug-of-war over *chilenidad* and rural images saw Liberals and Conservatives anchoring one end of the rope, leftist groups that formed the FP anchoring the opposite end, the PR grabbing on somewhere in between, and other political groups trying to join the contest. Politicians and intellectuals to the right of the PR seized on rural imagery with great enthusiasm, though it is impossible to say with certitude when this first occurred.[77] It is clear, however, that images of *huasos* and allusions to the cultural worth of the countryside became most apparent in the early 1930s across the board.

On the far right, the MNS, despite being the most nonrural party one could possibly imagine, used the *huaso* to make a political point in the 1930s (though the image of the urban ruffian, or "*roto*," was more prevalent in National Socialist propaganda). A cartoon published in the party's magazine, *Acción Chilena*, depicts a teeter-totter with a gluttonous capitalist on one side and a hammer- and sickle-wielding Marxist on the other. A *huaso*, which represents the MNS, approaches the teeter-totter and violently knocks the capitalist and Marxist to the ground. The message is clear: the MNS—a truly Chilean party and defender of the nation's interest—offers a third way.[78] To be sure, the more mainstream political groups of the 1930s used rural imagery to a much greater extent than did the National Socialists.

Within the *alessandrista* camp, conservative nationalists, especially members of the landowning elite associated with the National Agricultural Society (SNA), were particularly motivated to use rural social relations as an example of the authentic Chile, given the fact that unionization began to spread to the countryside during the 1920s. Landowners acknowledged *criollismo*'s aesthetic appeal and used it. To the traditional elite, the language of reformers and, in some cases, reform itself became political exigencies. No circumstance convinced landowners of this reality more than rural unionization.

Although Chilean rural society was bereft of far-reaching structural change during the 1920s and 1930s, it nonetheless saw the beginning of what, by the 1960s, became one of Latin America's most formidable labor movements enthused by revolutionary ideas. The rumbles of lower-class mobili-

zation in the countryside certainly caught the attentions of the major political interests between Alessandri's first administration and the FP. Of course,
different political groups responded to incipient unionization in the countryside in different ways. As one would think, traditionalist Liberals and
Conservatives grew worried over the prospect of union organizers swarming
throughout the campo. At the same time, the organized Left (and, from time
to time, the Radicals) lauded the onset of what the newspaper *Frente Popular*
called "the conquest of the campo."[79] Thus, although the working and living
conditions of urban workers had dominated political discussion about the
social question since the latter decades of the nineteenth century, political
groups and their media resources increasingly discussed rural labor after
about 1920, especially during periods of depressed agricultural production.[80]

Scholars such as Brian Loveman have studied unionization and varying
responses to it during the 1920s and 1930s. Without reproducing their detailed findings here, it is apparent that the legalization in 1924 of labor
organizing in the countryside began a period of labor conflict that lasted
into the latter half of the century, though Loveman likely overstates the
reach of rural unionism before 1940.[81] The only union to be granted legality
under the law was the Professional Syndicate of the Livestock and Cold-
Storage Industry (Sindicato Profesional de la Industria Ganadera y Frigo-
rífico) of Magallanes. No purely agricultural-based union was formed until
the promulgation of the Labor Code of 1931, though the FOCh remained
busy rallying support among campesinos during the final decade of the Parliamentary Republic.[82] With a new labor code on the books during the early
years of Alessandri's second term, unions became more visible in the countryside. Among the more prominent rural unions was the Poor Campesino
National Defense League (Liga Nacional de Defensa de Campesinos Pobres),
founded in 1935 by Emilio Zapata, a Trotskyist and congressional deputy. In
response to rural unionization efforts, the SNA officially lobbied the Alessandri government to amend the Labor Code of 1931. In the meantime, landowners personally sought to curtail labor organizing on their properties.[83]

Alessandri's posture toward rural labor was, in many ways, a mixed bag of
status quo politics and reformist aspirations. In 1933, the newly established
Ministry of Labor, in the spirit of the Labor Code of 1931, began granting
legal status to all qualified rural unions via an application process. The SNA,
the most powerful landowner-based organization in the country, expressed
its opposition in no uncertain terms, but two government review boards
upheld the grants of legality.[84] Yet Alessandri, concerned with the impact of
rural unionization on landowners and their support for his government,

temporarily suspended the legal inscription of agricultural unions. In 1935, Alessandri proposed rural reform measures in part to make up for his decision to suspend legalization proceedings. By the mid-1930s, the Left and reformist groups (including the PR) supported the idea of agrarian reform by way of subdividing haciendas, and many within the SNA agreed that some social reforms were needed to mitigate the possibility of social revolution.[85] They already had endorsed the concept of creating "new small-property owners, who, as such, constitute the best base for social tranquillity." This was to be done largely by "colonizing" lands not in use rather than by expropriating existing properties.[86] What Alessandri had in mind, however, was not acceptable to SNA landowners. A new rural reform statute was enacted that granted the government more authority over land and strengthened its hand in matters of expropriation.[87] In practice, though, little became of talk to alter land tenure in the countryside in the 1930s. The same could be said of the FP's policy toward rural matters during the presidency of Aguirre Cerda.

The specter of rural unionization and campesino radicalization was a major concern of the Alessandri government as the Left became more organized, memories of the Socialist Republic remained fresh, and landowners pressured Alessandri regarding the legality of rural unions. The Alessandri administration was particularly troubled by police reports of the spread of Marxist ideas among the rural working poor. For decades, antirevolutionary governments had dealt with urban manifestations of revolutionary thought, and Alessandri himself had established limits to Left-oriented social protest during his first administration (the massacre at San Gregorio, for example). During Alessandri's second presidency, administration officials routinely investigated landowner complaints regarding "*agitadores*" (urban unionists who "stirred up" revolutionary sentiment) in the countryside and sought to curtail their activities whenever possible.[88] Landowners, meanwhile, also expressed concern that not enough workers were on hand to harvest the crops of Central Valley haciendas owing to ongoing urbanization.[89]

While attempting to protect their socioeconomic power amid unionization and calls for rural reforms, landowning *alessandristas* cast themselves both as campesinos and as authentic representatives of *chilenidad*.[90] The SNA, for example, demonstrated in April 1933 the importance of forging discursive and symbolic ties to the rural worker and *chilenidad* by changing the name of its journal, the *Boletín de la Sociedad Nacional de Agricultura*, to *El Campesino*. The fact that *El Campesino* was a journal dedicated to the concerns of landowners suggests that large landowners identified themselves with (or even as) campesinos—just ones with land titles and unmitigated power. Middle-class intellectuals had accentuated the countryside's *chilenidad*, and landowners found personal significance in that idea, regardless of its original intent. Thus, landowners could easily arrive at the conclusion that Marxists who wanted to unionize the countryside were alien to the campo and were anti-Chilean for seeking to disrupt time-tested rural lifeways and traditions. Reformers shared this opinion to some extent but found a place for campesino lifeways and traditions in a populistic discourse that differed from the status quo discourse of *alessandrista* landowners.

By the early 1930s, *criollista* stories and *huaso* imagery were common in the pages of *El Campesino*. In a decade that saw the short-lived Socialist Republic of 1932 and the founding of the PS the next year, some notions found in *criollismo*, such as dedicated labor and tranquillity, appealed to the landowning elite searching for some way to defend their political turf and justify rural socioeconomic relations. In *El Campesino*, the SNA turned to *criollista* short stories to make its own, interpreted political and nationalist statement. Federico Gana's "La señora," a story written in 1899 that was included in the 1916 anthology *Días de campo* and published in *El Campesino*'s April 1933 edition, describes a visit to a Central Valley hacienda where the *mayordomo*, the *huaso* Daniel Rubio, was raised by the estate's señora.[91] Found destitute as a young boy, Rubio was fed, educated, and unofficially adopted by the landowning family. Rubio never left the estate, never married, and later assumed full care of the señora after her husband's death. The visitor, impressed by the harmony and interpersonal commitments of hacienda life, remarks that he is touched in some profound way: "The birds sang with happiness. The fresh morning air seemed to infuse me with liveliness, a strange force. I thought that this happiness, which seemed to overflow with the first rays of the sun, had come from the outstretched hand of that man."[92] Gana's *huaso* protagonist reflects a singular morality and unmatched sense of responsibility considered typical of the rural experience. The SNA's landowners, it seems, found in "La señora" a defense of deference and paternalism, a facet of *inquilino-patrón* socioeconomic relations that had contributed to rural stability (and *inquilino* subservience) since the colonial period. The vision of an authentic pastoral life served the discursive needs of the landowning class, which at that time was defending traditional rural society amid unionization and calls for agrarian reform.[93]

Oligarchs and middle-class reformers established not only a precarious political accord in the early 1930s but also a superficial meeting of the minds regarding what constituted *lo chileno*; both groups found great national and cultural value beyond the city's edge. A 1932 editorial in the *Boletín de la Sociedad Nacional de Agricultura*, for example, states that a "return to agriculture today seems a unanimous aspiration. Everyone focuses their sight on mother earth with the hope that she returns to us good times lost during these years of universal ruin." The editorial calls for a "return to the search for the simple life."[94] Yet, as *La chica del Crillón* broke book-selling records in the mid-1930s, the political alliance between reformist mesocrats and the more conservative *alessandristas* crumbled. The rupture between reformers and *alessandrismo* included a rush by both blocs to stake claims to rural imagery. Landowners, conscious of the mesocracy's political intentions in the upcoming presidential election of 1938, began to criticize "urban" conceptions of *lo rural* and claimed the campo as their exclusive domain. By doing so, landowners believed their candidate, Gustavo Ross Santa María, would be considered an authentic national persona—a true leader of the *real* Chilean people, the campesinos.

In an October 1937 address over the SNA-owned radio station, a landowner spokesman suggested that urban intellectuals seeking to capture the essence of rural life were participating in a somewhat bogus venture. He stated that "for the *huasos* of the *Cordillera* [the Andes], the city man is a *gringo*" and that "to go to the countryside with the perception of a Kodak [camera] serves to capture only exteriors, to produce imitations." Only landowners and rural workers, the speaker argued, really understood the campo's essence. The spokesman then posed a simple question: "Let us ask: does the writer have any mission to complete in the countryside?"[95] The comments are insightful when placed within the context of the growing political rift between *alessandrista* landowners and reformers of the urban middle class. Though the Conservative, Liberal, and Radical parties had combined to clinch Alessandri's victory over Socialist Marmaduke Grove and Communist Elías Lafertte in 1932, Radicals soon believed that Alessandri's failure to launch an extensive reform agenda represented a relapse of oligarchic rule reminiscent of the Parliamentary Republic. The *alessandrista* Right, meanwhile, increasingly feared the possibilities of a populist candidate and his electoral victory in the presidential elections of 1938. Aware that Radical reformers "with a mission to complete" could potentially curtail landowner power, the SNA made it clear that urban intellectuals visiting the campo (to arouse political support for *frentismo*?) or merely imagining the countryside were unwelcome gringos, a foreign species.

It must be noted that none other than Eduardo Barrios (1884–1963), a *criollista* who became a landowner in the Andean foothills east of Santiago in the 1930s thanks to high-paying civil service posts and money gained from winning two national lotteries, gave the SNA radio address in question.[96] Barrios was the most conservative *criollista* of the genre's second generation, and his political interests squared with those of the traditional landowning class after he became a self-made and self-styled *hacendado*. But Barrios's politics were never cut and dry, as his long ties to Ibáñez attest. The former *fundo* administrator was minister of education for the dictator Ibáñez in the late 1920s as well as during Ibáñez's elected presidential administration in the 1950s. Barrios also headed the National Library during his long public life. He began writing short stories in the 1920s but did not publish his most notable novel, *Gran señor y rajadiablos*, until 1948. In general, it was well received, but some reform-minded intellectuals, including Barrios's acquaintance Ernesto Montenegro, were critical of the novel's conservative overtones. As Montenegro recalled, "In my view, when Barrios invokes with exaggerated fervor the virtues of a paternalistic caste, like he does in *Gran señor y rajadiablos*, he has left the domains of his experience to rise to the level of abstraction, of political philosophy."[97] For our purposes here, taking Barrios into account reminds us that literary genres, by nature of their creative dimensions, seldom exhibit rigid uniformity, as Pierre Bourdieu suggests.[98]

As the 1938 presidential election approached, conservative landowning interests—and the *alessandrista* campaign in general—hoarded *huaso* imagery. In October, the SNA published a special issue of *El Campesino* to celebrate the association's one-hundredth anniversary. What was normally a publication devoted to more practical topics, such as labor and property issues, became a public relations portfolio of the nation's rural heritage. The *huaso* cowboy is visible throughout. An article on horses and horsemanship shows *huasos*, including children, in perfect command of their beasts.[99] Others are pictured sitting tall in their saddles, gazing over the rural landscape.[100] After thumbing through numerous pages of photos depicting hardworking and seemingly content *huasos*, one comes across an article on *inquilinos*. The piece, an excerpt from the book *Agricultura chilena* by Luis Correa Vergara, flatly states that "the *inquilino* system is not as bad as many people think." It goes on to cite Claudio Gay, who favorably compared *inquilinos* to other *fundo* laborers in the mid-nineteenth century. In short, the SNA sought to convince the ever expanding reading public that *huasos* and other campesinos were doing just fine, regardless of what *frentistas* were saying about poor rural conditions.

The landowning class and its candidate went so far as to embrace the *huaso* as an unofficial campaign symbol for the election. At campaign stops, horse-men whom the press and Ross's political operatives called *huasos*—perhaps *inquilinos* "invited" to the events by their landowners, or the landowners themselves—often greeted the *alessandrista* candidate.[101] In August, during Ross's final campaign swing through the southern Central Valley, some thirty-five hundred *huasos* are said to have paraded in Linares in his honor. *El Diario Ilustrado* reported that *huasos* from numerous nearby *haciendas* gathered at the city's athletic field to pay homage. The newspaper, a vo-ciferous supporter of Ross, quoted Linares's PL leader Nicanor Pinochet as saying: "Here [in the countryside] we all know that the Popular Front is the enemy of the *patria*."[102] Pinochet construed urban space—with all its problems, including the social question—as the FP's domain. Moreover, in Maule, the native land of Latorre, Ross witnessed a twenty-minute proces-sion of *huasos*. *El Diario Ilustrado* reported that "*huasos* paraded behind a large Chilean flag . . . and passing in front of the balcony where Ross was located, the parading *huasos* lifted their *sombreros* and burst out in cries of victory."[103] In this way, then, images and symbolism so typical of the *criollista* imagina-tion were discursive elements of a conservative nationalism that the SNA, *alessandristas*, and *rossistas* habitually professed during the 1930s. The un-abashed cosmopolitanism so typical of the Parliamentary Republic's aristoc-racy had, over the course of a few years, given way to a nationalism espoused by an oligarchic establishment desperate to sustain hegemony.

The FP was quick to comment on Ross's *huaso* support. The newspaper *Frente Popular*, reporting on Ross's stop in Curicó, stated that pro-Ross *huasos*, "sent there from neighboring *fundos*, assaulted the local office of the PS, located a few meters from Curicó Station and the police station." The *huasos* then "defaced the house of a known *frentista*, which, according to his report, belongs to Mr. Gregorio Contreras."[104] Clearly, some *huasos* operated under the influence of their Ross-supporting landowners, *Frente Popular* indicates. A year earlier, the newspaper had called the rural lower class a realm of "reaction" but inferred that overbearing and oppressive landowners were to blame, not workers.[105] Bellicose and apparently obedient *campesinos* aside, FP intellectuals and politicians viewed *huasos* in a rather positive light. With the PR on board after 1936, *frentistas* employed the *huaso* mystique and ruralesque imagery in a populistic discourse that, among other things, in-cluded a call for the fundamental transformation of rural social relations and conditions.

The spectacle at the Caupolicán Theater in 1939, discussed at the begin-ning of this chapter, points to the high value placed on campesino heritage by the FP's intelligentsia. Another example of this tendency is a remarkable photo of *huasos* on horseback with clenched fists raised over their heads, which appeared in *Frente Popular* on the eve of the 1938 presidential election. The accompanying caption reads: "*Huasos* who came from Province of Coquimbo as authentic ambassadors of the rural lower class, who proclaimed Aguirre Cerda their candidate in the March for Democracy in La Serena under the banner 'Agriculturists will vote for an agriculturist.' [Aguirre Cerda came from a moderately successful landowning family.] Those pictured [in the photo] are part of the column from the Communist Party."[106] In essence, not only are the ubiquitous *huasos* displayed as representatives of the rural working class, but *Frente Popular* (primarily a mouthpiece of the Communist and Socialist parties) would have its readers believe that campesinos were participants in *frentismo*'s national(ist) movement and national political affairs.

As one would expect, moderate *frentistas* shied away from the notion of revolutionary *huasos*. They did, however, contribute to the ruralesque rhetoric that surrounded Aguirre Cerda's candidacy. Born in the village of Pocuro near the town of Los Andes in the northern Central Valley province of Aconcagua, Aguirre Cerda is known to have felt a certain affinity for his rural roots. Though primarily seen by his contemporaries as the candidate of the urban masses, Aguirre Cerda (also known as "Don Tinto," a reference to his ownership of a vineyard) drew praise for his supposedly authentic link to the campo. A late 1938 *Zig-Zag* article described the son of a small landowner in the following terms: "Don Pedro is the traditional Chilean, an archetype of our people. He is the Chilean who loves his country. . . . Chile lifts him to triumph because Chile is the people, the Popular Front; and Chile is also Don Pedro, born in the countryside of Pocuro." The edition goes on to state that "governed by him, we will feel more Chilean, more attached to our land and mountains" and that he represents "the Chile . . . of the *poncho*, the dark-skinned [*los morenos*], the rural, the hard-working, and the friend of liberty."[107]

With Aguirre Cerda's victory over Ross, mesocrats not only emerged as the dominant political force in the country but also could now fully employ the ever expanding governmental bureaucracy to champion *chilenidad* and encourage sentiments of national/cultural authenticity brought to public attention by the *criollistas*. Progressive nationalist representations of pastoral life—sanctioned by the state—became "official" components of Chilean national identity during the early years of the FP. In 1939, the new government published a compilation of freehand drawings and descriptive passages that essentially sanctioned the *huaso* as a national archetype. Written by Carlos del Campo for the tourist bureau of the Ministry of Development, *Huasos chilenos* hails the horseman as the cornerstone of society and identifies him as typically or authentically Chilean. Written in Spanish with accompanying English translation, *Huasos chilenos* includes mention of the festive rodeos, the *zamacueca*, and the skilled horsemanship of *huasos*. The cowboy is, according to del Campo, quite a hero: "With his wide-brimmed *sombrero*, his vividly colored *chamanto*, high boots and clinking spurs, he is, in the midst of our panorama, a handsome and energetic representative of the race."[108]

Rodeos and *Zamacuecas*

Ruralesque notions of *lo nacional* were not restricted to political discourses and electoral struggles. By the 1930s, they were detectable in everyday cultural practices, including those of the urban elite. What once was laughable became fashionable; what was rural became national and nationalist. The decade saw a tremendous assortment of spectacles with rural themes designed to lure urban audiences. In 1930, the anniversary celebration of the founding of San Bernardo (just south of Santiago) included *cuecas* danced by participants who showed a "real mastery for the classical national dance."[109] The 1935 Independence Day celebration in Santiago's Cousiño Park also had a notably rural flavor: "We noticed the presence of *huasos* on horseback," *El Diario Ilustrado* reported. "This year, there was a rejuvenation of the Chilean *cueca*, which is definitely banished from our aristocratic salons. We had seen it banished . . . [and] poorly replaced by tangos, fox trots, one-steps, rumbas, and *cariocas*."[110] The *zamacueca* may not have made it into the Union Club but nonetheless was given national importance by the conservative press.[111] Twenty-five years earlier, *El Diario Ilustrado* had reported entirely different Independence Day festivities. Among other things, the newspaper covered a government-sponsored centennial dinner (French cuisine was on the menu) and a symphony that played classical music atop Santa Lucía Hill in downtown Santiago.[112]

Zamacuecas were also important in another forum in which *lo rural* was celebrated: the rodeo. Large crowds of campesinos, middle-class professionals, and aristocrats filled midcentury rodeo arenas, cheering *huasos* who paraded the flag and danced *zamacuecas* before and after performing feats of

The *zamacueca* (or *cueca*), depicted in this early-twentieth-century illustration, became widely regarded as Chile's national folk dance during early decades of the century. Today, *cuecas* are danced at public and private celebrations of all sorts and figure prominently in the festive Independence Day celebrations each September. (Courtesy of the Consocio Periodístico, S.A. [Copesa], and *La Tercera*, Santiago)

horsemanship. The travel diary of Erna Fergusson describes the pageantry of a rodeo held in the early 1940s. The North American's detailed account begins with a horde of *huaso* horsemen, dressed in colorful patriotic attire, anxiously waiting inside the rodeo arena, or *medialuna*.[113] One by one, the horsemen took turns chasing young steers. Fergusson notes that they were "as handsome a lot of men as one would wish to see, completely at ease with their mounts, comfortable with each other and the onlookers."[114] By the time of Fergusson's trip, Chilean rodeos, which began during the colonial period as seasonal roundups of cattle from the outskirts of the haciendas, had been transformed from a laborious duty for *inquilinos* into a ritual thought to demonstrate cultural singularity and the nation's heritage. Today, *huaso* associations throughout the country regularly sponsor rodeos, including the remarkable Huaso Club of Arica, founded in 1968 in the once Peruvian, nonagricultural, and arid north! But there are no *inquilinos* among these contemporary *huasos*. Agrarian reform in the 1960s and 1970s did away with Chile's service tenantry, leaving "*huaso* tradition" in the hands of prominent families and urban professionals with small *parcelas* (plots) who, from time to time, give up their cellular telephones for bridles.

The Limits of Discourse

A hallmark of early *frentismo*, progressive nationalism's populistic and anti-imperialist underpinnings certainly dovetailed with the PR's strategies to combat the elite's power, further national economic development by curtailing foreign capital, and mobilize the lower classes in support of the FP. But as rural unionization expanded during the Aguirre Cerda presidency, Radicals proved there were strict limits to what lower-class Chileans could do as valued members of the *patria*. In late 1939 and 1940, Aguirre Cerda pleased landowners, including the SNA, by moving against "professional agitators" in the countryside and suspending rural unionization, in exchange for the former oligarchy's support in the Congress for *frentista* programs.[115] In the press, leftists ardently condemned any suppression of rural unionization, but the FP's Socialists and Communists nevertheless agreed with Radicals to suspend it. Socialists, in return, received important administrative posts, and a congressional proposal to outlaw the PCCh was defeated.[116] On the surface of things, the FP parties seemed to have made a short-term concession for long-term legislative gain. However, in the case of the PR's decision to suspend union organizing in the countryside, we should not underestimate the consequence of Radicalism's history of anti-Marxist sentiment. One can easily imagine Radical reformers of the early FP fearing that peons and *huasos* were in danger of being corrupted by detachments of very convincing rabble-rousers of revolution (Edwards Bello's *La chica del Crillón* warns of this very problem). One writer vigilant of labor organizing in the countryside observed in 1940 that "communist agitators have shown intelligence in attacking this stronghold of reaction first, for the *guaso* is, in reality, the bourgeois of the masses."[117]

As minister of the interior under Aguirre Cerda, *criollista* and Radical boss Guillermo Labarca signed a circular on August 17, 1940, that directed national police to make extraordinary efforts to arrest those in the countryside suspected of harboring or fomenting sentiments that, in his words, would "only lead to the creation of an environment of social unrest." In a written statement sent to police director Oscar Reeves Leiva, the *criollista* states that revolutionary elements also cause the "formation of unnecessary and unacceptable hatreds that bring with them grave consequences for our *patria*."[118] The countryside, he reasoned, should remain a tranquil place—as depicted in his *cuentos* published nearly four decades earlier. As faithful Radicals, Aguirre Cerda and Guillermo Labarca believed that state-based reform was the only acceptable political option. The *criollistas*, the reader will recall, did not sanction the idea of politicized campesinos. Like the outspoken Zola, who had vehemently defended Dreyfus in late-nineteenth-century France, Guillermo Labarca demonstrated that his art and politics were commensurate.[119]

In their many *cuentos* and novels, Guillermo Labarca and other middle-class intellectuals of the *criollista* movement conveyed ideas and sentiments with populistic intonations that were congruent to a Radical project that was antirevolutionary and antioligarchic. Some *criollistas* were members of the PR, and others were not, but collectively they participated in the molding of a new cultural and national consciousness that was considerably more democratic than conceptions of culture and "nation" prevalent among the elite of the Portalian and Parliamentary republics. While an urban readership consumed *criollismo* and many grew fond of the campo and its campesinos, reformers in the realm of public education were also busily rethinking and remaking Chile. They, too, profoundly shaped the cultural sphere and professed a nationalism that was progressive and populistic as they maneuvered between the forces of revolution and reaction.

Gobernar es educar.

VALENTÍN LETELIER, *La lucha por la cultura*, 1895

For Culture and Country   5
Middle-Class Reformers in Public Education

When reflecting on the education of the young Émile, Jean-Jacques Rousseau remarked that "plants are shaped by cultivation and men by education.... We are born weak, we need strength; we are born totally unprovided, we need aid; we are born stupid, we need judgment. Everything we do not have at our birth and which we need when we are grown is given us by education."[1] Like the eighteenth-century philosopher whose ideas helped shape the ideology of the French Revolution (and Latin American independence revolutions, for that matter), middle-class Chileans associated with the Radical Party (PR) and other reformist groups of the late nineteenth and early twentieth centuries were astutely aware of education's remarkable potential for molding present and future generations. Many prominent teachers, bureaucrats, politicians, and intellectuals shared the belief that education was a necessary component of modernization, a linchpin of liberal democracy, and a key to social peace across class lines. But properly executed instruction, they held, went beyond the teaching of reading, writing, arithmetic, history, foreign languages, physical education, or scientific knowledge; it entailed carefully orchestrated programs of ideological coaching that bestowed upon pupils concepts of Chilean singularity, national solidarity, and citizenship.

While reform-minded *criollistas* posed alternatives to elitist conceptions of culture and "Chile" in their short stories and novels about common laborers, reformers in public education likewise promoted a democratized cultural vision and a revised definition of "nation." But while most *criollistas* operated in the penumbra of politics, reformers in education fought in the political trenches and exercised considerable influence within Chile's burgeoning bureaucracy. Reformers in positions of power and influence moved to democratize culture through the expansion of state-directed schooling and, at the same time, sought to sculpt the proper citizen by way of nationalist teachings in and outside the classroom. Culture, in the pedagogical sense, was to be profuse and accessible; it would further erode the edifice of the elite's hegemony and curtail the forces of social revolution. The teaching of an inclusive nationalism, they believed, would inculcate students of varying ages and economic backgrounds with democratic and inclusive notions of nation and nationness, thus tempering "antisocial" political tendencies. *Criollismo*'s artistically communicated message was, therefore, accompanied by an institutionally oriented program, which, like the naturalist genre, was an element of a hegemonic project that left lasting imprints on Chilean society.

During the Parliamentary Republic, the reformist purveyors of "progressive nationalist" cultural politics in pedagogy, led by Radicals, focused on establishing a law of universal obligatory primary education. Leaders to the left of Radicalism, including Malaquías Concha and Luis Emilio Recabarren, also adhered to the idea of expanding public instruction and certainly contributed to the pressure that was brought to bear on the detractors of compulsory primary schooling, but they did not share in the cultural power that reformers amassed in pedagogical circles, especially in the Education Ministry. Broadly speaking, then, what unfolded was a decades-long debate that pitted influential reformers against conservatives with ties to the Catholic Church (which boasted a network of private schools and, as of 1889, the Pontifical Catholic University in Santiago) and their traditionalist Liberal allies in the oligarchic establishment. Radicals and like-minded anticlericals cast this cultural battle as one between enlightenment and ignorance, progress and reaction, nationalism and indifference. From the turn of the century until the passage of the Law of Obligatory Primary Instruction in 1920, reformers strongly championed the expansion of state-run education as national and nationalist imperatives and maintained this disposition thereafter. As one reformer explained in the journal of the National Education Association (AEN), "An intelligent democracy is the only protection against reactionary currents that want to drive us toward autocracy, on the one hand, and currents that push us toward disintegration, class-based hatred and anarchy on the other."[2]

The story of public education's gradual democratization during the Parliamentary Republic must necessarily begin with a discussion of pedagogical elitism in the nineteenth century and education's role in the consolidation of the ruling upper class. While a literature by and for the nineteenth-century elite circulated in the cultural marketplace, there also existed a pedagogical system that was inaccessible for the lower classes. As we have seen, elements of high society entertained confined and exclusive notions of culture and "nation" during the Portalian and Parliamentary republics, and such notions were manifested in the elite's cultural practices and conveyed through literature. In education, confined notions of culture and "nation" were evident in prevailing pedagogical theories and corresponding praxis until the final decades of the nineteenth century, when reformist mesocrats seized on public instruction as their own cultural domain. It is important to keep in mind that lines dividing social interests involved in education were often blurred during the period in question. Radicals, who had become central figures in the pedagogical bureaucracy by the end of the nineteenth century, maintained certain allies among the *parlamentarista* elite. Some notables who supported obligatory primary education, for example, came from the Liberal Party (PL), which included then Senator Arturo Alessandri. Furthermore, it is evident that some reformers were more conservative than others, and some traditionalists were more reformist than most. It was, therefore, not uncommon for a Radical and, say, a traditionalist Liberal to agree on a certain policy. Yet Radicals during and after the Parliamentary Republic remained committed to the idea of displacing the elite from the center of national affairs and never lost sight of this long-term goal despite short-term collaborations with the oligarchic establishment.

The Confines of Culture

The history of Chilean education extends back to the late colonial period and schools that were established by the Catholic Church in the eighteenth century. Primary schools taught basic reading, writing, and speaking skills, and so-called Latinity schools prepared students for higher education in convents and seminaries by teaching them Latin. After 1757, the Royal University of San Felipe, where students studied the philosophies of Saint Thomas and Saint Augustine, Justinian and canon law, Latin, mathematics, and medicine, provided higher education. In 1797, Manuel de Salas, who later became a founding father of the republic, established the Academy of San Luis, a school devoted to commercial and vocational education, in protest of colonial education's stress on metaphysics and the abstract. After creating a ruling junta in 1810, Creoles immediately turned to the issue of education. Inspired by Enlightenment principles and aware of the need to extend education to all classes and both sexes, the junta authorized the building of primary schools in every community larger than fifty inhabitants. The expense was to be shared by community members.[3] Though impractical and ineffective because of ongoing political instability and military conflicts during the earliest years of nationhood, the junta's education program inspired future reformers. The first government's most lasting and successful pedagogical invention was the National Institute, an elite academy founded in 1813 that instructed secondary school children, took on the teaching function of the Royal University, and produced an array of leading intellectuals and politicians.

Funded by the government, the institute was the most prestigious place of postprimary education of nineteenth-century Chile and was devoted to the socialization and consolidation of the new republican elite. Sixteen major areas of study were offered—including theology, civil law, and Latin—to students culled from the most affluent sectors of society. The National Institute, in short, was an exclusive cultural space of aristocrats who believed they, and they alone, constituted the nation (after all, it was called the *National* Institute). Although the institute assigned itself the task of educating all classes, it fell far short of that goal. By the 1830s, the school had become an environment dedicated to the creation of "an elite which the state would train for public service."[4] The grooming of future leaders also went beyond the classrooms of the institute; at times, for example, Diego Barros Arana and others hosted *tertulias* in their homes for selected pupils.[5]

The founding of the University of Chile in 1843 signaled a change in the institute's role in the pedagogical system, but not in its commitment to educating the sons of high society. At first, the university was a nonteaching institution charged with research and the validation of examinations. Its rector—a government appointee—oversaw all state-operated instruction with the help of the Council of the University of Chile (Consejo de la Universidad de Chile), later renamed the Public Instruction Council (Consejo de Instrucción Pública) in 1879. The Ministry of Public Instruction, fused with the Justice Ministry, had only a secondary role in national pedagogical affairs at this time. The institute continued to offer university-level courses into the 1870s, when the university finally assumed all higher public instruction. Thus, the institute slowly was transformed during the mid-nineteenth century into a national preparatory school for affluent children who aspired to enter the University of Chile.[6] In terms of fiscal policy, the institute received a large percentage of the nation's public education budget throughout the nineteenth century when compared with funds allocated for secondary and primary education. In 1850, for example, the school received 12 percent of the education budget, while secondary education was allocated 15 percent and primary schooling 16 percent. The institute secured 16 percent of the budget in 1860; 26 percent went to secondary instruction and 31 percent to primary education.[7]

The notion that all Chileans were not equals and therefore did not deserve equal educational opportunities was widely shared among midcentury intellectuals. Andrés Bello, the Venezuelan-born educator and the first rector of the University of Chile, expressed this neo-Aristotelian notion when he stated that "not all men are to have equal education, for each has his own way of contributing to the common felicity."[8] This approach to public education guided policy making for the remainder of the nineteenth century and into the Parliamentary Republic, as many in the oligarchic establishment were steadfastly against a more inclusive education system.

Primary instruction in the nineteenth century did not venture beyond rudimentary skills and moral lessons given the fact that most pupils were not expected to enter secondary schools, which were primarily private.[9] Of 78 primary schools operating in Santiago in 1841, only 8 were municipal; 7 were in convents, 3 were functioning in parishes, and other private parties maintained another 60. The numbers were more balanced at the national level. In 1853, there were 280 public primary schools and 281 private schools, but only 10 percent of primary school–age children were enrolled overall. After the government of Manuel Montt declared in 1860 that primary instruction would be free but not obligatory, the number of public primary schools swelled to 598 in 1861, while the number of private schools rose to 335. That year, 15 percent of primary school–age children were matriculated with no law of obligatory primary education on the books.[10] The above enrollment figures most likely reflect the matriculations of children from more affluent families, and, if socioeconomic distinctions were taken into account, the percentage of children from urban or rural working-class families enrolled in primary schools surely would be much lower.

Secondary education outside the National Institute was also exclusive. If financial and geographic conditions permitted, nineteenth-century parents in the provinces sent their children to *liceos* (public secondary schools), which became popular educational options for landowning and mine-owning families. *Liceos* were established only in important provincial centers, including La Serena and Concepción in 1830, Talca in 1831, Coquimbo in 1834, Cauquenes in 1837, and San Felipe in 1838. By 1849, ten public secondary schools were functioning throughout the country (including the National Institute). Eight more were founded between 1851 and 1879.[11] Complementing the *liceos* were the *escuelas superiores*, which provided three years of postprimary instruction at no cost to students. Though certainly more accessible than the National Institute, the elongating chain of *liceos* and *escuelas superiores* nonetheless served the urban and rural elite. As the conservative Ignacio Domeyko reasoned in the mid-nineteenth century, secondary schools were to remain the domain of affluent Chileans, and the poor were to be relegated to basic primary education.[12] One option for students of lower socioeconomic status, however, was to enter normal schools, where they would be trained to become primary school teachers. In 1842, the government established the country's first Normal School for Preceptors and appointed its director, Argentine-in-exile Domingo Faustino Sarmiento.

Although education was primarily an affair of the elite during the Portalian Republic, figures show a gradual increase in public literacy, which corresponded to a rapid growth in the number of primary and secondary schools after about 1850. The adult literacy rate increased from 13.5 percent in 1854 to 23 percent in 1875.[13] During the later decades of the nineteenth century, moreover, an expanding urban sector saw the development of a middle class that demanded quality and accessibility in education.

Cultural Politics and the *Estado Docente*

It is evident that by the eventful 1880s public education was undergoing a gradual, but significant, metamorphosis. That decade saw marked increases in public education spending and enrollment figures during the ill-fated government of José Manuel Balmaceda and witnessed the emergence of prominent Radicals as leaders in pedagogical matters.[14] The realization of the *Estado docente,* or "teaching state," seemed to be within the grasp of Radicals and reform-minded Liberals, who fervently sought to expand the state's role in Chile's cultural life. Not all reformers agreed on every idea or issue, but together they initiated a national conversation about culture and "nation" with long-term effects in the public sphere. Valentín Letelier was the most visible leader of the education reform movement during the country's transition from Portalianism to *parlamentarismo*.

As Amanda Labarca Hubertson appropriately argued in the 1930s, Valentín Letelier was the most important pedagogical figure of the late nineteenth and early twentieth centuries.[15] A graduate of the National Institute and PR member, he worked as a lawyer and professor of history and literature in Santiago before being elected to his first congressional seat in 1879. In the 1880s, Letelier spent six years in Germany as part of the Chilean diplomatic legation in Berlin, where he closely studied that country's primary and secondary education systems. After returning from his stay in central Europe, Letelier was again elected to the Chamber of Deputies in 1888 to represent Talca, and he later went on to serve in the prestigious post of rector of the University of Chile. His political ideas placed him in the PR's left wing, which meant he was not endearing to Radical chieftain Enrique Mac-Iver and more conservative Radicals. In fact, Letelier successfully championed a more "socialist" approach to dealing with social matters in a debate with a Mac-Iverist faction during the Radical convention of 1906 in Santiago.[16]

After years of observing education methods in Europe, Letelier returned to Santiago in 1886 with the intent to restructure the Chilean system. His primary concern was his country's pedagogical backwardness in comparison with the education systems of the Old World, particularly that of Bismarck's Germany. Letelier's basic pedagogical principles were associated with a stern belief that Chile's modernization—intellectual and political as well as socioeconomic—was inexorably bound to the modernization of education. He, like Rousseau, saw young children as empty voids, or sponges, capable of absorbing the knowledge that all good citizens should possess. That knowledge, Letelier argued, came by way of a liberal and ardently secular "humanistic" education modeled after Germany that concentrated on the humanities and sciences. For much of the nineteenth century, however, Chilean secondary schools had a distinctly French flavor. As in France, Chile's *liceos* generally taught one subject at a time, and subjects changed as students progressed from one grade to the next. Inspired by the German system, Letelier and his allies (including educator Claudio Matte) successfully argued that *liceos* should adopt a "concentric" structure, whereby many subjects were taught simultaneously. Each student, then, would advance in a given subject each year for six years of secondary education. The government adopted this system in January 1889, and the Liceo of Santiago became the first concentric-oriented *liceo* in the nation (it was later renamed the Liceo Valentín Letelier).[17]

Letelier gave significant attention to elementary education as well. Although the National Institute and the *liceos* had been of central interest to the University of Chile and the Ministry of Justice and Public Instruction, the Radical recognized that, in a given student's life, primary instruction was the foundation on which all other knowledge rested. He therefore called for a concentric model for primary schools as well. But for all his emphasis on reinventing Chilean education, Letelier viewed primary instruction in much the same manner as many mid-nineteenth-century intellectuals did. Primary school students, Letelier argued in his *Filosofía de la educación* (1891), were best served by general knowledge, given that most would not pursue secondary schooling; the *liceos*, special postprimary technical schools, or the university were naturally meant for more affluent students from which the nation's future leaders would someday emerge. It would be unfair, however, to equate Letelier with Bello or Domeyko. *Filosofía de la educación* reflects Letelier's belief that social mobility was possible in Chilean society, but only if schools relayed the individualist ethos inherent in liberal, humanistic instruction. In essence, then, we see in Letelier's ideas a transformation that was occurring within the PR as the turn of the century neared. The party moved toward a more populistic and progressive posture—what Letelier considered "socialist"—and away from the more conservative sensibility of Radicalism's old guard led by Mac-Iver.

It was always clear to his supporters and detractors that Letelier was a firm believer in state intervention in cultural matters. He was a fervent defender of secular instruction and adamantly believed that the state provided a more effective education than any parish or convent. Of course, Letelier realized that an effective state-run education system depended on the presence of a highly trained and dedicated pool of teachers. To that end, Letelier led the fight for the creation of a national teacher's school for secondary instruction—one that would complement the normal schools that trained primary-level teachers. In 1889, the same year of Letelier's victorious campaign for concentric education, the Balmaceda government heeded the distinguished Radical's call and founded the Pedagogical Institute (Instituto Pedagógico) in Santiago. It graduated its first class of twenty-nine teachers in 1893. Areas of study included Spanish, Latin, Greek, German, history, geography, mathematics, and the natural sciences.[18] Over the next few years, top positions at the Pedagogical Institute went to Germans in light of the fact that "few Chileans possessed the technical competence [formal pedagogical training] to hold these posts during the institute's early years."[19] Alejandro Venegas, the author of *Sinceridad* and graduate of the National Institute, was among the few Chileans who taught at the Pedagogical Institute during its first decade.[20] Letelier naturally was delighted to have Germans involved in Chilean education but soon faced stiff opposition within his own party regarding the centrality of foreign teachers.[21]

With concentric education under way and the Pedagogical Institute in operation, Letelier continued to champion state-run public schooling. In 1895, he published his most renowned book, *La lucha por la cultura*, a compilation of speeches and articles. Here we see that Letelier viewed public education not only as the creator of moral and individualistic citizens but also as a cultural glue capable of mitigating social tensions. "To govern is to educate, and every good political system is a true educational system, just as every general education system is a true political system," Letelier insists. "The purpose of education in society is . . . the convergence of all its hearts on the same proposition and all the understandings on the same faith, with the deliberate intent to produce the harmonious development of all of society's active elements."[22] The book does not pinpoint a "proposition" on which all hearts would converge, but the body of his work and his political loyalties suggest that liberal democracy is that proposition—a system that Letelier and other reformers believed to be the key to the "harmonious development" of society.

La lucha por la cultura also attacks those whom Letelier undoubtedly regarded as foes of democracy: traditionalists who criticized his and the Radicals' ideas about public instruction. Letelier chastises adversaries who called him a "red authoritarian" for expanding state power in the cultural sphere, and he locates them squarely in the camp of "reaction."[23] "They are the ones," Letelier writes, "who intend to paralyze national development."[24] He goes on to praise various organizations founded by Liberals and Radicals, including the Society for Primary Instruction (1855), the Society of the Friends of Progress (1872), and the Academy of Fine Arts (1873), for their ongoing efforts against the "centers of reaction entrusted with recruiting and stirring up proselytes against the culture of the republic."[25]

Although reformers enthusiastically backed Letelier's pedagogical ideas, especially his secular stance, a small group led by the spirited Radical *correligionario* Eduardo de la Barra condemned the employment of foreign teachers at the Pedagogical Institute and elsewhere as fundamentally anti-Chilean.[26] Thus, a nationalism brewing within the PR surfaced in de la Barra's newspaper columns and other writings published in 1899 under the title *El embrujamiento alemán* (The German bewitchment). His trepidation anticipated the guarded suspicion of foreigners that informed Palacios's

Raza chilena. "Is Chile for the Germans or for the Chileans?" de la Barra asks. This rhetorical question is accompanied in *El embrujamiento alemán* by a detailed assault on the German professors of the Pedagogical Institute and the education establishment's open acceptance of German theories and practices, including Letelier's program of concentric education. De la Barra, who had the support of Tancredo Pinochet Le-Brun, among others, explains that the Germans had bewitched many educators who were nothing but "adorers of everything German."[27] He also questions why Chilean teachers were being paid in paper currency (during an era of increasing inflation rates) while the government satisfied its debts to the Germans with gold. In addition, de la Barra found personal insults particularly satisfying. He makes the unverified assertion that some members of the institute's six-man German contingent were guilty of maltreating students and were mentally unstable. De la Barra remarks that one professor, a linguistics expert, spoke French like a "waiter in a German beer hall" and produced laughable studies on Chile's colloquial Spanish and the Araucanian language.[28] Although his verbal assault on the German professors often breached the etiquette that typified debates over education during that period, de la Barra nevertheless denied being a xenophobe.[29]

De la Barra essentially found it repugnant that Chileans looked to Europe for guidance regarding domestic cultural matters. It is apparent that Letelier perpetuated a certain cultural cosmopolitanism that many Parliamentary Republic reformers, including *criollistas*, found offensive. But unlike cosmopolitan oligarchs who sustained exclusive spaces of cultural interaction (such as the Municipal Theater, Gath y Chaves, or the Casa Pra), Letelier seized on foreign cultural ways to create a more structured and progressive education system for Chilean children of different socioeconomic backgrounds, though schooling in the late nineteenth century was largely divided along class lines.

With Letelier's "humanistic" model firmly in place at the turn of the century, a new debate began to churn pedagogical circles at the General Congress of Public Education in 1902. There, a handful of intellectuals questioned the value of liberal humanism as the guiding spirit in Chilean education and proposed a more "practical" or "economic" pedagogical agenda.[30] Letelier's detractors suggested that curricula not venture into abstract concepts, become mired in literary interpretations, or devote much time to the teaching of philosophy or Latin.[31] They instead argued for an education that would prepare students for jobs in business and industry.[32] The issue was debated, but nothing came of the discussions. Nearly a decade after the 1902 congress, however, Francisco A. Encina published the most powerful and effective arguments in favor of a more "practical" education.

The late historian Carl Solberg, in his description of Chile's intelligentsia in the early twentieth century, stated that many were "deeply concerned with social and economic questions" and they "argued that the theoretical and humanistic orientation pervading Chilean secondary education gave the students little training for business life."[33] The fate of economic development, these intellectuals believed, depended on the molding of a citizenry capable of creating and perpetuating a modern, industrialized society. Thus, Chilean workers, businessmen, and industrialists, rather than foreigners, would direct the nation's economy and developmental path. A strong spirit of economic nationalism guided these thinkers, and Encina expressed it in no uncertain terms. Encina published two highly influential books in 1911 and 1912 (with the patronage of the AEN) that influenced the growing nationalist movement and spurred a flurry of publications critical of the Parliamentary regime's education policies. Encina's *Nuestra inferioridad económica*, as the reader will recall, constructs a pessimistic portrait of a turn-of-the-century Chilean economy and society dominated by "superior" foreign civilizations that retarded the development of domestic industries and nationalism. His antihumanist pedagogical ideas, published in the form of *La educación económica y el liceo* in 1912, were in much the same vein.

In *La educación económica y el liceo*, Encina argues that European education methods were perfectly suited for German or French children but not Chileans: "Secular education has remained, in large part, in the hands of wise men, of philosophers, of the erudite, of the well read, all individuals in which intellectual faculties predominate.... An understanding of the world and of real life are lacking in these people.... [They are] enclosed in their laboratories and their libraries, isolated from the manifestations of human activity."[34] He states that humanism is, indeed, a proper educational approach in fully industrialized countries but that Chileans are in need of a more rudimentary form of instruction: an "economic education." Encina explains that secondary schooling lacks the basic training necessary for graduates to excel in an industrializing and modernizing society—an opinion shared by the Manufacturing Promotion Society (Sociedad de Fomento Fabril, or SOFOFA), an organization of industrialists.[35] Vocational skills and the inculcation of a work ethic are touted by Encina as critical pedagogical elements; philosophy or Latin, on the other hand, serve no social purpose until a given society has achieved a certain level of material comfort.[36] Encina states that "the flowering of the sciences and of the liberal arts in a poor country does not lead to a utopia."[37]

Encina recognized that all nations were not equally suitable for the educational program pushed by Letelier and the German instructors (a humanist and highly intellectual approach).[38] Certain national characteristics peculiar to Chile—its status as a developing nation, its racial composition, ethnic heritage, and so on—made the act of "copying" European educational methods problematic. As Encina notes, "That which constitutes the nerve and the strength of the entire educational system, the soul that gives it life, we have not been able to import nor copy. . . . The soul of the whole educational system is the same as the soul of the community that created it."[39] Nationalism, Encina believed, was an aspect of the Chilean soul that should guide the development of a productive education system, but his concept of nationalism was largely limited to economic matters. It is important to point out that Encina does not suggest in *La educación económica y el liceo* that education serves a greater purpose outside the economic realm, nor does he acknowledge that morals and ideology should be pedagogical imperatives. Encina, it seems, did not champion education as a social mortar but instead viewed it as a means to develop national industry and achieve economic independence.

One of Encina's most ardent critics was Enrique Molina, a member of the PR, ally of Letelier, and professor at the Pedagogical Institute. Molina's *La cultura i la educación jeneral*, a collection of conference presentations, argues that Encina's stress on pedagogical practicality reflects a conservatism and anti-intellectualism that negates a humanistic tradition in Chilean society perpetuated by Lastarria, Barros Arana, and reformers like Letelier.[40] Encina's failure to address the church's meddling in education is offered by Molina as an example of anachronistic traditionalism: "He doesn't devote a single line to, among other things, the actions of the church. This silence is inexplicable if one considers the social and political influence that the church exerts in Chile, which is superior to that in all the cultured countries on Earth, such as England, Germany, France, the United States. . . . In his numerous criticisms of secondary instruction, he talks only of the *liceos*, and never about the congregational secondary schools."[41]

The prevailing nationalist rhetoric woven throughout Encina's books also drew Molina's ire. Both *Nuestra inferioridad económica* and *La educación económica y el liceo* suggest that humanistic instruction is antinationalist in that it does not promote the development of Chilean industry. Molina, who later became the rector of the University of Concepción, sees this as simply preposterous: "One does not find the enemy of the spirit of nationality in humanism," he asserts, "but in Epicurean individualism without ideals."[42] Molina does not want to be construed as antinationalist and explains that Chilean education has always had, and should always have, a nationalist character. He notes that "the songs that our children sing are the martial hymns that filter through their souls" and that other aspects of instruction relay to students the "triumphs and struggles of the men that make up the race" despite the pedagogical influences of foreigners in the Chilean system.[43] Moreover, Molina indicates that Encina's obsession with economic development and economic nationalism reflects a worldview that transforms humans into simple components of a productive system. Despite Molina's arguments, Encina's ideas about "economic education" began to seep into reformist discourse during the final years of the Parliamentary Republic, as Radicals and others turned to a more protectionist economic posture under difficult fiscal conditions.[44] It was not until the dictatorship of Carlos Ibáñez del Campo that a more "practical" pedagogical scheme became public policy.[45] Liberal humanism, however, was not displaced as a guiding theme in education.

In the Name of Unity: Cultural Democracy and Primary Education

The intellectual battle between Encina and Molina, though representative of a larger struggle over the definitions of culture and "nation," took a secondary position during the early twentieth century to the most important and dynamic pedagogical controversy since independence: the debate over obligatory primary education. Radicals and dissident Liberals led the fight for secular and mandatory primary schooling against Conservatives, who defended Catholic instruction, and many traditionalist Liberals who harbored contempt for the expansion of the state's power in society. Armed with nationalist catchwords, proponents of obligatory primary schooling argued that cultural democratization would soothe class-based tensions, serve to build a truly modern society, and safeguard democracy. The PR first officially embraced the idea at its inaugural national convention in 1888 and never dropped it as a central ideological pillar before the Law of Obligatory Primary Instruction was approved in August 1920 and executed soon thereafter.[46] Conservatives countered by asserting that parents and private bodies, not the state, should maintain the right to educate children and that the expansion of public instruction would negatively effect nonpublic school-ing. This debate, which reached its zenith during the Sanfuentes administra-tion (1915–20), demonstrates that culture was a battleground on which op-posing political blocs waged war over social and political power. Reformers in education, like the *criollistas* in literary culture, rethought the parameters of culture and expressed a nationalist ethos based on inclusion and soli-darity. Oligarchs vigorously defended their cultural power but could not hold back the rising tide of pedagogical reform.

As we have seen, public education was, for the most part, the cultural space of affluent Chileans during the nineteenth century. Primary education was not obligatory, and thus many children of working-class families ended their academic lives at very young ages in order to seek work (if they attained any formal schooling at all). Many leading intellectuals, including Bello and Domeyko, suggested that children of working-class families were simply not credible candidates for a more rigorous and protracted educational experi-ence. Primary instruction did not become a notable priority of the state until the Balmaceda administration. Balmaceda's large-scale school con-struction program—paid by nitrate revenues—translated into higher ma-triculation figures at both the primary and secondary levels.[47] It is not sur-prising, then, that the PR adopted a plank regarding obligatory primary education at the height of Balmaceda's presidency.

Proponents of elementary-level reforms who wished to stir public sup-port pointed to low literacy rates. In 1896, PR member Armando Quezada Acharán complained that only two of every three Chileans, school-age and older, were literate—2.3 million illiterates overall. Among children four to sixteen years old, Quezada cited 650,000 illiterates, while only 150,000 chil-dren were matriculated in all primary and secondary schools, both public and private.[48] Radicals like Quezada constantly complained that illiteracy was a fundamental social ill that not only slowed national development but also crippled any prospect of social unity. A resolution passed by the Radical Youth of Copiapó in 1901 captured this sentiment . It called for free, secular, and obligatory primary education "for all the children of both sexes older than six years of age," which would guarantee "the happiness of the Chilean family and the progress and greatness of the *patria* in all manifestations of human activity."[49] This was a common theme in the reformist press well into the twentieth century.

A measure regarding obligatory primary education was first proposed in the Senate by Pedro Bannen, a Radical, in 1900. Without support from the administration of President Federico Errázuriz, a traditionalist Liberal, and in light of the oligarchy's majority in both houses of Congress, the proposal largely fell on deaf ears. The reformist *La Lei* attacked Errázuriz's "reactionary" cohort for waging a de facto "war against instruction" by not supporting elementary-level reform, noting that "the instruction given in our primary schools does not reach, in terms of benefit, the children of those individuals who form the lowest social layer, of those who live in the greatest misery and most complete ignorance."[50] At the same time, the newspaper cites Bannen's personal struggle to make education more accessible to working-class children in the face of the oligarchy's intransigence. *La Lei* praises the Radical for founding the School of Workers (Escuela de Proletarios) in a poor Santiago neighborhood known as Cañadillas, where 120 primary-level pupils were enrolled as of January 1900.[51] Bannen used his own funds to open the school, which then relied on donations from the public.

The founding of the AEN in 1904 gave a new impetus to the reform movement's push for cultural democratization. Headed by a PR member and physician, Dr. Carlos Fernández Peña, the association considered obligatory primary education its highest goal.[52] Other objectives included the creation of "common" primary schools in which children of all socioeconomic backgrounds would be classmates. The AEN boasted a distinguished membership that included Nicolás Palacios, the *criollista* Guillermo Labarca Hubertson, Amanda Labarca Hubertson, Pedro Aguirre Cerda (vice president of the association in 1920), Darío Salas, Encina, Guillermo Subercaseaux, Luis Barros Borgoño, Eliodoro Yañez, Armando Quezada Acharán, Tancredo Pinochet Le-Brun, Malaquías Concha, Manuel Guzmán Maturana, and Lucila Godoy (Gabriela Mistral). In its foundational manifesto, the association declared that education "should be a continuous process without interruption by an imagined dividing line, in a way in which all proceed through the public school, which is the most effective medium for preventing wars between classes that endanger our current social condition. Instead of deepening social divisions, the school would predicate a spirit of concordance between the diverse classes as well as tolerance and absolute respect for all beliefs, thus combating fanaticism and fortifying the sentiment of social unity [*el sentimiento social*]."[53] The AEN saw in cultural democratization the unique opportunity to create a Chile absent of class-based animosity that fueled the pernicious forces of revolution and reaction. Inventing a new Chilean citizen was, according to the AEN, a pressing need of national and nationalist importance to be realized in the cultural sphere. Thus, when the association applied for its juridical personality, it identified its mission as the "elaboration and implantation of an educational system that responds to our social, economic, and political necessities; it will develop all of the energies of the race, forming the individuality of the child; familiarizing him with governing himself through a solid moral and civic education; preparing him to be an energetic, honest, and honored citizen in the broader community he will find outside his school."[54] AEN partisans were convinced that only through obligatory primary schooling could the nation produce such energetic, honest, and honored citizens.

The AEN soon became the most prominent education-related organization in the country. Along with the PR and other reformist groups, the pedagogical association took on traditionalist intellectuals allied to the Catholic Church who moved to block state-orchestrated cultural democratization.[55] The opponents of obligatory primary instruction proved quite effective in the Congress. No only did Bannen's 1900 bid for a law fail, but so did another attempt in 1906 led by Radical deputy Agustín Gómez.[56] Facing vigorous criticism, Conservatives defended their belief that compulsory primary schooling was not the solution to Chile's cultural problems but stressed that they were not foes of public education in general. "There surely is no other service that urgently beckons the constant attention of the government," *El Diario Ilustrado* explained in 1907. "The success of the new generations depends on public instruction."[57] Another column pointed to the relative failure of the obligatory primary instruction law passed in France in 1882. It cites the conservative French journal *Le Journal des Debats*, which asserted that French literacy rates showed no marked increases after the law's promulgation.[58] Moreover, *El Diario Ilustrado* later blamed reformers for wrongly convincing many Chileans that compulsory primary education was a "panacea."[59] The Radical newspaper *La Lei*, furthermore, reported that the Conservative Assembly of Santiago declared to liberals that "now begins the fight" and resolved to "take the Sacred Cross to all the schools."[60]

Instead of expanding secular education, advocates of conservativism suggested to parents that they send their children to private schools. They pointed to the Catholic Church's Victoria Prieto School in downtown Santiago as a shining example of private instruction. The conservative press argued that the school satisfied the intellectual, material, and spiritual needs of the next generation: "With souls fed in the church with orations and prayers, stomachs satisfied in the dining room with healthy and nutritious food, the students go to the different classrooms . . . where the various directors of the school personally teach elemental knowledge."[61] Religious instruction, of course, formed the core of congregational schools, and its defenders went so far as to propose that all public schools have compulsory

Dr. Carlos Fernández Peña, the longtime president of the National Education Association, was a principal leader in the campaign for obligatory primary instruction. He presided over the AEN for more than three decades. This caricature of Fernández Peña appeared in 1912. (Courtesy of the Archivo Fotográfico, Museo Histórico Nacional, Santiago)

religious instruction. This idea was presented in 1904 to the Public Instruction Council, the oversight committee associated with the University of Chile, which was controlled by Radicals. Not surprisingly, the concept was abruptly rejected.[62]

Reformers routinely and unabashedly lashed out against their conservative adversaries for their "crusade against the schools" and their war against "culture and liberalism."[63] *La Lei* exclaimed that clerics had failed to attract large numbers of children to their private schools because most parents remained convinced that "congregational instruction is not the best for preparing good citizens, excellent professionals, active industrialists, and businessmen."[64] At one point, the conservative press responded to such attacks by noting a glaring discrepancy between the rhetoric and practices of its cultural foes. In a stinging 1904 article, *El Diario Ilustrado* listed the names of forty-seven prominent Radicals and Liberals whose children were enrolled in Catholic educational institutions, including the schools Sagrado Corazones, San Jacinto, San Pedro Nolasco, and San Ignacio.[65] The reformist press offered only a weak rebuttal.[66] Such exchanges over public instruction's orientation and content demonstrate the continuation of nineteenth-century conflicts over church-state relations and most certainly show the Conservatives' deep contempt for the Radicals' *Estado docente.*

The debate over obligatory primary education remained lively as the Parliamentary Republic went on. With the growing support of working-class organizations, Radicals and the AEN continued to lead the charge for cultural democratization at the time of the centennial, while roadblocks erected by oligarchs in the Congress and La Moneda fed the ongoing frustration of reformers. Obligatory primary education was again proposed in the Congress in 1911 but failed once more despite a degree of interest shown by Aníbal Letelier, a Liberal-Democrat and minister of justice and public instruction under President Ramón Barros Luco. The AEN, in the wake of yet another defeat, did not curtail its cultural campaign. In 1912, the association resolved that "education is the most secure method for progress and reform that any country may adopt" and that elementary education formed the basis of any pedagogical system.[67] Three years later, the organization's *Revista de Educación National* lauded itself for tireless efforts in the name of culture: "Our journal . . . has energetically fought against our educational, political, and social ills," an editorial explains. "It is profoundly nationalist."[68]

Though tired of the elite's intransigence and legislative inertia, reformers found new energy during the administration of Liberal-Democrat (or Balmacedist) Juan Luis Sanfuentes. Sanfuentes, unlike the majority of his presidential predecessors, believed that government had an important role to play in cultural matters. He recognized that Radicals were highly qualified in the era of pedagogy and were becoming dominant players in party politics, and he chose the Radical *correligionario* Aguirre Cerda to head the Ministry of Justice and Public Instruction in April 1918. Aguirre Cerda was succeeded in November by Luis Orrego Luco, a Radical and author who had served in the same capacity during the administration of Ramón Barros Luco in 1912. In the seventeen cabinets convened by Sanfuentes during the course of his administration, more Radicals took the post of minister of justice and public instruction than in any other presidential cabinets of the Parliamentary Republic.[69] It comes as no surprise, then, that obligatory primary education became a reality under Sanfuentes, though very late in his presidency.

The Sanfuentes years saw a boom of publications and speeches related to public education and, specifically, obligatory primary schooling. In the press, *La Nación*, founded in 1917 by Eliodoro Yañez as a voice of Liberalism's dissident wing, became the standard-bearer of the campaign after *La Lei* closed in March 1910, while the AEN continued to publish articles in its *Revista de Educación Nacional*.[70] The social question remained a central topic of conversation, and reformers continued to herald cultural democratization as an elixir. In 1916, for example, the *Revista de Educación Nacional* complained that Chile was passing through a period of "decline" and racial "degeneration," and it again proposed expanding instruction.[71]

To reformers, racial and cultural salvation depended on the immediate extension of public education to members of the working class. Among the notable supporters of obligatory primary instruction during the later years of the Parliamentary Republic were Darío Salas, an influential educator, Radical, and member of the AEN, and then Senator Arturo Alessandri Palma. Both expressed progressive nationalist ideas when addressing education's role in mitigating tensions between classes, while traditionalists zealously defended the church's cultural power and expressed little interest in expanding public instruction.

Writing in an era of large-scale urban strikes, the unionization efforts of revolutionaries, and the oligarchic establishment's intransigence in matters of reform, Salas published *El problema nacional* in 1917, a renowned book in which he calls for an expanded education system to safeguard "democracy" and strengthen the Chilean "collective." Salas cites as his motivation "a profound faith in the virtues of our race and in the efficacy and perfectibility of our institutions" and thanks both the AEN and a leading teacher's union of the era, the National Society of Teachers (Sociedad Nacional de Profesores, or SNP), for their strong support.[72] *El problema nacional* flatly asserts that "opportunities to receive instruction should be the same for everyone and, furthermore, that education would prepare each person to participate in a *correct* manner in democratic life."[73] Salas points to Chile's high illiteracy rate and inadequate education budgets as national travesties in dire need of correction and places blame squarely on nineteenth- and twentieth-century oligarchs who deliberately blocked the average Chilean's access to culture and, as a consequence, contributed to the frailty of what Palacios called in a different context the "spirit of nationality."[74]

Salas explains that moving away from an education system founded by and for the affluent would bridge social chasms that endanger Chile's order and progress: "We want to be a democracy, and the equality of educational opportunity does not exist, and one cannot even speak of it under the current regime without referring only to a small portion of the population." He adds that "half of our adult population lacks the essential instrument for incorporation into civic life—suffrage—and among the rest a large number find themselves incapable of using it in an intelligent way. . . . We want social peace but we do not base it upon the solidarity of all."[75] This statement echoes much of what early-twentieth-century reformers, and Radicals in particular, believed about the elite as well as members of the lower classes. It is the responsibility of enlightened educators, Salas suggests, to rescue their illiterate and otherwise uneducated compatriots—souls without command of their basic faculties—from vice. A major vice of lower-class Chileans, Salas and others believed, was the tendency to vote for traditionalists or harbor revolutionary loyalties (it was not uncommon, as the reader will recall, for *huasos*, the uneducated horsemen of rural society, to support conservative candidates at the behest of their landowner. In addition, the growth of urban unions during the Parliamentary Republic convinced reformers that revolutionary opportunists were misleading uneducated workers). The Radical essentially argues that Chileans of lesser means, if properly educated, not only would contribute to the material progress of the nation but also would become nationalists with clear conceptions of civic duty. Salas contends that "education needs to make future citizens feel and understand that the *patria*, apart from what is means physically, is a symbol and a bond: a symbol of our resolution to pursue happiness, living all for one and one for all, and a bond that ties us at once to the past and to the future, obligating us in a unified manner to respect the tradition of our dead and to ensure a better future for our posterity."[76] The state, he points out, is the only entity capable of implementing a massive cultural plan to "make each member of the collective a citizen and a patriot" and "increase the vigor of the race."[77]

The arguments presented by Salas in *El problema nacional* were not necessarily new; nor were they very different from those offered by reformers since the late nineteenth century.[78] The book's timing, however, could not have been better, given the political circumstances of the Sanfuentes years. After the election of Sanfuentes, reformers enjoyed a louder voice in the Congress and were no longer denied the courtesy of germinating debate on its floors regarding the expansion of public education. Thus, the PR introduced a proposal for obligatory primary instruction (the fourth in nearly two decades) in the Senate and Chamber of Deputies in 1917. Within the Senate, which, unlike the lower house, remained in the hands of Liberal and Conservative traditionalists during the last two years of the Sanfuentes administration, one of the most vocal representatives in favor of obligatory primary education was Alessandri.

By 1919, Alessandri was the most influential dissident Liberal of the Parliamentary Republic who supported Salas's call for pedagogical reform. Arguing in defense of the "national soul," Alessandri endorsed the proposal in a series of Senate speeches. Like the AEN and Salas, he saw merit in public instruction's capacity for mitigating the maelstrom of social discord in a modernizing country. In a Senate address Alessandri asked, "What is, Mr.

President [of the Senate], the principal objective of education? To form within each man a social purpose, exercise each and every one of his faculties to convert him into a moral force, and make him economically useful in the society in which he lives. To reach this objective it is indispensable to give all the educated a mental orientation that is homogeneous so that their spirits converge and merge into a common and harmonious truth. That is why primary instruction cannot be dispersed, it cannot obey diverse criteria, diverse orientations. If that occurs, far from contributing to social organization and the homogeneity of the national spirit, [the nation] will move toward disintegration, disorder, and chaos."[79] Here, Alessandri suggests that expanding public schooling not only would create more "useful" citizens ready to participate in the economy but also would foster a certain ideological homogeneity. It is fair to assume that Alessandri believed his own ideas and values were kindred to a "common and harmonious truth" upon which all "spirits" would converge. In another speech, Alessandri pointed to a persistent social malaise caused by the Parliamentary Republic's oligarchy and a debilitated sentiment of national unity. He complained, "There exists a sickness among us with symptoms that we can diagnose as chronic pessimism. . . . [A] dense and dark shadow of pessimism darkens all of our acts and judgments. Pessimism is a negative force and as a consequence is destructive and damaging."[80] Pointing to the figure of 1.6 million illiterate adults, Alessandri argued that a national education strategy, based on obligatory primary instruction, would restore optimism and create a "social equilibrium" between classes to keep the nation "advancing on the shining path of aggrandizement and progress."[81]

Alessandri's rhetoric effectively rallied support for obligatory primary education in the Congress among dissident Liberals, while more conservative parliamentary oligarchs, sensing that passage of the proposed law was imminent with or without their endorsement, expressed lukewarm support for it as the presidential election of 1920 drew closer.[82] When the legislative branch passed the measure by a slim margin in the winter of 1919, *El Diario Ilustrado*, a longtime foe of obligatory primary education, struck a notably conciliatory tone: "The country will receive profound satisfaction from this news, which meets its desire for moral and intellectual improvement."[83] Yet many conservative groups remained bitter, including the National Association of Catholic Students, an organization associated with the Pontifical Catholic University of Chile (founded in 1889 under Bishop Joaquín Larraín), which lashed out against Radical anticlericalism and the expansion of the secular state.

In a 1920 manifesto, the Catholic association stated that reformers were reviving church-state animosity that, to some extent, had been soothed during the late nineteenth century. It chided the PR for believing it is "Chile's intellectual axis" and argued it "has not yet reached the cultural level of respecting the conscience of others, making it clear that its patriotism has been too weak for it to refrain from expressing unjust hatred against the church." On secularization of Chilean society, the association noted, "As patriots we reject it, because we know that all of the great labors in Chile have been done with the decisive cooperation of the church. . . . To us, the *patria* without religion would not be what it is today."[84] This statement captures the conservative bloc's belief that God and nation were wed. Any notable expansion of the secular state was considered a threat to the very underpinnings of the *patria*. National salvation in the face of the social question and cultural problems, conservatives thought, had a religious solution. As the reader will recall, intellectual Juan Enrique Concha, a leading defender of church power, argued that the "teaching of Christ, practiced by the individual and respected and supported by the State and its laws" could save Chile from disintegration.[85]

To the chagrin of its conservative opposition, the passage of the Law of Obligatory Primary Instruction on August 26, 1920, which took effect exactly six months later, forever expanded the secular state's power in Chilean culture, while President Alessandri's close attention to pedagogical matters gave reformers great hope regarding cultural democratization.[86] Cheering crowds took to the streets of Santiago on August 29, including a large group of teachers and students from local normal, primary, and secondary schools that triumphantly marched to La Moneda.[87] One joyful reformer, writing in the government's *Revista de Educación Primaria*, noted in early 1921 that the new law "has been established and has struck a hard blow to ignorance." The state's new education policy, he goes on to state, is "in harmony with the vigor of the race, with the fertility of our valleys, with the enormous wealth of our soil, with the inexhaustible springs of our rugged mountains."[88]

It is certainly difficult to gauge whether or not obligatory primary education dealt an immediate "hard blow" to illiteracy, given that literacy climbed steadily during the nineteenth and twentieth centuries. The adult literacy rate already had risen from 13.5 percent in 1854 to approximately 25 percent in 1885. It stood at 50 percent in 1920, 56 percent in 1930, and climbed to roughly 85 percent by 1960.[89] What these figures do not show, however, is that literacy made a marked advance within the lower classes during the early twentieth century, while the elite held a monopoly on literacy during much of the

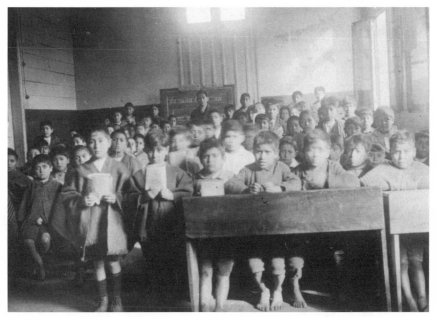

Children assembled for a photo at a public primary school, ca. 1920. The school's location is unknown. (Courtesy of Eduardo Devés)

nineteenth century. The law did have an instantaneous effect on matriculation figures. In August 1920, there were 289,148 pupils officially enrolled in primary schools. The number rose to 376,930 by August 1921.[90] Darío Salas, the author of *El problema nacional*, served as general director of primary instruction during this enrollment boom.

The Law of Obligatory Primary Instruction was far more effective in cities than in rural areas, where enforcement proved difficult. The law stipulated that all *hacendados* with properties larger than 2,000 hectares and valued over 500,000 pesos were required to operate, mostly at their personal expense, a primary school if the number of elementary-age children on their land numbered more than twenty. Many landowners skirted this responsibility. In 1924, the Ministry of Justice and Public Instruction admitted that the new law "has not borne the fruits that were expected" and asked provincial governors, intendants, and mayors to coordinate with local carabineros in matters of enforcement.[91] Bureaucrats continued to complain about enforcement problems in 1930. Juan Saavedra, the director of education of the province of Bío-Bío, for example, wrote to the ministry in June of that year about the *fundo* Santa Rosa, owned by María Gana, widow of a Mr. Dufeu. It was a property of more than 4,000 hectares and was valued at 2 million pesos and did not have a primary school. The report states that more than 100 young children went without education—a clear sign of the owner's "lack of interest in the well-being of the children of her *inquilinos*."[92] Other landowners, however, immediately complied with the law, including one Luis Mitrovich, owner of the haciendas San Vicente and Santa Rosa in the province of Aconcagua.[93] Such rural schools established on *fundos* under the Law of Obligatory Primary Instruction were free, subject to periodic inspections by government officials, and received a modicum of material support from the ministry.

The extended conflict over cultural democratization in the form of obligatory primary education demonstrated a division between members of social blocs who thought about culture and "nation" in different ways. In public debates, many reform-minded proponents of the measure espoused a "progressive nationalism" that included members of the lower classes in their imagined national community. In response, traditionalists defended their cultural privilege and, at times, questioned the patriotism and political motives of reformers. Despite such efforts to the contrary, cultural democratization was making great headway by the end of the Parliamentary Republic, and obligatory primary schooling was an important element. The idea of requiring elementary-level instruction, however, did not command all the energy of reformers during the three decades it was debated. They also worked to open night schools for adults and similar centers of cultural diffusion, as did others concerned with educating the working class.

Proletarians as Pupils: Night Schooling and Popular Libraries

It was a widely shared opinion among pedagogical reformers, including Letelier, that children were essentially dry sponges waiting to be soaked with academic knowledge, analytic tools, and, as we shall see, ideology. Adults, on the other hand, were rightly considered the product of personal experience, observation, and deliberate instruction realized over the course of many years. Although reformers understood that children were ideal subjects for socialization and acculturation, they did not want to abandon adults to what they considered to be the malfeasance of ignorance, which facilitated the pernicious programs of both manipulative revolutionaries and reactionaries. Thus, reformers actively engaged in adult education through mostly unofficial channels during the Parliamentary Republic as part of their cultural political project. It is important to stress here that Radicals were not alone on this crusade. Recabarren, the founder of the Socialist Workers Party, was an outspoken supporter of education for both children and adults of the working class, and unions and federations, often with the assistance of the Chilean Federation of Students, or FECh, formed their own small schools. Indeed, working-class organizations, mutual aid societies, and other groups initiated important literacy programs among workers.[94]

The idea of adult education for workers was first proposed in an official setting by reformers at the National Pedagogical Congress in 1889. In attendance were the major education figures of the era, including Dr. Federico Puga, minister of justice and public instruction for President Balmaceda. Coupled with a resolution that called for obligatory primary education, the pedagogical congress endorsed the idea of state-run adult night schools with the same basic curricular structure as public primary schools. It was suggested, moreover, that such adult schools could work in conjunction with working-class organizations to spur matriculation and, if enrollments remained low, prizes and other incentives could be offered to lure students.[95] As was the case with required elementary instruction, night schooling for working adults did not materialize in the short term despite the minister's direct participation in the pedagogical congress. Frustrated but not defeated, many reformers took night schooling into their own hands. The absence of obligatory elementary instruction before 1920 and the relative exclusivity of the *liceos* motivated reformers to find alternate means of educating the masses. In 1895, *La Lei* called on all liberals of good conscience to join its campaign for adult night schools for members of the working class, the "only solid base for political power and all civilizing and progressive projects." The newspaper also declared, "The slogan on our glorious flag should be 'Work for Popular Instruction.'"[96] With little interest shown by government leaders regarding adult education, the founding of private night schools became a common occurrence. Radicals proved especially successful in this cultural endeavor.

On an autumn day in 1907, the Radical Assembly of Nuñoa (a middle-class barrio of Santiago) met to discuss important national issues. Education was on the agenda, and talk soon gravitated to the importance of adult night schools. In the midst of the exchange, one member suggested that, given the state's indolence, the assembly should establish a night school of its own. Strongly enthused by the suggestion, assembly members immediately organized a collection drive at the local Radical Club, where party members often met to socialize, dine, and imbibe *con gusto*. The first classes at the Radical Assembly's adult school—presumably taught by party volunteers—were held at the Radical Club that same night.[97] In light of the fact that Nuñoa had no working-class neighborhoods or, for that matter, an industrial capacity, Radicals most likely found it difficult to recruit prospective students, though there were some rural workers in the surrounding area (given the barrio's location on the then outskirts of the capital). While Radicals taught adults in Nuñoa, the University of Chile and the AEN offered special courses and conferences for workers at night and on weekends. With strong support from the university's rector, Valentín Letelier, the University Extension program began in 1907 and soon merged with the AEN's program of "popular conferences," which was established that same year under the direction of Amanda Labarca Hubertson, renowned educator, feminist, AEN member, Radical, and wife of the *criollista* Guillermo Labarca Hubertson. The extension's corps of teachers was large, and a great many conferences were offered during the mid- and late Parliamentary Republic.[98]

In 1911, the University Extension, in conjunction with the AEN, offered instruction in five areas—Chilean history, civic education, the "sociability of workers," domestic economy, and industrial education. Instruction took place at various locales established by working-class organizations, such the La Unión Artisan Society and the La Universal Society, and was imparted by teachers who "have contributed in the most noble and exalted way to the culture and the enhancement of the *patria*." As Amanda Labarca described, the AEN enthusiastically assisted the extension "as a means to expand and carry through our action in the bosom of the working-class community, creating closer ties between it and professors, and to give an exclusively superior character to the courses and conferences of the University of Chile."[99] Among the courses offered in 1912 were "Economic Patriotism" taught by Alberto Edwards (a Liberal chieftain); "Theater as an Educational Institution" by Víctor Domingo Silva (author and Radical); "Chilean Life on the Nitrate Pampa" by the *criollista* Baldomero Lillo; "Nationalist Politics" by Guillermo Subercaseaux; "The New Phase of Science in Chilean Teaching and Education" by Encina; and "Socioeconomics" by Aguirre Cerda.[100] The total number of conferences organized by the extension in Santiago during the middle and later years of the Parliamentary Republic is very impressive, as are attendance figures. Between October 1907 and January 1917, there were 178 conferences (regrettably, no attendance figures are available for those years). From 1917 through 1920, thirty-four conferences reportedly drew 31,050 people, while during the years 1921–25 another thirty-six conferences recorded a total audience of 36,750. Thus, according to figures compiled by the AEN, the average University Extension conference between 1917 and 1925 drew just under 1,000 people.[101]

As the Parliamentary Republic's demise drew nearer, private adult schools continued to function alongside the University Extension.[102] In July 1918, the Francisco Bilbao Center, an organization of teachers in the city of Los Angeles, successfully petitioned the Ministry of Justice and Public Instruction for use of a primary school for adult instruction at night. The teachers asked for permission on the grounds that they realized the "ignorant state in which the working classes live" and desired to contribute to the "progress of our masses." The center, moreover, pledged to install electrical lighting at the school at no cost to the government. Minister Aguirre Cerda gave final approval to the plan.[103] A year later, the Third Company of Firemen of Santiago declared its intention to open a night school on the premises of the Alberto Reyes Primary School in the name of "justice and liberty." The ministry's director of primary instruction, Darío Salas, endorsed the idea, which was later authorized by Aguirre Cerda.[104] Along with the aforementioned School of Workers established by Pedro Bannen at the turn of the century, such privately operated schools complemented the pedagogical mission reformers assigned as their own.

Privately organized night schools were joined by state-operated night schools during Alessandri's first administration. By 1936, forty-three public night schools around the country maintained an enrollment of 2,857, while eighty-eight private establishments boasted a total of 5,687 students.[105] In the large scheme of Chilean education, the number of night schools and their enrollments were but minuscule portions of the country's pedagogical complex. This does not mean, however, that night schooling was irrelevant. The University Extension and the AEN did not operate schools but nonetheless offered courses and conferences that served a similar pedagogical role during the later years of the Parliamentary Republic (such events were not officially sanctioned by the ministry). Together with the University Extension and AEN, night schools taught literacy skills and basic knowledge to many workers who, in the nineteenth century, would not have been offered the promise of education. Reformers, especially Radicals, were leaders in this area.

Assisting night school teachers in their cultural project were the founders and operators of "popular libraries," which generally catered to the marginally literate members of the working class. Although no official count of popular libraries was undertaken, the number most likely remained small during the Parliamentary Republic.[106] One such library was the Santa Lucía popular library, opened by Onofre Herrera Labbé in 1906. This downtown Santiago site, which was personally funded and staffed by Herrera, operated from 8 to 10 P.M. and averaged about fifteen readers per night. In 1908, Santa Lucía accommodated 3,327 readers (including returning users), was open 223 days, and boasted a total of 5,000 volumes. No fees were required. Herrera's devotion to after-hours education drew strong praise from the reformist press: "Among the gold medallions they are stamping out in La Moneda for the upcoming centennial celebration, one should be destined for this self-sacrificing educator and public servant."[107]

To those like Salas and Alessandri who fought for obligatory primary education, or members of Nuñoa's Radical Assembly who surrendered their evenings to teach adults, or the operator of the Santa Lucía popular library, cultural democratization was a necessary factor in the creation of an inclusive democracy and interclass cohesion in a modernizing society. The diffusion of literacy and basic knowledge, they believed, served to level Chile's cultural playing field and create a stronger nation—a nation that included the once dismissed lower classes. Thus, reformers in the pedagogical sphere, much like the *criollistas* in literary culture, articulated a cultural politics that redefined the parameters of culture and "nation" by eschewing traditionalist constructions of both that pervaded society during the Portalian and Parliamentary republics. This criollo *Kulturkampf* of the late nineteenth and early twentieth centuries saw conservatives defend the Catholic Church's cultural role in society and once again underscored the lingering discord between conservatives and liberals in Chilean political culture. Liberal Party members tended to side with Radicals on matters of cultural democratization but were, for the most part, quiet partners (Alessandri was the most important exception). Radical bureaucrats, politicians, intellectuals, and teachers led the protracted effort that ultimately scored major gains in public policy. These gains may be seen not only as pedagogical and cultural advances but also as political ones. That is to say, middle-class reformers benefited directly in terms of their class's political power from the state bureaucracy's amplification, which, of course, accompanied the greater reach of public instruction.

It is more than reasonable to assert that *parlamentarista* oligarchs generally displayed little interest in domestic cultural matters, although Conservatives vociferously fought to protect the Catholic Church's customary cultural domain. Radicals became leading figures at the University of Chile and controlled its Public Instruction Council, which oversaw public schooling at the secondary level. Outside the government, both the AEN and the SNP (founded in 1909) were laden with PR members. Some *correligionarios*, such as Salas, Aguirre Cerda, and Guillermo Labarca, were members of both organizations.[108] Leftist leaders, who worked within their mutual aid societies and syndicates to spread literacy, were absent from top posts in the pedagogical establishment and key pedagogical associations during most of the Parliamentary Republic. It was not until the 1920s that leftist educators formed significant unions, such as the General Association of Teachers (Asociación General de Profesores, or AGP), while others joined the SNP.

Parliamentary-era reformers not only used their considerable influence within the pedagogical complex to pursue cultural democratization but also moved to infuse nationalist teachings into the official curriculum. Nationalism, they believed, would neutralize revolutionary ideas, restrain the forces of reaction, and perpetuate Chile's singular Latin American democracy. At the *liceo* level, the Radical-dominated Public Instruction Council made the final decisions regarding course offerings and guidelines and used this power, at the behest of the AEN and other interests, to instate "civic education"—a course on citizenship with decidedly nationalist overtones—officially as a core subject in 1912. What followed was a slew of decrees and protocols governing nationalist instruction in the classroom that culminated with the so-called Plan de Chilenidad (Chileanness Plan), which was inaugurated in 1941 by the FP government of Aguirre Cerda.

Debemos recordar que la base angular de las primeras
nacionalidades del mundo ha estado en la escuela.

La Nación, July 24, 1920

Teaching the "Nation" 6

When middle-class reformers of the Parliamentary Republic argued in favor
of obligatory primary instruction, they enveloped their appeals in the recog-
nizable idiom of nationalism. For more than three decades, members of
the National Education Association (AEN), Darío Salas, Arturo Alessandri
Palma, and others defended cultural democratization on the grounds of
promoting national and racial fortitude. They imagined a Chile in which
culture, in the pedagogical sense of the term, would somehow counteract
modernization's centrifugal social forces. But reformers were convinced that
nationalism was more than a discursive weapon to be wielded on the battlefield of cultural politics. Like culture, nationalism was viewed by many as
a social mortar—an ideological link between Chileans who may otherwise
have shared little in common.

As early industrialization and the growing export sector rapidly diversified
the country's socioeconomic landscape, revolutionary ideas made headway
in the cities as the social question intensified and the state proved that
repression remained a political option. In response to the changing conditions around them, reform-minded mesocrats called for the incorporation
of nationalist (or what often was referred to, in that era, as "patriotic")
teachings into the required curriculum. Public schooling, they believed, not
only fought the plague of ignorance to ensure democracy, order, and progress but also was a cultural instrument capable of inculcating children of
diverse socioeconomic backgrounds with notions of national solidarity and

citizenship. Radicals, associates of the AEN, and other leaders in pedagogy were principal architects of this campaign for "nationalist" socialization, which, in the words of AEN president and Radical Party (PR) member Dr. Carlos Fernández Peña, sought to "lift up the hearts of our fellow citizens, inspiring in them a love for our race."[1] From their positions of influence, middle-class nationalists lobbied for "civic education," a subject with nationalist overtones that concentrated on civic duties and rights, both before and after it was approved as a required course in 1912. By the 1920s, nationalist teachings had expanded beyond the parameters of civic education classes. The flow of ministerial directives regarding nationalist instruction reached its zenith in 1941 with the promulgation of the Plan de Chilenidad, which was orchestrated by the Radical-led Popular Front (FP).

It is clear that governments of different ideological persuasions from the late Parliamentary Republic to the FP endorsed nationalist instruction in the public classroom. Each regime, whether *alessandrista*, *ibañista* or *frentista*, naturally had a vested interest in perpetuating the state's authority and deference to its institutions. But because reformers, and Radicals in particular, nearly monopolized positions of influence within the pedagogical complex as teachers, bureaucrats, and administrators, the nationalism imparted in public schools demonstrated a "progressive" inclination by the end of the 1930s. Progressives and traditionalists agreed that nationalist instruction served to undermine working-class mobilization, but progressive nationalists also perceived an antioligarchic dimension in nationalist instruction. After the promulgation of the Law of Obligatory Primary Instruction in 1920, youngsters of varying socioeconomic origin—including working-class children—were told of *their* national and racial singularities. Thus, they were discursively and symbolically included in an imagined community that was certainly more democratized than the one entertained by the nineteenth- and early-twentieth-century elite. In essence, reform-minded nationalists in pedagogy, like literature's *criollistas*, not only sought to redefine the parameters of culture but also offered a democratized understanding of "nation." Reformist mesocrats, in education and elsewhere, therefore worked to rupture oligarchic power while they strove to build their own hegemonic project.

Civic Education and the New Citizen

Reform-minded nationalists, who saw themselves as social mediators between elements of revolution and reaction, pushed for civic education during the first decade of the twentieth century. Their efforts coincided with the tirades unleashed by antiparliamentary nationalists and *criollismo*'s emergence as an important literary genre. The scope of this initial campaign for nationalist instruction was, in general, limited to secondary schooling, which, at that time, was directed by the University of Chile (under the rectorship of Valentín Letelier) and its Public Instruction Council. After the approval in 1920 of the Law of Obligatory Primary Instruction, which greatly amplified the state's reach in Chilean society, nationalists turned to the implementation of nationalist instruction at the primary level.

In light of the fact that secondary instruction largely remained within the purview of upper- and middle-class youngsters during the Parliamentary Republic, an important question must be posed: Why would the earliest efforts to instate nationalist teachings concentrate on secondary rather than primary schools, where most working-class children reached their highest levels of instruction? Reformers held that achieving at least a semblance of unity across class lines entailed more than assuaging working-class radicalism; it also depended on the proper socialization of more affluent sectors by way of nationalism. As the reader will recall, many nationalists, especially those in the PR, contended that Chile's problems largely stemmed from a *parlamentarismo* perpetuated by the country's highest socioeconomic echelon. Many considered its *"politiquería,"* for example, a symptom of nationalism's debility. In the eyes of many nationalist detractors of *parlamentarismo*, the strengthening of nationalism in the public sphere, including its reinforcement among young aristocrats, would therefore counteract the system's divisive tendencies and buttress liberal democracy. In addition, Chile's *liceos* rapidly were becoming a bastion of the urban mesocracy during the Parliamentary Republic and thus became an important space in which reformers reproduced their social constituency's worldview. Consequently, the effort made by reformers to accentuate civic education was not entirely altruistic but a component of a developing hegemonic project.

Although no discrete course on civic education existed until 1912, the subject nonetheless was a component of pedagogy in the nineteenth century, albeit in an amorphous and diffuse form. Civic education—the teaching of civic rights and responsibilities, citizenship, and the state's basic juridical structure—played an important role in the consolidation of the postcolonial ruling class by grooming young aristocrats for careers in government as presidents, ministers, ambassadors, congressional representatives, diplomats, and civil servants. In this way, civic education bolstered the state-based patriotism that permeated the upper class for much of the nineteenth century. But nationalists of the Parliamentary Republic imagined a more amplified mission for civic education; rather than it persisting as a contributor to the elite's power, it was, either directly or indirectly, to become a program of *national* relevance.

As in the campaign for obligatory primary schooling, the AEN provided important leadership in the area of civic education and nationalist instruction. Its mostly middle-class membership, led by Fernández Peña, endorsed civic education in the reformist press and in the AEN's *Revista de Educación Nacional*, which routinely addressed education's link to nationalism and the national spirit. Some of the AEN's earliest statements regarding nationalist instruction appeared in the PR's *La Lei*, a leading critic of the oligarchy. In late 1905, Fernández Peña and AEN secretary Guillermo González sent two letters on behalf of the organization to Antonio Huneeus, minister of justice and public instruction for President Germán Riesco Errázuriz and member of the Liberal Party (PL), regarding the issue of nationalism in education. Both pieces of correspondence, which were reprinted in the same edition of *La Lei*, are excellent examples of nationalist sentiments that permeated the mesocracy during the middle years of the Parliamentary Republic and directly influenced the education curriculum.

In one letter, the AEN complains that civic education, like public instruction in general, had not received the attention it deserved at the highest levels of government. With a tone similar to that of Enrique Mac-Iver's, the Radical leader who drew attention to the nation's "moral crisis" in his well-known speech in 1900, the correspondent asserts that "one of the most characteristic signs of the moral crisis through which this country passes is, without a doubt, the debilitation of patriotism, the foundation of the nation's moral unity. Among many other factors, the negligence with which the teaching of civic education has been treated in the schools, and above all else in the *liceo*, is perhaps one of the most powerful determining causes of that debilitation."[2] Here, the AEN criticizes the Parliamentary hierarchy for failing to pursue nationalist instruction in the classroom. Thus, the organization suggests that oligarchs are partially to blame for the "moral crisis" that gripped the country (anarchists and communists likely were considered two of the "other factors" alluded to by the AEN). The organization also makes reference to *Raza chilena*, one of twentieth-century Chilean nationalism's seminal works, when criticizing the Parliamentary Republic's leadership.

The letter states that Palacios's popular book, which had been published a year earlier, exemplifies what messages should be imparted through civic education. The racial identity elaborated in *Raza chilena*, as previously discussed, transcended issues of class and party politics and promoted a radical way of imagining the national community. The AEN then calls on the ministry's budget commission to set aside funds to acquire copies of *Raza chilena* for use in schools and for the book's inclusion in popular libraries.[3] The letter, moreover, mentions an abridged version of *Raza chilena* that Palacios apparently was preparing for classroom use, though no such edition is know to have been completed before the author's death in 1911. The association's proposition demonstrates that reformers understood civic education's nationalist overtones.

Another letter to the minister opens with a simple request from the AEN's general assembly: a government grant of four thousand pesos for the purpose of supplying national flags to schools of the republic. The rationale behind the organization's solicitation is then divulged: Chile is in dire need of nationalism, and schools are the ideal setting for its propagation. As the AEN explains, "The school, for the civic education it imparts to transform the child into a citizen, may be considered a temple dedicated to the cult of patriotism. That is how the school's labor has been understood in the United States, in Japan and, within the last few years, in Argentina, where salutes to the flag symbolize the cult of its institutions and the national soul. . . . Today, as doctrines are proposed that tend to destroy patriotism, that is to say, the nation's moral unity, the most vital thing a nation has, this expenditure [for the flags] is necessary, as well as the prohibition of using [the flag] in any places that dishonor or stain the name of the *patria*."[4] This excerpt illustrates the AEN's faith in the efficacy of education and nationalism in the creation of citizens untainted by political doctrines or activities reform-minded mesocrats considered profane. It also indicates that civic education existed in some form before it was established as an official subject in 1912, but, in the eyes of nationalist reformers, its expansion was a pedagogical imperative. In sum, both letters convey a sense of urgency in the face of perceived threats to Chile's "moral unity" and "national soul."

As the AEN formulated its grim diagnoses of nationalism's health, it began to foster nationalism among schoolchildren without the official participation of the state. In September 1905, just weeks before *La Lei* published the AEN's letters to the minister, the association joined with the Society of Primary Instruction (Sociedad de Instrucción Primaria)—a private association of reformist educators that established numerous primary schools around the country during the nineteenth century—to sponsor a *dieciocho* (Independence Day, September 18) celebration for young *santiaguinos*. This

"*fiesta escolar*" was held at the Santa Lucía Theater and drew students enrolled in the society's schools.[5] It is important to note here that such celebrations of important historical events were not exceptional. The *dieciocho* and
other festivities marking significant episodes, including the so-called Combate Naval de Iquique (a momentous War of the Pacific naval battle between
Chilean and Peruvian warships) of 1879, drew large crowds, which surely
included school-age children, during the nineteenth century.

Aside from publishing the AEN's opinions regarding civic education and
news of AEN-sponsored activities, the PR's *La Lei* independently praised the
concept of nationalist instruction. In October 1907, for example, the newspaper applauded yet another statement issued by the AEN regarding the
expansion of civic education and blamed the Parliamentary Republic's political climate for negatively affecting nationalism. When discussing nationalism's debilitated state, *La Lei* expressed its gratitude to AEN members for
having "identified an enemy that threatens, at its moral base, the soul of our
race [and] the Chilean nation." Civic education, the newspaper explained, is
a measure that "must be realized in the schools to counteract the work of
those who demolish the ideals of the *patria* [and] to conserve that group of
elemental ideals and desires that constitute our Chilean soul."[6]

A 1909 *La Lei* editorial reflected the opinion shared by reformers that
destroyers of the "ideals of the *patria*" were not only operating within the
ranks of the working class but also were found in high society. The newspaper lashed out against *parlamentarismo*'s aura of elitism, its rampant "*politiquería*" (to which the Radicals certainly contributed), and the absence of
political morality. The editorial explains that "the lack, or better yet, the
forgetting of the civic spirit among Chileans, which constituted one of most
accentuated and noble qualities of their temperament, has, for many years,
and is today, the cause of great errors and misguided acts. . . . It is the civic
spirit that has disappeared or has become lethargic due to sordid interest in
the fever of business, in pittance, in the joy of obtaining money by any
means, to the point of losing honor or dignity."[7] This assertion is particularly revealing. It demonstrates the consensus among reformers that an
unchecked capitalism was detrimental to the "civic spirit," or notions of
unity and collective belonging. In this way, *La Lei* echoed Radical *correligionarios* like Valentín Letelier who called for the state's intervention in social
and economic matters when he promoted a *socialismo de Estado* at his party's
convention in 1906. In addition, the newspaper states that ideologues with
narrow political interests, whether revolutionary or reactionary, are respon-

sible for the troubles vexing Chilean society (reformers, of course, believed their politics was in the nation's best interest).

The AEN, with support in the reformist press, remained committed to civic education as the Parliamentary Republic progressed. In June 1911, less than a year after the centennial celebrations, the organization once again complained of nationalism's sorry state and the importance of fostering what it called "civic virtues." An editorial in the AEN's journal, in a way reminiscent of the letters the association sent to Minister Antonio Huneeus in 1909, underscores the nationalism-education nexus. It explains that "if the cult of patriotism and the qualities of citizenship somewhere have an altar, that place must be, without a doubt, the school" and that the class-room is where "the souls and minds of future citizens are shaped."[8] The tireless efforts of the AEN and other reformers finally paid off in 1912, when the Public Instruction Council, the University of Chile's committee in charge of secondary schooling, approved civic education as a required course in all public secondary schools.[9] It allotted two hours of civic education per week for students in their fifth and sixth years of secondary-level study (equivalent to high school juniors and seniors in the United States). When compared with the other core subjects, civic education was granted a signifi-cant portion of the fifth- and sixth-year curricula. The natural sciences, physics, chemistry, and philosophy, for example, were assigned two hours each, while history and geography, foreign languages, Spanish, and mathe-matics were each taught three hours per week.[10] The measure became popu-lar enough by 1917 to warrant the establishment of civic education as a required course in private secondary schools as well.

The original civic education curriculum approved in 1912 by the council was considered a nationalist project by its architects. It established outlines for teaching the rights and responsibilities of citizenship, the constitutional and institutional underpinnings of the republic, and the legal system.[11] Domingo Amunátegui Solar, a historian and Liberal who succeeded Valen-tín Letelier as rector of the University of Chile, later recognized the national-ist values that were imparted to students during the early years of the civic education program. Civic education, Amunátegui explained, combated "the disturbing work of books, magazines, newspapers, and agitators adverse to patriotic sentiments, which have thrown public opinion into convulsions, not only among us, but throughout the civilized world, as a result of the displeasing happenings of the Great War."[12]

The council immediately went about the task of training teachers to wage such a war against elements "adverse to patriotic sentiments." Since the Pedagogical Institute did not offer civic education as an area of specialization before 1912, there were no teachers with special training in that subject to fill the new positions in the *liceos* immediately. Thus, the council drew from a pool of social science teachers and instructors with legal backgrounds who had graduated from the institute. One such teacher was Pedro Aguirre Cerda, who accepted a teaching position in civic education in 1913.[13] The Pedagogical Institute, and its single faculty member assigned to civic education, expeditiously began training specialists after the subject's implementation (civic education constituted a field of specialization within the "humanities" subject area, and civic education instructors received bachelor's degrees in *humanidades* rather than civic education). In 1919, a second faculty member was added to the institute's civic education field.[14]

One of the earliest and most widely used texts for civic education, *Instrucción cívica*, was first published in 1917 by Amador Alcayaga and Eliodoro Flores, both teachers in public schools.[15] It touches on such topics as governmental structures at all levels, the rights of citizenship, and penal procedures. Aside from explaining the legal configuration of the republic, the text quotes the Declaration of the Rights of Man, the fundamental statement of the French Revolution of 1789, and the Magna Carta, which established legal restrictions on monarchical power in thirteenth-century England. The inclusion of these texts (especially the Declaration) strongly suggests that Alcayaga and Flores entertained a liberal sensibility—one that saturated the largely middle-class teachers corps during the Parliamentary Republic—that they believed should be imparted in the *liceos*.[16] It may be noted here that many Chilean reformers (Radicals and Masons in particular) also fancied themselves as Latin American cousins of nineteenth-century French Radicals.

Guidebooks for civic education teachers accompanied texts for children. In 1920, the year in which the Congress passed the Law of Obligatory Primary Instruction, Malaquías Concha, the leader of the Democratic Party and consistent ally of the Radical cause, published a new edition of his *Cartilla de educación cívica*, which sought to inform teachers as to the subject's pedagogical and national value. In his introduction to the book, which apparently was endorsed by the Riesco administration in 1904 (when civic education was not a separate subject), Concha explains that "love for the *patria* and of liberty, the self-sacrifice for the family and for fellow citizens, the respect for law and justice, and the ardent desire to contribute to the public good" are among the highest qualities any citizen may possess.[17]

Accordingly, he considered civic education a means of inculcating those qualities in students.

The idea of *patria* is highlighted in the book's first chapter, which reads as if it were a lecture to students (sample questions conclude the chapter). One passage explains: "One of the sweetest and most powerful sentiments that has always made the human heart resonate is love for the *patria*." Another states that "a good citizen owes all to the *patria*. . . . The *patria* has a right to all our abnegation." Concha goes on to suggest that "cosmopolitans" endeavor to "erase the frontiers of nations, to only love humanity as a whole. . . . Cosmopolitanism is the indifference in matters of nationality [and] the suppression of nationality very much goes against progress just as the suppression of the family would as well."[18] What follows are chapters on national sovereignty; forms of government (democracy gets preferential status); liberty, equality, and fraternity (again, the French Revolution is an important theme); the constitution; the separation of powers; constitutional history; and labor, which exposes Concha's very positive appraisal of unions.

The campaigns for civic education and obligatory primary instruction during the first two decades of the twentieth century should be considered tandem elements of a nationalist mesocratic reform movement. Reformers, in essence, recognized the link between culture, politics, and nationalism and sought to exploit it for the purposes of "order," "progress," liberal democracy, and the building of hegemony. Civic education represented the first stage, though a somewhat limited one, of what became a substantial program to disseminate nationalism in Chilean schools. That program, which expanded far beyond civic education classes by the end of the Parliamentary Republic, was propelled, in large part, by Alessandri's first administration in response to ongoing class-based tensions. But before exploring decrees and protocols designed to enhance nationalism, we must cast our eyes upon the streets of Santiago in mid-1920, when civil unrest reached a fevered pitch. Amid anarchist-led demonstrations, protests by university students, and the rumblings of reactionaries, many complained of nationalism's debility, and some sought a pedagogical solution to Chile's social conundrum. Civic education at the secondary level, it seemed, had not helped stem the tide of social discord. Thus, as the Ministry of Justice and Public Instruction began to implement the Law of Obligatory Primary Instruction, nationalists no longer would rely on civic education as a subtle conduit of ideology. They began to formulate measures to stimulate nationalism more overtly at both the primary and secondary levels. All told, the campaign for the amplification of civic education undoubtedly contributed to the eventual development of decrees and protocols that firmly established nationalism's formal place in a pedagogical environment commanded by middle-class reformers.

A Call to Arms

Hearing cries of *"Viva Chile!"* and the melody of the national hymn, the army regiments of Buin and Pudeto, both based in the capital's metropolitan area, marched by cheering crowds on July 20, 1920, as the units made their way through Santiago to the Estación Yungay train depot. The two detachments later boarded rail cars bound for the Peruvian and Bolivian borders in the arid Norte Grande, as had numerous other units throughout the country.[19] Only days before, Bolivian revolutionaries had seized control of La Paz, ousted President Gutiérrez Guerra, and allegedly issued threats (supposedly echoed by their Peruvian allies) regarding the "recovery" of the nitrate- and copper-rich desert region taken by Chilean troops during the War of the Pacific.[20] "Natural and spontaneous" patriotic celebrations, as one Santiago newspaper described them, drew thousands throughout the country despite rumors that fears of an imminent invasion were largely unfounded.[21] Scuttlebutt circulated that war minister Ladislao Errázuriz Lazcano, a traditionalist Liberal and a conspicuous member of the Parliamentary Republic oligarchy, was personally profiting from sales of war provisions to the government and was purposefully dramatizing and inflating the Bolivian situation. A political game was afoot. Just two weeks before troops were mobilized by Errázuriz, Liberal Alliance (AL) candidate Alessandri had gained a majority of the electoral college in the presidential election but had garnered slightly fewer popular votes than Barros Borgoño of the Unión Nacional (UN). Thus, as a Tribunal of Honor deliberated the final outcome of the contest, Errázuriz and his UN partners wisely shipped Santiago's regiments—along with their *alessandrista* sympathies—to a faraway place. For these reasons the deployment became known as "Don Ladislao's War."

In the end, Peruvian, Bolivian, and Chilean soldiers did not fire a single shot during the supposed standoff in the north. A different confrontation, however, began to rage in Chile's capital. Violence erupted in Santiago at the height of Don Ladislao's War when progovernment conservative youths, revolutionary activists, and antiwar protesters with leftist sympathies (including university students) occupied the downtown area. Responses to the events of mid-1920 expressed in the Santiago press by UNistas and reformers—nationalists of differing stripes—reflected the chasm separating political blocs and the continuing importance given to nationalism as a pedagogical tool. Thus, the social violence of July, which included the highly publicized deaths of two young students, serves us as yet another access point into the realm of cultural politics and nationalist ideas of early-twentieth-century Chile and beckons substantive attention here.

Passing through the downtown area after attending a pro-troop lunchtime rally at a nearby train station on July 21, a group of young, rightist Chileans—most in their late teens and twenties, apparently—paused in front of the headquarters of the Chilean Federation of Students (FECh), the country's largest student union with ties to the Communist-led Chilean Workers Federation (FOCh). Aware of the union's politics, its participation in anti-war protests that same week, and its decidedly pacifistic stance toward the Bolivia-Peru situation, they proceeded to harass the FECh members inside.[22] According to police reports, the pro-"war" youths attempted to enter the establishment with the peaceful intent of chanting of *"Viva Chile!"* A handful of students responded by throwing bottles. One FECh leader, Pedro Gandulfo Guerra, apparently resorted to a more serious measure; he fired three shots from a pistol toward the clamoring crowd outside. No one was injured. (Gandulfo eventually was captured, arrested, and jailed on charges of firing his weapon and trespassing after he leaped onto the roof of a neighboring house owned by Arturo Lyon of the Lyon clan, a wealthy family of French descent.)[23]

Angered by the FECh members' actions, the defenders of Don Ladislao's War stormed the locale. Furniture, books, and other items were thrown into the street before police arrived. It was reported in *El Mercurio*, which had criticized the FECh on previous occasions, that two portraits—one of the Peruvian president, the other of Leon Trotsky—had been found inside the headquarters after police ended the brouhaha, demonstrating in an unambiguous manner the FECh's negative intentions.[24] FECh members later complained that certain important books were intentionally destroyed. Alfredo De María, the federation's president, reflected on the incident days later in a statement to union members: "What does the material death of the federation matter if its idealist spirit survives among you, my beloved comrades? What does the persecution, the calamity, the injustice and jail matter to us, the students, while we can count on the confidence of the proletariat?"[25] Members of the FECh soon took to the streets to protest the attack on their headquarters and the Chilean military's mobilization. A day of violence in the capital had only just begun.

Eight hours after the assault on FECh headquarters, Julio Covarrubias Freire, a twenty-four-year-old army reservist, died on a sidewalk outside the Military Club in downtown Santiago from a single gunshot wound to the heart. He had been the flag bearer of another group of youths parading in favor of Don Ladislao's War. The gunman was Carlos López Marchant, possibly an anarchist student, who was arrested by police soon after the incident.[26] In the days after Covarrubias's death, nationalists of both the UN and the reformist AL lashed out against "antipatriotism" and the alleged revolutionary and anarchistic activities of some university students. The AL, however, was quick to criticize the Sanfuentes government for creating an Inquisition-like political environment and for fanning the flames of reaction in a presidential election season.

Nationalists of conservative and progressive inclinations complained in the press that Covarrubias's murder and student involvement in the protests of July 21 illustrated the fundamental lack of sentiments of *chilenidad* among many *santiaguino* youths. The conservative and clericalist *El Diario Ilustrado* described Covarrubias's death as "the first blood" in a violent struggle against the forces of revolution. Commenting on the tensions on the Bolivian border that led to the ruckus in the downtown area, one editorial writer blamed Chile's public education system for the nation's ideological maladies. "Blood has been spilled as a result of old disputes with Peru [he uses "Peru" to denote Peru and Bolivia, as if Bolivia retained the name "Upper Peru" from the colonial period]; the victim is Julio Covarrubias Freire and the culprit another Chilean, a student," he said. "To see that an antipatriotic virus has infiltrated our secondary schools and the university [the University of Chile], that thousands of young people do not love their *patria*, and that fanaticism has reached the point of assassinating the bearer of the national flag, quivers of horror run through the body."[27] Don Ladislao himself also spoke out on the Covarrubias case, stating that the youth was "treacherously assassinated" and that the young man died "in defense of that noble sentiment, love for the *patria*, so profoundly rooted in the bosoms of our fellow citizens."[28] In addition, an editorial in the July 22 edition of *El Diario Ilustrado* indicated that Chile was in dire need of a "prophylactic" to protect against harmful foreign viruses. "The carriers of the microbes [revolutionary ideas] are the foreign propagandists: Russians and Peruvians, Argentines and Peruvians, Spanish and Peruvians, all the nationalities and Peruvians. Not to mention the IWW [the anarchist Industrial Workers of the World], the organization kicked out of the United States . . . and that comes to set up shop in Santiago," the writer warned.[29] Moreover, in the political climate of an election year, UN supporters simply could not resist implicating the AL as a contributor to the unrest. Former president and Nationalist Union member Germán Riesco Errázuriz, in a statement that reflects deep resentment toward the AL, suggests that reformers were allies of revolutionaries by noting that "the names Gandulfo [the FECh pistoleer] and Alessandri are mentioned in the same phrase; that is why they [antigovernment demonstrators] voiced their support for this candidate after committing the homicide [of Covarrubias]; and that is why they chose the Radical Club as a meeting place before the blow."[30] UN supporters, moreover, added the Masons to their list of culprits.[31]

The reformist press also addressed the events of July with an antirevolutionary tone.[32] *La Nación*, a voice of Alessandri's dissident Liberals and the AL, called the Covarrubias murder a symptom of an "antipatriotic illness" and lamented that antipatriotism "is a sickness of this century and perhaps the most salient symptom of the decline of the Latin races."[33] But reformers quickly responded to UN supporters who suggested that Radicals and Masons backed the rebellious students. Such insinuations in the UNista press, *La Nación* observed, represented a "voice of division" that "goes directly against patriotism and [the nation's] most sacred interests." It also stated, in a defiant tone, that "martyrs like Julio Covarrubias are not emblems of division, but are emblems of unity and glory for all of the sons of our people."[34]

La Nación also criticized the state for the heavy-handed tactics it used to control street demonstrations. It described the plight of former FECh president Pedro León Loyola Leyton, a professor at both the National Institute and the Pedagogical Institute, who was assaulted and arrested by police for no apparent reason during a large "revolutionary" protest organized by workers and students on June 27. Ironically, Loyola Leyton had abandoned all ties to the FECh in 1919 after being alarmed by its "extremism."[35] *La Nación* scorned the Sanfuentes government for infringing upon the bystander's "public liberties" and called police actions in the wake of the Covarrubias murder "arbitrary" and rife with "abuses of power."[36] Another observer reacting to the maltreatment of protesters following the Covarrubias murder stated in *La Nación*, "The action of the government [of Sanfuentes] and that of the leaders of the parties seems to be fatally oriented toward the provocation of the dissociation of the distinct elements of the country. . . . One does not see the conciliatory hand nor does one hear the voice of tranquillity and peace, which bring the fortitude to weigh this grave moment in which we find ourselves and the necessity to prepare ourselves in a fraternal way to go forward from this stage in our national life. . . . At this time, patriotism imposes duties upon us that no one may excuse themselves from carrying out."[37] Reformers also took more practical and symbolic steps to distance themselves from conservative nationalists. La Nación, for instance, organized a fund-raising drive to help rebuild the FECh headquarters. Within a week, the newspaper had received some 1,000 pesos, including a check for 100 pesos from PR member and the up-and-coming writer Joaquín Edwards Bello.[38] All the while, however, reformers were concerned about the germination of revolutionary sympathies within the FECh and kept a careful eye on the group, though they certainly did not share the rancor of Parliamentary Republic traditionalists.[39]

The political firefight between the AL and the UN over the Covarrubias case left the FECh complaining that the government and the opposition had lost sight of the true victim of the July 21 unrest. De María, FECh president and medical student at the University of Chile, claimed that his union, not Covarrubias, was the most notable casualty. De María also denied allegations that his organization fanned the flames of antipatriotism. He instead argued that patriotism (perhaps in the way Recabarren understood it?) was a strong and widely shared sentiment among students.[40] However, La Nación published a FECh manifesto, coupled with commentary from Guillermo Subercaseaux, university professor, former member of the UNA/PN, AL supporter, and soon-to-be minister of finance under Alessandri, to counter De María's assertion that the FECh was an innocent and patriotic organization. The manifesto, dated June 24, reads: "[The FECh] believes that one of the primary causes of international conflicts is the current social organization of states based on capitalism, and it would be very difficult to achieve universal peace while the forces of production are not socialized and are not organized internationally." Subercaseaux commented that sovereignty is the basis of all nations and that "the idea of patria is sacred for today's peoples." He then labeled radicalized students as "petulant" youths drunk with the "fantasies of communism."[41]

Despite the fact that reformers expressed concern and condolence over Covarrubias's murder, it is clear that conservative nationalists sought to claim the young man as their exclusive martyr. But by late September, the reformist press was drawing attention to another victim of the unrest, Domingo Gómez Rojas, who became a martyr of progressive nationalists.

Gómez was a second-year law student at the University of Chile, member of the FECh, a poet, member of the PR, and a participant in the Radical Propaganda Center and was also taking a course at the Pedagogical Institute.[42] During the week of July 20, police arrested Gómez for his alleged participation in the antigovernment demonstrations that shook Santiago. Under suspicion for being a member of the IWW, he languished in jail for two months—with little food, according to reports—until he contracted meningitis and died on September 29. What followed were outcries from reformers who viewed the Sanfuentes administration's response to the demonstrations as brutal and excessive.

The pro-AL *La Nación* condemned the government's comportment in the Gómez case, expressed emotional praise for the deceased student, and denied the police's claim that the young Radical was involved in revolutionary activities and public demonstrations. "Writer, orator, and poet, he never towed the subversive line. It was bad luck to have found himself having lunch at the federation's headquarters on the day of its assault, of which he was a victim," one columnist wrote, noting that Gómez suffered a bout of hysteria during his unjust incarceration.[43] While praising the government's stance against "foreign spies who continue breathing among us," the newspaper also criticized the Sanfuentes administration for continuing to detain Chilean citizens with cases similar to that of Gómez.[44] In addition, the Radical Assembly of Santiago, under its president, Aguirre Cerda, issued a strongly worded resolution in response to Gómez's death. "The Radical Assembly of Santiago, upon the death of the *correligionario* Domingo Gómez Rojas, caused by the poor treatment of which he was a victim in jail, resolves to point out, in front of the country, the cowardly way in which the oligarchy conducts itself against citizens who have the courage to express their progressive ideas."[45] The conservative press, meanwhile, remained unremarkably subdued regarding the Gómez matter.

As noted above, *El Diario Ilustrado* accompanied its appraisal of the Santiago situation with an indictment of public education. The events of July, UNistas believed, demonstrated that public schools, especially the *liceos*, had failed the country by not graduating students with heightened sentiments of nationality. Accordingly, wayward youths increasingly had embraced revolutionary ideas and contributed to such grave happenings as the death of Covarrubias, a graduate of the Pontifical Catholic University. This assessment was a thinly veiled denunciation of reformist mesocrats, given that traditionalists understood that public schooling was, in general, controlled by Radicals and other progressive interests with ties to the AL. By pointing out public education's failure to produce citizens imbued with nationalism, UN proponents indirectly questioned the nationalist conviction of their electoral rivals.

Reformers, too, drew attention to the relationship between education and nationalism but did not blame public instruction—their cultural domain—for the tumult of July. Instead, reformers adopted a more proactive stance. The most eloquent statement on this matter appeared in *La Nación* on July 24. An editorial writer argued that "the necessity to educate the spirit of the new generations about the most pure sentiments of *patria* and civic conscience" beckoned government initiatives for the "renovation of these great and ancient virtues that have gradually been becoming weak during thirty years of absolute peace and relative prosperity." He added, "We need to finally counteract, with arguments and reason, never with violent acts, the pernicious propaganda of those few elements who exaggerate amongst themselves with their loud uproars while the great mass of our citizens is patriotic and calm."[46] Reformers essentially believed the state could do more regarding the pedagogical application of nationalism, and the newspaper gives the impression that all Chileans, not just the working class, would benefit from the amplification of nationalist teachings. Moreover, *La Nación* once again condemned "violent acts" such as the assault on the FECh's headquarters by young conservatives and the government's implicit approval of police crackdowns on protesters. At the same time, the newspaper demonstrated the antirevolutionary sensibility that typified reformist discourse.

In sum, responses articulated in the press regarding the civil unrest of mid-1920 demonstrate that conservative and progressive nationalists, UNistas and AL reformers, were embroiled in a heated conflict over political power. Conservative and progressive nationalists agreed that the revolutionary impulse needed to be curtailed and that schools should convey a nationalist ethos, but each questioned the other's commitment to the *patria*. Conservative nationalists blamed progressive nationalists, especially Radicals, for tacitly supporting revolutionary interests and for contributing to the youthful fanaticism that led to the killing of Julio Covarrubias. Progressive nationalists, in turn, contended that aggressive and intransigent traditionalists only made a bad situation worse. Regardless of who was right, it is clear that nationalist reformers in positions of pedagogical and political influence assumed for themselves the task of devising a more nationalistic education system after complaints were aired about nationalism's frailty in schools.

Everyday Forms of Nationalist Instruction
under the Liberal Alliance

The events of July 1920 fueled a sense of urgency in the pedagogical sphere regarding the implementation of nationalist teachings. Although the idea of formulating a more nationalist education system at the turn of the century led to the adoption of civic education as a core secondary-level subject, few guidelines existed before 1920 that governed the most conspicuous mode of nationalist instruction: the theatrics of commemoration. In short, nationalist educators considered student participation in spectacles an integral part of nationalist indoctrination. The remainder of this chapter explores nationalist theatrics of commemoration and other forms of nationalist instruction in Chilean public schools from the late Parliamentary Republic through the FP presidency of Aguirre Cerda.

As we have seen, the Radical-dominated Public Instruction Council of the University of Chile adopted civic education as a core subject in 1912 after reformers, including many members of the AEN, convinced the council that a nationalist sensibility imparted through civic education would promote social peace and political stability. While reformers concentrated on civic education, the Ministry of Justice and Public Instruction, which controlled primary schooling, remained notably silent on the issue of nationalism's pedagogical importance for the bulk of the Parliamentary Republic. The only consequential decree before 1920 involving nationalist theatrics of commemoration was promulgated on May 21, 1909, the thirtieth anniversary of the Combate Naval de Iquique. All primary schools were ordered to celebrate, from then on, both May 21 and September 18 (Independence Day) by order of the president, Pedro Montt, and his minister of justice and public instruction, PR member Jorge Huneeus, brother of former minister Antonio Huneeus.[47] The decree also called for teachers and students to mark the occasions by embarking on "trips into the countryside" and "public acts," which were subject to ministerial approval.[48] No details regarding motives or ideological rationale were included in the ministry's decree.

Another significant guideline for activities thought to incite nationalism was not instituted until July 1920, at the onset of Don Ladislao's War. This time, the AL-controlled Chamber of Deputies—not the president or his Ministry of Justice and Public Instruction—took the lead. In late July, the Chamber voted on a bill (first introduced in January by Radical deputy Alejandro Rengifo) regarding a mandatory flag ceremony for Chile's schools. The measure, which was authored by the AEN, stipulated that directors of all public and private schools would "hoist the flag at their respective establishments at the start of the school day and lower it when the school day ends." This meaningful act, moreover, would take place in the presence of a school's student body. The measure also prohibited the use of the national flag and "civic emblems," portraits of heroes and presidents, and other items of national significance in houses of prostitution, places where illicit "meetings" took place, locations where alcoholic beverages were served and consumed, and in vehicles in which said libations were transported. Violators, the measure went on to state, would face a 10- to 200-peso fine or a jail sentence of no more than five days if the fine went unpaid.[49] After the AEN explained that the secular ritual would "inculcate youths with love for the *patria* and the belief that as long as they study, work, and develop themselves, they are cooperating in her enhancement," the Chamber unanimously passed the plan on July 29. It then received the support of the Senate. The first ceremonies took place on August 1.[50]

The AEN praised the law's passage and expressed faith that such daily ceremonies would advance nationalist sentiments among students. The association resolved that "all of the educators and all of the students should work for our flag, because neither age nor social position are obstacles to serving the *patria*. . . . This law marks the glorious beginning of the nationalization of our education system."[51] Minutes of the AEN's proceedings of August 1, moreover, record self-congratulations among members of the association for "having fought many years" for the infusion of nationalist elements into the curriculum.[52] Yet the AEN continued to harbor concern regarding nationalism's weak state in the public sphere. In a letter to President Alessandri dated September 29, 1921, the AEN complained, "There has been a profound collapse of our civil morality, manifested as a lack of appreciation for patriotic labor; for the indifference in which national traditions are maintained and continued." The organization explained, "It is vital to defend and maintain the idea of *patria*; a people may lose battles and provinces, and nevertheless rise again, but it has lost everything, and will never rise again, when it loses the sentiments that nurture its national soul." It went on to state: "We lack love for the institutions of the *patria* and respect for the constitution and its laws. The lack of democracy and of social justice in our hearts has, through ignorance or evil, allowed for the diffusion of ideas of dissolution that have substituted for noble affection for *patria* and family, to the point of forgetting what we should most love."[53] Alessandri took the AEN's plea seriously.

Little more than a year had passed since Don Ladislao's War when the Ministry of Justice and Public Instruction under President Alessandri promulgated the most detailed decree of its kind. On October 29, 1921, Minister Tomás Ramírez Frías, a dissident Liberal, issued Decree 5582, which established protocols for commemorations of "civic festivities" that intended to "stimulate the sentiment of nationality [*sentimiento patrio*] as a fundamental goal of education in establishments of public instruction." The decree, in its opening paragraph, ordered all teachers and students to participate in celebrations of national and nationalist importance. It then proclaimed:

> 2. On September 18, the students of public primary schools and *liceos* will convene to sing the national hymn, in Santiago at the foot of the monument to Bernardo O'Higgins; in Valparaíso at the monument to the navy; in provincial capitals, at sites that will be indicated by the provincial governors; and other communities and in the countryside, at places that will be indicated by the Visitor of Schools;
>
> 3. The students of these educational establishments will also make an annual visit with their teachers to monuments or to the tomb of the Heroes of the *Patria*, and an excursion to historic national sites that may be in close proximity;
>
> 4. Preference will be given to patriotic hymns and national hymns in general in musical instruction at said establishments.[54]

Such measures, the government later said, were necessary for the creation of a more harmonious society. The ministry, moreover, observed in 1922, "The flag's form, color, and movement [in the wind] awakens patriotism in the child. . . . Neither age nor social position are obstacles to serving the *patria*. Our flag is a symbol of what we are and what we want to be." It explained that the "government should soothe the discord between capital and labor, between the weak and the strong, between the individual and the corporation, between the poor and the rich. The government should give guarantees against all injustice for individuals as well as the collective; it should give a legal medicine for all ills."[55] Aguirre Cerda, then a senator, expressed a similar view in the reformist press by noting that the "man of labor indispensably needs order, justice, and respect for authority, and to contribute, along with the community, to the maintenance of those principles that are keys to national progress."[56] In short, reformist mesocrats of the AL believed that a pervasive sense of nationality and nationness, the legal protection of all citizens, and the steady evolution of institutions, rather than abrupt change, contributed to social justice and ensured tranquillity across class lines.

After the promulgation of Decree 5582 in 1921, a number of schools informed the Ministry of Justice and Public Instruction about scheduled patriotic celebrations and relayed plans for acts of "patriotic service." An August 1922 letter from the Liceo de Niñas No. 2 (Girls' Secondary School) of
Santiago asked the ministry to allow its students to host a celebration for
veterans of the War of the Pacific. Twenty-five teachers—all women—signed
the letter, hoping to give their students "an objective lesson about how one
should practice a real patriotism."[57] The Liceo de Niñas No. 12 of Talca
also asked permission from the ministry in 1922 for its participation in a
benevolence project to benefit War of the Pacific veterans. In Punta Arenas,
moreover, the Liceo de Niñas informed Minister Róbinson Peredes that it
planned a "patriotic evening" on Independence Day to satisfy Supreme Decree 5582. *Liceo* director Hilda Rojas stated in a memorandum that by bringing together parents, teachers, and students, the school would enhance "patriotic sentiments" in a region where "the great majority of pupils are
children of foreigners."[58]

The ministry undoubtedly was pleased to learn of the activities organized
by such schools as the Liceo de Niñas of Punta Arenas. Education officials,
however, learned that some schools, including the Liceo de Niñas of Valparaíso, the Liceo de Hombres (Boys' Secondary School) of Valparaíso, the
Liceo de Niñas of Viña del Mar, and the Commercial Institute of Valparaíso,
did not participate in the 1922 *dieciocho* ceremonies as stipulated in Decree
5582. The office of the regional intendant (or governor), a presidential appointee, headed a brief investigation into the matter. In the case of the Liceo
de Niñas of Valparaíso, an investigator found that administrators and teachers did not attend and did not require the participation of their students. In
a letter to the intendant, the school's director, Clara L. de Sanhueza, explained that teachers had a right to "enjoy their vacation" and take advantage of free time to "consult a doctor" or see to other necessities. The director, however, added that she asked both teachers and parents to participate
in future *dieciocho* commemorations. In the end, no educator at the *liceo* was
sanctioned, though the intendant's investigator, in a letter to the school's
director, affirmed, "This is, madam, all about a patriotic act, which has, as a
fundamental goal, the lifting up of the civic spirit of our youth, and the
director and the teachers of your establishment, without a doubt, should set
an example to students regarding the virtues that, unfortunately, seem to be
getting the cold shoulder in our *patria*."[59]

Backed by the reformist AEN, the Alessandri administration's promulgation of Decree 5582 underscored the high degree of importance given to

nationalism in the pedagogical sphere.[60] Subsequent governments upheld the decree and, at times, amplified its scope and substance. All the while, reformers, and especially Radicals, remained in positions of power and influence in the education bureaucracy. As Chilean democracy wavered after the military coup of September 1924, middle-class reformers continued to encourage methods to strengthen Chilean nationalism.

As we have seen, Alessandri returned from exile in March 1925 to resume his presidency and immediately went about the task of overseeing the creation of a new constitution. During his brief return to power, which spanned only eight months, Alessandri and his minister of justice and public instruction, José Maza Fernández, a dissident Liberal, approved funding for a *"fiesta pro-raza"* ("celebration in support of the race") in Santiago on May 21 to commemorate the Combate Naval de Iquique.[61] The fiesta drew students from the capital's primary schools and *liceos*, who gathered at 10 A.M. At 10:30 sharp, directors from each school gave an "invocation for the race," which professed the state's "faith" in the Chilean youths assembled for the commemoration. Forty-five minutes later, columns of students, all with flags in hand, paraded in front of President Alessandri, who observed the fiesta from a balcony of the University of Chile.[62] Unfortunately, ministerial archives and newspapers do not reveal the content of the invocation, which was devised by the Ministry of Hygiene. Yet the very name of the celebration—the *fiesta pro-raza*—suggests that a racial identity (perhaps inspired by Nicolás Palacios's *Raza chilena*) permeated the event, which, of course, commemorated Chile's battle against another "race." The government continued to laud Chile's racial fortitude after Alessandri's resignation in October. Balmacedist (Liberal-Democrat) Emiliano Figueroa Larraín, a consensus candidate of the Conservative, Liberal, and Radical parties, easily won a hastily called election and headed a civilian government until February 1927. While Figueroa's minister of the interior, Carlos Ibáñez del Campo, waited in the wings for the opportune moment to take power, the Education Ministry remained committed to the *fiesta pro-raza* and nationalist teachings in general.

Figueroa's minister of justice and public instruction, Oscar Fenner, a captain of the carabineros, found great value in the commemorations of the Combate Naval de Iquique, including the *fiesta pro-raza*. Emphasis on the naval battle quite obviously stressed the importance of Chile's military history and furthered the military's legitimacy. With the approval of Figueroa, Fenner issued uniform standards for the yearly celebration of May 21, though none was terribly new. In a memorandum to administrators and teachers, the ministry states, "The glorious date of May 21, already consecrated by tradition as a civic festival in which we celebrate the maximum sacrifice and the indomitable courage that the love for the *patria* awakens in its sons, has been chosen for the youth to give solemn homage to the heroes, to the race, and to the institutions of the republic." The memorandum goes on to explain, "The government therefore desires that, along with the celebrations of the Combate Naval de Iquique, children should remember not only the heroic manifestations of patriotism [such as Captain Arturo Prat's long-remembered death in the battle] but also their obligation to praise Chile and to satisfy their superior duties to the race and to the institutions of society. . . . And given that education is the most important medium for preparing the citizen for civilized forms of material and intellectual labor, it is logical to associate, in the spirit of the student, the supreme ideal of the *patria* and the sentiments that accompany efforts of personal interest."[63] Clearly, it was in the interests of both civilians and military officers to laud sentiments thought to buttress the "institutions of society" in light of the political situation. As we have seen, unions were gaining steam in the cities, union recruiters made their way into the countryside, and leftist political groups became more organized in the 1920s. In addition, it is fair to infer that civilians of the major political parties, who were concerned with the military's involvement in government, surely considered the Congress or the electoral system as prized "institutions of society." Officers like Ibáñez and Fenner, on the other hand, likely counted the army, navy, and the carabineros among the most important institutions of the republic.

Public Schooling, *Patria*, and "Antipatriotism": The Ibáñez Years

The Education Ministry of the Ibáñez regime, which succeeded the Figueroa experiment in 1927, continued in the tradition of previous administrations by promoting nationalism as a pedagogical tool. The Ibáñez years, however, witnessed a new approach by the state for ensuring the proper implementation of nationalist teachings. As nationwide scholastic celebrations of important events continued, the Ibáñez regime turned its attention to the teachers' corps and those whose nationalism the ministry questioned. Thus, the government increasingly sought to identify teachers suspected of possessing political loyalties it said were contrary to the principles of authority, order, and nationalism.

At the time, the Ibáñez presidency was the most impressive period of government-sponsored education reform since the Law of Obligatory Primary Instruction (it also saw the division of the Ministry of Justice and Public Instruction into two separate cabinet departments). The education budget grew markedly before the onset of the Great Depression (it doubled between 1925 and 1930), and the entire public education system was restructured to fit what Ibáñez deemed the needs of the nation. As part of Ibáñez's social legislation package, the government issued Supreme Decree 7500 in 1927, which overhauled the structure of primary education, wrested secondary instruction from the University of Chile, and adopted a theoretical approach to Chilean pedagogy much like that of Francisco A. Encina. Influenced by the ruminations of former UNA/PN member Luis Galdames, a teacher and graduate of the National Institute, the decree, its architects explained, contributed to "the development of high patriotic and nationalist spirits" and fortified the "virtues of our nationality."[64]

Supreme Decree 7500 dealt a blow to the "humanistic" educational philosophy of Valentín Letelier, which had lingered in Chilean pedagogical circles, by promoting "technical" (vocational) instruction to "maximize productive capacity." In an explanation of the state's new pedagogical approach, José Santos Salas, head of the newly formed Ministry of Public Education, observed:

> A youngster without spiritual perspective, deprived of virile enthusiasm and of a social spirit and a capability for action, has been the lamentable product of a ruined educational system based on outdated conceptions absolutely not attached to the necessities of the era and the imperatives of reality. These [previous] generations [of students], without ideals and efficacy, have been transformed . . . into parasitic elements of the country's economic life and factors in the moral decay within political institutions and administrative organs of the state. It can be affirmed that among the determinant causes of the national crisis . . . [are] the tendencies and systems of the old public instruction from which thousands of individuals poisoned with absurd intellectualism have emerged.[65]

The Ibáñez years, therefore, saw the institutionalization of nationalist ideas regarding "economic education" that had become quite influential in the pedagogical sphere since Encina published *Nuestra inferioridad económica* and *La educación económica y el liceo* more than a decade earlier.

Aside from attending to structural elements of the education system, the ministry also encouraged nationalism among school children through civic education and the theatrics of commemoration and by endorsing student-produced propaganda.[66] Throughout, the Ibáñez administration, through the Education Ministry's *Revista de Educación Primaria*, routinely defended nationalism's pedagogical application. In 1928, for example, one contributor to the journal explained, "The government, animated by profoundly patriotic sentiments, presides over a nationalist resurgence, for which we all yearn. Only in this way will the school create a generation of vigorous men who love honor, who rise above parasitism, who feel a duty to work and who will cooperate so as to propel the country down the real avenues of progress."[67] In the same edition, Ibáñez himself declared that his government's education agenda was "inspired by sentiments of human solidarity and the love for labor and the *patria*."[68]

On the issue of propaganda, the ministry gladly received monthly issues of *Armonía Escolar* (Scholastic harmony), a newsletter published by the Escuela Completa No. 2 (a joint primary and secondary school) of Quillota, a small inland town near Valparaíso. The publication, composed entirely by members of the school's all-female student body, debuted in September 1928. Its inaugural edition, which coincided with the *dieciocho* and sold for twenty centavos, is replete with prose that expresses love for, and adherence to, the *patria*. An essay written by student Aida Alarcón, for example, proclaimed, "*Patria!* Such a lovely name to the Chilean. . . . We, students, how can we demonstrate our love for the *patria*? By being studious, fulfilling the duties that our *patria* asks of us, and appreciating the favors it bestows on us." Another student, Mercedes Zamora, explained, "We consider our national hymn as a garden seeded with beautiful flowers which exude an exquisite perfume. . . . We should not permit anyone to spoil it, much less have it sung in inadequate places, because it is sacred and because it represents our *patria*."[69] In addition to such essays, the edition includes short, one-sentence passages on the bottom of each page, such as "To be a patriot is to be honorable, laborious, and virtuous"; "We shall honor the *patria* with actions and not words"; "A people are not great when its men are not honorable and laborious"; and "A student who since birth becomes accustomed to being loyal and austere, will be a good citizen and lover of his *patria*." When analyzed together, these essays and passages demonstrate that, at least by the late 1920s, students easily dealt with abstract concepts such as "*patria*" or "virtue" with remarkable ease and stylistic grace. The publication, moreover, reflects a certain hostility shared by reformers and traditionalists toward elements that seemingly threatened the *patria*.

The Ibáñez government undoubtedly found *Armonía Escolar* engaging. It was far less amused by signs that some teachers held ideas that, according to the regime, were decidedly anti-Chilean. The government therefore embarked on a campaign to root out teachers with questionable ideological orientations. In short, the Ibáñez regime employed an investigative apparatus never before seen in the pedagogical sphere and established a precedence upon which subsequent administrations based their efforts to uncover teachers whose loyalties were, according to numerous government documents, "contrary to public order."

On April 14, 1928, in the southern city of Angol, investigators searched the home of teachers Pedro Figueroa, Fernando Inapaimilia, Teodoro Cid, and Raúl Rettig under the authority of the regional governor, an Ibáñez appointee.[70] The instructors, the governor's office claimed, had engaged in promoting "the propaganda of the journal *Izquierda* ["The Left"], which is published in Buenos Aires" among their colleagues. Documents in the case underscored the fact that Inapaimilia was president of the local teachers' union and Figueroa served as secretary of the organization. Three days later, the governor, without consulting the Ministry of Public Education, suspended Inapaimilia, who was accused of selling ten editions of *Izquierda*, and Figueroa, who was charged with "threatening teachers who were testifying in the investigation," for engaging in "subversive activities." But after a subsequent investigation by the Education Ministry, both teachers were absolved and reinstated. In a letter to the minister, the regional office of education stated, "The innocent teachers have proven to us that they were not involved in any activity that may be characterized as subversive."[71]

Leading teachers' unions of the era also fell under ministerial scrutiny. In late 1928, for example, pro-Ibáñez *criollista* and education minister Eduardo Barrios sent a letter to provincial education directors and all public school teachers explaining that the government, in its effort to curtail "political action and proselytism," had stripped two major unions of their juridical personalities. Without furnishing many details, the ministry accused the General Association of Teachers (AGP) of "diverting the energies of [its members] to propaganda contrary to the principles of authority, order, and nationalism" and the National Society of Teachers (SNP), formerly headed by Aguirre Cerda, of working against "the principle of unity . . . that the government considers one of the fundamentals of the Reform [Supreme Decree 7500]."[72] In an effort to prevent any future infractions, Barrios explained that all "teachers in service to the state are prohibited from belonging to political parties and participating in struggles, polemics, and actions of social, political, or religious propaganda." Furthermore, the government made it illegal for teachers to become members of the aforementioned unions. As we shall see, Barrios's actions—though extraordinary at the time—were not unlike measures taken by the second Alessandri government, a decidedly more conservative administration than the Liberal's first presidency, to identify and punish teachers suspected of "dangerous" activities. While Ibáñez was placing restrictions on teacher conduct, the government also acted to instate hiring practices that it believed would further ensure nationalism's presence in the classroom.

In a move that addressed concern voiced by Eduardo de la Barra some three decades earlier, the ministry in April 1929 ordered that all teachers of Chilean history and geography in secondary schools were required to be Chilean nationals.[73] Although no data are available on the number of teachers affected by the directive, evidence suggests that those teachers who were unable to prove Chilean citizenship were either dismissed or transferred to posts involving other disciplines. The government concluded that foreign history and geography teachers could not be trusted with reproducing a vital ideological mortar: the national patrimony.

When assessing the nationalism of *ibañismo* during the years 1927–31, it becomes clear that the regime's education policies were cloaked in a nationalist rhetoric not unlike that of the AEN, Salas, or Alessandri. But liberal and reformist progressive nationalists, especially Radicals like the *criollista* Guillermo Labarca Hubertson, had little patience for Ibáñez's strong-arm tactics, which included crackdowns on unions (including the SNP and AGP), the stifling of party politics, the exiling of the dictator's political foes, the closure of newspapers, and the limiting of civil liberties.[74] It is important to note, however, that early in 1927 some Radicals tacitly supported the spirit of *ibañismo*. Luis Orrego Luco, in a letter to Aguirre Cerda, explained: "I, like you, believe that it is necessary to support Colonel Ibáñez and this sentiment is clearly indicated by the course our party has taken. It can't be that we are such boobs that we cry because the pious [the clericalist conservatives] and the Balmacedists are not in power, and because the financial hawks of the caliber of Alberto Edwards aren't in charge of the public treasury. It's better that way."[75] Although, in general terms, *ibañistas* and reformers employed— at least in the pedagogical sphere—a similar nationalist lexicon, their general political dispositions were notably dissimilar.

On the issue of government investigations of teachers and unions, reformers remained remarkably quiet. This, of course, comes as no surprise given the Ibáñez regime's propensity toward repression. But one must not, however, overlook the presence of antirevolutionary sympathies within the reformist camp as a reason for such silence. In fact, some reformers fueled the prevailing climate of inquisition by expressing impatience for "anti-patriotisms." Francisco Araya Bennett, a Radical and director of education for the province of Aconcagua, was one of the more outspoken nationalist educators during the Ibáñez regime. In an April 1928 article in *La Unión* of Valparaíso, a writer drew attention to Araya's establishment of "Navy Week" in all provincial schools (the week of May 21) and lauded his efforts to revive a nationalism, which "has declined in the school for various causes . . . that are on the minds of everyone: the confusion of party politics [a symptom of *"politiquería"*] and cosmopolitan communism."[76] The article takes a confrontational turn when it assigns blame for nationalism's debility. It blasts teachers who are politicized—such as those who serve on political party committees—and educators who are members of "corruptive political groups." The article ends by blessing Araya's move to fuse patriotism and education in Aconcagua Province, noting that all schools should be "formally and eminently patriotic, affirming nationalist ideals and nurturing patriotic sentiments in school youths."[77] Araya, like many reformers and traditionalists, feared certain consequences of rapid social change, which in early-twentieth-century Chile included the rise of a politicized urban working class. It is likely, too, that Araya witnessed the proliferation of working-class activism firsthand in his native city, Valparaíso, and thus came to believe that public schools could steer youngsters toward nationalism rather than internationalism ("communist cosmopolitanism").

The Great Depression, and especially its effects on Chile's nitrate exports and employment, brought down the Ibáñez regime. When Chilean democracy resurfaced in 1932, the second Alessandri government's approach to nationalism and education demonstrated a certain continuity that had much to do with the popularity of Marxist ideology and the political organizations professing it. In addition, until the PR split from Alessandri to join the FP, middle-class reformers retained positions of importance in the pedagogical establishment. As participants in the Alessandri administration and later as leaders of *frentismo*, these reformers sustained a hegemonic project that seemed fully realized with Aguirre Cerda's victory in 1938.

Alessandri, Nationalism, and Education in the 1930s

Alessandri's resounding victory in the presidential election of 1932 filled reformers with a certain nostalgia for days past. It had been a dozen years since the AL's momentous win over the UN, which signaled the mesocracy's arrival at the pinnacle of political power and the eventual collapse of *parlamentarismo*. But much had changed in Chile since 1920. The Communist Party had gained strength since its founding in 1922, the abbreviated Socialist Republic of 1932 had animated the Left in general, and the PL had refused after its bifurcation in the years before the 1920 election. Together with Conservatives and Radicals, Alessandri's Liberals put Chile back on the democratic road. Reformers, however, soon realized that their political fortunes lay down a different path than the *alessandristas* of the 1930s.

In the pedagogical sphere, the Alessandri government maintained the policies of its predecessors regarding nationalist theatrics of commemoration and civic education. Despite mounting concerns regarding the growth of organized communism and socialism and the continued expansion of urban unions in the late 1920s and early 1930s, the Alessandri administration remained in stasis regarding the further development of nationalist teachings for Chilean schools. It may very well be that Alessandri and his ministerial officials were content with decrees and protocols already in place, such as Decree 5582 of 1921, and thus saw no need for new directives.[78] A close inspection of ministerial records, however, reveals that the Alessandri government did, in fact, recognize the Left's mounting power. But instead of approaching the problem by way of amplifying nationalist instruction, it sought to locate "subversive" teachers who supposedly lacked the nationalist convictions necessary for carrying out the proper instruction of Chilean youngsters. For Alessandri, who used the well-armed members of his so-called Republican Militia to contain both leftists and rightists between 1933 and 1936, this was a more subtle way of combating his suspected enemies.

During the opening years of Alessandri's second administration, education minister Domingo Durán, a Radical and Mason, oversaw a bureaucracy that identified and investigated numerous teachers suspected of harboring "subversive," and certainly "antinationalist," ideas. When the PR split from *alessandrismo* to join Socialists and Communists in the FP in 1936, a bout of selective amnesia struck many Radicals. In the press, reformers joined with their *frentista* allies in attacks on Alessandri for ruining, or at least damaging, the careers of many fine "nationalist" educators. Teachers with suspected ties to the Communist Party, especially those associated with the newly founded and Communist-supported Federation of Teachers (Federación de Profesores), were the Alessandri administration's targets of choice in the 1930s. One of the more significant cases involved primary school teachers who attended the Federation of Teachers convention of 1933, which was held in the southern city of Concepción.[79] Some 160 educators who participated in the meeting were summarily dismissed from service by Alessandri's Education Ministry—headed by Durán—for entertaining what Alessandri himself later called a "communist ideology" that threatened "representative democracy."[80] Archival evidence, though sketchy, suggests that many of the teachers in question had earlier participated in a December 1932 strike in Concepción over the poor conditions of their respective schools and the government's failure to ameliorate them.[81]

In September 1936, amid the Radicals' official split from Alessandri, PR deputies Rudecindo Ortega and Fernando Maira met with the president with the hope of arranging the teachers' reinstatement. More than three years had passed since the mass firing, and dozens of teachers remained destitute. Alessandri steadfastly refused.[82] After noting that the fired teachers had demonstrated a political disposition "contrary to national interests and the well-being of all our citizens," the president reminded Ortega and Maira that "it was a Radical minister who, in accordance with these principles and reasons, adopted the course of action that you now ask me to suspend."[83] Unfazed by the apparent contradiction, Radicals, together with their new FP allies, assailed Alessandri for refusing to rehire teachers who always had maintained an "eminently democratic and nationalist" sensibility.[84] The newspaper *Frente Popular*, which had earlier attacked the Alessandri government for perpetuating a climate of "inquisition" in pedagogy (no doubt a reference to the president's clericalist supporters), lashed out against "feudal lords of the land" who ignored "a half-million children, who through their illiteracy pay their contribution to the ultramontane reaction."[85] It is important to note here that *Frente Popular* pointed to a connection between a properly conceived nationalism and antioligarchism by describing the teachers in question as "nationalists" while berating the forces of "ultramontane reaction." This was a central theme of the FP.

As the presidential election of 1938 drew nearer, the pedagogical application of nationalism became an important theme in the campaign of *alessandrista* candidate Gustavo Ross Santa María. Two months before the vote and sounding much like the AEN and reform-minded ministerial bureaucrats of the Parliamentary Republic, Ross told supporters at the Central Theater in Concepción (the host city of the much maligned Federation of Teachers convention in 1933), "We need to inject education with the sentiment of 'nation'; the systematic degeneration of the *patria*, of its institutions and its government, constitutes a widespread illness that is sapping the patriotism of our race [and] destroying the ties of social solidarity."[86] The conservative newspaper *El Diario Ilustrado* added, "Our education system requires a new road regarding its intellectual and moral aspects," and argued that a more nationalistic education system, aside from creating stronger social bonds, would free Chile from its "economic dependence" on foreign powers.[87] On the eve of the election, moreover, the *alessandrista* press praised Ross's *chilenidad* by noting that the former treasury minister "incarnates the characteristics of the race and has a profound love for that sublime mother we call the *patria*."[88]

By focusing attention on nationalism's supposed weakness in the educational sphere, the *alessandrista* camp indirectly questioned the nationalist convictions of reformers, who maintained a great deal of influence in the pedagogical complex during the previous decades. The UN, as discussed earlier, used this tactic to criticize reformist mesocrats of the AL at the height of Don Ladislao's War in July 1920. The Radical-led FP movement, in response to comments like those published in the *Diario Ilustrado*, warned that *alessandristas*, if elected, would instate an education system that was "hateful and sectarian." *Frente Popular* explained that such a negative and divisive pedagogical disposition would run "contrary to the national conscience" and lead to further "fanatical persecutions" of innocent teachers.[89] The war of words between *alessandristas* and *frentistas* did not end when votes finally were cast on October 25; what did end, however, was the *alessandristas*' hold on executive power. After Aguirre Cerda took office on Christmas Eve, the FP immediately went about assessing the pedagogical needs of the nation. Nationalism was identified as one such need. After a lull during the second Alessandri administration in terms of the formulation of guidelines for nationalist instruction, the Aguirre Cerda government moved to make nationalism—a progressive nationalism—a more conspicuous part of the education curriculum, but without its antirevolutionary edge owing to the coalition's composition.

The Popular Front and *Chilenidad* in the Classroom

In the minds of many, and middle-class reformers in particular, Aguirre Cerda's triumph over Ross—the candidate who *alessandristas* believed incarnated the "characteristics of the race"—represented a victory for Chile's only genuinely nationalist social, political, and cultural movement. That movement's nationalist core coalesced within Chile's mesocracy during the Parliamentary Republic, and those in it elaborated a nationalist imagination in literature and the pedagogical sphere that eschewed the elite's constructions of "nation" and culture. While the Chilean Left remained relatively disorganized and distant from cultural and political power before 1932, reformers had responded to the social question and the persistence of oligarchic power by disseminating a recast national identity through *criollismo*, spearheading a campaign for cultural democratization by way of obligatory primary education, and leading efforts to promote national solidarity through civic education and nationalist teachings in public classrooms. What became the "official nationalism" of the Aguirre Cerda presidency and the FP, then, was profoundly mesocratic in origin and resoundingly populistic, reformist, and "progressive."

With victory in hand, mesocrats immediately began to legitimize the FP's victory using the language of nationalism. One supporter, writing in the magazine *Zig-Zag*, pointed to Aguirre Cerda's personal characteristics that made the former civic education teacher, and not Ross, a Chilean archetype. "One of the major and most accentuated factors [that led] to the triumph of Don Pedro Aguirre Cerda was, without a doubt, the *chilenidad* of the Popular Front candidate, his defined nationality, so pure, so unchallenged," he said. "Don Pedro is the traditional Chilean, an archetype of our people. . . . He is the Chilean who loves his country and he showed it with his sacrifices as a teacher. . . . Chile is for Don Pedro an obsession. . . . Governed by him we will feel more Chilean, more attached to our land and our mountains. In his dark face [*cara morena*] and in his tense eyes, the people see and recognize themselves. . . . Chile is Don Pedro."[90] The article goes on to link Aguirre Cerda's *chilenidad* with imagery popularized by the short stories and novels of the *criollistas*. It notes, "It would not be strange to see spurs on Don Pedro—our Don Pedro. Don Pedro is Chile," and includes a photo of a *huaso* mounted on a horse.[91] Making citizens "feel more Chilean" became, as the excerpt above foretold, an imperative of the FP. Radicals at the helm of the Education Ministry renewed the state's commitment to nationalist teachings, while dramatically reducing—but not entirely eliminating—the climate of inquisition that characterized public education in the late 1920s and 1930s.

Within months of Aguirre Cerda's victory, education minister Rudecindo Ortega, a Radical and one of the Chamber deputies who in 1936 asked Alessandri to reinstate teachers fired for "subversive" activity, ordered the investigation of the "penetration of Hitlerism" in Chilean education. Ortega's move, which was endorsed by the *frentista* press, resulted in the closure of a small private primary school in Peñaflor, near the capital, where "enemies of Chile" supposedly disseminated Nazi propaganda.[92] Of most concern, however, were private schools operated by German immigrants or their descen-

Pedro Aguirre Cerda, the victorious presidential candidate of the Popular Front in 1938, is flanked by youths soon after the momentous election. His motto, "To govern is to educate," though first made popular among reformers by Valentín Letelier, became a hallmark of Aguirre Cerda's administration, which was cut short by his death in 1941. (Courtesy of the Consocio Periodístico, S.A. [Copesa], and *La Tercera*, Santiago)

dants in the southern provinces. *Frente Popular* warned of "anti-Chilean work that is done in the schools directed by Germans who are nothing but members of the Gestapo and take orders from Berlin."[93] *Frentismo's* virulent anti-Nazi discourse waned with the signing of the Nazi-Soviet Non-Aggression Pact in August 1939. However, the Ministry of the Interior, led by Radical and *criollista* Guillermo Labarca, continued to keep a close eye on Germans in the south and elsewhere. Provincial officials, for instance, were required to report the names and activities of local German families.[94] While *frentistas* warned of the pernicious activities of "anti-Chilean" Nazis, no reference was made to the country's own National Socialist Movement, which, in the heat of the 1938 presidential election, supported Aguirre Cerda and the FP over an *alessandrismo* tainted by the blood of the Social Security building incident on September 5. In general, the Aguirre Cerda government was not terribly preoccupied by subversion, relatively speaking. Its attention, it seems, was primarily fixed on the diffusion of nationalism in the pedagogical sphere as part of the administration's populistic and reformist agenda.

One of the Education Ministry's first moves to solidify nationalist instruction concentrated on a time-honored ritual: the singing of the national hymn. Citing that there existed a "virtual anarchy" throughout the country vis-à-vis variations in the hymn from school to school, the government acted in May 1939 to establish uniformity for the important rite. On the advice of director of primary education Luis Galdames (architect of the Ibáñez government's Supreme Decree 7500), the ministry established a national commission charged with developing one official version for the classroom and reviewing other patriotic songs that could be used. Commission members included the director of the National Conservatory of Music, the band director of the military, a teacher of pedagogy, a music teacher, and one teacher each from a secondary school and a normal school.[95] The commission's founding was a small, initial step in what became the most far-reaching state-sponsored campaign to fortify nationalism to that date. Two main elements of this campaign were the Defensa de la Raza y Aprovechamiento de Horas Libres (Defense of the Race and the Utilization of Free Time), established in 1939, and the aforementioned Plan de Chilenidad, which was promulgated by the Education Ministry in mid-1941.

As the reader will recall, early-twentieth-century reformers seeking to promote social stability and liberal democracy opened and supported night schools and popular libraries so that adults would have access to cultural resources. President Aguirre Cerda created the Defensa de la Raza in August 1939 with the same general intent.[96] The administration proclaimed that the organization would "cultivate in the conscience the value of 'nation' and of patriotic honor," and it defined the Defensa de la Raza as "a national organization, apolitical but eminently patriotic, with the principal mission of elevating the physical, moral, intellectual, and social coefficient of all Chileans."[97] Chaired by former military officer Humberto Donoso, the institution sought, in the words of one reformer, to correct "the negatives that were deteriorating the Chilean race."[98] Instead of returning home after a day at school or at work, members of working-class families were asked to meet at special centers established by Defensa de la Raza.[99] Branches were opened in Santiago, as well as in more remote locations, such as the El Teniente mine in the mountains southeast of the capital.[100] At such centers, participants could involve themselves in "friendly gatherings, physical exercise, conferences about hygiene and morals, and music." The centers, which were thought to possess educational value, thus gave the state yet another environment in which to "impregnate the soul with . . . more dignified, more noble emotions . . . for their [the workers'] physical and moral betterment."[101] Services at the centers, moreover, were rendered at no cost but were not "free"; participants were required not to engage in conversations about politics, world affairs, or religion.[102]

The Ministry of Public Education, though not the organization's designer, played a significant role in Defensa de la Raza activities that were thought to strengthen the "race" and nationalism. In May 1940, the organizers of Defensa de la Raza in Santiago asked the ministry to allow Defensa participants to join the capital's public school students at Plaza Bulnes to commemorate the Combate Naval de Iquique. In a letter to the minister, Donoso stated that the event would be "the first in a series of directed acts for the auspices of youth unity inspired by a healthy patriotism with high and noble ideals."[103] The call for a "healthy patriotism" was again made in December, when Donoso notified the ministry about how many teachers nationwide had either "forgotten" or "not used" the national flag on a regular basis, which was stipulated in a law passed by Congress in July 1920. Donoso called for a "crusade of rehabilitation and respect in support of this insignia" that had brought "so many glories" to the republic.[104]

Owing to its rhetoric of inclusion and national fraternity, Defensa de la Raza drew wide praise in *frentista* circles. Maximiliano Salas Marchán, a PR standout and former student of Aguirre Cerda, stated that the program reflected the president's "patriotic" commitment to "cementing the national greatness [and] the re-exaltation of public values."[105] The pro-Radical *La Hora* called Aguirre Cerda's initiative "beautiful and patriotic" and praised the leader for creating a program that "cares for and protects the moral and spiritual interests of the proletarian and middle classes."[106] *Frente Popular*, aligned with the coalition's left wing, also was a strong supporter of the president's project. One contributor observed that Defensa de la Raza reflected the fundamental ideals of *frentismo* by countering the effects of "one hundred years of oligarchic politics."[107] That same antioligarchic spirit inspired another contributor to *Frente Popular* to state: "Before [the FP], the Chilean flag was not of major significance to the Chilean people. The oligarchy, while it talked about nationalism and of national glories, sold the country to foreigners. That false nationalism was odious to the people. Now it is the people who vindicate nationalism for itself, the glories of the *patria*, its heroes, and the Chilean flag."[108]

As Defensa de la Raza centers opened their doors to the working class, the Education Ministry formulated the most significant measure in the area of nationalist instruction since Decree 5582 of 1921. In early 1941, the ministry began composing a plan to stimulate "Chileanness" in the classroom. Recognizing that "our pride as Chileans" had diminished since the heyday of nationalism when "Chile was, perhaps, the premier republic in South America," the government moved to consolidate previous nationalist directives and establish new guidelines in one swift blow supposedly to cure Chile's "anemic illness."[109] A major supporter of the idea of teaching *chilenidad* was the National Institute, which, since the early part of the century, had increasingly catered to the middle class.

In May, the school's *Boletín del Instituto Nacional*, directed by César Bunster, a PR member, textbook author, and Education Ministry bureaucrat, published an editorial that endorsed *chilenidad* as a pedagogical theme and gave examples of what it considered to be components of Chileanness. The journal explained that "*chilenidad* should be understood and defined in concrete terms. Chile, politically, is a territorial domain, a geographical concept. To Chileanize is to give a Chilean character to something, to impregnate it with Chilean custom. *Chilenidad* is the exaltation of the root of those customs, of those principles, of those foundations." It goes on to state that "Chile has symbols, institutions, and human values. Symbols, in a concrete way, represent even the most abstract of those principles: the hymn, the [national] shield, the flag."[110] Later in the same edition, the rural *zamacueca* folk dance is offered as an example of *chilenidad*. The journal hails the *zamacueca* as "the great organ of popular lyricism" that "awakens the fervor of the race" and proclaims it the "alma mater of our race."[111]

Leaders in higher education echoed the National Institute's endorsement of *chilenidad*'s educational value. The Commission of University Rectors informed the ministry in May 1941 as to its perception of *chilenidad*: "It is not enough [for any Chilean] to love the *patria*; one must feel the satisfaction, the pride of being a Chilean. To love the *patria*, one only needs to know our history. But if we want children of this land to feel the satisfaction of being Chilean, not only for what the nation has been but also for what it is, it is not enough to teach them the doings of our heroes, the glorious deeds of the past; they need something else: that all of them may live, materially and morally, in such conditions that life, for them, to a lesser or greater degree, is a joy.... We must, therefore, concern ourselves with improving the material conditions of the inhabitants of this country. Our standard of living is, shamefully, too low."[112] *Chilenidad*, the rectors essentially argued, was not merely a collection of emotions and passions but was tied to a political program to promote socioeconomic improvement among the lower classes. The letter clearly expresses the opinion that nationalism and reformism went hand in hand, as they had within middle-class circles since the late nineteenth century.

After months of preparation and anticipation, the Ministry of Public Education under Juan Antonio Iribarren, a Radical, introduced the Plan de Chilenidad (Supreme Decree 3791) on July 28, 1941. In the decree's preface, the ministry affirmed

> that the sentiment of *patria* figures among the most noble human sentiments . . . that it is an obligation of the government to stimulate love of the *patria* and its institutions, heroes, savants, artists, illustrious leaders, and even the beauty and wealth it boasts . . . that it is not enough to have patriotic sentiments, but it is necessary to show them in such ways as respect for national authorities, institutions, and symbols . . . that the national flag and hymn are the spiritual symbols *par excellence* that should be honored by all Chileans . . . that the true and rightly understood sentiment of *chilenidad* is incompatible with any other sentiment that makes the love of the *patria* an equal to sentiments felt for another nation or ideology . . . that the action of teachers in the diverse fields of public education constitute one of the elements of greatest importance in developing real spiritual values.[113]

The plan's architects, as this statement demonstrates, imagined a Chile in which nationalism, rather than "any other sentiments . . . for another nation or ideology," informed individual and collective action. But if we concur that nationalism is a political phenomenon, and, indeed, nationalisms are dimensions of political ideologies, then the Education Ministry established one official nationalism with one official ideology, that of liberal reformism.

The plan's guidelines were similar to those issued by previous governments. It ordered primary school students to "initiate their weekly tasks with a brief civic act devoted to emphasizing a name, deed or circumstance that lifts patriotic sentiments and develops among the students the pride of *chilenidad*." Such an act could include paying homage to Bernardo O'Higgins or a discussion concerning the heroism of Arturo Prat at the Combate Naval de Iquique. A related provision states that "all establishments of public education in the country will start and end each school session with a solemn act of homage to the flag" while accompanied by the singing of the national hymn. It also ordered schools to abstain from "exhibiting at public places, assembly halls, classrooms, cafeterias, dormitories or grounds foreign symbols, images or effigies." In addition, the plan prohibits that any foreign flags be flown or posted next to the Chilean flag. Furthermore, the ministry declared, "The directors and personnel of establishments of primary, secondary, and special public education, in harmony with the programs they develop and in accordance with the capacities of their students, will produce the greatest possible understanding of our great public men and of those who have had success in their labors and completed their duty."

Aside from expanding upon previous directives, the plan entailed the creation of a curriculum that centered on cultural aspects of *chilenidad*. The ministry's *Revista de Educación* announced a plan to teach Chilean folklore, a "true science" that "understands the manifestations of the popular spirit and all the characteristic forms of the people's life." Devised by educator and ministry official Dr. Gonzalo Latorre Salamanca (no apparent relation to the *criollista* Mariano Latorre), the pedagogical manifesto states with a populistic inflection that "the genius of a race, its creative capacity, artistic sensibility, and its psychological tendencies are only deeply understood when you look at the roots of the people's life and you study its principal forms of expression." The study of Chilean folklore, Latorre surmised, would therefore "accentuate the sentiment of *chilenidad*" through the exploration of "our old tales and traditions" as well as "games, myths, legends, sayings and proverbs, popular songs, and music." Latorre reasoned that "if education is to be considered the first and vital function of the community . . . the campaign to accentuate *chilenidad* should consider folklore as one of its allies with the most efficacy. The song, the game, the dance, the stories, etc. will be the natural roads [leading to an accentuated *chilenidad*] and are the methods most technically proper."[114]

The implementation of this folklore policy relied on the use of texts for classroom use that were chosen by the ministry. As Gonzalo Latorre states, "the new reading books and auxiliary texts that will need to replace the current ones to further the campaign of *chilenidad*" included *La Lola*, a legend about "the Atacama desert that shows the lives, superstitions, boldness, and adventurous spirit of our miners."[115] The worker, in short, was directly associated with *chilenidad*. Not only were texts chosen for students, but teachers also were given a list of recommended texts to further their knowledge of *chilenidad*. A list published in the *Revista de Educación Pública* includes *Panorama y color de Chile*, a 1939 anthology of short essays edited by Antonio

Rocco del Campo that portrays campesinos and their cultural traditions. A passage in the book by contributor Víctor Domingo Silva, a poet and Radical, concerns a rural celebration on Independence Day and a proud *huaso*: "Glory and happiness of September! The *guaso* even shined his best weapon and today he proudly shows it off in the tent put together in plain sun and in the open countryside."[116] In addition, a brief description of the *zamacueca* folk dance written by the *criollista* and PR member Joaquín Edwards Bello, celebrated author of *El roto* and *La chica del Crillón*, explains that "the *cueca* is intoxicating music and no criollo can listen to one without feeling inebriated."[117] Other titles on the list of useful books for teachers are *Cuentos chilenos* by Blanca Santa Cruz Ossa, *Cuentos populares chilenos* by Ramón Laval, and an assortment of publications from the Institute of Rural Information (Instituto de Información Campesina). Once teachers were fully educated on the intricacies of *chilenidad*, they were asked to lead discussions in their classroom on a variety of topics related to the concept. The "utilization" of folklore in education, the manifesto states, could take the form of an "hora del cuento" (story hour), an "hora de leyendas" (the hour of legends), or an "hora literaria" (literature hour) or could include having the children dress in the "typical clothes" of the nation. By engaging in these activities, teachers would be furthering a "culture that belongs to us all" and completing "a pleasant patriotic obligation."[118]

Naturally, Aguirre Cerda's closest supporters praised the Plan de Chilenidad. In its laudatory remarks about the program, the pro-Radical *La Hora* proclaimed that there was "no emotion higher or more dignified" than *chilenidad*.[119] A strong voice of approval also came from the AEN, which made sure to congratulate itself, as it did on previous occasions, for "maintaining and defending the ideal of *patria*" during the course of its existence.[120] The association credited Aguirre Cerda for calling on "all the sectors of public opinion to support the sentiment of *chilenidad* by way of a plan of vast proportions" and placed the responsibility for *chilenidad*'s ultimate fate on teachers.[121] Such endorsements reflected the profound importance that *frentistas*, and Radicals in particular, bestowed upon the pedagogical application of nationalism.

The plan also was warmly received at the lower end of the social spectrum, including by the workers at the El Teniente copper mine near Rancagua (owned by U.S.-based Braden Copper). In his brief discussion of the plan's influence at the enormous mine, Thomas Klubock shows that workers understood the populistic and anti-imperialist overtones of the *chilenidad* campaign to mean their genuine inclusion in a national and nationalist project.

As the miners' newspaper explained, it "is Chilenidad to go to union meetings, to help out in the resolution of our problems for the good of our class, to elevate our social, cultural and political economic level, and in order that indirectly and as a true support for Chilenidad, we should contribute to make Chile a country of freedom and respect, welfare, regrowth . . . a full and serene democracy."[122] But after the death of Aguirre Cerda, the miners accused the FP leadership (and President Juan Antonio Ríos, a Radical) of violating the spirit behind the *chilenidad* plan by increasing the price of wheat. The workers' union argued that the move went against the interests of the popular sectors and was an offense to the memory of Aguirre Cerda.[123] As the reader will recall, a somewhat similar instance of inconsistency existed in 1940 when *criollista* and interior minister Guillermo Labarca, a man who demonstrated a certain passion for his country's campesinos, ordered the carabineros to arrest any and all rural workers active in, or suspected of, revolutionary activity and unionization. Quite simply, it was becoming clear to workers that there were limits to their power and participation in the national community imagined by reformist mesocrats.

When considered in tandem, the Defensa de la Raza and the Plan de Chilenidad captured the basic tenets of reformism and certainly attracted the leftist element of the FP because of their inclusive and popular overtones, though the Left remained aware of *frentismo*'s programmatic boundaries set by Radical leaders. Both programs stressed the need for solidarity and democratization, accentuated the role of education in national life, and reiterated the importance of lower-class material conditions, traditions, and lifeways in the perpetuation of nationalism, *chilenidad*, and the *"raza chilena."* With Radicals in charge, notions of culture and "nation" fostered by middle-class reformers since the turn of the century essentially became axial components of Chile's "official nationalism" during the Aguirre Cerda years.

As we have seen, many reformers had exercised their cultural power in the pedagogical complex to promote their nationalist imagination during the half century before Radicals captured the presidency. They pursued cultural democratization by way of compulsory primary instruction, promoted civic education as a core subject at the *liceo* level, and were leading figures in the development of nationalist teachings in the public schools. In the literary sphere, as earlier chapters demonstrated, reform-minded participants in the *criollista* movement advanced progressive nationalist ideas as they eschewed elite-established parameters of "nation" and culture. Ties between *criollista* aestheticism and pedagogy are clearly seen in folklore instruction under the Plan de Chilenidad. The inclusion of Joaquín Edwards Bello in a suggested text, for example, indicates that nationalist reformers in education understood, or at least appreciated, the ideological weight of *criollismo* and the cultural capital of its crafters and integrated the genre's message into the official nationalism imparted in classrooms. It is not surprising, then, that *criollismo* and variants thereof also appeared in popular textbooks of the 1920s to 1940s, including a series titled *El lector chileno*, which was assembled and published by Manuel Guzmán Maturana, a teacher, member of the AEN, and Radical. Ministry-approved textbooks provided reformist mesocrats with yet another conduit for their nationalist imagination and stood as projections of their cultural political agenda and hegemonic impulse.

El niño ha de trabajar, de andar, de estudiar, de

ser fuerte, de ser hermoso.

José Martí, "A los niños que lean *La edad de oro*," 1889

The Three *Rs*

7

Readers, Representations, and Reformism

For any scholar interested in the history of ideas, a book's content is always easier to evaluate than its effects on readers. In the case of school textbooks (as well as novels, poems, and so forth), there is, simply put, no way to ascertain definitively the degree to which they have stirred ideological sentiments, including nationalism, in any society. But books imply reading, and reading connotes the internalization of images, perceptions, and sentiments. As Bourdieu and Passeron have observed, "because every pedagogic action that is exerted commands by definition a pedagogic authority, the pedagogic receivers are disposed from the onset to recognize the legitimacy of the information transmitted and the pedagogic authority of the pedagogic transmitters, hence to receive and internalize the message."[1] We have seen that acceptance of *criollismo*'s images, perceptions, and sentiments transformed political discourses and shaped the way many Chileans thought about themselves and their nation during the first half of the twentieth century. Thus, with certainty we may assume that textbooks, as well as other forms of nationalist instruction, influenced students in consequential ways. One need only recall our discussion of *Armonía Escolar*, published by the Escuela Completa No. 2 of Quillota in 1928, to emphasize nationalism's transference from the teacher to the taught. Of interest to us here, then, are those nationalist images, perceptions, and sentiments discernible in scholastic textbooks of the years following the Parliamentary Republic. By establishing the presence of themes and patterns in those textbooks, we may further our understanding of everyday forms of nationalism in a classroom environment largely molded by middle-class reformers as part of their ongoing effort to construct an ideological consensus among Chileans—a meeting of the minds with hegemonic ends.

In the United States during the late nineteenth and early twentieth centuries, as Gladys Wiggin tells us, nationalism constituted a prominent dimension of education, and authors of textbooks played a special role in nationalism's pedagogical manifestation by "creating images of America and the good American." These writers "have helped to enforce such national symbols as the flag, the Constitution and heroes. They have painted the ideal America and American partly through contrast with and comparison to other countries and peoples."[2] The central assumption of U.S. educators, then, was that nationalism needed to be constantly reproduced in the public classroom—the state's cultural domain—for the purpose of molding good citizens. Such was the general disposition of reformist mesocrats in Chile who, through the cultural conduits of textbooks, sought to diffuse and fortify the cardinal tenets of their nationalism and their ideas about culture in the public sphere. Like the *criollistas* in the literary realm, these educators perpetuated a national self-image with characteristics that supposedly identified proper citizenship and the authentic Chilean, and they put forth a contrasting collection of attributes that presumably negated national solidarity and *chilenidad*. Thus, whether in a modern nation with global power, such as the United States, or a modernizing nation on the outskirts of South America, educators valued nationalism's applicability and utility and considered the textbook an effective medium for its transmission.

A great variety of Chilean textbooks were employed in state-directed instruction during the 1920s and 1930s, when middle-class reformers maintained their hold on the pedagogical establishment and endeavored to actualize a hegemonic objective. In light of the amount of available material, what follows is not a scientific sampling of all the texts that circulated in Chilean schools but rather an examination of volumes that best demonstrate the nationalist discourse and ideological coaching orchestrated by reform-minded mesocrats in three pedagogical environments: adult night schools, *liceos*, and primary schools. During the period in question, all three settings underwent significant expansion, which necessitated the adoption of new reading materials. By way of allegories, anecdotes, essays, poems, and portrayals found in widely used textbooks, educators defined parameters of citizenship and fostered ideas about culture and "nation" that were reinforced by the Radical-led Popular Front (FP).

Night Schooling and Nationalism

In addition to the ongoing activities of private night schools, such as those founded by Radicals during the middle years of the Parliamentary Republic, the consolidation of state-directed night schooling for adults became an important ministerial pursuit in the 1920s and 1930s. As we have seen, reaching out to the culturally disenfranchised was cast as a nationalist campaign by reformist mesocrats who sought to mitigate the social question and explode elite-defined parameters of culture and "nation." They also believed that acculturation entailed more than building literacy skills or grasping basic academic knowledge; it involved the creation of upstanding citizens and ideal Chileans. Thus, nationalism not only constituted a high pedagogical priority in primary and secondary schools but also formed an integral part of adult education. The textbook *El lector del obrero chileno* (The Chilean worker's reader), a compilation of essays published in 1925, reflects nationalism's place in state-operated night schools for workers.

After Alessandri's brief return to the presidency ended with his second resignation in October 1925, a provisional government led by Luis Barros Borgoño (Alessandri's electoral foe in 1920 who later became the president's interior minister and vice president) warmly endorsed *El lector del obrero chileno*, a text compiled by schoolteachers Carlos Prado Martínez, who later became the director of secondary education during the final months of the Ibáñez regime, and Jenaro Torres for use in public night schools. As the government explained in its decree, the text was congruous with the "state's duty to contribute, by all means possible, to the diffusion of the concepts of moral health and civic education." A friend of the authors added in the prologue, "The sound mentality of each page shines to illuminate the mind and heart of our masses." In a short preface to their volume, the authors outline their motives for publishing a text for night schools. They complain that nocturnal instruction relied on texts approved for elementary schools and that such books were, in some cases, fifty years old. A newer and more appropriate text, they argue, was needed to address "the real necessities of the country" and convey to adults a better "comprehension regarding the ideals of the nation and the race." Prado and Torres then beckon all with "interest in the education of the people and the country's progress" to share in the "sound aims behind this book's conception."[3] What follows is an emotional (and somewhat backhanded) appeal to the text's intended audience.

The authors open by expressing their sympathies to the intended readership. Using the *vosotros* grammatical form, which relays respect, Prado and Torres tell readers they understand the "suffering" and "involuntary errors" of workers and that "you are our blood brothers of our heroic race, in a battle for life and for the happiness of the people we love, in a struggle for the enhancement of our beloved *patria*, in the effort to make it more prosperous and felicitous every day." The authors go on to explain, "We know your life from close up, we appreciate your qualities in all their valor, we comprehend your defects; because your suffering has made us suffer, because we have seen the immortal soul of our race in the noble traits of your heart, because we know your defects are born only as a result of a lack of adequate knowledge, of unawareness of healthy principles, and not of perverse inclinations, we publish this book with the hope that it will be your counselor, a sincere friend who only wants what is good for you."[4] With that said, the text proceeds to short essays on a wide range of topics. Interspersed among essays on milk, water, carpentry, agriculture, and history are passages regarding the idea of *patria*, the significance of the national flag, and qualities inherent in hard work. One arrives at the impression that "*patria*," the flag, patrimony, and labor are just as vital in life, and to life, as nourishment and shelter.

In the brief essay titled "La Patria," the authors inform workers that loving the *patria* entails "the love of our land that gave us life, the love of our families, the remembrance of our beloved dead, the cult of our heroes, our affection we feel toward our similarities that tightly unite us with the same language, by the same traditions, by the same beliefs, by the same aspirations for progress and perfection, and even by the same blood. The love of the *patria* informs all our acts, all our loves, all of the loves that should warm the human heart. It is one of the sweetest feelings, sweeter and more vigorous than any that have shook the human soul throughout time."[5] This appeal not only is made on the grounds of language, blood, and sentiment but also rests on the premise of family. Prado and Torres add that "the man who does not love his *patria* is a worthless individual; he is a much more worthless being than an ingrate who does not love his parents, his siblings, his companion in life, his children."[6] The nation, in short, is portrayed as the ultimate family unit and takes precedence over other forms of social organization. Of course, one's family is worth defending against any threat. The passage points to "foreigners" as dangerous actors that could possibly damage or destroy national unity, noting that love of the *patria* "obliges the people to rise up valiantly against foreign enslavers" of it.[7] In all, "La Patria" reflects the tremendous appeal of nationalist concepts and constructs that were circulating in the public sphere and within pedagogical circles during the Parliamentary Republic. "Progress," "blood" (or "*raza*"), and "*patria*" all were key components in the nationalist lexicon of liberal reformism; such terms denoted, at least among progressive nationalists, the inclusion, rather than exclusion, of "*el bajo pueblo*" in the imagined community.

The textbook's nationalist inclination also is evident in the essay "Nuestra Bandera" (Our flag), which hails the red, blue, and white symbol as one that "we gather around in the most solemn moments of the nation." The authors, in the spirit of the law passed in July 1920 that governed flag etiquette and Alessandri's Decree 5582 of 1921, declared that "she [the flag] is the image of the *patria*. When a soldier makes his way through the smoke on a battlefield, and comes across the flag, he exclaims 'Here is Chile!' The Chilean who crosses the oceans to arrive at places thousands of leagues from our country, to see our banner high atop our legation's building, yells with happiness and joy 'There is my *patria!*'"[8] They go on to describe how aspects of the flag represent distinguishing characteristics of the *patria*: red "indicates the intensity with which we should love Chile, our *patria* [and] its liberty, for which many heroes generously spilled their blood"; white "tells us to have pure and noble sentiments"; blue "is the color of our sky and signifies to us the ideals of moral and material progress"; and the white star, "the polar star of the south . . . indicates Chile's location at the extremity of the world."[9] The colors of the Chilean flag are recurring motifs in poems and essays in a multitude of textbooks from this period.

Aside from such essays with overtly nationalistic implications, the text subtly imparts a nationalist message in passages related to civic education, which, by the late 1920s, was firmly implanted into the required curriculum at the *liceo* level. A passage on government, for example, outlines the responsibilities of citizens (respect leaders, obey the law, and pay taxes) and the state's obligations to the governed (protection from foreign aggressors, domestic tranquillity, justice, education, public works, the protection of national industry, and the promotion of public health).[10] In addition, a poem by one José A. Soffia underscores "Los deberes del chileno," or the "Duties of a Chilean." Like other nationalistic poetry of this era, Soffia's piece describes with idealist overtones the physical landscape upon which Chileans have achieved greatness. The author writes:

In our beautiful *patria* there are no slaves!
A titanic legion of brave people
broke the servitude of their chains:
with blood in their veins
poured forth in harsh combat, our grandparents
the sacrosanct liberty they sealed,
and when they accomplished their magnanimous desires,
life, greatness, and *patria* they bequeathed us.

And across the Andes and the veiled ocean,
this happy *patria* lives enchanted
amidst the centuries-old forests
a hundred rivers like oceans
fertilize the countryside; beautiful flowers
carpet its expanses, and wherever
one looks he sees wonder, and the shining beauties
of an uninterrupted spring

In our blue sky, the red glow
glares off the sun; the white peaks
of the colossal Andes rise proudly.
Let the majestic brightness
of the evening star
flow brightly from the serene blue,
Immense in size, splendid in colors
you will see the radiance of the *tricolor* [the three-color flag]!

As this brilliant and pure *tricolor* is
formed by God himself, so is the future
that awaits the *patria*. In your hands,
virtuous citizens,
make haste. . . . In your daily work, give a noble example
of austere patriotism, and our land
will be a temple of grandiose liberty

Let no one in the *patria* be a vain member
rise to live the life of a citizen,
elevate the good and combat the bad.
If ingrate fortune
bears down on your life,
if the fierce storm rumbles angrily,

serene in danger lift your head high,
and if it is necessary to die, die like a man![11]

The poem essentially calls for workers to contribute to the "beautiful *patria*" by meeting the obligations of citizenship, appreciating Chile's geographic extravaganza, exhibiting a disciplined patriotism, coveting the flag, and dying, if need be, in defense of the nation. Workers, the poem suggests, are full members of the nation by virtue of being the posterity of heroic founders who freed Chile from the chains of Spanish colonialism. Readers, moreover, are told they are not slaves to anyone or anything; it may be inferred from this passage that Prado and Torres wish to convey the notion that workers are not slaves to their bosses, capitalism, and the bourgeoisie, as Recabarren and other Marxists of that era argued. Instead, the text hints that workers are to remain devoted to their labors because of their strong sense of nationalism.

Working-class adults enrolled in night schools learned from the text that they could contribute to the "beautiful *patria*" through dedicated labor, which stands as "a joy in and of itself."[12] The short essay titled "El amor al trabajo" (The love for work) makes a resounding call for a "happy" workplace: "The love of work is conducive to perfecting labors because it is known that we cannot have perfection until we are inclined to feel good about what we do. . . . The love of work often times transforms into a passion from which large fortunes and businesses are born."[13]

One gathers from "El amor al trabajo" and other elements of the volume that "love of work," coupled with "love of the *patria*," would contribute to social harmony and the material progress of all Chileans, including members of the lower classes. There is also the assertion that upward mobility is a possibility when one labors hard and well, though the impossibility of striking it rich must have crossed the readers' minds. Nevertheless, this text sought to convince workers that they were valued components of the imagined community, and thus *El lector del obrero chileno* is a significant example of how nationalism was applied in the classroom. The textbook's title yields its fundamental message; Prado and Torres tell the reader that workers are, first and foremost, Chilean—not members of a transnational labor corps with common origins, shared characteristics, a similar plight, and collective goals. They owe singular allegiance to the *patria* and, as members of the nation, must fulfill their obligation of dutiful labor. Nationalism instead of working-class internationalism (directed by Moscow or the Industrial Workers of the World) is the key theme. Allegiance and obligation are notions that also permeate state-approved textbooks that were read by primary and secondary students during the 1920s and 1930s, including books compiled by reformers Manuel Guzmán Maturana and César Bunster.

Pupils for the *Patria*

For obvious reasons, many more textbooks were developed for the primary and secondary levels of public instruction than were published for use in adult night schools. Among texts that were employed in primary and secondary education were sets of reading books with editions specifically designed for each grade level. Two of such series were *El lector chileno* (The Chilean reader), compiled by teacher and AEN member Manuel Guzmán Maturana, and *El niño chileno* (The Chilean child), published by Radical education bureaucrat César Bunster. Both collections enjoyed wide circulation during the immediate post-Parliamentary years and are representative of the types of reading materials that students used on a daily basis in the classroom and at home. They enforced images and ideas promoted by reform-minded nationalists in the pedagogical sphere, and, as we shall see, the rural aestheticism popularized by the *criollistas* constituted a conspicuous part of the nationalist imagination exposed in primary- and secondary-age textbooks.

Guzmán's long career as a textbook author began in 1905, with the appearance of the anthology *Primer libro de lectura para preparatoria* (First reading book for primary school), which established the basic structure he later employed in the *El lector chileno* series.[14] The *Primer libro de lectura para preparatoria* underwent an evolution in terms of content during its nearly three decades in print and demonstrates the steady infusion of *criollista*-inspired imagery into the classroom during the first half of the twentieth century. In a later edition of the text, for example, Guzmán included the short story "Las viviendas" (The dwellings; no author is cited), a *cuento* that tells of Jorge, a campesino boy who "prefers the goings-on of the countryside to the bustle of the city or the roar of the ocean" and ventures across the landscape on horseback. "The campos of green wheat look to him like an emerald rug," the story describes.[15] The essay "La labranza" (Farming) reinforces the rural aestheticism of "Las viviendas" by proclaiming, "What a beautiful countryside of farmlands!"[16]

The text also includes elements that later appeared in the *El lector chileno* series, such as the poem "¡Soy chileno!" (I am a Chilean!), which imparts the notion of self-sacrifice for the national good. The poem reads:

Where are you going?, said Fame
to Chile, and History said:
I will conquer glory;
I go where duty calls.

Far away . . . the ocean . . . I am a sailor!
And the mines? I am a miner!
And the fire engines? I am a fireman!
And the desert? It is my way.

And danger? I am a soldier!
And death? I am a Chilean!
I would die loyal and well
for my adored Chile![17]

The glory of the nation and Chile's historical destiny, the poem contends, rest on the shoulders of dutiful mariners, miners, and firemen (nonelite people, obviously), and youngsters should, someday as soldiers, be prepared to make the ultimate sacrifice for their "adored Chile" if dangerous circumstances demand it. Here, then, we see a populistic vision of Chile—democratized and inclusive. Moreover, mention of the desert (presumably the Norte Grande) and the additional reference to paying the ultimate sacrifice for the *patria* relate to the ongoing animosity between War of the Pacific combatants.

Considerable demand for the *Primer libro de lectura para preparatoria* apparently motivated the government to put Guzmán under contract to craft *El lector chileno*, a series that remained part of the official reading curriculum in Chilean schools into the 1960s.[18] The first book of *El lector chileno*, written for students in their second year of primary instruction, was published in 1929 and went through twelve more printings over the next twenty-one years. Guzmán then followed with texts for the third, fourth, fifth, and sixth years of primary instruction and the first, second, and third years of secondary schooling.

The second book of the *El lector chileno* series (for third-year primary students) communicates a nationalist sensibility by way of the poem "¡Soy chileno!" by Ismael Parraguez (the poem shares the same title as the one discussed above). This contribution to the text reflects two main aspects of progressive nationalist discourse—a mestizo identity (though the term never appears) and the embracing of the working classes as vital elements of the *patria*—that permeated middle-class circles during the early twentieth century. Parraguez's poem includes the verses:

> I am a Chilean! I base my glory
> in my warrior ancestry
> whose deeds history sings:
> the brave Indian and the Spaniard.
>
> If the enchantments of peace reflect
> over the countryside of my country,
> I work in the gold and silver mines,
> I sow, singing, seeds of wheat and corn. . . .
>
> And if the *patria* calls me to war,
> I throw down the sickle and pick up a gun.
> The [nitrate] pampa knows, the mountains know
> that victory follows me.
>
> I am a Chilean! If Chile is small,
> our men make it look large;
> through work we make it rich
> and our chests give it power.[19]

Here, again, we see references to the mixing of Araucanian and Spanish blood and the centrality of laboring Chileans (rural workers and miners) in the building of a strong *patria*. It is interesting to note yet another mention of war, which reflects the pervasive tension surrounding Chile's incorporation of the formerly Bolivian and Peruvian northern provinces in the late nineteenth century.

The same Guzmán text also includes an anonymous poem about the indigenous leader Lautaro, who "was as strong as an oak tree" and "was astute and intelligent like a fox" while defending his people against encroaching Spaniards during the Conquest.[20] Moreover, the short poem "Caupolicán" by renowned Nicaraguan poet Rubén Darío, who spent a great deal of time in Chile during the early years of the twentieth century, is in the same vein.[21] By drawing attention to Chile's valorous indigenous past—a consequential aspect of the nation's racial development—these selections point to the ongoing importance of ideas found not only in Ercilla's sixteenth-century *La Araucana* but also in Palacios's twentieth-century *Raza chilena*.

The *"raza"* motif appears quite clearly in the edition intended for sixth-year primary students. An essay titled "Voz de la raza" (Voice of the race) written by J. Gustavo Silva tells students to "listen to the voice of the *raza*, which imperiously strikes at your conscience and wants to stir the fiber of your spirit. . . . Listen!" Silva then explains that "two populations, two continents [Europe and South America], the people of two worlds, fusing they were, over centuries, to put into circulation a torrent of generous blood in your veins: blood of navigators and conquistadores, of brave *toquis* and *caciques* [indigenous leaders]; blood of heroes and of military commanders, who in Spain were called Don Pelayo and Rodrigo Díaz de Vivar, and in the forest of Arauco were called Colo-Colo, Caupolicán, and Lautaro. And your race emerged, inheritor of the virtues, of all the energies, of all the virile boldness of your progenitors."[22] Silva lists outstanding members of the *raza*, including Bernardo O'Higgins, Benjamín Vicuña Mackenna, José Victorino Lastarria, and Radical educator Valentín Letelier, whom children are told to venerate and study. Not surprisingly, all political figures and leading intellectuals listed by Silva, with the exception of President Manuel Montt, were foot soldiers of Chilean liberalism. Montt, who served from 1851 to 1861, may have been included in the passage for his criticisms of the Catholic Church. Along with Antonio Varas and other secular conservatives, Montt founded the National Party in 1857, which soon became known simply as the *montt-varista* party. Montt, moreover, was a proponent of state intervention in the economy and oversaw changes in the state's institutional structure that amplified the Congress's power in limited ways.

The cultivation of nationalism is also pursued by the poems "Los colores de la Bandera" (The colors of the flag) by future Nobel laureate Gabriela Mistral and "A la Bandera" (To the flag) by Manuel Magallanes Moure. Mistral's poem in the text for fourth-year primary students resonates with a racial identity and fortifies the flag's place in school-based theatrics of commemoration, which, at the time of the appearance of the Guzmán volume in which the poem is reproduced, constituted a central part of nationalism's pedagogical application:

CARDINAL [red]: Blood of my race,
coagulated on this sacred linen.
BLUE: Clear as an extended sky,
caring and sweet, like a robe.
WHITE: Garment of God, who has descended
to dress the naked Andes.

Child who reads, have you recognized me?
I am the *tricolor*! I am the flag![23]

Here, Mistral gives us yet another example of the importance of race in a Chilean identity championed by elements of a middle class to which the author belonged. The reader also will notice the presence of a religious motif in this poem—one that runs through most of Mistral's well-known short works. It was, of course, not the goal of reformers to rid Chile of religion and religiosity but rather to divorce the Catholic Church from major state affairs.[24] Thus, passing references to divine grace are periodically found in textbooks devised for public primary and secondary schools, though reformers clearly rejected any role for Catholicism in the general orientation and practical organization of schooling. Magallanes's poem, found in Guzmán's volume for fifth-year pupils, conveys an emotional message similar to Mistral's. An excerpt reads:

Noble and sacred symbol
which brings to memory
so many remembrances of glory
so much past greatness
when our gaze fixes
upon you, our courage
wakes and grows, and it appears
like a streak of heroism,
descending from heaven itself,
that trembles our souls.[25]

Together, the poems of Mistral and Magallanes stress the spirituality of the flag and the *patria* by using such words as "sacrosanct," "sacred," and "souls." Children were essentially advised to entertain intangible concepts symbolized by a tangible artifact: the flag.

The textbooks designed by Guzmán for use in primary schooling also include essays related to civic education, which was a required subject in the fifth and sixth years of *liceo* instruction. Youngsters were prepared for future civic education courses by such essays as "Soy ciudadano chileno" (I am a Chilean citizen), an anonymous contribution in his 1932 textbook for fourth-year elementary students. It reads: "Our *patria* is Chile. Here we have been born; here we have our parents, our siblings, our friends. The house in which we live, the school that educates us, the city that we inhabit, its buildings, its plazas, its gardens; all that is around us makes up our *patria*.

Chile, the *patria*, is the mother of all her children. Laws are wise advice that the *patria*, like a good mother, instills in all her citizens. We have been fortunate to be born in this beautiful land of Chile, and our greatest pride is to call ourselves Chilean citizens."[26] Obeying the law, the essay suggests, is akin to obeying one's mother (the *patria*), who always knows what is best for her child (the citizen). Guzmán's text for fifth-year primary students makes a similar correlation: "The child should have two loves above all other loves: his mother and his native people. . . . The *patria* is the greatest mother, the common mother of all Chileans."[27]

The value of proper citizenship is also stressed in Guzmán's text for sixth-year primary instruction, first published in 1931, which includes the poem "Deberes del chileno" by José A. Soffia, the very same selection that appeared in Prado and Torres's night school text *El lector del obrero chileno*. In addition, Guzmán incorporated the anonymous essay "La Patria" in the sixth-year text. It informs students that "love for the *patria* is composed of all of the affections of a good citizen: love for family and friends, love for society, love for the soil that saw our birth and that supported our first steps. . . . All honorable men should contribute to the progress of the *patria*." The essay explains that "the Chilean child proves his love for Chile and is a good citizen if he accomplishes all of his duties as a student." With a tone much like that of *El lector del obrero chileno*, "La Patria" continues by noting that "it does not matter what sort of work one does to serve the *patria*: it equally honors and extols the modest worker who helped build a house, the architect that thought up the plans or the owner who paid for its construction." Not all are honored and extolled, however. Some are afflicted with "laziness, vices, [and] bad habits. These men do not deserve to be Chilean citizens because they do not know how to love the *patria*."[28]

A place where the *patria*'s best traits were expressed was the countryside, or so Guzmán sought to convince readers of his textbooks. The short piece "El trabajador de los campos" (The worker of the countryside), an anonymous essay found in the 1932 volume for fifth-year primary students, promotes the valuable labor of rural Chileans with "valiant hearts." The essay exclaims: "Campesino of valor! Leave working with iron or inert stone to the workers of the cities. You work the live and fertile soil! . . . You give life to humanity!"[29] The same text includes a short story (no author cited) of the "honorable and just" *patrón* Don Francisco, who, despite the small size of his hacienda, paid his workers well and "attended to their needs." Don Francisco, the essay suggests, is an ideal landowner who does not rely on heavy-handed tactics to maintain order on his property but rather understands the reality of campesino life and addresses its necessities.[30] This story reminds one of "La señora," the *cuento* written by the *criollista* Federico Gana, which stresses the benevolence of the *patrona* and the devotion of the *huaso* Daniel Rubio. In essence, these stories expose a reformist sensibility by suggesting that problems in rural society—or society in general—could be resolved through the fair treatment of workers and mutual understanding between employer and employee, rather than repression or social revolution.

Social unity and nationalism also constituted underlying themes of the textbook series *El niño chileno*, which was compiled by César Bunster, a Radical who served as a visitor of schools under the Ibáñez regime and directed both the *Boletín del Instituto Nacional* and the government-sponsored *Revista de Educación* (formerly the *Revista de Educación Primaria*). A friend of Pedro Aguirre Cerda's, Bunster was a longtime employee of the National Institute and served as a high-ranking bureaucrat in the Ministry of Public Education during the early years of the FP.[31] In the 1930s, he published volumes for both the primary and secondary levels, and, like Guzmán's *El lector chileno*, volumes in *El niño chileno* were used in public schools well into the 1960s.

While serving in the ministry, Bunster published his only work not intended for a young audience, the brief *Reflexión sobre la inquietud actual* (1939). In this analysis of Chile's sociopolitical environment, Bunster addresses the need for "cultured souls" in an era marked by global uncertainty. With fascism on the rise and world war imminent, Bunster, like any good Radical, believed in striking a balance between liberal individualism and collective consciousness. He explains that "when our educational system is capable of creating fruitful individuals that act like vital forces for social cohabitation, the future will stop making us feel uncertain."[32] Clearly, creating "cultured souls" imbued with nationalism was a primary motive behind his *El niño chileno* series. Each text is an anthology of essays, stories, poems, and drawings that offers valuable insight into how students were exposed to images of Chile and the good Chilean on a regular basis in the public classroom. Bunster's 1931 volume for first-year *liceo* students, for example, includes the essay "Chile" by PR member Senator Alberto Cabero. It hails the country's majestic geology and topography, which has "given an energy, austerity, a tenacious motivation" to the Chilean people. Cabero praises the "pride of our race" and goes on to state, "The harmonious rhythm of the physical surroundings makes our ground a promised land. All that is remaining—capital, effort, and labor—is the work of the *raza*. Blessed be our land!"[33] The same text contains the poem "La tierra chilena" (Chilean land) by Mistral, who also praises the landscape's richness.[34]

Supplementing poems about Chile's physical singularities is "Voz de la Raza" by PR member Amanda Labarca Hubertson, who describes the genetic qualities of the nation. The essay, published in Bunster's 1934 text for third-year students at male secondary schools, suggests that students "ignore the discouraging teachers who preach the inferiority of your *patria* compared to the other American countries." Moreover, she explains: "Don't lend an ear to the preachers of pessimism. You know that your race carries the sign of superior destinies. It values itself for what it is, not for what it has. A homogeneous and strong race is yours. Blood of conquerors and the blood of indomitable fighters [Araucanian Indians] runs through your veins. Forged on the anvil of adversity and poverty, it is rigorous and brave. . . . Don't listen, youngster, to the discouraging speakers."[35] It remains unclear exactly who Amanda Labarca considers "preachers of pessimism" (revolutionaries or reactionaries, or both?), but the substance of her essay, like that of others published in Guzmán's and Bunster's textbooks, discloses an important characteristic of progressive nationalism. While reformers of the mesocracy openly identified apparent national maladies, they often maintained a characteristically positive outlook regarding the common Chilean, or at least the idea of the common Chilean. Amanda Labarca thus explains that the voices of Chile's mountains and oceans tell students to "have faith . . . for millions of years we have taken care of you, love us with constancy, love us with effort, love us with all of your intelligence and heart, love us triumphantly and the future shall be yours, oh child of the mountain and the sea!"[36]

Afflictions such as oligarchism and revolutionary thought, reformers believed, harmed an otherwise noble, unsullied, and conscientious community destined for greatness, and many mesocrats championed civic education as a vehicle for such greatness. Bunster conveys principles of civic education in the essay "El verdadero ciudadano" (The true citizen), which tells juvenile readers of an ideal child who "was a real citizen. He loved Chile above all else. . . . [He] felt a cherished satisfaction every time he finished good work; [he] respected the laws of his *patria* and obeyed the orders of his superiors. . . . He was always prepared to complete his duty." Such a child, the essay goes on to state, "never has an absurd remark on his lips."[37] If the essay points to a "real" citizen—one who respects law and order and puts the *patria* ahead of all other concerns—it, logically, suggests the existence of "unreal" citizens who fail to meet their civic responsibility and must not love the *patria*. In the volume's appendix, therefore, Bunster asks teachers to help create proper citizens by organizing "a club or society with the goal that children will become like the exemplary child discussed in the text."[38] In sum, "El verdadero ciudadano" is yet another example of how middle-class reformers subsumed the idea of "citizen" within a nationalistic construct of "Chilean" during the first half of the twentieth century.

Constructions of "Chilean" and *lo chileno*, as the reader will recall, were primary elements of literary *criollismo*, the fiction genre forged by middle-class intellectuals with largely reformist political sensibilities. Bunster, who recognized the literary importance of the *criollistas*, included in his texts short works (not necessarily along the *criollista* vein) written by Marta Brunet, Luis Durand, Joaquín Edwards Bello, Federico Gana, Guillermo Labarca Hubertson, Mariano Latorre, Baldomero Lillo, and Rafael Maluenda. Accompanying the contributions by these writers are poems, essays, and short stories by Víctor Domingo Silva, Diego Dublé Urrutia, Pablo Neruda, Gabriela Mistral, and others who were influenced to varying degrees by the *criollistas*. Although the many *criollista*-authored and *criollismo*-inspired works compiled by Bunster are too brief to relate the substance and ideological complexity of, say, *Zurzulita* or *La chica del Crillón*, they nevertheless convey a rural aestheticism that permeated the intellectual milieu of the middle class. That rural aestheticism—a component of an alternative nationalism—surely contributed to the shaping of a new Chilean self-image among young readers of textbooks in public schools.

The essay "Pascua chilena" (Chilean Christmas), by Edwards Bello, which is found in Bunster's 1933 textbook for students in their second year of secondary instruction, is an excellent example of *criollismo*'s place in public instruction.[39] It describes a scene in which campesinos enter Santiago to sell goods. As Edwards Bello describes, "the campo has set upon the capital; one becomes accustomed to seeing a *huaso* on horseback on the Alameda [Santiago's main avenue], as if he was a reprimand on this civilization of 'snobs.'"[40] Also present are *huasitas* (a gendered derivative of "*huaso*" used by the author to denote "campesinas"), including Chepita from Parral, who "has a red bow on her straw hat that provokes looks" from curious *santiaguinos*. Her attire, Edwards Bello explains, "is not the elegance of Paris, but the *chiquilla* [young girl] is rather noble."[41] Important here is that a woman, Chepita, is ascribed the "nobility" normally reserved for *huasos*—an intriguing sign that women had a place in the nation imagined by reformers.

The anonymous essay "Ranchos y rascacielos" (Thatched huts and sky scrapers), which appears in Bunster's volume first published in 1935 for sixth-year primary students, is another example of a contribution that instructs young readers about Chile's exemplary rural heritage. The piece establishes a direct link between rural society and national greatness by explaining that in the countryside of the late eighteenth and early nineteenth centuries "there began to form the Republic and the People of the future. From the *ranchos* emerged the men who fought for national ideals, for liberty, for independence, for progress, for civilization." Despite such valor, the essay notes, "today, in the large cities, who remembers those humble *ranchos* of the past, with their fragile walls that shook in the wind of the Cordillera [the Andes]?"[42] The author then seeks to impart the importance of the *ranchos* in the making of modern Chile: "When one thinks that skyscrapers are the descendants of *ranchos*, one cannot but contemplate with respect and admiration about the strength of our people, about the glory of our civilization, about the cities born in the *campos*, about the great united and free *patria*, working for the present and for the future. Each *rancho* that remains in our countryside is a small temple of the past; each skyscraper that rises over our streets is an altar to the future."[43] This passage not only underscores the symbolic importance of *lo rural* in the nationalist imagination of reformist mesocrats but also captures the impulse for progress (skyscrapers as altars to the future) that typified progressive nationalist discourse in early-twentieth-century Chile.

The textbooks examined in this chapter convey to readers images, symbols, and meanings that reinforced the cultural politics and nationalism of *criollistas* and reform-minded educators who sought to democratize culture, spread nationalism in the public sphere, and, by extension, realize a hegemonic project between revolution and reaction. Such texts divulge constructs of *patria* and *lo chileno* that suggested to both adults and children that they, regardless of socioeconomic status, were part of an imagined community based on notions of liberty, fraternity, equality, hard work, order, and progress and shared a patrimony that included a racial dimension. "Class," on the other hand, is a concept that remains without elaboration in these reading materials, though contributors to the texts certainly understood the importance of class in their rapidly changing country. Many contributors found imaginative ways to discuss society using other terms—"*raza*," "citizens," and so on—that did not necessarily carry with them a discursive imprint of the Left, as "class" did. This underscores the populistic principles of collectivity and solidarity, as well as the antirevolutionary sensibility, that permeated reformist discourse in pedagogy.

For reformers, texts such as *El lector del obrero chileno*, *El lector chileno*, and *El niño chileno* served a vital role as precipitators of consent, though it is impossible to gauge to what exact degree students incorporated and internalized the ideas and iconography in them. What is certain, however, is that these textbooks were read and, like examples of *criollismo* and nationalist curricula, became part of the everyday lives of thousands of Chileans during the twentieth century. Coincidence or not, the generation of young schoolchildren who read the above-mentioned texts in the 1930s, 1940s, and 1950s included many who went on to defend democratized notions of "nation" and culture in the 1960s and 1970s as part of Unidad Popular's *vía chilena al socialismo*. They spoke of the *patria*, of liberty, of solidarity. It must be pointed out, however, that many of the same generation also found discursive weight in such concepts when endorsing Popular Unity's toppling in September 1973 and the subsequent seventeen-year military regime. Indeed, among the dictatorship's most ardent supporters were members of the right-wing group Patria y Libertad.

Hay por delante una tarea ineludible de afirmación,

de saneamiento, de revaluación de las posibilidades

y excelencias de que está llena nuestra raza.

DOMINGO MELFI, *Indecisión y desengaño de la juventud, 1935*

Epilogue _____

An epilogue, rather than a conclusion, seemed most appropriate for this book, given that the middle-class reformist project examined in the preceding chapters was far from any conclusion in the early 1940s. The ideal epilogue, however, would extend hundreds of pages. It would, for example, address the evolution of reformist cultural politics from the Aguirre Cerda years through the Popular Unity (UP) era (1970–73) and beyond; follow the trajectories of progressive and conservative nationalisms in the public sphere into the latter decades of the century; explore the roots and manifestations of what may be called the "revolutionary nationalism" of the Left during 1960s and 1970s, including that of the UP and its leader, Salvador Allende; and assess the peculiar origin and cultural politics of reform Catholicism and the Christian Democrat Party.[1] But given the practical limitations of this narrative medium, I must leave such themes for another time or for other scholars. The objective here is to outline briefly the most consequential ideological aspects and long-term implications of the rise of Chile's middle class and the cultural politics and nationalist imagination of reformers.

Before proceeding further, the reader should be reminded that any study's periodization is, of course, an author's prerogative. This does not mean that periodizations should go without explanation and defense. In this case, the Parliamentary Republic—an era in which middle-class reformism became a formidable socioeconomic, political, and cultural force—constituted our starting point; the early 1940s seemed an appropriate terminus for two principal reasons. Of most significance was the reformist camp's capture of political primacy upon the victory of Aguirre Cerda, which inaugurated Radicalism's roughly thirteen-year control of La Moneda. Aguirre Cerda's government gave utmost attention to matters of public education and in mid-1941 promulgated the most comprehensive strategy for nationalist instruction to that date: the Plan de Chilenidad. Second, the early 1940s saw a steady decline in the production and popularity of *criollismo*, which had emerged during the Parliamentary Republic and may have reached its literary zenith with Edwards Bello's *La chica del Crillón* (1935). Although the most important examples of the naturalist genre were reprinted over the following decades, other intellectuals with differing literary tastes and strategies gradually eclipsed the aging *criollistas* in the cultural marketplace. The *criollista* Generation of 1900 and its neophytes gave way to the so-called Generation of 1938, an amalgam of fiction authors and poets that included Stella Corvalán, Juan Donoso, Nicomedes Guzmán, Nicanor Parra, Luis Merino Reyes, Gonzalo Rojas, Roque Esteban Scarpa, María Silva Ossa, and Volodia Teitelboim. The 1930s also saw the arrival of Pablo Neruda and Gabriela Mistral as prominent literary figures. Both went on to win the Nobel Prize. The writers of this post-*criollismo* generation were influenced by *criollismo*'s naturalist inclination toward the examination of society's underbelly but ventured beyond the genre's thematic and structural limits.

During the extended period covered in the preceding chapters, reformist mesocrats strove to implement an agenda of cultural politics framed by a nationalist discourse native to their class and Chile's troubled belle epoque. Their ideas about culture and "nation" were best expressed in literature and public education—in the colorful and somewhat tedious narratives of the *criollistas*, debates over obligatory primary instruction, pedagogical policies designed to stir nationalist sentiments, and ministry-approved textbooks that promoted a national and nationalist self-image in Chilean classrooms. In doing so, nationalist reformers demonstrated that they, like defenders of oligarchism and aristocratic hegemony, maintained a firmly antirevolutionary political disposition throughout the opening half of the twentieth century. At the same time, *criollistas* and progressive educators associated with, or with sympathies for, the organized political forces of reformism affirmed an antioligarchic program that gradually eroded the cultural and political joists of the elite's hegemony. Simply put, Chilean reformers asserted and applied their antirevolutionary and antioligarchic political schema in the cultural realm and forged a hegemonic project amid accelerated social, political, economic, and cultural change.

The reformist movement discussed in this book created lasting impressions on Chilean society, politics, culture, and institutions of the state. We have seen, for example, that conservative nationalists of the National Agricultural Society and the *alessandristas-rossistas* of the 1930s, as well as Marxists of the early Popular Front (FP) years, embraced images of rural life largely popularized and disseminated by the *criollistas*. These cases, as well as caricatures found in the satire magazine *Topaze* and in the propaganda of the National Socialist Movement, demonstrate the remarkable extent to which rural aestheticism had permeated the nation's political culture. In addition, the *huaso*'s "official" status as a national archetype during the Aguirre Cerda government (as seen, for example, in the pages of Carlos del Campo's *Huasos chilenos*, published in 1939 for the Ministry of Development's tourist bureau) further solidified the *criollista* vision's place in the public sphere. *Criollismo*, moreover, influenced the way many Chileans viewed their culture, as *zamacuecas* and rodeos became respected cultural practices in the minds of urban folks. Chilean *criollismo*'s idiosyncrasies notwithstanding, similar nativist and *costumbrista* (literally "customist") intellectual projects emerged in other Latin American nations during this era.

In the late nineteenth and early twentieth centuries, Chileans witnessed many of the same socioeconomic transformations that were experienced by other Latin Americans. As literature (be it newspapers, magazines, books, or *folletines*) became a highly visible and widely used means of communication between those sharing in an imagined community, Argentines, Bolivians, Brazilians, Peruvians, and others expressed their political and cultural concerns and hopes in both fiction and nonfiction. When comparing late-nineteenth- and early-twentieth-century intellectual movements in general terms, one finds that Chilean *criollismo* shares certain common characteristics with other literary/political trends, including Andean *indigenismo*, which sought to redefine "nation" by looking to the American Indian subject—his or her culture, history, economy, and society—cast aside during a century of postcolonial oppression. The Chilean *criollistas* likewise amplified a previously restricted concept of what was, and who were, considered elements of the *patria* by eschewing elite-generated constructions of nationhood. Some Brazilian intellectuals also sought the inclusion of marginalized populations under the rubric of "nation." Euclides da Cunha's classic *Os sertões* (1902), for instance, argues for the incorporation of the northeast region and its *sertanejos* (banditlike figures) into the imagined community, but only by way of a "civilizing" mission to stamp out backwardness. Furthermore, such notable writers as João Simonões Lopes Neto, the author of *Contos gauchescos* (1912) and *Lendas do sul* (1913), and Afonso Arinos (*Lendas e tradicões brasileiras*, 1917) entertained notions of cultural and national inclusion when discussing the gauchos of the pastoral southeast.

One finds important differences when comparing the Chilean and Argentine cases. Although the gaucho was first popularized as a folkish hero by José Hernández in his tragic epic *Martín Fierro* in the 1870s, the gaucho did not become a national symbol until the sight of immigrant hordes crashing ashore in Buenos Aires spawned nationalist fears after the turn of the century. With a largely reactionary and chauvinistic tone, Leopoldo Lugones, in his lectures on *Martín Fierro* at the capital's Odeón Theater that later formed his book *El payador* (1916), claimed the gaucho as a racial and cultural representative of an authentic Argentina that was progressively being debilitated by open immigration and liberalism in general. Since gauchos no longer roamed the pampas by the time the genre became popular during the first and second decades of the twentieth century, Lugones's *criollismo* did not seek to incorporate *existing* rural "others" into a more democratized vision of "nation." Instead, as a dualistic movement, early Argentine *criollismo* aimed either to alienate the immigrant or to establish a clearly defined pattern of what can be called "identity markers" that could be used by foreigners seeking social and cultural assimilation (Lugones preferred the former intent rather than the latter).[2] In addition, it is understandable that Argentine reformers did not entertain a nationalistic appreciation of their nation's gaucho heritage until later in the century because of the strong presence of immigrants in Argentina's Radical Party. Reformers, quite certainly, had no intention of alienating the many European-born immigrants in their ranks. In sum, Lugones simultaneously cast discursive stones at immigration policy, immigrants, and Argentine liberals who, in his assessment, were responsible for the decay of *argentinidad*. One area in which the Argentine and Chilean creolist movements demonstrate commonality is the issue of worker radicalism. During the first decades of the century, intellectuals from both countries—reformist mesocrats in Chile and conservatives in Argentina—entertained narrative strategies that (often subtly) criticized working class–based revolutionary ideologies. Andean *indigenismo*, in turn, was wed to social movements with revolutionary potential, such as Peru's American Revolutionary Popular Alliance (Alianza Popular Revolucionaria Ameri-

cana), which issued a program and disseminated a discourse based on concepts of economic, political, and social justice inspired by Marx.

While Lugones resurrected Hernández's tale of the gaucho Martín Fierro,
Da Cunha drew attention to the *sertanejos*, and the *indigenistas* offered alternative national projects in the Andes, many urban Chileans were drawn to
the *huaso* and today remain conscious of the figure and what he represents.
The term *"huaso"* is akin to "campesino" in contemporary Chile, but small
landowners of the Central Valley and more southern areas of the country are
also commonly referred to as, and call themselves, *huasos*. This occurs despite
the fact that *"huaso"* has not completely shed its original, nineteenth-century
connotation: bumpkin. The phrase *"huaso bruto"* (brutish *huaso*), for example, is sometimes employed when criticizing a person's lack of manners,
education, intelligence, and so on. But the *huaso* figure, though associated
with some negative traits, nevertheless evolved as an overwhelmingly positive construct in *criollismo* and popular culture. One writer was so enthused
by the cowboy legend that he went so far as to construct a history of the
"real" *huaso*, with his flamboyant dress and shining silver spurs—certainly a
far cry from the *inquilino* examined by traveler Claudio Gay or Chilean historian Mario Góngora. René León Echaiz wrote in 1955 that "with his *chamanto*
of vivid colors that fans out in the wind . . . the *huaso* constitutes an essential
element of the countryside. Common and typical in some regions, scarce in
some and unknown in others, he nonetheless is the absolute and total
Chilean. That is how they knew him long ago in colonial times, that is how
he lived during the confusing days of national independence and that is how
he is among us."[3] The ongoing magnetism of the *huaso* myth is considerable.

Los Adobes de Argomedo, a downtown Santiago restaurant with a countryside ambience, indulges its diners with a spectacle considered typically
chileno. Within the locale's whitewashed, mud-brick walls, dancers dressed as
huasos perform spirited *zamacueca* folk dances and proudly exclaim "¡Viva
Chile!" while waving the nation's flag. Los Adobes de Argomedo is but one
public forum at which *huaso* iconography is commodified and a ruralesque
cultural authenticity is defined and reproduced in contemporary Chile.
Each year, Las Condes, an upper-middle-class municipality of the capital,
sponsors a highly publicized week of festivities, *La Semana de Chilenidad*
(Chilenidad Week), to celebrate Independence Day. The municipality, which
is recognized as an important banking and commercial center, hosts a parade of *huasos* on horseback, and crowds flock to a rodeo to mark the week-
long, and sometimes inebriating, occasion. Las Condes mayor and recent

presidential candidate Joaquín Lavín of the conservative Independent Democratic Union (Unión Demócrata Independiente), rationalizing the juxtaposition of the "rural" and the "urban," explained in 1995, "It is our intention to bring the community closer to *huaso* traditions. We want the people to immerse themselves in the traditional values of the countryside."⁴ Although these examples may suggest that *huaso* imagery is confined to affluent venues, the cowboy legend is a mass phenomenon in popular culture. A more "popular" independence celebration held annually at O'Higgins Park in greater Santiago is strongly imbued with the *huaso* mystique and rural imagery. In fact, a celebrant may visit the park's Museum of the Chilean Huaso while eating empanadas (meat, cheese, or seafood turnovers so typical of Chilean "criollo" cuisine) purchased at a nearby stand.

In the 1970s and 1980s, the Pinochet dictatorship offered its own political interpretation of the *huaso* that, according to Mario Sznajder, underscored "values that supporters of the military government depict as an antique, fine, and transcendent rural culture that served as a basis for the establishment, stability, and growth of the Chilean Republic in the nineteenth century [based on Portalian constitutional authoritarianism]."⁵ But what of the origin of this more conservative and traditionalist understanding of the *huaso*? We may, perhaps, trace the *pinochetista* interpretation to the pages of *El Campesino* and Gustavo Ross Santa María's 1938 presidential campaign. Such wide incorporation and appeal of the *huaso* figure and the *criollista* vision stems from rural aestheticism's integration into Chilean cultural identity and the political discourses of the early twentieth century. The *huaso* mystique and nationalist representations of pastoral life persist in popular culture long after their principal instigators—middle-class reformers—failed to avert a revolutionary social rupture (and, accordingly, the sledgehammer of reaction). Indeed, the *huaso* character survives decades after the agrarian reforms of the 1960s and early 1970s and *pinochetista* agrarian commercialization of the 1980s, which together ended *inquilinaje* in the Chilean countryside.

In pedagogy, middle-class educators, using nationalism as their discursive anchor, campaigned for what became the Law of Obligatory Primary Instruction (1920), which extended public education's reach to tens of thousands of primary-age working-class children. Reformers who entertained Valentín Letelier's notion of a *socialismo de Estado* viewed the amplification of the state's role in culture as a positive step in the development of a modern country. They also were keenly aware that expanding the education bureaucracy augmented the power of the reformist movement (the dominant political constituency in the pedagogical establishment at that time), further eroded the cultural power of the elite, and served to mitigate revolutionary ideas and the social question, which they considered cultural problems as well as socioeconomic and political ones.

Angel Rama, when reflecting on the middle class and the expansion of public education during the late nineteenth and early twentieth centuries in Latin America, observes that nationalist "pride and education for everyone were causes that challenged the values—intellectual universalism and elite enrichment—characteristic of the period of modernization, but the goal was not to eliminate these values, only to complement them and create a broader social base for them. . . . In some ways, this was a democratic analogue of the much more elitist demands made by intellectual spokesmen years before." He goes on to state that this new nationalism did not "imply a precise ideological orientation" and "it served as a bulwark against both rapacious imperialism and poor immigrants, and tended to justify an indolent resistance to new ideas from outside the country."[6] Indeed, the champions of reformism in pedagogy did not eschew the fundamental underpinnings of capitalist modernization; they most certainly did not condone the return to premodern conditions. Yet, at the same time, nationalist reformers pursued a hegemonic project that, when compared with the aims and practices of oligarchs, represented a dramatic departure on social, political, and cultural fronts. Democratic it was; a mere analogue it was not. As we have seen, reform-minded mesocrats articulated a progressive nationalism in their debates and policies and were central figures in the promulgation of nationalist curricula that buttressed notions of *patria* and democracy in a conflictive social environment. Their project was undeniably nationalist in discourse and scope and corresponded to a distinct political ideology that permeated a great portion of the expanding middle class.

In 1920, the newspaper *La Nación*, a fervent supporter of the Liberal Alliance and presidential candidate Arturo Alessandri Palma, captured a primary theme of a mesocracy-contrived alternative nationalism in one short passage. A columnist told readers that nationalism was an absolute necessity in the "biological defense of the national organism against a corrosive that is beginning to harm its entrails" and that resolute sentiments of nationness and nationality affirmed the "moral vigor" of Chilean society and combated "doctrines that are considered dangerous." The newspaper essentially warned that pernicious political elements, if left unchecked, would rot the *patria* from the inside out. But in a departure from the rants and ravings of traditionalists, *La Nación* argued that nationalism, properly conceived, was conciliatory, just, and democratic. It stood in contrast to the ethic of "violent repression, which tends toward arbitrary behavior [and gives] more strength to antisocial ideas and sentiments."[7] To this core belief the *criollistas* and reformist educators added interpretations of "nation," nationness, and culture that, at least discursively, included lower-class Chileans in the imagined community. This study sought to demonstrate that the nationalist principles shared by such people as the contributor to *La Nación* noted above, the *criollistas*, and reformist educators were largely indigenous to a class constituency that tasted political power in the early 1920s and ultimately wrested it from an insistent oligarchy in 1938.

Although its members shared a well-defined socioeconomic layer and demonstrated similar cultural tastes, the ascending middle class certainly was not ideologically homogeneous. Radical-led reformism was but one option among many in a diversifying political arena, and it was not remarkable for early-twentieth-century middle-class Chileans to join the ranks of traditionalist Liberals, Catholic Conservatives, National Socialists, and Marxists. As the Radical Party (PR) declined in the 1950s and 1960s, many people of middle-class stock signed on to Christian Democracy, others to a reborn and populistic *ibañismo*, and still others to the Popular Action Front (Frente de Acción Popular, or FRAP) and UP, both Marxist-led coalitions. It remains clear, however, that reformism was the dominant ideological strain among middle-class Chileans during our period of interest; the cultural capital they amassed and utilized, their prevalence within the state bureaucracy, and Radicalism's electoral triumphs stand as testimonies to their power. The long-term importance of early-twentieth-century nationalist reformers, however, goes beyond the number and kinds of books they published, teaching positions they occupied, pedagogical ideas they entertained, ministerial appointments they enjoyed, or election results they celebrated.

Nationalist reformers of mesocratic origin and predilection, led by the writers, educators, and politicians examined in this study, were the principal contributors to the withering of the elite's political and cultural power during the late nineteenth and early twentieth centuries. As a movement that endeavored to alter cultural production and reproduction as well as extend the conceptual borders of "nation" beyond those drawn by the affluent few, middle-class reformism was a progressive alternative to the elite's hegemony before Socialists and Communists became consequential participants in party politics and affairs of state in the 1930s and 1940s. That is to say, nationalist reformers buttressed liberal democracy after the demise of the Portalian Republic and were leaders in the democratization of Chilean society and thus contributed to the eventual rise of other movements, including UP's "*vía chilena al socialismo*," by creating apertures never before seen in that country's body politic and cultural life. The parties of the Left availed themselves of those openings with the blessing of middle-class reformers (primarily during the very early phase of the *frentista* experiment) or without such support, which was most often the case. Reformers found it perfectly reasonable to limit the expression and actions of leftists when they deemed it necessary for the good of the *patria* and "their" class's interests. Of course, organized Marxist parties, mutual aid societies, and leaders such as Recabarren and Allende were the seminal forces in the emergence and success of the Left; they made the movement what it was. Yet, when assessing the coalescence of what became one of Latin America's most inspiring Marxist movements, the tremendous importance of reformist mesocrats in the creation of a "new" Chile in the twentieth century—one to which the Left certainly contributed and in which it proliferated—should not go unnoticed or understated.

In essence, then, UP's rise to power in 1970, which led to the polarization of Chile's political landscape between Left and Right, not only constitutes evidence of middle-class reformism's eventual demise but also may be seen as an indication of its legacy. PR-led reformism's significant role in the country's political and cultural evolution did not escape President Allende, a Mason and middle-class professional himself, who recognized the place of liberal reformers in the forging of a recognizably different Chile. In a 1971 interview with Régis Debray, the Socialist leader of UP explained, "All my uncles and my father were Radical Party militants at a time when being a Radical meant that one held advanced views. My grandfather founded the first lay school in Chile and his political views earned him the nickname of 'Red Allende.' . . . Since then, the family has maintained the tradition."[8]

Notes

Abbreviations

AN	National Archive (Archivo Nacional)
ARSC	Archive of Raúl Silva Castro (Archivo de Raúl Silva Castro)
ASXX	Archive of the Twentieth Century (Archivo del Siglo XX)
BN	National Library (Biblioteca Nacional)
CPAC	Pedro Aguirre Cerda Collection (Colección Pedro Aguirre Cerda)
MEP	Ministry of Public Education (Ministerio de Educación Pública)
MI	Ministry of the Interior (Ministerio del Interior)
MIP	Ministry of Public Instruction (Ministerio de Instrucción Pública)
MJ	Ministry of Justice (Ministerio de Justicia)
b.	Box
doc./docs.	Document/Documents
f.	Folder

Introduction

1. Rama, *Transculturación narrativa*, 15. Rama was referring to Latin America's middle classes in general.

2. Thompson, *Making of the English Working Class*, 9–10.

3. Ibid., 11.

4. Rama, *Literatura y clase social*, 10.

5. Forgacs and Nowell-Smith, *Antonio Gramsci*, 41.

6. Williams, *Marxism and Literature*, 75.

7. Early notions of hegemony are discussed in Perry Anderson, "The Antinomies of Antonio Gramsci," *New Left Review* 100 (November 1976–January 1977): 5–78.

8. Consult Gramsci, *Selections from the Prison Notebooks*. The Bolsheviks did not assign such consequence to culture in their formulation of hegemony.

9. Williams, *Marxism and Literature*, 112.

10. Ibid., 112–13. Williams adds that the "most interesting and difficult part of any

cultural analysis, in complex societies, is that which seeks to grasp the hegemonic in its active and formative but also its transformational processes."

11. Jay, *Marxism and Totality*, 165.

12. Carlos Silva Cruz, "El progreso de la cultura musical en Chile," *Revista de Educación Nacional* 11 (June–July 1915): 231, 233.

13. Altamirano and Sarlo, *Literatura/Sociedad*, 64.

14. Rama, *Lettered City*, 75.

15. Consult Simon Miller, "Urban Dreams and Rural Reality: Land and Landscape in English Culture, 1920–45," *Rural History* 6 (April 1995): 89–102. Also see Genet, *Rural Ireland, Real Ireland?*, and for Argentina, Prieto, *Discurso criollista*. In addition, Williams examines the complex relationship between rural and urban spheres in *Country and the City*.

16. Benedict Anderson convincingly argues that nations are "imagined communities" in which individuals and market conditions create and perpetuate a collective national consciousness. See Anderson, *Imagined Communities*.

17. Lowenthal, *Literature, Popular Culture, and Society*, xi, xv.

18. Randal Johnson, "Editor's Introduction: Pierre Bourdieu on Arts, Literature, and Culture," in Bourdieu, *Field of Cultural Production*, 12–13. See Goldmann, *Hidden God* and *Towards a Sociology of the Novel*.

19. Johnson, "Editor's Introduction," 12.

20. Forgacs and Nowell-Smith, *Antonio Gramsci*, 108.

21. Bernstein, *Class, Codes, and Control*, 3:158. Also consult Apple, *Ideology and Curriculum*, and Bourdieu and Passeron, *Reproduction*.

22. Hobsbawm, *Nations and Nationalism since 1780*, 91–92.

23. Pike, "Aspects of Class Relations in Chile," 17–18. Johnson, Pike, and other scholars interested in Latin American middle classes are also discussed in Parker, *Idea of the Middle Class*.

24. Pike, "Aspects of Class Relations in Chile," 22–23. Pike drew this conclusion after examining *El Mercurio*, which, as the journalistic organ of the Liberal Party, maintained a strongly oligarchic sensibility during the Parliamentary Republic. In addition, Pike's characterization of the middle class partly stems from his attention to the rather inconsequential Middle Class Federation (Federación de la Clase Media), which in 1919 put forth a platform that "although containing a mild warning to the oligarchy to refrain from some of its more notorious abuses said absolutely nothing about aiding the lower classes."

25. See Luis Ratinoff, "The New Urban Groups: The Middle Classes," in Lipset and Solari, *Elites in Latin America*, and José Nun, "A Latin American Phenomenon: The Middle-Class Military Coup," in Petras and Zeitlin, *Latin America*. See Parker, *Idea of the Middle Class*.

26. See, for example, Graciarena, *Poder y clases sociales*; Parker, *Idea of the Middle Class*, 3–5.

27. I use the term "Portalian Republic" to denote the period from the conservatives' final victory over the liberals in 1831 to the approval of a new constitution in 1891. The Portalian Republic may be divided into two periods: the conservative period (1831–61) and the liberal period (1861–91), which began with the election of Chile's first Liberal president, José Joaquín Pérez.

28. Among Barros Arana's major works are *Historia jeneral de Chile* and *Un decenio de la historia de Chile*.

29. See, for instance, Barría, *Breve historia del sindicalismo chileno*, *El movimiento obrero en Chile*, and *Los movimientos sociales de Chile desde 1910 hasta 1926*; Jobet, *Ensayo crítico del desarrollo económico-social de Chile* and *Luis Emilio Recabarren*; and Ramírez, *Historia del movimiento obrero en Chile*.

30. Aware of it or not, conservative historians, including Mario Góngora and Jaime Eyzaguirre, countered this historiographical current by focusing on a colonial past during which politically organized proletarians and Marxists were nowhere to be found. See Góngora, *Origen de los "inquilinos" de Chile central* and *Encomenderos y estancieros*, and Eyzaguirre, *Historia de Chile*.

31. See Salazar, *Labradores, peones y proletarios* and *Violencia política popular en "las grandes alamedas."*

32. Consult Halperin, *Nationalism and Communism in Chile*.

33. Solberg, *Immigration and Nationalism*, ix. This argument is also advanced in Houseman, "Chilean Nationalism."

34. Mallon develops the concept of "alternative nationalisms" in *Peasant and Nation*.

35. See Patricio Quiroga Zamora, "Dos casos del nacionalismo autoritario en Chile," *Documentos* 11 (1994): 1–70; Valdivia Ortiz de Zárate, "Camino al golpe," *Nacionalismo chileno en los años del Frente Popular*, and "Las nuevas voces del nacionalismo chileno: 1938–1942," *Boletín de Historia y Geografía* 10 (1993): 119–39.

36. Consult Hobsbawm, *Nations and Nationalism since 1780*.

Chapter 1

1. *El Diario Ilustrado*, November 28, 1908.

2. *La Lei*, September 18, 1903.

3. Collier, *Ideas and Politics of Chilean Independence*, 324.

4. Zeitlin, *Civil Wars in Chile*, 100.

5. Bauer, *Chilean Rural Society*, 152.

6. Zeitlin, *Civil Wars in Chile*, 84, 125.

7. Edwards, *Fronda aristocrática*, 181.

8. Pinto Lagarrigue, *Balmaceda y los gobiernos seudo-parlamentarios*, 26–27.

9. Loveman, *Chile*, 184.

10. Sociologist Maurice Zeitlin asserts that the civil war of 1891 was actually a "bourgeois revolution that never was" and that it was a conflict between a bourgeoisie seeking to bolster domestic industry and an oligarchy unwilling to do so. See Zeitlin, *Civil Wars in Chile*, 74, 89. Differing views are found in Encina, *Presidencia de Balmaceda*, and Heise, *Historia de Chile*.

11. *La Lei*, July 8, 1894.

12. Ibid., June 21, 1894.

13. Góngora, *Ensayo histórico*, 74–75.

14. Harold Blakemore, "From the War of the Pacific to 1930," in Bethell, *Chile since Independence*, 68; Scully, *Rethinking the Center*, 47; Valenzuela, *Political Brokers in Chile*, 202. García counts 121 different cabinets and 530 ministers for the period 1891 to 1920. García, *Partido Radical y la clase media*, 32.

15. Loveman, *Chile*, 194.

16. Drake, *Socialism and Populism in Chile*, 101.

17. Edwards, *Fronda aristocrática*, 214.

18. Vera, *Evolución del radicalismo chileno*, 73–75.

19. *La Lei*, June 10, 1894.

20. Sepúlveda, *Radicales ante la historia*, 76.

21. Góngora, *Ensayo histórico*, 105.

22. Sepúlveda, *Radicales ante la historia*, 77–79.

23. Ibid., 77.

24. *La Lei*, December 2, 1909.

25. Ibid., March 5, 1908.

26. Vial, *Historia de Chile*, 2:694–95.

27. To Pedro Aguirre Cerda, Héctor Arancibia Laso, and Enrique Oyarzún from Arturo Alessandri Palma, March 17, 1920. CPAC, AN, vol. 14, docs. 263–64 (1920).

28. Heise, *Historia de Chile*, 2:315.

29. Vial, *Historia de Chile*, vol. 1, pt. 1, pp. 12–18.

30. DeShazo, *Urban Workers and Labor Unions*, 57–59; Vial, *Historia de Chile*, vol. 1, pt. 2, p. 502.

31. To Pedro Aguirre Cerda from the Federation of Employees of Antofagasta, April 2, 1921. CPAC, AN, vol. 20, docs. 13–15 (1921).

32. Vial, *Historia de Chile*, vol. 1, pt. 2, p. 537.

33. DeShazo, *Urban Workers and Labor Unions*, 68–69.

34. Russell, *Visit to Chile*, 192; Ramírez, *Historia del movimiento obrero*, 278.

35. Ortiz, *Movimiento obrero en Chile*, 78.

36. *La Lei*, October 30, 1903.

37. Heise, *Historia de Chile*, 2:123.

38. *El Pueblo*, April 9, 1892; Ramírez, *Historia del movimiento*, 258.

39. Heise, *Historia de Chile*, 2:330, 336; Barría, *Movimiento obrero en Chile*, 50.

40. *La Lei*, June 22, 1894.

41. Ibid., October 30, 1903.

42. To Pedro Aguirre Cerda from the Nitrate and Railway Company of Agua Santa, March 17, 1921. CPAC, AN, vol. 19, doc. 404 (1921).

43. To Pedro Aguirre Cerda from Alejandro Gonzáles, president of the Radical Assembly of Curanilahue, April 30, 1921. CPAC, AN, vol. 20, docs. 468–69 (1921).

44. Edwards Bello, *Crónicas del Centenario*, 49.

45. *La Lei*, October 24, 1905.

46. Ibid., October 26, 1905.

47. Ibid., September 3, 1907.

48. Vera, *Evolución del radicalismo chileno*, 140, 142.

49. "El Señor Diputado don Alejandro Huneeus G.H.," *Chile Ilustrado* 2 (December 1903): no page numbers.

50. Morris, *Elites, Intellectuals, and Consensus*, 123.

51. *El Diario Ilustrado*, August 1, 1918.

52. Ibid., September 4, 1919.

53. Ibid., January 10, 1907.

54. Vicuña Urrutia, *París americano*, 54–55.

55. *El Porvenir*, April 21, 1900.

56. Bernardo Subercaseaux, *Fin de Siglo*, 63.

57. Silva, "Expansión y crisis nacional," in Villalobos, *Historia de Chile*, 670.

58. Edwards Bello, *Crónicas del Centenario*, 73.

59. Ibid., 76.

60. Balmaceda Valdés, *Mundo que se fue*, 100.

61. Silva, "Expansión y crisis nacional," 669.

62. Ibid.

63. Balmaceda Valdés, *Mundo que se fue*, 115.

64. Godoy, *Carácter chileno*, 332; Silva, "Expansión y crisis nacional," 676.

65. Godoy, *Carácter chileno*, 332.

66. Balmaceda Valdés, *Mundo que se fue*, 143.

67. José Joaquín Brunner, "Cultura y crisis hegemónicas," in Brunner and Catalán, *Cinco estudios sobre cultura y sociedad*, 30.

68. Balmaceda Valdés, *Mundo que se fue*, 321; Godoy, "Salones literarios y tertulias intelectuales en Chile: Trayectoria y significación," in Agulhon et al., *Formas de sociabilidad en Chile*, 142.

69. Orrego Luco, *Memorias del tiempo viejo*, 1:173.

70. Godoy, "Salones literarios y tertulias," 144–45; María Angélica Muñoz Gomá, "Tertulias y salones literarios chilenos: Su función sociocultural," in Agulhon et al., *Formas de sociabilidad en Chile*, 243–45.

71. Edwards Bello, *Crónicas del Centenario*, 89.

72. Balmaceda Valdés, *Mundo que se fue*, 124.

73. *La Lei*, March 8, 1906.

74. Sepúlveda, *Radicales ante la historia*, 11.

75. *La Lei*, February 13, 1896.

76. Mac-Iver, *Discurso sobre la crisis moral de la República*, 4–5.

77. *La Lei*, September 5, 1903.

78. Ibid., October 20, 1905.

79. Ibid., June 10, 1894.

Chapter 2

1. On the emergence and nature of the bourgeois pubic sphere in Europe, see Habermas, *Structural Transformation of the Public Sphere*. In Chile, the number of books and pamphlets rose from 692 in 1888 to 1,279 in 1902, while the number of periodicals increased from 193 in 1888 to 406 in 1902. Bernardo Subercaseaux, *Historia del libro en Chile*, 108–9.

2. Given the fluidity of ideas in the intellectual environment and the existence of points of cooperation between "progressive" and "conservative" nationalists, the reader should consider these categories as elastic classifications rather than definitive results of any rigid scientific typology.

3. Brading, *First America*, 39.

4. Ibid., 5.

5. Collier, *Ideas and Politics of Chilean Independence*, 22.

6. Ibid., 23.

7. Ibid., 25. Molina coined the phrase.

8. Ibid., 28.

9. Ibid., 208.

10. Ibid.

11. Hobsbawm, *Nations and Nationalism since 1789*, 86.

12. Consult Woll, *Functional Past*.

13. Yeager, *Barros Arana's Historia jeneral de Chile*, 71.

14. Collier, "From Independence to the War of the Pacific," in Bethell, *Chile since Independence*, 26; Collier and Sater, *History of Chile*, 103.

15. "Necrología," *Revista Pedagógica* 7 (June 1911): 224.

16. See Carl Solberg, "A Discriminatory Frontier Land Policy, Chile 1870–1914," *Americas* 26 (October 1969): 115–33.

17. Palacios, *Raza Chilena*, 3.

18. Ibid., 4.

19. Ibid., 248–50.

20. Dirección General de Estadística, República de Chile, *Censo de población de la República de Chile*, I, 276.

21. *La Lei*, July 12, 1905.

22. Solberg, *Immigration and Nationalism*, 162–63.

23. Ibid., 160.

24. Ibid., 163.

25. Yeager, *Barros Arana's Historia jeneral de Chile*, 143.

26. Vial, *Historia de Chile*, 2:436.

27. Palacios, "Decadencia del espíritu de nacionalidad," in Arce Eberhard et al., *Pensamiento nacionalista*, 164.

28. Ibid., 165–68, 178.

29. Anonymous, "Don Nicolás Palacios," *Revista de Educación Nacional* 7 (October 1911): 425. One advertisement later called *Raza chilena* "the book for all Chilean patriots." *El Diario Ilustrado*, July 4, 1918.

30. It remains unclear when "*raza*" or "*raza chilena*" became widely used terms. As early as 1858, one Chilean newspaper boldly declared: "People of invincible spirit! Privileged race in Spanish America!" Collier and Sater, *History of Chile*, 103.

31. Pinochet, *Conquista de Chile*, 66.

32. Ibid., 101.

33. Ibid., 66. In his memoirs, Pinochet describes an intellectual evolution that led him to question the elite's privilege and the aristocracy's overly robust sense of importance. See Pinochet, *Autobiografía de un tonto*, 46–64.

34. Ibid., 236.

35. Ibid., 102–4.

36. Ibid., 209.

37. Valdés Cange, *Sinceridad*, xi.

38. Amunátegui Solar, *Letras chilenas*, 356–57.

39. Valdés Cange, *Sinceridad*, 3.

40. Ibid., 205–6.

41. Ibid., 10–11.

42. Vial, *Historia de Chile*, 2:436.

43. Valdés Cange, *Sinceridad*, xiii.

44. *El Mercurio*, September 18, 1910.

45. Valdés Cange, *Sinceridad*, 7.

46. Encina, *Nuestra inferioridad económica*, 15, 221.

47. Ibid., 210.

48. Ibid., 223.

49. It is evident that Encina also incorporated elements of Palacios's racial, nativist thinking in his own sociopolitical philosophy. Encina, for example, refers to "*la raza*" when citing Chile's national character in *La educación económica y el liceo*, a study that shares the thematic emphases of *Nuestra inferioridad económica*. In addition, in Encina's voluminous *Historia de Chile*—published between 1940 and 1952—"the race and [national] heritage are the determining factors that explain and give order to the apparent chaos of historical reality." In this case, the indigenous element of the *raza* is presented by Encina in a negative manner. José Vicente Mogollón, "Francisco Antonio Encina: Su personalidad y sus ideas sobre la raza, la economía y la educación. Escenario: Chile, 1910," published as a corollary to *Atenea*, no. 405 (1965): 11.

50. Encina, *Nuestra inferioridad económica*, 220.

51. Ibid., 222.

52. *El Mercurio*, November 13, 1916.

53. Guillermo Subercaseaux, "Política nacionalista," *Revista de Educación Nacional* 9 (August 1913): 263.

54. *El Mercurio*, December 10, 1915.

55. Ibid.

56. Ibid., November 15, 1916.

57. *El Diario Ilustrado*, June 18 and 20, 1913.

58. Ibid., October 9, 11, and 14, 1915.

59. Encina, representing the Nationalist Union, sat on the board of directors of the so-called Unión Liberal, which allied with the Conservative Party to form the Unión Nacional. *La Nación*, May 4, 1920. Also consult *La Nación*, March 18, 1920.

60. Pinochet, *Oligarquía y democracia*, 77.

61. Ibid., 17–19.

62. Ibid., 180.

63. Jobet, *Luis Emilio Recabarren*, 7. The *folleto* is a transcription of Recabarren's talk titled "Ricos y pobres a través de un siglo de historia republicana," which he presented in Rengo (south of Santiago near the city of Rancagua) on September 3, 1910. Vial, *Historia de Chile*, 2:512.

64. Eduardo Devés and Ximena Cruzat painstakingly assembled 639 published articles and fragments authored by Recabarren between 1898 and 1924 in a four-volume anthology. See Devés and Cruzat, *Recabarren*.

65. *El Trasandino*, September 19, 1909; Devés and Cruzat, *Recabarren*, 2:139.

66. *El Trasandino*, September 19, 1909; Devés and Cruzat, *Recabarren*, 2:139.

67. *El Despertar de los Trabajadores*, August 29, 1912; Devés and Cruzat, *Recabarren*, 2:175–76.

68. Jobet, *Luis Emilio Recabarren*, 39.

Chapter 3

1. Gazarian Gautier, *Interviews with Latin American Writers*, 70.

2. Latorre, "Autobiografía de una vocación," in Latorre, *Memorias y otras confidencias*, 59.

3. The term *"criollismo,"* which is also used in Argentina to describe ruralesque literature, apparently originated from a 1904 review of Baldomero Lillo's story *Sub-Terra* by the writer Augusto Thomson (also known as Augusto D'Halmar). Thomson noted that Lillo's description of life in mining communities was *"criollo* to the last" and "is, in reality, Zola-ist [*zolaína*]." *La Lira Chilena*, October 2, 1904; Raúl Silva Castro, "Apéndice," in Lillo, *Obras completas*, 39–45; Muñoz and Oelker, *Diccionario*, 86; Dieter Oelker, "El criollismo en Chile," *Acta Literaria* 8 (1983): 38.

4. The "creolist" tendency also appeared in the visual, plastic, and musical arts during the early twentieth century. Of note are the painters of the so-called Generation of 1913 who furthered the "national" aesthetic established by earlier artists, including Pedro Lira and Juan Francisco González. In addition, folkloric poetry and music were subjects of examination by such figures as Ramón Laval and Julio Vicuña Cifuentes, as Chileans increasingly sought to explore and express what they understood as Chile's criollo essence. These and other figures are placed in the broader cultural context in Collier and Sater, *History of Chile*, chap. 7. The literary *criollistas*, however, set the cultural tone during this period and literally outproduced other forms.

5. The name *huaso* may have evolved from the Quechua word *wasu*, meaning "rustic man." See Subercaseaux, *Diccionario de chilenismos*. The Argentine term *gaucho* is thought to be related.

6. Lastarria, *Recuerdos literarios*, 105. The book first appeared in 1878.

7. Corse, *Nationalism and Literature*, 7; T. D. MacLulich, "Thematic Criticism, Literary Nationalism, and the Critic's New Clothes," *Essays on Canadian Writing*, no. 35 (1987): 17–36.

8. Silva Castro, *Panorama literario de Chile*, 346. Silva Castro focuses on the works of Lastarria, but his statement applies to the movement in general. Also see Francisco Santana, "Hombres de 1842," *Atenea*, no. 203 (1942): 290–325. This collection of intellectuals has also been called the "Lastarria Generation," the "Bello Generation," the "Romantic Generation," and the "Generation of 1842." Goic, *Novela chilena*; Domingo Melfi, "La generación de Lastarria," *Atenea*, no. 141 (1937): 235–83; Raúl Silva Castro, "Introducción a la historia literaria de Chile," *Finis Terrae* 7, no. 25 (1960): 3–27. In this case, I shy away from the "generation" classification not only because some intellectuals who are assigned membership were notably older than others (Bello was sixty-one at the time, for example) but also because the category of "generation" suggests greater congruence of purpose and activity than those in question shared, though they agreed on the need for a "national" literary tradition.

9. Lastarria, *Miscelánea histórica y literaria*, 1:vi.

10. Consult Woll, *Functional Past*.

11. Ibid., 20–21.

12. Muñoz and Oelker, *Diccionario*, 40.

13. Blest Gana, *Martín Rivas*, 20.

14. Valenzuela, *Chilean Society As Seen through the Novelistic World of Alberto Blest Gana*, 79–80.

15. Blest Gana, *Martín Rivas*, 37.

16. Ibid., 81.

17. Ibid., 73.

18. See the essay on Blest Gana in Sommer, *Foundational Fictions*.

19. Goic, *Novela chilena*, 57.

20. Blest Gana, *Martín Rivas*, 19.

21. Latorre, *Autobiografía*, 42.

22. Ibid.

23. Ricardo Latcham, "La historia del criollismo," in Latcham et al., *El criollismo*, 12.

24. Vicuña Subercaseaux, *Ciudad de las ciudades*, 510.

25. Some thirty thousand copies of the *folletín* were sold. Subercaseaux, *Historia del libro en Chile*, 90–91.

26. Latorre, *Autobiografía*, 43.

27. Edwards Bello, *Recuerdos de un cuarto de siglo*, 207.

28. Rama, *Lettered City*, 55.

29. Bauer, *Chilean Rural Society*, 5–6.

30. Góngora, *Encomenderos y estancieros*, 15.

31. Gay, *Historia física y política de Chile*, 184.

32. Ibid., 156–57.

33. Manuel José Balmaceda, *Manual del hacendado chileno*, 127.

34. Gilliss, *U.S. Naval Astronomical Expedition*, 357. Also see Bauer, *Chilean Rural Society*.

35. Gilliss, *U.S. Naval Astronomical Expedition*, 359.

36. Ibid., 346.

37. Gay, *Historia física y política de Chile*, 153.

38. Atropos, "Inquilino en Chile," 201.

39. Bauer, *Chilean Rural Society*, 55.

40. Rumbold, *Reports to Her Majesty's Secretaries*, 387.

41. Thomas Wright, "Agriculture and Protectionism in Chile, 1880–1930," *Journal of Latin American Studies* 7 (February 1975): 47. Also consult Bauer, *Chilean Rural Society*.

42. Harold Blakemore, "From the War of the Pacific to 1930," in Bethell, *Chile since Independence*, 62.

43. Wright, *Landowners and Reform in Chile*, 31.

44. Bauer, *Chilean Rural Society*, 168.

45. See Tancredo Pinochet Le-Brun, "Inquilinos en la hacienda de Su Excelencia," in Corvalán, *Antología chilena de la tierra*, 81–112. Pinochet first published this indictment as a serial in the Santiago newspaper *La Opinión*.

46. Wright, *Landowners and Reform in Chile*, 31–37.

47. Loveman, *Struggle in the Countryside*, 31.

48. Ibid., 75.

49. Corse, *Nationalism and Literature*, 7.

50. Montenegro, *Mis contemporáneos*, 47, 150.

51. Cedomil Goic, "Generación de Darío," *Revista del Pacífico* 4 (1967): 25; Oelker, "Criollismo," 41.

52. *El Siglo*, June 6, 1954.

53. Ibid.

54. *Claridad*, September 15, 1923.

55. Montenegro, *Mis contemporáneos*, 37. Among Lillo's friends were literary notables Diego Dublé Urrutia, Mariano Latorre, Fernando Santiván, and Víctor Domingo Silva.

56. MIP, ASXX, Providencias, vol. II, no. 78, 1922.

57. Guillermo Labarca Hubertson, Address to the Federación de Estudiantes de Chile, 1907. ARSC, BN, b. 32, f. 356.2.

58. In a 1900 newspaper article, Labarca praised Zola's intent to relay how the common person weathers the sometimes harsh realities of life and rises to forge sociopolitical change. Labarca hailed Zola's depiction of people who are "reborn with more strength now that the collective has the means to make itself heard and to influence the organization of governments." *La Prensa*, January 14, 1900. Many reformers in Labarca's day found inspiration in Zola, who defended Dreyfus during the famous Dreyfus Affair in France. Following the 1898 suicide of Colonel Henry, who admitted he falsified documents in the Dreyfus case, *La Lei* praised Zola for seeking justice: "The figure of Zola radiates in these times the prestige of a hard-fought triumph with the sole expectation of vindicating justice." *La Lei*, September 28, 1898. The Frenchman's political battles and travels through Europe were followed closely in the reformist, Radical press. See *La Lei*, May 3, 1895. Zola, moreover, was praised by the literary club Ateneo in 1903 to mark the first anniversary of the Frenchman's death. See *La Lei*, October 1, 1903.

59. *El Mercurio*, November 18, 1964; ARSC, BN, b. 32, f. 356.

60. See Labarca's "Último contento," *Luz y Sombra*, no. 38 (1900); "Cita," *Luz y Sombra*, no. 10 (1901); "Apunte," *Luz y Sombra*, no. 86 (1901); "De luengas tierras," *Zig-Zag*, no. 129 (1907); and "Ñico," *Zig-Zag*, no. 253 (1909). His earliest stories, though not highly touted by critics, caught the fancy of renowned poet Carlos Pezoa Véliz. Pezoa told Labarca in a 1901 letter that his work was imbued with a "harmonious fluidity that delights the ear." Letter to Guillermo Labarca Hubertson from Carlos Pezoa Véliz, 1901 (no specific date stipulated). ARSC, BN, b. 32, f. 356.

61. Twelve short stories are in the anthology: "En la campiña," "Despues del trabajo," "Al son de la vihuela," "Vida del campo," "El ídolo," "Nunca mas," "La siembra," "En el hogar," "Jente serrana," "La grieta," "El acriminado," and "El Pirulo." The *cuento* "Jente serrana" won first place in a literary contest sponsored by *El Mercurio* in 1900.

62. Guillermo Labarca Hubertson, *Al amor de la tierra*, 16.

63. Ibid., 55.

64. Ibid., 38.

65. *La Lei*, December 16, 1905.

66. *El Mercurio*, November 18, 1964.

67. Letter to Pedro Aguirre Cerda from Guillermo Labarca Hubertson. CPAC, AN, vol. 41, doc. 303 (1926), and ARSC, BN, b. 32, f. 356. Labarca is eulogized in David Perry, "Guillermo Labarca Hubertson," *Atenea*, nos. 353–54 (1954): 107–14.

68. Maluenda, *Escenas de la vida campesina*, 1.

69. He edited a full page in *El Mercurio* devoted to Alessandri's campaign and the Liberal Alliance in 1919 and 1920.

70. *El Mercurio*, October 16, 1938.

71. Maluenda joined his uncle in admiring the naturalists. Maupassant and Daudet were among his favorites. *Las Últimas Noticias*, November 5, 1960.

72. Maluenda, *Escenas de la vida campesina*, 88.

73. This assessment was reprinted in *El Diario Ilustrado*, June 14, 1959.

74. *Últimas Noticias*, October 11, 1941; ARSC, BN, b. 34, f. 378. Stated by Mariano Picón-Salas.

75. Promis, *Novela chilena del último siglo*, 21.

76. ARSC, BN, c. 34, f. 376.

77. *El Mercurio*, March 9, 1939; Luis Merino Reyes, interview with author, Santiago, September 1996; Luis Durand Jr., interview with author, Santiago, September 1996.

78. *Últimas Noticias*, October 18, 1941; Oelker, "Criollismo," 43.

79. *Últimas Noticias*, October 20, 1943.

80. Oelker, "Criollismo," 43.

81. Latorre, *Autobiografía*, 12.

82. Domingo Melfi, "Mariano Latorre," *Revista de Educación* 1 (December 1929): 672.

83. Latorre, *Autobiografía*, 32, 35.

84. Mariano Latorre, "Génesis y evolución del cuento chileno," *Anales de la Universidad de Chile*, nos. 27–28 (1937): 12; Latorre, *Autobiografía*, 71–72; Merino Reyes, interview with author; Durand, interview with author. Bret Harte, Latorre stated, gave "a model of the adventurer, torn from the block of an almost colonial society." Oelker, "Criollismo," 44.

85. Latcham, "Aspectos del criollismo en América," in Latcham et al., *Criollismo*, 62.

86. *Últimas Noticias*, October 20, 1943.

87. Latorre, *Cuentos del Maule*, 67.

88. Ibid., 33.

89. Ibid., 33–34.

90. ARSC, BN, b. 34, f. 378.

91. Raúl Silva Castro, unpublished manuscript (no title or date), ARSC, BN, b. 34, f. 377.

92. *El Mercurio*, July 25, 1926.

93. ARSC, BN, b. 34, f. 378.

94. Santiván, *Confesiones de Santiván*, 96. Gana contributed to such publications as *La Tribuna*, *La Actualidad*, *Zig-Zag*, and *La Revista Ilustrada*.

95. Silva Castro, *Panorama literario de Chile*, 353–54.

96. *La Nación*, October 10, 1926.

97. Ibid., August 8, 1926.

98. Gana, *Días de campo*, 104.

99. For a more substantial treatment of Gana's literary motivations, see Guerra-Cunningham, *Texto e ideología en la narrativa chilena*.

100. See Szmulewicz, *Pablo Neruda* and *Vicente Huidobro*.

Chapter 4

1. *El Diario Ilustrado*, January 22, 1930.

2. *Frente Popular*, January 12, 1939.

3. See Anderson, *Imagined Communities*, chap. 6.

4. Anonymous, "La vuelta a la tierra," *Boletín de la Sociedad Nacional de Agricultura* 64 (August 1932): 381.

5. *La Nación*, October 28, 1920.

6. Alessandri, *Recuerdos de gobierno*, 1:31.

7. Virginia Krzeminski, "Alessandri y la cuestión social," in Orrego et al., *Siete ensayos sobre Arturo Alessandri Palma*, 249.

8. Harold Blakemore, "From the War of the Pacific to 1930," in Bethell, *Chile since Independence*, 69.

9. Loveman, *Chile*, 203.

10. Vial, *Historia de Chile*, 3:230–37.

11. Ibid., 235–36.

12. Nunn, *Chilean Politics*, 2.

13. Alessandri, *Recuerdos de gobierno*, 1:365.

14. Ibid., 2:348.

15. Ibid., 452.

16. ARSC, BN, b. 32, f. 356.2.

17. The political ramifications of the depression are discussed in Monteón, *Chile and the Great Depression*.

18. Sofía Correa Sutil, "Arturo Alessandri y los partidos en su segunda administración," in Orrego et al., *Siete ensayos sobre Arturo Alessandri Palma*, 436. Police, for example, stormed the office of the leftist newspaper *La Opinión*. Its editor, Juan Bautista Rosseti, was banished to the island of Quinchao, off the coast of Chiloé. The Chilean Nazi Party newspaper, *Trabajo*, also was ransacked.

19. Snow, *Radicalismo chileno*, 79; Correa, "Arturo Alessandri y los partidos en su segunda administración," in Orrego et al., *Siete ensayos sobre Arturo Alessandri Palma*, 437.

20. *La Hora*, May 23, 1937.

21. Aguirre Cerda resigned from a government commission in 1933. To Pedro Aguirre Cerda from Gustavo Ross Santa María. CPAC, AN, vol. 44, doc. 3 (1933).

22. *El Diario Ilustrado*, May 28, 1938; Verónica Valdivia Ortiz de Zárate, "Las nuevas voces del nacionalismo chileno," *Boletín de Historia y Geografía* 10 (1993): 122. Also see Valdivia Ortiz de Zárate, *El nacionalismo chileno en los años del Frente Popular*.

23. *Trabajo*, September 17, 1937.

24. Ibid., September 16 and 25, 1937.

25. Jorge González von Marées, "El alma de la raza," *Acción Chilena* 4, no. 2 (1935): 73–74.

26. *Trabajo*, January 27, 1938. The newspaper blamed *alessandristas* for unjustly portraying the MNS as anti-Semitic.

27. *Frente Popular*, June 8, 1938.

28. Ibid., October 20, 1938.

29. *El Diario Ilustrado*, August 21, 1938.

30. *La Opinión*, October 26, 1938.

31. Aguirre Cerda chose the Socialist Salvador Allende to head the Health Ministry.

32. Latorre, *Zurzulita*, 135. "*Zurzulita*" means turtle dove.

33. Ibid., 19.

34. Ibid., 83.

35. Ibid., 29.

36. Ibid., 125.

37. Edwards Bello, *Recuerdos de un cuarto de siglo*, 134.

38. After the success of *Zurzulita*, Latorre went on to produce many books and published in leading periodicals and newspapers, including *La Nación* and *Atenea*.

39. Anonymous, "Luis Durand," *Atenea*, nos. 351–52 (1954): 2. Durand directed *Atenea* before his death.

40. ARSC, BN, b. 7, f. 161.

41. Luis Durand Jr., interview with author, Santiago, September 1996; Julio César Jobet, "Recuerdo de Luis Durand," *Occidente* (April/May 1955): 42. Julio César Jobet notes that Durand joined the Popular Socialist Party during the administration of Gabriel González Videla (1946–52) and then moved to the short-lived Frente del Pueblo. Some rumored that Durand flirted with the idea of joining the Communist Party. Frederick Pike noted that the author eventually abandoned middle-class reformism because of what Durand deemed its betrayal of the lower classes during the early years of the Popular Front. Pike, "Aspects of Class Relations in Chile," *Hispanic American Historical Review* 43 (February 1963): 25.

42. Luis Durand, "Humitas," *Zig-Zag* 23, no. 1186 (1927): no page numbers given.

43. Ibid. During this period, the term "gringo" generally referred to Europeans and North Americans alike.

44. He developed similar themes in the anthology *Campesinos*, published in 1932. Durand also wrote columns for the Santiago newspaper *Últimas Noticias* in the 1940s.

45. Durand, *Alma y cuerpo de Chile*, 114.

46. Durand, *Paisajes y gentes de Chile*, 166, 164.

47. Ibid., 165.

48. Durand, *Don Arturo*, 180.

49. Durand, interview with author.

50. On the issue of political affiliation, Brunet commented in 1961, "I belong to the Radical Party without having ever signed its membership list. I have always given it my support. I never officially joined because they soon would have thrown me out for being undisciplined." *La Tercera*, November 20, 1961.

51. Both men and women workers, however, did take pleasure in celebrating harvest's end. On payday, "groups of *campesinos* [presumably *huasos*] arrived on horseback," sporting their clinking spurs, *mantas* (much like a *chamanto*), and large hats. They passed in a "picturesque parade," Brunet writes. Brunet, *Montaña adentro*, 55–56.

52. *El Mercurio*, December 13, 1923.

53. Anonymous, "¿Como, cuando y porqué se hizo Ud. escritor?," *Zig Zag* 30, no. 1586 (1935): no page numbers given.

54. Brunet, "Trasto viejo," *Zig-Zag* 21, no. 1059 (1925): no page numbers given.

55. *El Diario Ilustrado*, June 17, 1930. For discussions of Güiraldes's novel from varying methodological and thematic angles, see Kirkpatrick, *Don Segundo Sombra*.

56. *La Nación*, August 10, 1934.

57. Angel Cruchaga Santa María, "El nacionalismo literario," *Revista de Educación* 1 (July 1929): 320–22.

58. *El Diario Ilustrado*, March 15, 1931.

59. *La Nación*, October 4, 1962.

60. More than six thousand copies were sold within the first week after publication. *La Nación*, August 21, 1920. The first part of *El roto* appeared in Paris in 1918 with the title *La cuna de Esmeraldo*.

61. Edwards Bello, *El roto*, 9–10.

62. Emilio Vaisse (Omer Emeth) stresses this point in his review of *El roto*. *El Mercurio*, August 2, 1920.

63. Ibid.

64. *La Nación*, July 11, 1933.

65. Ibid., September 22, 1932.

66. Ibid., September 18, 1932.

67. Ibid., February 7, 1937.

68. Coll, *Chile y los chilenos en las novelas de Joaquín Edwards Bello*, 179.

69. Silva Castro, *Panorama literario de Chile*, 274–75.

70. Orlandi and Ramírez, *Joaquín Edwards Bello*, 26–27. Edwards Bello took his own life in 1968.

71. Edwards Bello, *Chica del Crillón*, 262.

72. Ibid., 269. Emphasis added.

73. *El Diario Ilustrado*, February 11, 1935.

74. The highly influential *criollistas* did not go without some criticism from within literary circles. A debate erupted in the late 1920s between critics loyal to *criollismo* and those allied to the *"imaginista"* movement, a small but growing cadre of literary vanguardists, who had grown tired of *cuentos* about the rural countryside and campesino protagonists. *Criollismo* survived the debate without permanent injury and remained the most popular fiction genre in the country. Consult Dieter Oelker, "La polémica entre criollistas e imaginistas," *Acta Literaria*, no. 9 (1984): 163–64. The debate appeared in *La Nación*, *El Diario Ilustrado*, *El Mercurio*, and the magazine *Letras*. It included such notable critics as Manuel Vega, Ricardo Latcham, Raúl Silva Castro, and Emilio Vaisse.

75. *Topaze* 4, no. 216 (1936): no page number.

76. Ibid., vol. 7, no. 320 (1938): no page number.

77. In 1915, a gallery filled with Santiago's aristocrats witnessed a *"gran rodeo"* in the capital's Cousiño Park. *"Jinetes"* (horsemen) paraded their steeds around a rodeo arena, or *medialuna*, built for the event. These *jinetes* were predominantly landowning notables of high society, and many of them were accompanied by "servants"—apparently *huasos* from their Central Valley haciendas—who assisted them as they displayed equestrian skills. A journalist in attendance commented that the event, a fund-raiser for an organization called the Protection of Women's Work, "depicted the most genuine customs of our rural life." *El Mercurio*, October 23, 1915. Questionable is the suggestion that landowners actively participated in livestock roundups or other important forms of labor on their estates. Moreover, well-to-do Chileans dressed in *huaso* attire were seen in Cousiño Park on Independence Day in 1919. *El Diario Ilustrado*, September 20, 1919.

78. *Acción Chilena* 2, no. 8 (1934): 340–41.

79. *Frente Popular*, March 3, 1937.

80. The reformist press, especially *La Lei*, focused attention on working and living conditions among the rural lower class during the early years of the Parliamentary Republic. In 1907, for example, *La Lei* complained that rural workers had not shared any of the modest improvements seen by urban workers. *La Lei*, March 26, 1907.

81. See Loveman, *Struggle in the Countryside*.

82. Ibid., 113, 133–69.

83. See Loveman, *Struggle in the Countryside*, chap. 5.

84. Wright, *Landowners and Reform in Chile*, 154.

85. Ibid., 131.

86. *El Diario Ilustrado*, March 31, 1930.

87. Wright, *Landowners and Reform in Chile*, 133–34.

88. On many occasions, carabineros and landowners reported suspicious activity on hacienda land, and such reports led to more substantive investigations. See MI, Carabineros de Chile, Dirección General. Copies in MEP, ASXX, Oficios, vol. 1, no. 552 (1937); Loveman, *Struggle in the Countryside*, 56.

89. Higher wages were being paid to miners, and many campesinos migrated to Iquique, Antofagasta, and surrounding areas. The resulting demographic shift was a "grave ill" that threatened the "basis of life for a people." *El Diario Ilustrado*, February 17 and 18, 1930.

90. Heise calculates that 70 percent of Conservative Party members were landowners. Heise, *Historia de Chile*, 2:315.

91. Published in a 1935 *El Campesino* edition, Luis Durand's "La riña de Los Pretiles" features the friendship of two *huasos* who, after a period of time without contact, find themselves working for the same *patrón*. The *huasos*, Clodomiro and Ernesto, speak the poor Spanish of a rustic campo—using, for example, *"iñor"* instead of *"señor"*—and are presented as hard workers who converse, as Durand writes, "about all those little things that are of interest to the simple and good people of the countryside." Durand, "La riña de Los Pretiles," *El Campesino* 67 (June 1935): 291.

92. Federico Gana, "La señora," *El Campesino* 65 (April 1933): 246.

93. Landowners, aware that some social reforms were necessary, preferred a paternalistic approach to improving the conditions of the lower classes. Nunn, *Chilean Politics*, 14.

94. Anonymous, "La vuelta a la tierra," *Boletín de la Sociedad Nacional de Agricultura* 64 (August 1932): 381.

95. "Los intelectuales y la vida campesina," *El Campesino* 69 (November 1937): 552.

96. Durand, *Gente de mi tiempo*, 149.

97. Montenegro, *Mis contemporáneos*, 116.

98. See Bourdieu, *Field of Cultural Production*.

99. *El Campesino* 60 (October 1938): 304–5.

100. Ibid., 445.

101. An April 1938 *Topaze* cartoon, which shows a *patrón* on horseback leading his workers to the polls, made a similar point six months before the election. See *Topaze* 6, no. 297 (1938).

102. *El Diario Ilustrado*, August 29, 1938.

103. Ibid., August 27, 1938.

104. *Frente Popular*, September 6, 1938.

105. Ibid., October 25, 1937.

106. Ibid., October 19, 1938.

107. *Zig-Zag*, no. 1761 (1938): 29.

108. Del Campo, *Huasos chilenos*, 1.

109. *El Diario Ilustrado*, February 17, 1930.

110. Ibid., September 20, 1935.

111. The *zamacueca*'s long history is discussed in Acevedo Hernández, *La cueca*.

112. See *El Diario Ilustrado*'s editions of September 15–20, 1910.

113. The name *medialuna* is derived from the facility's design. A curved fence divides the circular area where the horsemen compete, thus giving the appearance of a crescent or half-moon.

114. Fergusson, *Chile*, 180. The national championship is held in Rancagua, south of the capital, each autumn.

115. Loveman, *Chile*, 248–50. The Aguirre Cerda administration received numerous written complaints from landowners and rural police regarding union gatherings and other manifestations that were registered with the Ministry of the Interior. See, for example, MI, ASXX, Oficios, vol. 2, nos. 272, 233 (1940).

116. The Left's hostility toward Labarca's actions is evident in the newspaper *Frente Popular*'s editions of August 26 and 27, 1940. Also see Loveman, *Chile*, 248–49.

117. Subercaseaux, *Chile, o una loca geografía*, 171.

118. MI, ASXX, Oficios, vol. 5, no. 963 (1940).

119. For Zola's defense of his political activism, consult Zola, *Dreyfus Affair* and *Naturalist Novel*.

Chapter 5

1. Rousseau, *Émile*, 38.

2. *Revista de Educación Nacional* 16 (May 1920): 97.

3. Anguita, *Leyes promulgadas en Chile desde 1810 hasta el 10 de Junio de 1913*, 1:36; Silvert and Reissman, *Education, Class, and Nation*, 108.

4. Gertrude M. Yeager, "Elite Education in Nineteenth-Century Chile," *Hispanic American Historical Review* 71 (February 1991): 76.

5. Yeager, "Elite Education," 91.

6. Ibid., 77–78.

7. Ibid., 83.

8. Silvert and Reissman, *Education, Class, and Nation*, 114.

9. Yeager, "Elite Education," 78.

10. Amunátegui, *Estudios sobre la instrucción pública*, 2:103–5; Silvert and Reissman, *Education, Class, and Nation*, 112.

11. Silvert and Reissman, *Education, Class, and Nation*, 119–20. The first *liceos* for girls were not established until 1877 (Valparaíso and Copiapó). These schools were originally established as private institutions and later were operated by the state. Vial, *Historia de Chile*, vol. 1, pt. 1, p. 172.

12. Silvert and Reissman, *Education, Class, and Nation*, 120.

13. Collier and Sater, *History of Chile*, 101.

14. Public instruction received a whopping one-seventh of the national budget in 1888. School enrollment increased from 79,000 in 1886 to 150,000 in 1890. Harold Blakemore, "From the War of the Pacific to 1930," in Bethell, *Chile since Independence*, 46.

15. Labarca Hubertson, *Historia de la enseñanza en Chile*, 193.

16. Sepúlveda, *Radicales ante la historia*, 76.

17. Labarca Hubertson, *Historia de la enseñanza en Chile*, 181; Campos, *Desarrollo educacional*, 84.

18. Labarca Hubertson, *Historia de la enseñanza en Chile*, 196.

19. Solberg, *Immigration and Nationalism*, 76.

20. Vial, *Historia de Chile*, vol. 1, pt. 1, p. 159.

21. Letelier describes late-nineteenth-century German pedagogy in *Escuelas de Berlín*. He calls the German education system, among other things, "a technical bureaucracy that imposes itself more by merit than authority" (11).

22. Letelier, *Lucha por la cultura*, 45.

23. Ibid., 3, 16.

24. Ibid., 29.

25. Ibid., 233.

26. Conservatives also questioned preferences given to foreign, especially German, teachers. The newspaper *El Porvenir*, for example, warned its conservative readers in 1891 of the "fantastic danger of Germanization to the Chilean public." Their primary concern was that German teachers were unquestionably secular. Vial, *Historia de Chile*, vol. 1, pt. 1, p. 160. Also see Letelier, *Lucha por la cultura*, 413–15.

27. On support for de la Barra, see Vial, *Historia de Chile*, vol. 1, pt. 1, p. 193; de la Barra, *Embrujamiento alemán*, iv, 6.

28. De la Barra, *Embrujamiento alemán*, 37, 97.

29. Ibid., 16.

30. Labarca Hubertson, *Historia de la enseñanza en Chile*, 228.

31. Pedro Aguirre Cerda, who was a young student at the turn of the century, defended the humanistic orientation of Chilean education in his *Estudio sobre la instrucción secundaria*.

32. After voicing its support for Letelier's position in 1902, the reformist press argued in 1907 that "practical" education should find its way into the national curriculum but that such a change should happen gradually rather than suddenly. *La Lei*, March 1, 1902, and February 8, 1907.

33. Solberg, *Immigration and Nationalism*, 28.

34. Encina, *Educación económica y el liceo*, 24.

35. *El Mercurio*, September 3, 1910.

36. Encina, *Educación económica y el liceo*, 18.

37. Ibid., 16–17.

38. Encina also argued his case in "Reforma de nuestra educación nacional," *Revista Pedagógica* 7 (March 1911): 4.

39. Encina, *Educación económica y el liceo*, 33–34.

40. Molina, *Cultura i la educación jeneral*, 21–22.

41. Ibid., 13, 18.

42. Ibid., 53.

43. Ibid., 50, 137.

44. The AEN endorsed Encina's ideas in 1912 but did not reject the need for a moral component in Chilean education. *Revista de Educación Nacional* 8 (April 1912): 75.

45. Before Ibáñez's government, Encina's ideas were supported by the conservative press, which criticized Chile's "French" (i.e., humanist) education system. *El Diario Ilustrado*, September 23, 1919.

46. Sepúlveda, *Radicales ante la historia*, 64.

47. In 1860, 486 primary schools had 23,882 students. In 1900, 1,547 establishments taught 111,410 pupils. Labarca Hubertson, *Historia de la enseñanza en Chile*, 229.

48. *La Lei*, August 27, 1896.

49. Ibid., December 8, 1901.

50. Ibid., January 3, 1900.

51. Ibid., January 3, 1900, and June 1, 1900.

52. Fernández was a vocal member of Santiago's Radical Assembly. Letter to Pedro Aguirre Cerda from Carlos Fernández Peña. CPAC, AN, vol. 25, doc. 233 (1921).

53. *La Lei,* April 2, 1904.

54. MJ, ASXX, Decretos, vol. 16, no. 1864 (1904).

55. The AEN reported an active membership of 357 in 1911. The number climbed to 380 the next year. These figures are impressive if one considers the modest size of Chile's intelligentsia at the turn of the century. *Revista de Educación Nacional* 8 (April 1912): 67, and 8 (June 1912): 228.

56. Campos, *Desarrollo educacional,* 28.

57. *El Diario Ilustrado,* March 5, 1907.

58. Ibid., March 22, 1907.

59. Ibid., January 31, 1908.

60. *La Lei,* July 9, 1907.

61. Ibid., November 1, 1908.

62. *La Lei,* August 23, 1904.

63. Ibid., March 31, 1908, and September 26, 1903.

64. Ibid., May 9, 1909.

65. *El Diario Ilustrado,* December 13, 1904.

66. Consult *La Lei,* December 14, 1904.

67. *Revista de Educación Nacional* 8 (August 1912): 366–67. The *Revista Pedagógica* was renamed the *Revista de Educación Nacional* in 1912.

68. Ibid., vol. 11, no. 2 (1915): 41.

69. Between 1891 and 1920, eight different Radicals served as ministers of justice and public instruction. Four served under Sanfuentes: Aguirre Cerda, Orrego Luco, Pablo Ramírez, and Javier Gandarillas. In general, the majority of all Sanfuentes ministers were Liberals and Radicals. Vial, *Historia de Chile,* 2:694–95.

70. The *Revista de Educación Nacional* was directed by some of the leading political and pedagogical figures of the era, including Luis Galdames (1913), Maximiliano Salas Marchán (1913–14), and Guillermo Labarca Hubertson (1914).

71. Anonymous, "La decadencia de la raza," *Revista de Educación Nacional* 12 (June 1916): 145.

72. Salas, *Problema nacional,* 29. The newspaper *El Mercurio,* which supported the Liberal Party during the late Parliamentary Republic, praised Salas's push for obligatory primary education. An anonymous reviewer of *El problema nacional* wrote, "It is a motive for happy satisfaction to contemplate that during an era such as this one, in which politics is the only preoccupation that absorbs and wastes the best energies of the country, there are people like the author of the book . . . who dedicate their talent . . . to our national problems." *El Mercurio,* June 9, 1917. In a June 16, 1917, edition of *El Mercurio,* the educator Luis Galdames notes that the title Salas chose for the book aptly describes the magnitude of Chile's pedagogical dilemma.

73. Salas, *Problema nacional,* 215. Emphasis added.

74. Ibid., 32. Proponents of obligatory primary education were also angered by decreases in education spending immediately after the outbreak of World War I, when a strong recession gripped Chile. Government oligarchs said reductions were

necessary because of falling revenues. Spending for primary education dropped from 12,471,844 pesos in 1914 to just over 12 million pesos in 1915. See *Revista de Educación Nacional* 8 (June 1912): 179, and 11 (March 1915): 21. Also consult *El Diario Ilustrado*, January 10–12, 1915.

75. Salas, *Problema nacional*, 41.

76. Ibid., 219.

77. Ibid., 220.

78. Tancredo Pinochet Le-Brun also calls for the expansion of public education in his *Oligarquía y democracia*, in which he blames oligarchs for rampant illiteracy.

79. Alessandri, *Instrucción Primaria Obligatoria y Laica*, 162.

80. Ibid., 61.

81. Ibid., 17.

82. Another influential book in support of obligatory primary education was González Echenique, *Verdades amargas*.

83. *El Diario Ilustrado*, September 12, 1919.

84. Secretariado General de la Unión Social Católica de Chile, *Separación de la Iglesia y el Estado*, I, 15–16.

85. Morris, *Elites, Intellectuals, and Consensus*, 123.

86. The Law of Obligatory Primary Instruction was the first national law of its type. On the local level, the municipality of Magallanes enacted an obligatory elementary instruction law in 1916. MEP, ASXX, Providencias, vol. 9, no. 9385 (1930).

87. *La Nación*, August 30, 1920.

88. J. Felix González Rocuant, "La educación primaria obligatoria," *Revista de Educación Primaria* 31 (March–April 1921): 5–6.

89. Harold Blakemore, "From the War of the Pacific to 1930," in Bethell, *Chile since Independence*, 61; Collier and Sater, *History of Chile*, 290; Labarca Hubertson, *Historia de la enseñanza en Chile*, 276.

90. *Revista de Educación Primaria* 31 (July–August 1921): 235. While student enrollments climbed, teachers with at least ten years of service enjoyed a 20 percent pay increase, which was approved by the ministry in 1919. MIP, ASXX, Decretos (copies), vol. 1, no. 238 (1919).

91. MI, ASXX, Circulares, no. 10 (1924), reproduced in MIP, ASXX, Providencias, vol. 4, no. 2850 (1924).

92. MEP, ASXX, Oficios, vol. 7, no number (1930).

93. MIP, ASXX, Providencias, vol. 4, no. 2672 (1921).

94. Ortiz, *Movimiento obrero en Chile*, 118; the FECh alone maintained eleven of such schools. Vial, *Historia de Chile*, vol. 1, pt. 2, p. 524.

95. Vial, *Historia de Chile*, vol. 1, pt. 1, p. 148.

96. *La Lei*, February 9, 1895.

97. Ibid., March 31, 1895. The school was founded on March 29.

98. Workers also had the option of associating with the Popular University (Universidad Popular), which was established in 1905. It was patterned after the Popular University founded in France in the late nineteenth century. Émile Zola was among its more famous lecturers. *La Lei*, August 16, 1905, and October 22, 1907.

99. *Revista de Educación Nacional* 8 (April 1912): 70.

100. Ibid., vol. 9, no. 9 (1913): 500.

101. MEP, ASXX, Providencias, vol. 8, no. 6235 (1937).

102. In 1915, Eliodoro Yañez, a dissident Liberal, headed the extension, while Francisco Encina served as vice president. At that time, Pedro Aguirre Cerda and the *criollista* Mariano Latorre were members of the extension's committee. *Revista de Educación Nacional* 11 (April 1915).

103. MIP, ASXX, Oficios, vol. 5, no. 475 (1918).

104. Ibid., vol. 5, no. 458 (1919). Much like the Masons, firemen had a distinguished history as liberal activists. See Gazmuri, *"48" chileno.*

105. Labarca Hubertson, *Historia de la enseñanza en Chile,* 278.

106. This is inferred from a 1933 petition to the Ministry of Public Education regarding the need for more popular libraries. MEP, ASXX, Providencias, vol. 20, no. 12984 (1933).

107. *La Lei,* September 22, 1909.

108. Aguirre Cerda was president of the SNP during the 1920s. The union's founding platform was reprinted in *La Lei,* September 18, 1909. In general, the program restated the AEN's declaration of principles of 1904.

Chapter 6

1. *La Lei,* November 19, 1905.

2. Ibid.

3. Ibid. Unfortunately, no information on the proposal's fate is found in ministerial records.

4. Ibid.

5. Ibid., September 17, 1905.

6. Ibid., October 1, 1907.

7. Ibid., September 2, 1909.

8. Anonymous, "El patriotismo i las virtudes cívicas en la educación," *Revista Pedagógica* 7 (June 1911): 186.

9. MIP, ASXX, Providencias, vol. 1, no. 143 (1922). The Ministry of Justice and Public Instruction, moreover, approved in 1912 the sum of 53,000 pesos for, among other things, the purchase of Chilean flags for classroom use. *Revista de Educación Nacional* 8 (April 1912): 80.

10. Consejo de Instrucción Pública, *Plan de estudios,* 7–8; MIP, ASXX, Providencias, vol. 1, no. 143 (1922).

11. Consejo de Instrucción Pública, *Plan de estudios,* 223–25.

12. MIP, ASXX, Providencias, vol. 1, no. 143 (1922).

13. CPAC, AN, vol. 42, doc. 187 (1927).

14. MIP, ASXX, Providencias, vol. 1, no. 143 (1922).

15. The text was used in establishments such as the Liceo Valentín Letelier in Santiago, the Liceo of Curicó, the Liceo de Niñas of Coquimbo, the Liceo Amunátegui in Santiago, the Liceo de Niñas of Viña del Mar, and the Liceo de Niñas No. 1 of Valparaíso. See MIP, ASXX, Providencias, vol. 8, no. 29 (1921), Providencias, vol. 8, no. 36 (1921), Providencias, vol. 8, no. 697 (1921), Providencias, vol. 8, no. 10 (1924), Providencias, vol. 8, no. 1869 (1924), and Providencias, vol. 8, no. 20 (1924), respectively.

16. Alcayaga and Flores, *Instrucción cívica.* A second and identical edition was published in 1920.

17. Concha, *Cartilla de la educación cívica*, 6. The Education Ministry's endorsement is included in the 1920 edition. It remains unclear whether this book appeared in a previous form prior to that year.

18. Ibid., 11, 13–14.

19. *El Mercurio*, July, 21, 1920.

20. *El Diario Ilustrado*, July 21, 1920.

21. *El Mercurio*, July 21, 1920.

22. *La Nación*, July 23, 1920; *El Mercurio*, July 21, 1920.

23. *El Mercurio*, July 22, 1920; *El Diario Ilustrado*, July 22, 1920.

24. *El Mercurio*, July 22 and 24, 1920. The conservative press had warned of the FECh's "agitators" a year earlier. See *El Diario Ilustrado* editions of September 6, 8, 17, and 19, 1919.

25. *La Nación*, July 27, 1920.

26. Ibid., July 22, 1920. It was reported in the July 22 edition of *El Mercurio* that López was employed as a machinist. His exact status as a student, then, remains unclear.

27. *El Diario Ilustrado*, July 22, 1920. Traditionalists were, therefore, happy to learn of the government's cancellation of the FECh's juridical personality on July 24. See *El Diario Ilustrado*, July 25, 1920.

28. *El Mercurio*, July 24, 1920.

29. *El Diario Ilustrado*, July 22, 1920. The reformist press also reflected on the possible "infiltration" of two thousand IWW members expelled by the United States. *La Nación*, August 1, 1920. In addition, the Sanfuentes government moved to track foreign residents in Chile. Officials began to gather names for the "Register of Foreigners" at the height of the disturbances of July, 1920. See *El Mercurio*, July 20, 22, and 27, 1920.

30. *El Diario Ilustrado*, July 23, 1920.

31. *La Nación*, July 23, 1920.

32. Although it is likely that traditionalists and reformers overstated the threat of social revolution, their concerns over student-worker collusion were not entirely unfounded. On July 25 (four days after the ransacking of the student union's headquarters) the FOCh and the FECh announced a forty-eight-hour general strike set to begin the next day. The strike was quickly condemned in the moderate and conservative press but was viewed in a lackadaisical manner by some. An *El Mercurio* editorial, for instance, regarded the strike as just another needless interruption of work that would gain nothing—as usual. *El Mercurio*, July 26 and 27, 1920.

33. *La Nación*, July 23, 1920.

34. Ibid., July 24, 1920.

35. Vial, *Historia de Chile*, 3:102.

36. One of the more vocal critics of police tactics was Radical congressional deputy Pedro Aguirre Cerda. *La Nación*, July 28, 1920.

37. *La Nación*, July 28, 1920.

38. Ibid., July 27, 1920.

39. The University of Chile and its rector, Domingo Amunátegui Solar, maintained surveillance of the FECh well after the unrest of July 1920. See MIP, ASXX, Providencias, vol. 1, no. 1890 (1921), and vol. 6, no. 645 (1923).

40. *El Mercurio*, July 24, 1920. See the discussion of Recabarren and patriotism in chapter 2.

41. *La Nación,* July 24, 1920.

42. Ibid., September 30, 1920.

43. Ibid., October 1, 1920. FECh president De María and Radical poet Víctor Domingo Silva were among the speakers at Gómez's funeral.

44. Ibid.

45. Ibid., September 30, 1920. Aguirre Cerda, like many reformers, took a more personal approach to the Gómez case by donating 50 pesos to a fund for the student's family. Ibid., October 1, 1920.

46. Ibid., July 24, 1920.

47. This decree was restated in Law No. 2977, promulgated in January 1915. Cited in MIP, ASXX, Oficios, vol. 2, no number (1925).

48. MIP, ASXX, Providencias, vol. 1851–75, no. 1870 (1909).

49. Ibid., Oficios, vol. 1, no number (1922); *El Mercurio,* July 20, 1920.

50. *El Mercurio,* July 20, 1920; *La Nación,* August 1, 1920.

51. "Memoria del Presidente de la Asociación de Educación Nacional [for 1920]," *Revista de Educación Nacional* 17 (March–July 1921): 40–41.

52. "Actas de la Asociación de Educación Nacional," *Revista de Educación Nacional* 16 (July–August 1920): 265.

53. MIP, ASXX, Oficios, vol. 1, no. 45 (1922).

54. Ibid., Decretos, vol. 74, no. 5582 (1921). Visitors of Schools were ministerial officials who oversaw public schooling in more remote areas of the country.

55. MIP, ASXX, Oficios, vol. 1, no number (1922).

56. *La Nación,* January 13, 1922.

57. MIP, ASXX, Oficios, vol. 3, no. 16 (1922).

58. Ibid., vol. 4, no. 30 (1922).

59. MIP, ASXX, Providencias, vol. 11, nos. 2898 and 2923 (1922).

60. The implementation of Decree 5582 coincided with booming school enrollments nationwide. More than 449,000 children were enrolled in public schools in 1924, while only 114,410 were enrolled in 1900. There were 3,427 public schools in 1924, up from 1,553 in 1900. Cabero, *Chile y los chilenos,* 378.

61. The sum of 2,000 pesos was approved by Darío Salas, director of primary education. MIP, ASXX, Oficios, vol. 2, no. 1985 (1925).

62. MIP, ASXX, Oficios, vol. 2, no number (1925), and vol. 2, no. 1985 (1925).

63. Ibid., vol. 4, no. 1112 (1925). Fenner established that educators would, as they did in 1924, lead "invocations for the race" at the May 21 event.

64. In a 1912 newspaper article in *La Unión,* Galdames states, "The Chilean race is not the German race, our mentality is not like the German, and so the German ways of teaching cannot be followed in Chile." Cited in Solberg, *Immigration and Nationalism,* 80.

65. MEP, ASXX, Decretos, no volume, no. 7500 (1927).

66. In the mid- and late 1920s, civic education remained a required core subject and was taught two hours per week to students in their fifth and sixth years of secondary school. The Pedagogical Institute, furthermore, maintained two faculty members (out of twenty-five to thirty) in the field of civic education. MIP, ASXX, Providencias, vol. 4, no. 37 (1924); vol. 6, no. 1798 (1925); vol. 10, no. 4197 (1925); vol. 6, no. 4528 (1927).

67. Anonymous, "Hora de prueba," *Revista de Educación Primaria* 35 (March 1928): 1–

2. The journal was renamed the *Revista de Educación* in December 1928. Volume numbers were changed on more than one occasion.

68. *Revista de Educación Primaria* 35 (March 1928): 19.

69. The September 1928 edition of *Armonía Escolar* is found in MEP, ASXX, Providencias, vol. 19007–19348, no. 19079 (1928).

70. Raúl Rettig, who fought a duel with Salvador Allende in the 1930s, became an esteemed Radical senator and went on, as an elderly man, to chair President Patricio Aylwin's National Commission on Truth and Reconciliation, which submitted its final report in 1991.

71. MEP, ASXX, Providencias, vol. 6290-7174, no. 6947, and vol. 15804-981, no. 15913 (1928). The regional governor made his initial report to the Ministry of the Interior. The case was then routed to the Education Ministry. Other examples of such tactics include the cases of Mrs. Carlota Vásquez, documented in MEP, ASXX, Providencias, vol. 14670–15201, nos. 151554–55 (1928); of Manuel Segovia and Zenobio Zambrano, Providencias, vol. 18028–18258, no. 18130 (1928); and various teachers in Colchagua, Providencias, vol. 10, no. 5132 (1929).

72. MEP, ASXX, Oficios, vol. 1501-2105, no. 1746 (1928).

73. Ibid., no volume, no. 1444 (1929).

74. ARSC, BN, b. 32, f. 356.2.

75. Letter to Pedro Aguirre Cerda from Luis Orrego Luco, February 20, 1927. CPAC, AN, vol. 42, doc. 91 (1927).

76. For some time, governments had been aware of the political activities of public school teachers, and many in the public sphere had questioned whether teachers should be overtly political. In 1916, Luis Galdames published a lengthy guest editorial in the Santiago press that addressed concerns that were circulating about teacher involvement in party politics. Even though they were employees of the state, Galdames argued, teachers were nonetheless highly educated people and should therefore be allowed to exercise their right to become active party members. *El Mercurio*, January 28, 1916.

77. *La Unión*, April 28, 1928.

78. Such was the administration's opinion on one occasion in July 1934, when the Education Ministry thanked the "Circle of Veterans of '79 and Retired Officers," an association of veterans of the War of the Pacific, for suggesting that primary schools engage in "acts of patriotic and educational character" to commemorate the Battle of La Concepción. The ministry responded by noting that many such events are celebrated each year, and it reassured the veterans' group that guidelines already existed for stirring "the true patriotic sentiments in all the schools of the country." MEP, ASXX, Oficios, vol. 7, no. 1743 (1934).

79. Other examples of government investigations and firings of "subversive" teachers may be found in MEP, ASXX, Oficios, vol. 2, no. 276 (1933); Providencias, vol. 3, no. 1987 (1934); Oficios, vol. 7, no. 1528 (1935); Providencias, vol. 1, no. 69 (1937); and Providencias, vol. 1, no. 509 (1938).

80. MEP, ASXX, Oficios, vol. 2, no. 633 (1937); *Frente Popular*, January 1, 1938.

81. MEP, ASXX, Oficios, vol. 7, no. 2720 (1932).

82. *El Mercurio*, September 18, 1936; *Frente Popular*, September 21, 1936.

83. MEP, ASXX, Oficios, vol. 2, no. 633 (1937).

84. *Frente Popular*, April 22, 1937, January 20, 1938.

85. Ibid., January 20, 1938.

86. *El Diario Ilustrado*, August 1, 1938.

87. Ibid., August 2, 10, 1938.

88. *La Nación*, October 8, 1938. *La Nación*, which had supported the Liberal Alliance in 1920, remained loyal to *alessandrismo* as the years passed.

89. *Frente Popular*, April 22, 1938.

90. Luis Enrique Délano, "Don Pedro Aguirre Cerda o la patria," *Zig-Zag*, no volume (December 1938): 29. The same issue includes a biography of Aguirre Cerda written by Radical and poet Víctor Domingo Silva.

91. Ibid.

92. *Frente Popular*, May 4, 1939.

93. Ibid., May 11, 1939.

94. See MI, ASXX, Oficios, vol. 5, nos. 801–81 (1940).

95. MEP, ASXX, Oficios, vol. 2, nos. 526, 574, 605 (1939).

96. Aguirre Cerda's program was not the first to use the phrase "defense of the race." The Education Ministry under Ibáñez operated the Office of the Defense of the Race, which was devoted to health matters. MEP, ASXX, Oficios, vol. 3, no. 738 (1930).

97. MEP, ASXX, Oficios, vol. 4, no. 1321 (1939). The organization had its own song, "Himno de la Defensa de la Raza," written by Radical Carlos Casassus and Javier Rengifo.

98. Maximiliano Salas Marchán, "La obra educacional de Don Pedro Aguirre Cerda," *Revista de Educación* 2 (August 1942): 10. The journal's volume numbers changed in 1941.

99. Salas Marchán, "Obra educacional," 10.

100. *La Hora*, July 9, 1940. This center was locally sponsored by the Braden Copper Syndicate and was named the El Teniente Defense of the Race Club.

101. Salas Marchán, "Obra educacional," 10.

102. MEP, ASXX, Oficios, vol. 4, no. 1321 (1939).

103. Ibid., vol. 1, no. 244 (1940).

104. Ibid., vol. 2, no. 870 (1940).

105. Salas Marchán, "Obra educacional," 11.

106. *La Hora*, January 16, 1940.

107. *Frente Popular*, August 22, 1939.

108. Ibid., July 10, 1939.

109. Salas Marchán, "Obra educacional," 12.

110. *Boletín del Instituto Nacional* 6 (September 1941): 3.

111. Eugenio Pereira Salas, "La zamacueca," *Boletín del Instituto Nacional* 6 (September 1941): 23.

112. *Anales de la Universidad de Chile: Boletín del Consejo Universitario* 11, no. 3 (1941): ccxxiii–ccxxiv.

113. MEP, ASXX, Oficios, vol. 1, no. 555 (1941).

114. Gonzalo Latorre Salamanca, "El folklore en la educación," *Revista de Educación* 1 (April 1941): 65–66.

115. Ibid., 67.

116. Rocco del Campo, *Panorama y color de Chile*, 297.

117. Ibid., 296.

118. Latorre Salamanca, "Folklore en la educación," 69.

119. *La Hora*, July 29, 1941.

120. "Memoria en cooperación al movimiento en favor de la chilenidad que propicia el S.E. el Presidente de la República," *Revista de Educación Nacional* 26 (April 1941): 3.

121. Ibid., 2.

122. Klubock, *Contested Communities*, 115; *Despertar Minero*, August 1, 1941.

123. Klubock, *Contested Communities*, 115.

Chapter 7

1. Bourdieu and Passeron, *Reproduction*, 21.

2. Wiggin, *Education and Nationalism*, 289.

3. Prado Martínez and Torres C., *Lector del obrero chileno*, i–iv. The endorsement was outlined in Decree 714, which was dated October 7, 1925 (within a week of Alessandri's resignation). It was issued by the Ministry of Hygiene, rather than the Ministry of Justice and Public Instruction.

4. Ibid., v–vi.

5. Ibid., 5–6.

6. Ibid.

7. Ibid., 6.

8. Ibid., 67–68.

9. Ibid., 68.

10. Ibid., 66–67.

11. Ibid., 129–30. The linguistic complexity of this poem suggests that Prado and Torres expected readers to possess well-developed literacy skills. Thus, *El lector del obrero chileno* may have been written with more advanced students in mind.

12. Ibid., 17.

13. Ibid., 18.

14. Guzmán also authored the novel *Don Pancho Garuya* (1933) and the anthology *Cuentos tradicionales en Chile* (1934).

15. Guzmán, *Primer libro de lectura para preparatoria*, 42–43.

16. Ibid., 171–72.

17. Ibid., 20. See also Guzmán, *El lector chileno: Libro primero para el segundo año de la escuela primaria*.

18. New editions of *Primer libro de lectura para preparatoria*, which first appeared in 1905, were published in Santiago in 1909, 1916, 1926, and 1929. The Liberal Alliance-controlled Chamber of Deputies, at the behest of the Education Ministry, voted in favor of Guzmán's plan for the *El lector chileno* series in August 1924. MIP, ASXX, Providencias, vol. 12, no. 2242 (1924). The *El lector chileno* series was used in public schools throughout the country. Requisitions for the book include those found in MEP, ASXX, Providencias, vol. 7, no. 5896 (1931); vol. 19, no. 21282 (1933); vol. 6, no. 6163 (1934); and vol. 8, no. 4501 (1939).

19. Guzmán, *El lector chileno: Libro segundo para el tercer año de la escuela primaria*, 194. This volume was reprinted eleven times through 1951.

20. It is likely that Guzmán authored the selections that do not assign authorship, though no evidence proves this supposition.

21. Guzmán, *El lector chileno: Libro segundo para el tercer año de la escuela primaria,* 117–19.

22. Guzmán, *El lector chileno: Libro tercero para el cuarto año de la escuela primaria,* 246–47.

23. Ibid., 200.

24. Mistral's reformist sensibility is clearly expressed in her personal correspondence. Consult Quezada, *Gabriela Mistral.* She was a close friend of Pedro Aguirre Cerda's.

25. Guzmán, *El lector chileno: Libro cuarto para el quinto año de la escuela primaria,* 233.

26. Guzmán, *El lector chileno: Libro tercero para el cuarto año de la escuela primaria,* 198. Ten editions of this text had appeared by 1961.

27. Guzmán, *El lector chileno: Libro cuarto para el quinto año de la escuela primaria,* 239–40. This edition was reprinted nine times by 1961.

28. Guzmán, *El lector chileno: Libro quinto para el sexto año de la escuela primaria,* 175–76. By 1951, seven editions of this volume were published.

29. Guzmán, *El lector chileno: Libro cuarto para el quinto año de la escuela primaria,* 116–17.

30. Ibid., 118–19.

31. To Pedro Aguirre Cerda from César Bunster. CPAC, AN, vol. 42, docs. 227–28 (1927); *Boletín del Instituto Nacional* 6 (November 1941).

32. Bunster, *Reflexión sobre la inquietud actual,* 8, 16.

33. Bunster, *El niño chileno: Libro auxiliar de lectura para el primer año de humanidades,* 94–95. This text was reprinted seventeen times between 1935 and 1956. Bunster published a total of eight texts in the *El niño chileno* series, which was endorsed by the Education Ministry.

34. One verse reads: "We dance on Chilean soil / more smooth than roses and honey / the soil that makes up men / of lips and chests without gall." Ibid., 9.

35. Bunster, *El niño chileno: Libro auxiliar de lectura para el tercer año de humanidades de los liceos de hombres,* 7–9. This text was reprinted twelve times between 1935 and 1957.

36. Ibid., 9.

37. Bunster, *El niño chileno: Libro auxiliar de lectura para el primer año de humanidades,* 98. The essay points to a Boy Scout as a model citizen.

38. Ibid., 260.

39. In most Spanish-speaking countries, the term "Pascua" translates as "Easter." This usage is prevalent in Chile, but Chileans also use "Pascua," as well as "Navidad," to denote Christmas.

40. Bunster, *El niño chileno: Libro auxiliar de lectura para el segundo año de humanidades,* 162–63.

41. Ibid., 163.

42. Bunster, *El niño chileno: Libro auxiliar de lectura para el sexto año de escuela primaria,* 17.

43. Ibid., 18.

Epilogue

1. Between 1964 and 1970, the ruling Christian Democrats and President Eduardo Frei Montalva in some ways echoed the Radicals' notion of *socialismo de Estado* when

promoting the government's "revolution in liberty," a policy of social reform in the defense of democracy. In fact, it seems as if Frei was reading from an old issue of *La Lei* or perhaps a Radical manifesto from the Parliamentary Republic in a 1964 speech in Valparaíso. He explained to the crowd that Christian Democracy stood between "reactionaries with no conscience" and "revolutionaries with no brains." *El Mercurio*, September 1, 1964; Collier and Sater, *History of Chile*, 308.

2. See Prieto, *Discurso criollista*.

3. León, *Interpretación histórica del huaso chileno*, 7.

4. *El Mercurio*, July 25, 1995. The *chilenidad* festival is now a yearly event.

5. Mario Sznajder, "Who Is Chilean?: The Mapuche, the Huaso, and the Roto as the Basic Symbols of Chilean Collective Identity," in Roniger and Sznajder, *Constructing Collective Identities*, 206. This essay's scope is largely limited to the Pinochet years. Moreover, the Pinochet regime underscored the value of the *cueca* folk dance. See Ministerio de Educación de Chile, *Cueca y danzas tradicionales*.

6. Rama, *Lettered City*, 101–2.

7. *La Nación*, May 31, 1920.

8. Debray, *Chilean Revolution*, 65–66.

Bibliography

Archives

Santiago, Chile
Archivo de Alfonso Calderón, Biblioteca
  Nacional
Archivo de Raúl Silva Castro, Biblioteca
  Nacional
Colección Pedro Aguirre Cerda, Archivo
  Nacional

Ministerio de Educación Pública (formerly
  Ministerio de Justicia e Instrucción
  Pública), Archivo del Siglo XX
  Oficios, Providencias, Decretos
Ministerio de Justicia, Archivo del Siglo XX
  Oficios, Providencias, Circulares
Ministerio del Interior, Archivo del Siglo XX
  Oficios, Providencias, Circulares

Newspapers

Claridad, 1937–38
Diario Ilustrado, El, 1907–41
Frente Popular, 1936–40
Hora, La, 1935–41
Lei, La, 1894–1910
Lira Chilena, La, 1904
Mercurio, El, 1910–41
Nación, La, 1920–41

Opinión, La, 1932–38
Porvenir, El, 1900
Prensa, La, 1900
Siglo, El, 1938–41, 1954
Tercera, La, 1961
Trabajo, 1937–38
Últimas Noticias, Las, 1940–43
Unión, La, 1928

Annals/Journals/Magazines

Acción Chilena
Acta Literaria
Americas
Anales de la Universidad de Chile
Boletín de Historia y Geografía
Boletín del Instituto Nacional

Campesino, El (formerly *Boletín de la Sociedad
  National de Agricultura*)
Chile Ilustrado
Documentos
Finis Terrae
Hispanic American Historical Review

Historia
Journal of Historical Sociology
Journal of Latin American Studies
Luz y Sombra
Mapocho
Nueva Atenea (formerly *Atenea*)
Pacífico Magazine
Revista Católica
Revista de Chile
Revista de Educación (formerly *Revista
    de Educación Primaria*)

Revista de Educación Nacional (formerly
    Revista Pedagógica)
Revista de la Sociedad de Escritores de Chile
Revista del Pacífico
Revista Radical
Rural History
Topaze
Zig-Zag

Primary Literature

Aguirre Cerda, Pedro. *Estudio sobre la instrucción secundaria (memoria de prueba para optar al grado de Licenciado en la Facultad de Leyes i Ciencias Políticas, Universidad de Chile)*. Santiago: Imprenta Aurora, 1904.

Alcayaga, Amador, and Eliodoro Flores. *Instrucción cívica*. Santiago: Casa Editorial Minerva, 1917.

Alcayaga, Amador, and Guillermo Gandarillas. *Educación cívica*. Santiago: Imprenta Universitaria, 1938.

Alessandri, Arturo. *Instrucción Primaria Obligatoria y Laica: Discurso del Senador por Tarapacá en las sesiones del 23-28-29-30 de Julio y 4 de Agosto de 1919*. Santiago: Imprenta Fiscal de la Penitenciaría, 1919.

——. *Recuerdos de Gobierno*. Vol. 1. Santiago: Editorial Universitaria, 1952.

——. *Recuerdos de Gobierno*. Vols. 2–3. Santiago: Editorial Nascimento, 1967.

Anguita, Ricardo, ed. *Leyes promulgadas en Chile desde 1810 hasta el 10 de Junio de 1913*. 6 vols. Santiago: Imprenta Barcelona, 1912–18.

Ara, Guillermo, ed. *El Payador y antología de poesía y prosa*. Caracas: Biblioteca Ayacucho, 1979.

Arancibia Laso, Héctor. *La doctrina radical: Programa de gobierno*. Santiago: Imprenta y Litografía Antares, 1937.

Arce Eberhard, Alberto, et al. *Pensamiento nacionalista*. Edited by Enrique Campos Menéndez. Santiago: Editorial Nacional Gabriela Mistral, 1974.

Balmaceda, Manuel José. *Manual del hacendado chileno*. Santiago: Imprenta Franklin, 1875.

Balmaceda Valdés, Eduardo. *Un mundo que se fue*. Santiago: Editorial Andrés Bello, 1969.

Barros de Orrego, Martina. *Recuerdos de mi vida*. Santiago: Editorial Orbe, 1942.

Blest Gana, Alberto. *Martín Rivas*. Santiago: Zig-Zag, 1956.

Brunet, Marta. *Montaña adentro*. Santiago: Editorial Andrés Bello, 1991.

Bunster, César. *El niño chileno: Libro auxiliar de lectura para el primer año de humanidades*. Santiago: Imprenta Universitaria, 1931.

——. *El niño chileno: Libro auxiliar de lectura para el quinto año de la escuela primaria (quinta preparatoria)*. Santiago: Imprenta Universitaria, 1936.

——. *El niño chileno: Libro auxiliar de lectura para el cuarto año de la escuela primaria (quinta preparatoria)*. Santiago: Imprenta Universitaria, 1937.

——. *El niño chileno: Libro auxiliar de lectura para el segundo año de humanidades*. Santiago: Imprenta Universitaria, 1933.

——. *El niño chileno: Libro auxiliar de lectura para el sexto año de la escuela primaria (sexta preparatoria)*. Santiago: Imprenta Universitaria, 1935.

——. *El niño chileno: Libro auxiliar de lectura para el tercer año de humanidades de los liceos de hombres*. Santiago: Imprenta Universitaria, 1934.

——. *Reflexión sobre la inquietud actual*. Santiago: Imprenta Universitaria, 1939.

Cabero, Alberto. *Chile y los chilenos: Conferencias dictadas en la Extensión Cultural de Antofagasta durante los años 1924 y 1925*. Santiago: Editorial Nascimento, 1926.

Concha, Malaquías. *Cartilla de educación cívica*. Santiago: Imprenta, Litografía i Encuadernación Fiscal de la Penitenciaría, 1920.

Consejo de Instrucción Pública. *Plan de estudios: Programas de instrucción secundaria aprobados por el Consejo de Instrucción Pública para los liceos del Estado*. Santiago, 1916.

Corvalán, Antonio, ed. *Antología chilena de la tierra*. Santiago: Instituto de Capacitación e Investigación en Reforma Agraria, 1970.

Debray, Régis. *The Chilean Revolution: Conversations with Allende*. New York: Vintage Books, 1971.

de la Barra, Eduardo. *El embrujamiento alemán*. Santiago: Establecimiento Poligráfico Roma, 1899.

del Campo, Carlos. *Huasos chilenos*. Santiago: Servicios de Turismo del Ministerio de Fomento, 1939.

Devés, Eduardo, and Ximena Cruzat, eds. *Recabarren: Escritos de prensa*. 4 vols. Santiago: Nuestra América and Terranova, 1985–87.

Díaz Arrieta, Hernán [pseudo. Alone]. *Pretérito imperfecto: Memorias de un crítico literario*. Santiago: Editorial Nascimento, 1976.

Dirección General de Estadística, República de Chile. *Censo de población de la República de Chile levantado el 15 de diciembre de 1920*. Santiago: Imprenta y Litografía Universo, 1925.

Durand, Luis. *Alma y cuerpo de Chile*. Santiago: Editorial Nascimento, 1947.

——. *Campesinos*. Santiago: Editorial Nascimento, 1932.

——. *Don Arturo*. Santiago: Zig-Zag, 1952.

——. *Gente de mi tiempo*. Santiago. Editorial Nascimento, 1953.

——. *Paisajes y gentes de Chile*. Santiago: Zig-Zag, 1953.

——. *Sietecuentos*. Santiago: Editorial Nascimento, 1964.

Edwards Bello, Joaquín. *La chica del Crillón*. Santiago: Ediciones Ercilla, 1935.

——. *Crónicas del Centenario*. Santiago: Zig-Zag, 1968.

——. *Crónicas del tiempo viejo*. Santiago: Editorial Nascimento, 1976.

——. *El nacionalismo continental*. Santiago: Ediciones Ercilla, 1935.

——. *Recuerdos de un cuarto de siglo*. Complied by Alfonso Calderón. Santiago: Zig-Zag, 1966.

——. *El roto*. Santiago: Editorial Chilena, 1920.

Encina, Francisco A. *La educación económica y el liceo*. Santiago: Imprenta Universitaria, 1912.

——. *La literatura histórica chilena y el concepto actual de la historia*. Santiago: Editorial Nascimento, 1935.

——. *Nuestra inferioridad económica*. Santiago: Imprenta Universitaria, 1912.

Forgacs, David, and Geoffrey Nowell-Smith, eds. *Antonio Gramsci: Selections from Cultural Writings*. London: Lawrence and Wishart, 1985.

Galdames, Luis. *Educación económica e intelectual*. Santiago: Imprenta Universitaria, 1912.

Gana, Federico. *Días de campo*. Santiago: Ediciones de los Diez, 1916.

Gilliss, J. M. *The U.S. Naval Astronomical Expedition to the Southern Hemisphere during the Years 1849–50–52*. Vol. 1. Washington: n.p., 1855.

González Echenique, Guillermo. *Verdades amargas*. Santiago: Imprenta Cervantes, 1918.

Gramsci, Antonio. *Selections from the Prison Notebooks*. Edited and translated by Quintin Hoare and Geoffrey Nowell-Smith. London: Lawrence and Wishart, 1971.

Grez, Sergio, ed. *La "cuestión social" en Chile: Ideas y debates precursores, 1804–1902*. Santiago: Dirección de Bibliotecas, Archivos y Museos, 1995.

Guzmán Maturana, Manuel. *El lector chileno: Libro cuarto para el quinto año de la escuela primaria*. Santiago: Imprenta Universitaria, 1932.

———. *El lector chileno: Libro primero para el segundo año de la escuela primaria*. Santiago: Editorial Minerva, 1929.

———. *El lector chileno: Libro quinto para el sexto año de la escuela primaria*. Santiago: Sociedad Imprenta y Litografía Universo, 1931.

———. *El lector chileno: Libro segundo para el tercer año de la escuela primaria*. Santiago: Imprenta Universitaria, 1932.

———. *El lector chileno: Libro tercero para el cuarto año de la escuela primaria*. Santiago: Imprenta Universitaria, 1932.

———. *Libro de lectura para el primer año de humanidades*. 6th ed. Santiago: Editorial Minerva, 1937.

———. *Primer libro de lectura para la preparatoria*. 5th ed. Santiago: Sociedad Imprenta y Litografía Universo, 1927.

Instituto del Inquilino. *Cuecas y consejos del campo chileno*. Santiago: Zig-Zag, 1939.

Junta Central Radical (Santiago). *Programa, estatútos, reglamento: De convenciones y juntas provinciales*. Santiago: Imprenta La República, 1933.

Keller, Carlos. *La eterna crisis chilena*. Santiago: Editorial Nascimento, 1931.

Labarca Hubertson, Amanda. *Mejoramiento de la vida campesina*. Santiago: Empresa Letras, 1936.

Labarca Hubertson, Guillermo. *Al amor de la tierra*. Santiago: Imprenta Centro Editorial, 1905.

Lafertte, Elías. *Vida de un comunista*. Santiago: Talleres Gráficos Horizonte, 1961.

Lastarria, José Victorino. *Miscelánea histórica y literaria*. 2 vols. Santiago: Imprenta La Patria, 1870.

———. *Recuerdos literarios*. Santiago: Zig-Zag, 1968.

Latorre, Mariano. *Autobiografía de una vocación (Algunas preguntas que no me han hecho sobre el criollismo)*. Santiago: Ediciones de los Anales de la Universidad de Chile, 1954.

———. *Cuentos del Maule*. Santiago: Zig-Zag, 1912.

———. *Memorias y otras confidencias*. Edited by Alfonso Calderón. Santiago: Editorial Andrés Bello, 1971.

———. *Zurzulita*. 5th ed. Santiago: Editorial Nascimento, 1964.

Letelier, Valentín. *Las escuelas de Berlín: Informe elevado al Supremo Gobierno por la legación de Chile en Alemania*. Santiago. Imprenta Nacional, 1885.

———. *La lucha por la cultura*. Santiago: Imprenta i Encuadernación Barcelona, 1895.

Lillo, Baldomero. *Obras completas*. Santiago: Editorial Nascimento, 1968.

Mac-Iver, Enrique. *Discurso sobre la crisis moral de la República*. Santiago: Imprenta Moderna, 1900.

Maluenda Labarca, Rafael. *Escenas de la vida campesina*. Santiago: Imprenta Cervantes, 1909.

McBride, George M. *Chile: Land and Society*. New York: American Geographical Society, 1936.

Ministerio de Educación de Chile, Extensión Cultural. *La cueca y danzas tradicionales*. Santiago, 1981.

Molina, Enrique. *La cultura i la educación jeneral: Conferencias leidas en la Universidad de Chile en Septiembre de 1912*. Santiago: Imprenta Universitaria, 1912.

Montenegro, Ernesto. *Mis contemporáneos*. Editorial Universitaria, 1967.

Movimiento Nacional Socialista de Chile. *El Movimiento Nacional Socialista de Chile*. Santiago: Imprenta La República, 1934.

Orrego Luco, Luis. *Casa grande*. Santiago: Zig-Zag, 1908.

———. *Memorias del tiempo viejo*. Santiago: Ediciones de la Universidad de Chile, 1984.

Palacios, Nicolás. *Raza chilena*. 4th ed. Santiago: Ediciones Colchagua, 1988.

Partido Liberal. *Los deberes del Partido Liberal en la hora actual: Manifiesto de su presidente* (Ladislao Errázuriz Lazcano). Santiago: Cóndor, 1934.

——. *Programa y estatuto aprobados en la convención de Octubre de 1933.* Santiago: Editorial El Pacífico, 1934.

Partido Radical. *Manifiesto a los radicales del país: Programa del Partido Radical aprobado en la convención del partido de 1925, celebrada en Chillán.* Concepción: El Sur, 1931.

Pinochet Le-Brun, Tancredo. *La autobiografía de un tonto, sólo para mayores.* Santiago: Biblioteca de Alta Cultura, 1951.

——. *La conquista de Chile en el siglo XX.* Santiago: Imprenta, Litografía y Encuadernación La Ilustración, 1909.

——. *Oligarquía y democracia.* Santiago: Casa Editora T. Pinochet, 1917.

Prado Martínez, Carlos, and Jenaro Torres C. *El lector del obrero chileno.* Valparaíso: Fisher y Cía., 1925.

Programa mínimo provisional de la Organización Política, Económica, y Social de la Clase Media de Chile. Valparaíso: Imprenta Royal, 1934.

Quezada, Jaime, ed. *Gabriela Mistral: Escritos políticos.* Santiago: Fondo de Cultura Económica, 1994.

Rocco del Campo, Antonio. *Panorama y color de Chile.* Santiago: Ediciones Ercilla, 1939.

Rousseau, Jean-Jacques. *Émile.* Edited, translated, and notes by Allan Bloom. New York: Basic Books, 1979.

Rumbold, Horace. *Reports to Her Majesty's Secretaries of Embassy and Legation . . . on the Manufactures, Commerce, Etc.* London, 1876.

Russell, William Howard. *A Visit to Chile and the Nitrate Fields of Tarapacá, Etc.* London: J. S. Virtue and Company, 1890.

Salas, Darío. *El problema nacional.* 2d ed. Santiago: Facultad de Filosofía y Educación de la Universidad de Chile, 1967.

Salas Neumann, Emma, ed. *El pensamiento de Darío Salas a través de algunos de sus escritos.* Santiago: Ediciones de la Universidad de Chile, 1987.

Santiván, Fernando. *Confesiones de Santiván: Recuerdos literarios.* Santiago: Zig-Zag, 1958.

——. *Memorias de un tolstoyano.* Santiago: Zig-Zag, 1955.

——. *Obras completas.* Santiago: Zig-Zag, 1965.

Secretariado General de la Unión Social Católica de Chile. *Separación de la Iglesia y el Estado: Manifiesto de la Asociación Nacional de Estudiantes Católicos a la juventud chilena.* Santiago, 1920

Unidad Popular. *Programa básico de gobierno de la Unidad Popular.* Santiago: Horizonte, 1969.

Valdés Cange, Dr. Julio [Alejandro Venegas]. *Sinceridad: Chile íntimo en 1910.* Santiago: Imprenta Universitaria, 1910.

Vicuña Subercaseaux, Benjamín. *La ciudad de las ciudades.* Santiago: Sociedad Imprenta y Litografía Universo, 1905.

Zola, Émile. *The Dreyfus Affair.* Edited by Alain Pages. Translated by Eleanor Levieux. New Haven: Yale University Press, 1996.

——. *The Naturalist Novel.* Edited and introduction by Maxwell Geismar. Montreal: Harvest House, 1964.

Secondary Literature

Acevedo Hernández, Antonio. *La cueca: Orígenes, historia y antología.* Santiago: Editorial Nascimento, 1953.

Agulhon, Maurice, et al. *Formas de sociabilidad en Chile, 1840–1940*. Santiago: Fundación Mario Góngora, 1992.

Alarcón Pino, Raúl. *La clase media en Chile: Orígenes, características e influencias*. Santiago: Editorial Tegualda, 1947.

Alba, Víctor. *Nationalists without Nations: The Oligarchy versus the People in Latin America*. New York: Praeger, 1986.

Altamirano, Carlos, and Beatriz Sarlo. *Conceptos de sociología literaria*. Buenos Aires: Centro Editor de América Latina, 1983.

———. *Literatura/Sociedad*. Buenos Aires: Hachette, 1983.

Amunátegui, Miguel Luis. *Estudios sobre la instrucción pública*. 3 vols. Santiago: Imprenta Nacional, 1897–98.

Amunátegui Solar, Domingo. *Historia de Chile: Las letras chilenas*. Santiago: Establecimientos Gráficos Balcells & Co., 1925.

———. *Historia social de Chile*. Santiago: Editorial Nascimento, 1932.

Anderson, Benedict. *Imagined Communities: Reflections on the Origin and Spread of Nationalism*. London: Verso, 1983.

Apple, Michael W. *Ideology and Curriculum*. London: Routledge, 1979.

Apple, Michael W., and Lois Weis, eds. *Ideology and Practice in Schooling*. Philadelphia: Temple University Press, 1983.

Atropos. "El inquilino en Chile: Su vida: Un siglo sin variaciones, 1861–1966." *Mapocho* 5 (May 1966): 195–218.

Baily, Samuel, ed. *Nationalism in Latin America*. New York: Alfred A. Knopf, 1970.

Baraona Urzúa, Pablo, et al. *Chile: A Critical Survey*. Santiago: Institute of General Studies, 1972.

Barría Serón, Jorge. *Breve historia del sindicalismo chileno*. Santiago: Facultad de Ciencias Económicas de la Universidad de Chile, 1967.

———. *Chile en el siglo XX: Ensayos histórico social*. Santiago: Prensa Latinoamericana, 1973.

———. *El movimiento obrero en Chile*. Santiago: Ediciones de la Universidad Técnica del Estado, 1972.

———. *Los movimientos sociales de Chile desde 1910 hasta 1926: Aspecto político y social: Memoria de prueba para optar al grado de Licenciado en Ciencias Jurídicas y Sociales, Universidad de Chile*. Santiago: Editorial Universitaria, 1960.

Barr-Melej, Patrick. "Cowboys and Constructions: Nationalist Representations of Pastoral Life in Post-Portalian Chile." *Journal of Latin American Studies* 30 (February 1998): 35–61.

———. "Patria y pedagogía: Reformistas, nacionalismo y la búsqueda de una respuesta a la cuestión social en la educación pública chilena." *SOLAR: Estudios Latinoamericanos* (1998): 73–86.

Barros Arana, Diego. *Un decenio de la historia de Chile*. 2 vols. Santiago: Imprenta y Encuadernación Universitaria, 1905–6.

———. *Historia jeneral de Chile*. 16 vols. Santiago: R. Jover, 1884–1902.

Barros Lazaeta, Luis, and Ximena Vergara Johnson. *El modo se ser aristocrático: El caso de la oligarquía chilena hacia 1900*. Santiago: Ediciones Aconcagua, 1978.

Bauer, Arnold J. *Chilean Rural Society from the Spanish Conquest to 1930*. Cambridge: Cambridge University Press, 1975.

Bernstein, Basil. *Class, Codes, and Control*. 3 vols. London: Routledge and K. Paul, 1972–75.

Bethell, Leslie, ed. *Chile since Independence*. Cambridge: Cambridge University Press, 1993.

———. *A Cultural History of Latin America: Literature, Music, and the Visual Arts in the Nineteenth and Twentieth Centuries*. Cambridge: Cambridge University Press, 1998.

Bourdieu, Pierre. *The Field of Cultural Production*. Edited by Randal Johnson. New York: Columbia University Press, 1993.

Bourdieu, Pierre, and Jean-Claude Passeron. *Reproduction in Education, Society, and Culture*. London: Sage Publications, 1977.

Boyd, Carolyn. *Historia Patria: Politics, History, and National Identity in Spain, 1875–1975*. Princeton: Princeton University Press, 1997.

Brading, David. *The First America: The Spanish Monarchy, Creole Patriots, and the Liberal State, 1492–1867*. Cambridge: Cambridge University Press, 1991.

Bravo Elizondo, Pedro. *Cultura y teatro obrero en Chile, 1900–1930*. Madrid: Libros del Meridión, 1986.

Brunner, José Joaquín. *Un espejo trizado: Ensayos sobre la cultura y políticas culturales*. Santiago: Facultad Latinoamericana de Ciencias Sociales, 1988.

Brunner, José Joaquín, and Gonzalo Catalán. *Cinco estudios sobre la cultura y sociedad*. Santiago: Facultad Latinoamericana de Ciencias Sociales, 1985.

Campos Harriet, Fernando. *Desarrollo educacional, 1810–1960*. Santiago: Editorial Andrés Bello, 1960.

Castillo, Homero. *El criollismo en la novelística chilena*. Mexico City: Ediciones de Andrea, 1962.

Catalán, Carlos, et al. *Transformaciones del sistema cultural chileno entre 1920 y 1973*. Santiago: Centro de Indagación y Expresión Cultural y Artística, 1987.

Chartier, Roger. *Cultural History: Between Practices and Representations*. Translated by Lydia G. Cochrane. Ithaca, N.Y.: Cornell University Press, 1988.

Coll, Edna. *Chile y los chilenos en las novelas de Joaquín Edwards Bello*. San Juan: Ediciones Juan Ponce de León, 1965.

Collier, Simon. *Ideas and Politics of Chilean Independence, 1808–1833*. Cambridge: Cambridge University Press, 1967.

Collier, Simon, and William F. Sater. *A History of Chile, 1808–1994*. Cambridge: Cambridge University Press, 1996.

Concha Turri, Enrique. *Malaquías Concha, el político*. Santiago: Editorial Universitaria, 1958.

Coniff, Michael, ed. *Populism in Latin America*. Tuscaloosa: University of Alabama Press, 1999.

Corse, Sara M. *Nationalism and Literature: The Politics of Culture in Canada and the United States*. Cambridge: Cambridge University Press, 1997.

Cristi, Renato, and Carlos Ruíz, eds. *El pensamiento conservador en Chile: Seis ensayos*. Santiago: Editorial Universitaria, 1992.

Crowley, Cornelius. "Costumbrism in Chilean Literary Prose of the Nineteenth Century." Ph.D. diss., University of California at Berkeley, 1944.

Dahbour, Omar, and Micheline Ishay, eds. *The Nationalism Reader*. Atlantic Highlands, N.J.: Humanities Press, 1995.

Daitsman, Andy. "'The People Shall Be All': Liberal Rebellion and Popular Mobilization in Chile, 1830–1860." Ph.D. diss., University of Wisconsin, Madison, 1995.

DeShazo, Peter. *Urban Workers and Labor Unions in Chile, 1902–1927*. Madison: University of Wisconsin Press, 1983.

Donoso, Armando. *Conversaciones con Don Arturo Alessandri*. Santiago: Editorial Ercilla, 1934.

Donoso, Ricardo. *Alessandri, agitador y demoledor*. Santiago: Revista Occidente, 1951.

———. *El Instituto Pedagógico: Tres generaciones de maestros*. Santiago: Editorial Universitaria, 1963.

Drake, Paul. *Socialism and Populism in Chile, 1932–1952*. Urbana: University of Illinois Press, 1978.

Durán Bernales, Florencio. *El Partido Radical*. Santiago: Editorial Nascimento, 1958.

Edwards V., Alberto. *La fronda aristocrática*. 8th ed. Santiago: Editorial del Pacífico, 1976.

Encina, Francisco A. *Historia de Chile desde la prehistoria hasta 1891.* 20 vols. Reproduction
of original text. Santiago: Editorial Ercilla, 1983–84.
——. *Portales.* 2 vols. Santiago: Editorial Nascimento, 1934.
——. *La presidencia de Balmaceda.* 2 vols. Santiago: Editorial Nascimento, 1952.
Escobar, Roberto. *Teoría del chileno.* Santiago: Corporación de Estudios Contemporáneos,
1981.
Eyzaguirre, Jaime. *Historia de Chile: Génesis de la nacionalidad.* Santiago: Zig-Zag, 1965.
Faúndez, Julio. *Marxism and Democracy in Chile: From 1932 to the Fall of Allende.* New Haven:
Yale University Press, 1988.
Fergusson, Erna. *Chile.* New York: Knopf, 1943.
Fernández Fraile, Maximino. *Historia de la literatura chilena.* 2 vols. Santiago: Editorial
Salesiano, 1994–96.
Fuentealba Hernández, Leonardo. *Ensayo biográfico de Valentín Letelier.* Santiago: Escuela
Nacional de Artes Gráficas, 1956.
Fuentes, Walter. *La novela social en Chile (1900-1925): Ideología y disyuntiva histórica.*
Minneapolis: Institute for the Study of Ideologies and Literature, 1990.
García Canclini, Néstor. *Culturas híbridas: Estrategias para entrar y salir de la modernidad.*
Mexico City: Grijalbo, 1989.
García Covarrubias, Jaime. *El Partido Radical y la clase media en Chile, 1888-1938.* Madrid:
Michay, 1986.
Gay, Claudio. *Historia física y política de Chile: Agricultura.* Vol. 1. Paris, 1862.
Gazarian Gautier, Marie-Lise. *Interviews with Latin American Writers.* Elmwood Park, Ill.:
Dalkey Archive Press, 1989.
Gazmuri, Cristián. *El "48" chileno: Igualitarios, reformistas, radicales, masones y bomberos.*
Santiago: Editorial Universitaria, 1992.
Gellner, Ernest. *Nationalism.* New York: New York University Press, 1997.
——. *Nations and Nationalism.* Oxford: Blackwell, 1983.
Genet, Jacqueline, ed. *Rural Ireland, Real Ireland?* Gerrards Cross, U.K.: Colin Smythe, 1996.
Godoy, Lorena, ed. *Disciplina y desacato: Construcción de identidad en Chile, siglos XIX y XX.*
Santiago: Sur/Centro de Estudios de la Mujer, 1995.
Godoy Urzúa, Hernán. *Apuntes sobre la cultura en Chile.* Valparaíso: Universidad Católica de
Valparaíso, 1982.
——. *El carácter chileno.* Santiago: Editorial Universitaria, 1981.
——. *La cultura chilena.* Santiago: Editorial Universitaria, 1982.
——. *El oficio de las letras: Estudio sociológico sobre la vida literaria.* Santiago: Editorial
Universitaria, 1970.
Goic, Cedomil. *La novela chilena.* Santiago: Editorial Universitaria, 1968.
Goldmann, Lucien. *The Hidden God.* New York: Humanities Press, 1964.
——. *Towards a Sociology of the Novel.* London: Tavistock Publications, 1975.
Góngora, Mario. *Encomenderos y estancieros.* Santiago: Editorial Universitaria, 1971.
——. *Ensayo histórico sobre la noción de Estado en Chile en los siglos XIX y XX.* Santiago: Editorial
Universitaria, 1986.
——. *Origen de los "inquilinos" de Chile central.* Santiago: Editorial Universitaria, 1960.
Graciarena, Jorge. *Poder y clases sociales en el desarrollo de América Latina.* Buenos Aires: Paidós,
1967.
Graham, Richard, ed. *The Idea of Race in Latin America, 1870-1940.* Austin: University of Texas
Press, 1990.
Guerra-Cunningham, Lucía. *Texto e ideología en la narrativa chilena.* Minneapolis, Minn.:
Institute for the Study of Ideology and Literature, 1987.

Habermas, Jürgen. *The Structural Transformation of the Public Sphere: An Inquiry into a Category of Bourgeois Society*. Cambridge: MIT Press, 1991.

Halperin, Ernst. *Nationalism and Communism in Chile*. Cambridge: MIT Press, 1965.

Halperín-Donghi, Tulio. *Historia contemporánea de América Latina*. 13th ed. Madrid: Alianza Editorial, 1996.

Heise González, Julio. *Historia de Chile: El período parlamentario, 1861–1925*. 2 vols. Santiago: Editorial Universitaria, 1971–82.

Hernández, Roberto. *El roto chileno: Bosquejo histórico de actualidad*. Valparaíso: Imprenta Rafael, 1929.

Hobsbawm, E. J. *Nations and Nationalism since 1780: Programme, Myth, Reality*. Cambridge: Cambridge University Press, 1990.

Houseman, Philip Joseph. "Chilean Nationalism, 1920–1952." Ph.D. diss., Stanford University, 1960.

Hunt, Lynn, ed. *The New Cultural History: Essays*. Berkeley: University of California Press, 1989.

Jay, Martin. *Marxism and Totality*. Berkeley: University of California Press, 1984.

Jobet, Julio César. *Ensayo crítico del desarrollo económico-social de Chile*. Santiago: Editorial Universitaria, 1955.

——. *Luis Emilio Recabarren: Los orígenes del movimiento obrero y del socialismo chilenos*. Santiago: Prensa Latinoamericana, 1955.

——. *El Partido Socialista de Chile*. Santiago: Prensa Latinoamericana, 1973.

——. *Valentín Letelier y sus continuadores: Darío Salas, Luis Galdames y Pedro Aguirre Cerda*. San José, Costa Rica: Editorial Universitaria, 1954.

Johnson, John J. *Political Change in Latin America: The Emergence of the Middle Sectors*. Stanford: Stanford University Press, 1958.

Kirkpatrick, Gwen, ed. *Don Segundo Sombra*. Pittsburgh: University of Pittsburgh Press, 1995.

Klubock, Thomas Miller. *Contested Communities: Class, Gender, and Politics in Chile's El Teniente Copper Mine, 1904–1951*. Durham, N.C.: Duke University Press, 1998.

Labarca Hubertson, Amanda. *Historia de la enseñanza en Chile*. Santiago: Imprenta Universitaria, 1939.

Lagarrigue, Luis. *La cuestión social*. Santiago: Ercilla, 1895.

Lago, Tomás. *El huaso: Ensayo de antropología social*. Santiago: Ediciones de la Universidad de Chile, 1953.

Latcham, Ricardo, et al. *El criollismo*. Santiago: Editorial Universitaria, 1956.

León Echaiz, René. *Interpretación histórica del huaso chileno*. Santiago: Zig-Zag, 1956.

——, ed. *Pensamiento de Alessandri*. Santiago: Editorial Nacional Gabriela Mistral, 1974.

Lidtke, Vernon. *The Alternative Culture: Socialist Labor in Imperial Germany*. Oxford: Oxford University Press, 1985.

Lihn, Enrique, ed. *La cultura en la vía chilena al socialismo*. Santiago: Editorial Universitaria, 1971.

Lipset, Seymour Martin, and Aldo Solari, eds. *Elites in Latin America*. Oxford: Oxford University Press, 1967.

Loveman, Brian. *Chile: The Legacy of Hispanic Capitalism*. New York: Oxford University Press, 1988.

——. *Struggle in the Countryside*. Bloomington: Indiana University Press, 1976.

Lowenthal, Leo. *Literature, Popular Culture, and Society*. Palo Alto, Calif.: Pacific Books, 1961.

Mallon, Florencia. *Peasant and Nation: The Making of Postcolonial Mexico and Peru*. Berkeley: University of California Press, 1995.

Masur, Gerhard. *Nationalism in Latin America: Diversity and Unity*. New York: Macmillan Company, 1966.

Miller, Nicola. *In the Shadow of the State: Intellectuals and the Quest for National Identity in Twentieth-Century Spanish America*. London: Verso, 1999.

Monteón, Michael. *Chile and the Great Depression: The Politics of Underdevelopment, 1927–1948*. Tempe: Center for Latin American Studies Press (Arizona State University), 1998.

———. *Chile in the Nitrate Era*. Madison: University of Wisconsin Press, 1982.

Mörner, Magnus, ed. *Race and Class in Latin America*. New York: Columbia University Press, 1970.

Morris, James O. *Elites, Intellectuals, and Consensus: A Study of the Social Question and the Industrial Labor Relations System in Chile*. Ithaca, N.Y.: Cornell University Press, 1966.

Munizaga Aguirre, Roberto. *Algunos grandes temas de la filosofía educacional de don Valentín Letelier*. Santiago: El Imparcial, 1943.

———. *La educación en la época de O'Higgins y vigencia de la obra educadora de Bello*. Santiago: Ministerio de Educación Pública, 1989.

———, ed. *Educadores chilenos de ayer y de hoy*. Santiago: Editorial Universitaria, 1986.

Muñoz González, Luis, and Dieter Oelker Link. *Diccionario de movimientos y grupos literarios chilenos*. Concepción: Ediciones Universidad de Concepción, 1993.

Nugent, David. *Modernity at the Edge of Empire: State, Individual, and Nation in the Northern Peruvian Andes, 1885–1935*. Stanford: Stanford University Press, 1997.

Nunn, Frederick M. *Chilean Politics, 1920–1931: The Honorable Mission of the Armed Forces*. Albuquerque: University of New Mexico Press, 1970.

Olavarría Bravo, Arturo. *La cuestión social en Chile: Los partidos políticos chilenos frente a la cuestión social*. Santiago: Imprenta Penitenciaría, 1953.

Orlandi Araya, Julio, and Alejandro Ramírez Cid. *Joaquín Edwards Bello*. Santiago: Editorial del Pacífico, 1943.

Orrego, Claudio, et al. *Siete ensayos sobre Arturo Alessandri Palma*. Santiago: Instituto Chileno de Estudios Históricos, 1979.

Ortiz Letelier, Fernando. *El movimiento obrero en Chile, 1891–1919*. Madrid: Michay, 1985.

Parker, David S. *The Idea of the Middle Class: White-Collar Workers and Peruvian Society, 1900–1950*. University Park: Pennsylvania State University Press, 1998.

Peralta Pizarro, Ariel, ed. *Idea de Chile*. Santiago: Ediciones Universidad de Concepción, 1993.

Petras, James, and Maurice Zeitlin, eds. *Latin America: Reform or Revolution?: A Reader*. Greenwich, Conn.: Fawcett, 1968.

Pike, Frederick. "Aspects of Class Relations in Chile." *Hispanic American Historical Review* 43 (February 1963): 14–33.

———. *Chile and the United States, 1880–1962*. South Bend, Ind.: University of Notre Dame Press, 1963.

Pinto, Martín. *Alejandro Venegas y su legado de sinceridad para Chile*. Santiago: Editorial Universitaria, 1985.

Pinto Lagarrigue, Fernando. *Alessandrismo versus ibañismo*. Curicó: Editorial La Noria, 1995.

———. *Balmaceda y los gobiernos seudo-parlamentarios*. Santiago: Editorial Andrés Bello, 1991.

Plotkin, Mariano. *Mañana es Perón*. Buenos Aires: Ariel Historia Argentina, 1993.

———. "The Politics of Consensus in Peronist Argentina, 1943–1955." Ph.D. diss., University of California at Berkeley, 1992.

Prieto, Adolfo. *El discurso criollista en la formación de la Argentina moderna*. Buenos Aires: Editorial Sudamericana, 1988.

Promis, José. *La novela chilena del último siglo*. Santiago: Editorial La Noria, 1993.

———. *Testimonios y documentos de la literatura chilena, 1842–1975*. Santiago: Editorial Nascimento, 1977.

Rama, Angel. *La crítica de la cultura en América Latina*. Caracas: Biblioteca Ayacucho, 1985.

——. *The Lettered City*. Edited and translated by John Charles Chasteen. Durham, N.C.: Duke University Press, 1996.

——. *Literatura y clase social*. Mexico City: Folios Ediciones, 1983.

——. *Transculturación narrativa*. Mexico City: Siglo Veintiuno Editores, 1982.

Ramírez Necochea, Hernán. *Historia del movimiento obrero en Chile*. 2d ed. Concepción: Ediciones Literatura Americana Reunida, 1986.

——. *Origen y formación del Partido Comunista de Chile*. Santiago: Austral, 1965.

Remmer, Karen. *Party Competition in Argentina and Chile: Political Recruitment and Public Policy*. Lincoln: University of Nebraska Press, 1984.

Ríos, Juan Antonio. *Durante el gobierno del General Ibáñez*. Santiago: Establecimientos Gráficos Balcells & Co., 1931.

Ríos González, Tomás. *La cuestión social*. Santiago: Imprenta Universitaria, 1917.

Rivera, Jorge, ed. *Poesía gauchesca*. Caracas: Biblioteca Ayacucho, 1977.

Rock, David. *Authoritarian Argentina*. Berkeley: University of California Press, 1993.

Rodríguez Arancibia, Ezekiel. *La cueca chilena: Coreografía y significado de esta danza*. Santiago: Talleres Gráficos Casa Nacional del Niño, 1950.

Rojas Flores, Jorge. *La dictadura de Ibáñez y los sindicatos (1927–1931)*. Santiago: Dirección de Bibliotecas, Archivos y Museos, 1993.

Román-Lagunas, Jorge. *The Chilean Novel: A Critical Study of Secondary Sources and a Bibliography*. Lanham, Md.: Scarecrow Press, 1995.

Roniger, Luis, and Mario Sznajder, eds. *Constructing Collective Identities and Shaping Public Spheres: Latin American Paths*. Brighton, U.K.: Sussex Academic Press, 1998.

Salas Neumann, Emma. *Amanda Labarca*. Santiago: Ediciones Mar del Plata, 1996.

Salas Silva, Irma. "The Socioeconomic Composition of the Secondary School Population in Chile." Ph.D. diss., Columbia University, 1930.

Salazar Vergara, Gabriel. *Labradores, peones y proletarios: Formación y crisis de la sociedad popular chilena del siglo XIX*. Santiago: Ediciones Sur, 1985.

——. *Violencia política popular en "las grandes alamedas": Santiago de Chile, 1947–1987*. Santiago: Ediciones Sur, 1990.

Sater, William. *The Heroic Image in Chile: Arturo Prat, Secular Saint*. Berkeley: University of California Press, 1973.

Schorske, Carl E. *Fin-de-Siècle Vienna: Politics and Culture*. New York: Vintage Books, 1981.

Scully, Timothy R. *Rethinking the Center: Party Politics in Nineteenth- and Twentieth-Century Chile*. Stanford: Stanford University Press, 1992.

Sepúlveda Rondanelli, Julio. *Los radicales ante la historia*. Santiago: Editorial Andrés Bello, 1993.

Serrano, Sol. *Universidad y nación*. Santiago: Editorial Universitaria, 1994.

Seton-Watson, Hugh. *Nations and States: An Enquiry into the Origin of Nations and the Politics of Nationalism*. London: Methuen, 1977.

Shumway, Nicolas. *The Invention of Argentina*. Berkeley: University of California Press, 1993.

Silva Castro, Raúl. *Alberto Blest Gana*. Santiago: Imprenta Universitaria, 1941.

——. *Antología de cuentistas chilenos*. Santiago: Zig-Zag, 1957.

——. *Cuentistas chilenos del siglo XIX*. Santiago: Prensas de la Universidad de Chile, 1934.

——. *Don Eduardo de la Barra y la pedagogía alemana*. Santiago: Imprenta Universitaria, 1943.

——. *Eduardo de la Barra*. Santiago: Editorial Nascimento, 1968.

——. *Panorama literario de Chile*. Santiago: Editorial Universitaria, 1961.

——. *Paradoja sobre las clases sociales en la literatura*. Santiago: Imprenta Universitaria, 193?.

——. *Prensa y periodismo en Chile, 1812–1956*. Santiago: Ediciones de la Universidad de Chile, 1958.

Silva Maquieira, Fernando. *El radicalismo y sus nuevas orientaciones.* Valparaíso: Talleres de La Unión, 1918.

Silvert, Kalman, and Leonard Reissman. *Education, Class, and Nation: The Experiences of Chile and Venezuela.* New York: Elsevier, 1976.

Slatta, Richard. *Cowboys of the Americas.* New Haven: Yale University Press, 1990.

Smith, Anthony. *National Identity.* Reno: University of Nevada Press, 1991.

Snow, Peter G. *Radicalismo chileno: Historia y doctrina del Partido Radical.* Buenos Aires: Francisco de Aguirre, 1972.

Solar Correa, Eduardo. *La muerte del humanismo en Chile.* Santiago: Editorial Nascimento, 1934.

Solberg, Carl. *Immigration and Nationalism: Argentina and Chile, 1890–1914.* Austin: University of Texas Press, 1970.

Sommer, Doris. *Foundational Fictions.* Berkeley: University of California Press, 1991.

Stabb, Martin. *In Quest of Identity.* Chapel Hill: University of North Carolina Press, 1967.

Strawbridge, George. "Militarism and Nationalism in Chile, 1920–1932." Ph.D. diss., University of Pennsylvania, 1969.

Subercaseaux, Benjamín. *Chile, o una loca geografía.* Santiago: Editorial Ercilla, 1940.

Subercaseaux, Bernardo. *Fin de Siglo, la época de Balmaceda: Modernización y cultura en Chile.* Santiago: Editorial Aconcagua, 1988.

——. *Historia del libro en Chile (Alma y cuerpo).* Santiago: Editorial Andrés Bello, 1993.

Subercaseaux, Miguel. *Diccionario de chilenismos.* Santiago: Editorial Juvenil, 1986.

Sywak, William. "Values in Nineteenth-Century Chilean Education: The Germanic Reform of Chilean Public Education, 1885–1910." Ph.D. diss., University of California, Los Angeles, 1977.

Szmulewicz, Efraín. *Diccionario de la literatura chilena.* Santiago: Editorial Andrés Bello, 1984.

——. *Pablo Neruda: Biografía emotiva.* Santiago: Rumbos, 1988.

——. *Vicente Huidobro: Biografía emotiva.* Santiago: Editorial Universitaria, 1979.

Thompson, E. P. *The Making of the English Working Class.* New York: Vintage Books, 1966.

Urbistondo, Vicente. *El naturalismo en la novela chilena.* Santiago: Editorial Andrés Bello, 1966.

Uribe Celis, Carlos. *Los años veinte en Colombia: Ideología y cultura.* Bogotá: Ediciones Aurora, 1985.

Valdivia Ortiz de Zárate, Verónica. "Camino al golpe: El nacionalismo chileno a la caza de las fuerzas armadas." Serie de Investigaciones no. 11, Universidad Católica Blas Cañas. Santiago, 1996, pp. 5–69.

——. *El nacionalismo chileno en los años del Frente Popular, 1938–1952.* Santiago: Universidad Católica Blas Cañas, 1995.

Valdivieso, Jaime. *Chile: Un mito y su ruptura.* Santiago: Ediciones Literatura Americana Reunida, 1987.

Valenzuela, Arturo. *Political Brokers in Chile.* Durham, N.C.: Duke University Press, 1977.

Valenzuela, Víctor. *Chilean Society As Seen through the Novelistic World of Alberto Blest Gana.* Santiago: Talleres de Arancibia y Hnos., 1971.

——. *Cuatro escritores chilenos: Luis Orrego Luco, Emilio Rodríguez Mendoza, Baldomero Lillo y Federico Gana.* New York: Las Americas Publishers, 1961.

Varas, Augusto. *La formación del pensamiento político de Recabarren.* Santiago: Facultad Latinoamericana de Ciencias Sociales, 1983.

Vargas, Moisés. *Bosquejo de la instrucción pública en Chile.* Santiago: Imprenta y Litografía Barcelona, 1909.

Vargas Puebla, Juan. *Por los caminos de Recabarren.* Mexico City: Casa de Chile en México, n.d.

Vaughan, Mary Kay. *Cultural Politics in Revolution: Teachers, Peasants, and Schools in Mexico, 1930–1940*. Tuscon: University of Arizona Press, 1997.

Vázquez de Knauth, Josefina Zoraida. *Nacionalismo y educación en México*. Mexico City: Colegio de México (Centro de Estudios Históricos), 1970.

Vera Riquelme, Enrique. *Evolución del radicalismo chileno*. Santiago: n.p., 1943.

Vial Correa, Gonzalo. *Historia de Chile, 1891–1973*. 3 vols. Santiago: Editorial Santillana, 1981–86.

Vicuña Urrutia, Manuel. *El París americano: La oligarquía chilena como actor urbano en el siglo XIX*. Santiago: Universidad Finis Terrae, 1996.

Villalobos, Sergio. *Origen y ascenso de la burguesía chilena*. Santiago: Editorial Universitaria, 1987.

Villalobos, Sergio, et al. *Historia de Chile*. Santiago: Editorial Universitaria, 1993.

Vitale, Luis. *Interpretación marxista de la historia de Chile*. Santiago: Prensa Latinoamericana, 1967.

Whitaker, Arthur Preston. *Nationalism in Latin America: Past and Present*. Gainesville: University of Florida Press, 1962.

Wiggin, Gladys A. *Education and Nationalism: An Historical Investigation of American Education*. New York: McGraw-Hill Book Co., 1962.

Williams, Raymond. *The Country and the City*. London: Chaffot Windus, 1973.

———. *Marxism and Literature*. Oxford: Oxford University Press, 1977.

Woll, Allen. *A Functional Past: The Uses of History in Nineteenth Century Chile*. Baton Rouge: Louisiana State University Press, 1982.

Wright, Thomas. *Landowners and Reform in Chile: The Sociedad Nacional de Agricultura, 1919–1940*. Urbana: University of Illinois Press, 1982.

Wurth Rojas, Ernesto. *Ibáñez: Caudillo enigmático*. Santiago: Del Pacífico, 1958.

Yeager, Gertrude. *Barros Arana's Historia Jeneral de Chile: Politics, History, and National Identity*. Fort Worth: Texas Christian University, 1981.

———. "Elite Education in Nineteenth Century Chile." *Hispanic American Historical Review* 71 (February 1991): 73–103.

Zeitlin, Maurice. *The Civil Wars in Chile (or the Bourgeois Revolutions That Never Were)*. Princeton: Princeton University Press, 1984.

Index